The European Union and World Politics

Also by Andrew Gamble
THE SPECTRE AT THE FEAST

Also by David Lane
REVOLUTION IN THE MODERN WORLD (*co-editor with John Foran and Andreja Zivkovic*)

THE TRANSFORMATION OF STATE SOCIALISM

The European Union and World Politics

Consensus and Division

Edited by

Andrew Gamble
Professor of Politics,
University of Cambridge, UK

and

David Lane
Fellow of Emmanuel College,
University of Cambridge, UK

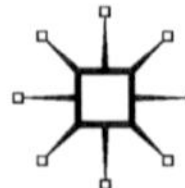

First published 2009 by
PALGRAVE MACMILLAN

Palgrave Macmillan in the UK is an imprint of Macmillan Publishers Limited, registered in England, company number 785998, of Houndmills, Basingstoke, Hampshire RG21 6XS.

Palgrave Macmillan in the US is a division of St Martin's Press LLC, 175 Fifth Avenue, New York, NY 10010.

Palgrave Macmillan is the global academic imprint of the above companies and has companies and representatives throughout the world.

Palgrave® and Macmillan® are registered trademarks in the United States, the United Kingdom, Europe and other countries.

ISBN: 978–0–230–22149–9   hardback

This book is printed on paper suitable for recycling and made from fully managed and sustained forest sources. Logging, pulping and manufacturing processes are expected to conform to the environmental regulations of the country of origin.

A catalogue record for this book is available from the British Library.

A catalog record for this book is available from the Library of Congress.

10 9 8 7 6 5 4 3 2 1
18 17 16 15 14 13 12 11 10 09

Printed and bound in Great Britain by
CPI Antony Rowe, Chippenham and Eastbourne

Contents

Acknowledgements

This book originated from the final conference of a series of workshops on the general topic of strategic elites and the enlargement of the European Union supported by the British Academy. Earlier workshops were organised in Budapest, Bremen, Prague, Kiev and Vienna. This particular workshop, which took place in Cambridge in March 2008, was concerned with the European Union and world politics. In addition to the papers in this book, which have been chosen from those presented by invited speakers, Mr Andrew Duff, the leader of the UK Liberal Democratic European Parliamentary Party, gave an introductory address. Other participants included: Geoffrey Edwards, Christopher Hill, Pieter Van Houten, Christel Lane, Julie Smith, Jochen Tholen, Helen Thompson and Bahri Yilmaz.

The editors are indebted to the British Academy for financial support for the conference and the other network events. We would also like to thank the Director of the Centre for Research in the Arts, Social Sciences and Humanities at the University of Cambridge for providing administrative assistance and a congenial venue for the hosting of the sessions and Michelle Maciejewska for her administrative assistance in organising the conference.

List of Tables

List of Figures

Contributors

Ben Clift is Senior Lecturer in Political Economy at the University of Warwick. His book, *The Comparative Political Economy of Global Capitalism* (Palgrave), is due out in 2009. He is author of *French Socialism in a Global Era* (Continuum, 2003), and has had articles published in the *British Journal of Political Science, Journal of Common Market Studies, New Political Economy*, and *Political Studies*.

Andrew Gamble is Professor of Politics and a Fellow of Queens' College at the University of Cambridge. He is a Fellow of the British Academy and joint editor of *The Political Quarterly*. He has published widely on British politics, public policy, and political economy. In 2005 he was awarded the PSA Isaiah Berlin prize for Lifetime Contribution to Political Studies.

Montserrat Guibernau is Professor of Politics at Queen Mary University of London and visiting fellow at the Centre for Global Governance, LSE. Recent publications include: *The Identity of Nations* (Polity Press, 2007) and *Catalan Nationalism: Francoism, Transition and Democracy* (Routledge, 2004).

Max Haller is Professor of Sociology at the University of Graz. He has written extensively on social stratification and the European Union.

Rosemary Hollis is Director of the Olive Tree Scholarship Programme at City University, London, where she also lectures on International Politics. Previously she was Director of Research and Head of the Middle East Programme at Chatham House. Her current publications include *Britain and the Middle East in the 9/11 Era* (2009).

Otto Holman is reader in International Relations and European Politics at the University of Amsterdam and member of the Amsterdam School for Social Science Research. He has written or (co)edited several books, book chapters and articles on international political economy and European integration. He is currently preparing a book on transformation processes in Central Europe and the European Union, and new patterns of core–periphery relations in an enlarged Union.

Martin Jacques is a visiting senior fellow at IDEAS, London School of Economics, and is a columnist for the *Guardian*. His book, *When China Rules the World: The End of the Western World and The Rise of the Middle Kingdom*, will be published in 2009. He has been a visiting professor at Renmin University, Beijing. He is a former editor of *Marxism Today*, and has worked for the *Independent*, the *Times* and *Sunday Times*.

David Lane is a Fellow of Emmanuel College, Cambridge University. Previously he was Professor of Sociology at the University of Birmingham. He has recently edited and contributed to *Revolution in the Making of the Modern World* (Routledge, 2008) and *Varieties of Capitalism in Post-Communist Countries* (Palgrave, 2007).

Mai Le is a post-doctoral researcher at Cardiff University and co-author of 'Joining the European Monetary Union – comparing first and second generation models of the open economy', *Open Economies Review*, 17 (3), 2006.

György Lengyel is professor at the Corvinus University of Budapest. His recent publications are *A magyar gazdasági elit társadalmi összetétele a 20. század végén* (*The Social Composition of the Hungarian Economic Elite at the End of the 20th Century*) (Akadémiai K., 2007) and *Restructuring of the Economic Elite after State Socialism* (edited with with D. Lane and J. Tholen, Ibidem V. Stuttgart, 2007)

Dr Georg Menz is Senior Lecturer in the Department of Politics at Goldsmiths College, London. His research interests are in political economy, EU politics, immigration and asylum. Recent articles have appeared in *The Journal of European Public Policy, Politique Européenne, Journal of European Social Policy* and *German Politics*. Recent works include *Varieties of Capitalism and Europeanization* (Oxford, 2005), and *The Political Economy of Managed Migration* (Oxford, 2008).

Patrick Minford is Professor of Applied Economics, Cardiff Business School, Cardiff University. From 1976 to 1997 he was professor of applied economics at Liverpool University. He was a member of the Monopolies Commission 1990–96 and of H.M. Treasury's Panel of Forecasters ('6 Wise Men') from January 1993 to December 1996. He was made CBE in 1996.

Eric Nowell is a research associate at Cardiff University, and the co-author of 'Nominal Contracting and Monetary Targets – Drifting Towards Indexation', *Economic Journal*, 113 (1), 2003.

Vivien A. Schmidt is Jean Monnet Professor of European Integration and Director of the Center for International Relations at Boston University as well as Visiting Professor at Sciences Po, Paris. Recent publications include *Democracy in Europe* (Oxford, 2006) and *The Futures of European Capitalism* (Oxford 2002).

Mario Telò is President of the Institute for European Studies, Université Libre de Bruxelles and member of the Royal Academy of Sciences, Belgium. He is Professor of International Relations and has served as an advisor to the European Union. Recent books include *EU and New Regionalism* (Ashgate, 2007) and *Relations Internationales. Une perspective européenne* (Université de Bruxelles, 2008).

List of Abbreviations

BDA	Bundesvereinigung der Deutschen Arbeitgeberverbände
CAG	Competitiveness Advisory Group
CAP	Common Agricultural Policy
CEE	Central and Eastern Europe
CEEC	Central and East European Countries
CEO	Chief Executive Officer
CFSP	Common Foreign and Security Policy
CGE	Computable General Equilibrium
CIS	Commonwealth of Independent States
CMEs	coordinated market economies
DG MARKT	Directorate-General Internal Market and Services
DGB	Deutscher Gewerkschaftsbund
EC	European Community
ECB	European Central Bank
ECJ	European Court of Justice
ECSC	European Coal and Steel Community
ECT	Energy Charter Treaty
EEA	European Economic Area
EMEs	emerging market economies
EMP	Euro-Mediterranean Partnership Programme
EMU	European Monetary Union
ENP	European Neighbourhood Policy
ERT	European Round Table of Industrialists
ESDP	European Security and Defence Project
ESM	European social model
ETUC	European Trade Union Congress
EU	European Union
FDI	Foreign direct investment
FSP	Common Foreign and Security Policy
GATT	General Agreement on Tariffs and Trade
GDP	Gross domestic product
IBEC	Irish Business and Employers Confederation
IEA	International Energy Agency
IG BAU	Industriegewerkschaft Bauen-Agrar-Umwelt
IG METALL	Industriegewerkschaft Metall
IMF	International Monetary Fund

IOC	International oil companies
IR	International relations
LI	liberal intergovernmentalism
LMEs	liberal market economies
LNG	Liquefied Natural Gas
LSP	liberalization of service provision
Medef	Mouvement des Enterprises en France
MENA	Middle East + North Africa region (Jordan included but Gulf countries not)
MLG	Multi-level governance
MMEs	mixed market economies
MNCs	multinational corporations
NAIRU	Non-Accelerating Inflation Rate of Unemployment
NATO	North Atlantic Treaty Organization
NGG	Nahrung-Genuss-Gaststätten
NIESR	National Institute for Economic and Social Research
NOCs	Nationally-owned Oil Companies
OECD	Organisation for Economic Co-operation and Development
OMC	Open Method of Co-ordination
OPEC	Organization of Petroleum Exporting Countries
PPP	Purchasing power parity
REU	Rest of EU (i.e., excluding UK)
RF	Russian Federation
ROW	Rest of World (i.e., excluding EU)
SEK	Swedish kronar
SIPTU	Services Industrial Professional and Technical Union
SMIC	salaire minimum interprofessionnel de croissance
SMP	Single Market Programme
SUI	Seamen's Union of Ireland
TCNs	third country nationals (non-EU citizens)
UK	United Kingdom
US	United States
USSR	Union of Soviet Socialist Republics
Ver.di	Vereinte Diesntlseitungsgewerkschaft
WEU	West European Union
WKÖ	Wirtschaftskammern Österreich
WTO	World Trade Organisation

Introduction

Andrew Gamble and David Lane

The European Union is a form of state for which there is no real precedent. As a result of the recent enlargements it now has 27 members. At the same time there has been further deepening of the union, most notably through the establishment of the single currency for some of the most developed and stable economies in the Union. But it remains far from clear what the ultimate destination of the EU will be, whether it will emerge as a global actor in other fields, including defence and foreign policy, in the way that it has emerged as a global actor in world trade. The setbacks to ratifying the constitutional treaty in 2005 and 2008 as a result of the referendum defeats in France, the Netherlands and Ireland have created a malaise in the EU. They have highlighted the disjunction that has emerged between the political elites and the electorates of the member states, and caused a lively debate about how the EU should develop in future, and whether it can overcome the present limitations on its ability to co-operate in new ways, and generate a truly common will and purpose. Unless it finds a way to do so, the EU is likely to remain secondary in power and influence to the United States and increasingly to some of the rising economic powers, such as China and India.

The chapters in this collection analyse different aspects of the EU and world politics, exploring some of the macro questions about the role it currently plays and the role it might conceivably play, as well as analysing the relationship of the EU to other major powers, and the behaviour and attitudes of EU elites at the micro level. The decentralised character of the EU polity make understanding of the EU and how it operates both internally and externally a complex task. By illuminating some of the key ideas and policies of the EU elites in relation both to the EU itself and to world politics, this book seeks to contribute to a better appreciation of both the strengths and weaknesses of this novel form of political association, and whether it provides a model which other parts of the world will increasingly seek to emulate, or whether it will come to be seen as an institutional form which is no longer relevant to contemporary conditions. Both views are expressed by contributors to this volume, as well as many views in between.

Many of the themes touched on by the contributors to this book have been thrown into sharp relief by the global financial crisis which began relatively slowly in the summer of 2007 but then erupted with explosive force in the last few months of 2008. The EU has passed through a number of phases in its development, and a number of enlargements which have altered its role in world politics. The global crash of 2008 seems set to inaugurate a new phase. The first moves towards European integration in the 1950s, culminating in the signing of the Treaty of Rome in 1956 and the establishment of a common market between the six signatories, took place against the background of the cold war in Europe, and the organisation of the Atlantic Alliance under United States leadership. The United States favoured European integration between the states of Western Europe in order to strengthen European defence, both militarily and by encouraging a zone of prosperity in Western Europe, which would underpin the legitimacy of its mostly Centre-Right governments. The recovery of Western Europe, and of West Germany in particular, was seen as necessary for US security. The same logic was behind the United States urging Britain to consider joining the EEC in the 1960s. But Britain's membership was held up because the French government perceived Britain to be too close to the United States, and therefore likely to prove unwilling to help forge an independent European political will and identity. Britain did not secure membership until General de Gaulle had departed, but de Gaulle's assessment of Britain's likely role within the Community proved prescient. As Vivien Schmidt shows in this book (Chapter 13), Britain always had a very different vision of the EU to the original members, one that was founded on a different conception of world politics, and on the purpose of the EU.

Britain's entry to the European Community in 1973 coincided with the onset of the first generalised recession since 1945. The decision of the United States to suspend the link between the dollar and gold, the oil-price shocks, accelerating inflation and stagnant output forced adjustments in every country, and a painful period of reconstruction. With all currencies floating against one another, the European Community sought to link its currencies together through the creation of the Exchange Rate Mechanism. This initiated a number of plans by the EC to deepen economic integration, partly in response to the breakdown of the Bretton Woods system. In the security field the member states of the EC remained very dependent on the United States, but in the economic field the EC became increasingly assertive in its bid to build an identity and a political will independent of the Americans. Britain was ambivalent, participating in some initiatives such as the single market, but not in others. As the economic integration gathered pace and was seen to confer advantages on the EC in coping with the uncertain global environment, so other plans came to the fore to turn the EC into a European Union, and equip it with more of the attributes of a state. One fruit of this evolution was the negotiations for what eventually became the Maastricht Treaty.

This evolution of the European Community was seen by some as tending naturally towards the creation of a state which might be in alliance with the United States, but would no longer necessarily be subordinate to it.

The idea of the EU as potentially a major player in world politics became a focus of attention in the third phase of its development after the signing of the Maastricht Treaty and the end of the cold war in 1991. The disappearance of the security threat in Europe and the reunification of Germany changed the relationships both within the EU and of the EU to the rest of the world. A key tension that now developed and was not resolved by the Maastricht Treaty was the tension between further enlargement of the European Union and deeper political and economic integration of the existing members. The EU attempted to pursue both objectives simultaneously, opening negotiations with the former communist states of Eastern Europe which was eventually to raise the membership to 27, and moving ahead with plans to establish a single currency. Different member states had different conceptions of the EU, and within political elites there were also divisions, as well as a growing divide between the EU political elite and EU citizens. Some of these tensions are explored from a number of different perspectives in this book.

The 2008 crash inaugurates a fourth phase in the development of the EU. The context of world politics will alter rapidly as a result of the political fallout from the crash and the global recession. If the global economy is to avoid lapsing into protectionism and a long period of stagnation of the kind that Japan suffered in the 1990s, it will be necessary to bring the rising economic powers, such as China, India and Brazil, into the institutions for governing the global economy, and new rules on currencies, financial markets and trade will need to be negotiated. The United States remains the leading economic and military power in the world, but the limits of its power have been exposed by recent events, and it may lack the capacity to re-establish itself. A major shift in the balance of world politics seems under way, and this will necessarily change the way the EU perceives the world and how it responds. It faces a major challenge to sustain the euro and even some of the basic principles of the common market such as the free movement of labour in the face of the political pressures which have arisen with the recession.

The essays in this book address these problems. In the first section, we consider Europe in the world context, with chapters on the United States, Russia and China. In the second section we focus on divisions within Europe, both between the elites and between elites and the public. In the third part we address the question of the type of capitalism that is arising in Europe. We conclude with two chapters which address the future of the European Union and the extent to which a European identity may be expected to develop.

Andrew Gamble sets the scene of the early postwar period, which involved Western Europe's willing subordination to the economic and military power of the US. The United States exercised a hegemony form of global power; legitimated by the notion of national self-determination, it effectively minimised the spheres of interest of other countries and enforced its power by an enormous military effort. Considering the role of the US in international politics, Gamble rejects the idea of empire – as the US does not seek to exert direct coercion (or the threat of coercion) over dependent states. Rather it is contended that hegemony is exercised through the United States's domination of the global economy, culture and the instruments of international politics.

Gamble points to the limitations of American unilateral power and the rise of a more multilateral and cosmopolitan world system operating through a global market. Since the 1980s, he notes a shift in the alliances of the US, with the rise of the 'Anglosphere' – shorthand for the English-speaking nations of the US, the UK, Ireland, Canada, New Zealand and Australia. 'The West' in this conception shifts from an embodiment of European values to an Anglo-American conception of politics, economics and culture. Three challenges to Anglo-American hegemony are considered in the first part of the book: from the European Union, the Russian Federation and China.

Mario Telò addresses the question of Europe as a civilian power. He shows how the EU is subject to many misunderstandings and misconceptions. Many of the dichotomies are false ones. He argues that there is merit in the notion of the EU as an 'unprecedented' power, but that it needs careful analysis. The idea of Europe as a civilian power needs disentangling both from realist and idealist currents in international relations theory. The idealist conceptualisation of civilian power fails to take account of the impact of 2001, or of the continuing reality of the international state system, or of the importance of internal socioeconomic and political divisions. Telò shows how the EU has been seen as a civilian power in three main ways. The first strand stresses not only the goals of the EU but also its means and internal democratic legitimacy. The second strand focuses on the EU as an example of soft power, while the third analyses how historically the individual member states of the EU have been reconstructed since 1945 as civilian powers. Telò also analyses the importance of internal divisions in explaining the limits and potential of the EU as a civilian power. He shows that, in contrast to federal states such as the US, internal divisions in the EU are relevant for high-politics international issues. Significant divisions are not limited to intergovernmental divisions, but extend to transnational cleavages. They are also not confined to conflicts between old and new member states. Telò concludes that the future of the EU will be shaped by the continuing contradiction between its nature as a regional multilateral entity and the need to have partnerships with both old and rising powers.

David Lane and Martin Jacques focus on two major 'others': Russia and China. Lane points to similarities with the Western European states in the position of the newly formed Russian Federation after the fall of the Soviet Union. In the early Yeltsin period, Russian policy was to accept American leadership – both with regard to the type of capitalism that was to develop in Russia as well as America's hegemony in international relations. However, Russia's economic and political weaknesses relatively quickly led to its isolation. NATO, under Washington's domination, expanded to areas previously in the Soviet Union's sphere of influence, which has led to conflict over such states as Kosovo and South Ossetia. It also became clear that membership, or even a close relationship, with the European Union would not be offered to Russia. Russian policy, however, changed considerably under the leadership of Presidents Putin and Medvedev who have asserted Russia's political and economic power. Lane considers that Russia's economic revival is positive, though he contends that this is misleading and proponents of Russia being a 'new world power' are mistaken. The Russian Federation has declined significantly from its word ranking as part of the former Soviet Union. Its recent economic revival has been driven by rising world prices for its major exports – raw materials. Its weaknesses are demonstrated with respect to the power and scope of its leading corporations, to the level of technology, research and innovation, and to the severe decline in human development – compared to its position in the former Soviet Union. Lane outlines Russia's place in the world economy and argues that it is a hybrid economy which in terms of levels of innovation and research cannot compete with that of the Western capitalist countries. The 'semi-periphery' of the world economy, to which Russia and China belong, should not be considered a transitionary formation, but one for further development outside of the hegemonic states. Russia's relatively limited participation in the world economy and its potential for state activity could give rise to an alternative political strategy.

Martin Jacques draws attention to the speed of China's rise, and to the new consciousness of China's power and potential in the rest of the world. He argues that China is once again becoming the centre of the East Asian economy as it used to be before the incursion of the Europeans into the region. China's strategy in contrast to that of Russia has been to become part of the international community and the global economy, which reflects the need of China for resources and markets outside its borders to maintain its very rapid economic growth. China's rise has so far been relatively free of tensions with other powers, but Jacques argues that this is unlikely to last. China is becoming so central to the global economy that it will increasingly assert itself and pursue its own interests and its own type of modernity. It will reject Western universalism and revive the idea of China as a civilisation state. This will present a severe challenge to Europe, not least to Europe's idea of itself, because it will undermine conceptions about their role in the world which Europeans have held for several centuries. Jacques explores the likely impact of China upon the EU in the period ahead, and how the EU might respond.

Answers as to whether Europe can provide an alternative political and social formation to American hegemony are provided by contributors to the second section of the book. The chapters here might lead one to conclude that the European Union is more characterised by division than consensus. Georgy Lengyel, basing his work on surveys of European political and European elites, considers divisions on some key aspects of European integration, particularly on issues of European identity, supranational institutions and visions of the nature of integration. He considers differences on an East–West basis (the West European 15 and the 10 new member states) and also between the core founder members of the EU and later additions. He reports that economic elites are more favourable to unification than political ones, who see integration as set in a nation-state context. A major finding is that economic elites in the new Eastern member states are rather more favourably disposed to the EU as a market driven entity compared to their own political elites and they also differed in this respect compared to the West European elites. The European Union is favoured as an economic redistributive institution more by the Mediterranean countries than the rest; a major contrast here is with the Visegrád states, the elites of which are strongly in favour of the EU as an institution promoting competition. Identity with the EU is greater for the original core members than the others. Taking as an example preferences for a European army, he finds that it is stronger for the Western elites than the Eastern ones; such support was also shown by more 'leftist' respondents and economic elites. There also appear to be major differences not only within the Western European countries (such as France and the UK) but also in the new member states. The Estonian and Czech elites join the ranks of the Euro-sceptics, while the Polish and Hungarian ones are more enthusiastic about the European identity and the idea of integration.

These issues are taken up in Max Haller's chapter, which focuses on differences in attitudes between elites and the public. He points to the extensive evidence that shows a growing gap between elites and the public over European integration. The process has been led by the elites but has received declining endorsement and enthusiasm from the European electorates. He documents the extent of this split, and the way in which it has deepened in recent decades. He discusses the rejection of the European Constitutional Treaty by clear majorities of French and Dutch voters in 2005. To explain these developments Haller explores two theses. The first is that European integration has been an elite process, and for the most part strongly supported by the elites, because of the advantages it has brought them and continues to bring. The second thesis is that such benefits are much less clear for the general population, and integration has had negative effects for particular groups. He seeks to substantiate these arguments with a survey of evidence from many different sources. His conclusion is that the gulf between political elites and citizens in Europe is not a transient phenomenon but deeply rooted in the structures of the EU as it has developed. Whether these differences are based on interests is taken up by Otto Holman who considers class structures in a later chapter.

Rosemary Hollis explores European policies and engagements in the Middle East and what they reveal about European elite assumptions. She employs the same definition of elites as that used by Max Haller, including both the member-state elites and the elites operating at the collective EU level. The Middle East, she argues, constituted a key element of the European neighbourhood, and she outlines the history of this region and its changing relationship with the European powers, particularly in the period of European imperial expansion, and later in the period of the cold war and the Arab-Israeli conflict. The end of the cold war and the collapse of the Soviet Union created a new context. The expansion of the EU created the need for a more definite policy towards the EU neighbourhood, particularly in regions such as the Middle East.

Hollis shows how EU policies on the Middle East are multifaceted, encompassing amongst other things defence and security, migration, human rights and democracy promotion, trade, investment and energy security policy. The EU's image of itself is as a civilian power, not interested in territorial expansion of any kind, but in issues such as conflict resolution, human rights, combating terrorism, and countering the proliferation of nuclear, chemical and biological weapons. Hollis examines the evidence from four case studies, the Barcelona Process, the Iraq crisis, the European Neighbourhood Policy and the Middle East Peace Process. She shows that in each case EU ideals were qualified by the pursuit of EU interests. Her conclusion is that EU policies are often introduced selectively and incrementally, which greatly limits their impact within the European neighbourhood. The Europeans resist real partnership and integration around the Mediterranean, being more concerned with maintaining their own heritage and identity, and at all times putting their security concerns above spreading their values abroad.

Many of the differences between the member states are captured by the papers in Part III of the collection dealing with the political economy of Europe. Some writers have considered that the underlying economic development has been a convergence towards the Anglo-American type of neo-liberal economy. Georg Menz, however, points out that the EU contains states with not only liberal market economies (LME) but also coordinated market economies (CME) – such as Germany's – Mediterranean mixed economies (MME) and emerging central and east European economies (EME). However, he points to the pervasive tendencies of deregulation which undermine national governance models. The Single Market Programme (SMP), he contends, has had the effect of weakening labour through the liberalisation of service provision. In addition, outsourcing and subcontracting also benefit capital at the expense of labour. Menz examines the institutional characteristics of countries and the ways that these shape national reactions to EU directives. He shows that EU liberalising initiatives are resisted; particularly by nationally organised trade unions, and that the strength of the response varies in relation to the degree of organisational centralisation, internal coherence, representation of clientele and access to government. In these respects, basing his conclusions on studies of a number of cases, he shows that European states have significant differences and are able to negotiate compromises with the EU over the imposition of liberalisation measures. These are defensive reactions which slow but do not fully mitigate the effects of neo-liberal policies. Attempts to impose neo-liberal policies are one of the most important reasons why many voted to reject the European Constitution.

Ben Clift makes clear that the European social model (ESM) is an ambiguous term covering 'diverse sets of economic, social and welfare policies and institutions, programmes and mechanisms that deliver them across Europe'. He also notes that 'an anachronistic blend of prevailing national peculiarity and isolated instances of European conformity characterises the (very) hesitant harmonising of European social policies'. Clift's chapter encompasses labour-market deregulation and flexibility. He points to different 'families' of welfare: Nordic, Continental/Bismarckian, liberal, and Mediterranean. A 'deep tension' exists, he contends, between national social protection and the logic of European integration. National and sub-national particularities remain deeply ingrained and difficult to dislodge. He stresses the limitations of the EU as 'convergence-inducing social policy actor'. Clift concedes that there may be commonalities in the direction of travel but that actors originate from widely divergent starting points. He contrasts Jacques Delors' view of a European model of society with that of the Anglo-Saxon neo-liberal one. Clift argues that the EU is not 'driving' a convergence of European welfare-state models. In considering the policy of full employment, he emphasises the importance of policy attempting to make a balance between flexibility and security. He holds that the 'tug of war' between national and supranational control of policy areas is being won by national policy elites in social policy and labour-market reform. The European Union as an entity is important but he points out that there are also other factors, such as globalisation and demographic change, which pull the other way. Outcomes, he concludes, are likely to be a continuation of national social models rather than convergence. The success of the UK in growth and employment comes at a high cost in terms of social equality. He sees the future as involving cross-fertilisation and hybridisation of models, and considers that there may even be a rebalancing of the relative merits of the regulated against the neo-liberal model in favour of the former.

In arguing that the EU has not been effective as a coordinating mechanism, Mai Le, Minford and Nowell adopt a more Eurosceptic position. The EU, they contend, has pursued protectionist policies in food and manufacturing. Moreover, it has had little effect on dismantling national forms of protection. They argue that, through its social interventionism, the EU has increased government costs and political integration has been prioritised at the cost of economic efficiency. Rather than introducing a neo-liberal economic policy, they consider that the European elites have limited world competition in order to protect domestic interests. Protection of the labour market has been pursued to ensure employment and to maintain welfare systems. 'Economic nationalism' rather than neo-liberalism is characteristic of the European Union.

Taking trade in manufactures and services as examples, the authors show the extent to which the EU acts to protect national interests against competition. They show that the EU is more protectionist against outsiders than the US. Cartels and restrictive policies, such as the Common Agricultural Policy, are promoted by the EU. They conclude that the cost of the EU's protectionist policy is approximately 3 per cent of its GDP. Widespread welfare lobbies within member countries press for social protection; and these countries have succeeded in achieving EU 'harmonisation' at a 'fairly high level'. They point to elite interests and consider that minority groups have the power to block change through their own national governments, as well as at the EU level.

As far as the interests of the UK are concerned, Mai Le, Minford and Nowell conclude that the EU is not neo-liberal enough: ' … its excessive interventions … [have] caused both unemployment and slow growth'. Following writers such as Mancur Olson, they argue that organised minorities have much to gain by securing protection, whereas individual citizens have a relatively small loss, though the sum of their total loss is greater than the benefit to the minority. Elites act to protect special interests rather than to implement policies that would secure the public good. They are not willing to confront the powerful domestic lobbies that are blocking reform. While the EU Commission is in favour of liberalisation of trade, as well as the deregulation of services, it is vetoed by nations whose principal industries would be damaged, even if the broader mass of their citizens would benefit from reforms. According to the authors the UK would be better off outside the EU and be able to determine its own economic policies, and to promote free trade, unhindered by the need to reach a consensus with its European partners.

A rather different interpretation is offered by Otto Holman, whose position is anchored on class analysis. He regards the deepening of European integration since its inception to be predicated on the coalescence of class structure, formation and agency. Elites are not alternatives to class analysis, but are the expression of class interests. Tracing developments to the formative coalition of national elites and the 'pan-European political elite' that brought about the European Community, he contends that national rivalries brought the process of unification to a halt in the 1960s and 1970s. It was replaced in the 1983–2003 period by a new consensus based on markets and monetary union.

The 21st century could usher in 'America's demise, Europe's rise', implying the rise of a new hegemony in the form of the European Union. Holman, however, like other writers here, remains sceptical on this score. Fundamentally, he argues, European integration was a strategy to change the welfare-state structure and transform corporatist mediation to regulation at a transnational level, thereby weakening democratic accountability at the national level. A form of 'transnational integration' by conscious design, he suggests, has occurred. Policies derived from this process stemmed the supposed 'ungovernability' of Western democracies (political acceptance of equality against freedom) as well as restoring bourgeois democracy. Organised labour as well as national parliaments were thereby marginalised and socioeconomic security and social inequality increased.

Following the arguments put forward elsewhere in this book, Holman argues that the 'democratic deficit' and lack of popular understanding and support gave rise to the votes against the Constitution and Treaty which have brought the development of the EU once more to a halt. Two reasons are at the root of Euroscepticism. First, the tensions arising from the loss of national identity consequent on enlargement from 12 to 27 states in addition to the possible future membership of Turkey and Ukraine. Second, the economic downturn and a perceived negative balance between costs and benefits of membership – as articulated by Le, Minford and Nowell in Chapter 11. The failure of the EU to consolidate its position may lead to another strategy – 'the [reassertion] of the EUs role as a global power', characterised by the use of 'soft' power (climate change, security concerns). But this position might be seriously questioned. The weakening of the European Union, concurrently with the crisis of neo-liberalistm, and the severe financial crises in 2008, could well lead to the opposite conclusion. Namely, a Eurosceptic outcome with a return to nationally based economics and politics, and a revival of national corporatism. Yet a third scenario is suggested by Holman – the EU may enter another period of 'eurosclerosis'.

A case study by Simon Bromley analyses EU energy policy. He starts with the 2007 EU energy policy, with its declaration that business as usual was not an option, and its ambitious targets for reduction in carbon emissions by 2020, and increase in energy production through renewables. Bromley questions the feasibility of such an ambitious EU-wide energy policy when there is still no integrated European energy market, and member states still have substantial sovereignty over energy policy. He discusses the position in the 1960s and 1970s when no energy policy at the EC level seemed necessary, and points to the oil crisis of 1973–4 as introducing a major change in attitude. He discusses the EU's relationship with the United States, and also with Russia, particularly in relation to gas, and the likelihood of an increase in conflict over energy resources in the future. Bromley believes that major changes will occur in the future in the way that oil reserves are calculated, which may trigger a move beyond conventional oil to other kinds of oil deposits, and to new extraction methods. He argues that there will be a strategic need for the EU to move beyond conventional oil, but that this will be difficult to do if it is left to liberalised markets.

In the final section of the book, Whither the European Union?, we consider possible future scenarios. In her paper Vivien Schmidt sums up the position of most of the contributors to this collection. The European Union is a heterogeneous collection of individual states having little common identity at the Union level: '... member-state sense of identity in the EU entails 27 very specific visions about the country in the EU – not to mention the divisions within the countries contesting those visions.'

Within this heterogeneity Schmidt identifies four basic discourses about the EU, which she terms: the pragmatic discourse of the EU as a problem-solving entity promoting free markets and regional security; the normative discourse of the EU as a values-based community ensuring solidarity; the principled discourse of the EU as a rights-based post-national union promoting democratisation; and the strategic discourse of the EU as a global actor that does international relations differently. The pragmatic discourse is most associated with Britain, Ireland and Scandinavia and some of the new member states from Central and Eastern Europe. These states often emphasise economic interests, although not exclusively. They also support enlargement. The states that deploy normative discourse, such as France, Germany, Austria, Belgium, the Netherlands and Luxembourg, are generally against further enlargement if it undermines the common values of the existing Community.

The rights-based discourse, with its emphasis on universal norms and strategic discourse, and with its emphasis on projects rather than processes, are often alternatives to the pragmatic and normative approaches, and have been developed by different sections of the political elites in the member states. They offer alternative ways of legitimating the European Union and imagining its future. Schmidt concludes that the heterogeneity that the different discourses display is not necessarily negative. There may be a way in the future of reconciling all four discourses in a strengthened Union, but this would require the acceptance of differentiated integration and an end to the pursuit of unanimity and uniformity.

Finally, Montserrat Guibernau addresses the crucial question of the formation of a European, as opposed to a national or ethnic identity. She cautions against a unilateral interpretation of 'European' values. She points out that Europe has had a history of different value systems. She poses the question of the sources of European identity and cultural diversity. The emergence of European identity requires political will to build a common project for the future. Such a project is located essentially in a commitment to liberal democracy and a liberal concept of capitalism. However, the formation of an EU identity faces formidable challenges in terms of religious values and cultural national forms of identification that are embedded in the histories of European states.

Guibernau points out that people may have shared identities at different levels: that of the nation state, their own ethnic or national identity, and supranational identities such as 'European'. The problem is to combine different identities in a successful way – to merge the allegiance to a nation state with a supranational identity of a European state. Currently, and following the findings of Gyorgy Lengyel's chapter, there is a great range of conflicting views among citizens of the EU as to the nature of the EU. The enlargement to the east has led to a rise of negative opinions concerning the EU and problematises cohesion. In Guibernau's view, European identity is best defined as an emergent 'non-emotional' identity, in contrast to the powerful and emotionally charged national identities. A problem here is the widening gap between the views of elites and masses about European identity, a gap reflected in the vote against the draft EU Constitution. National identity, she concludes, is the major focus of most citizens.

The contributions to this book illustrate that the world in the 21st century will not be a Eurocentric world, and Europeans will have to adjust to being a much less important part of the world than they have been used to being for the past three centuries. But the European Union will still be a very significant player. How it may respond, and how it may resolve some of its internal tensions and the different perceptions and interests of its members is the main subject of this book.

Part I
The International Context

1
The United States and the European Union: The End of Hegemony?

Andrew Gamble

After the collapse of the Soviet Union in 1991 the debate on US decline which had characterised the 1980s was succeeded by a debate on the new and unchallenged dominance of the United States, following the implosion of its one serious military rival. The end of the Cold War was an ideological and political triumph for the United States and was widely celebrated as a vindication of the long-term strategy of containment and pressure which the Americans had pursued over four decades. At the same time it created a vacuum in US policy, raising questions of whether the elaborate system of bases and the huge military budgets established during the Cold War were any longer necessary. Although there was some reduction in budgets, the overall contraction of US military capacity and reach in the 1990s was small, and instead a strong campaign was waged to consolidate and extend the unprecedented system of supremacy which the US had acquired. New doctrines of unilateralism, pre-emption, and primacy were formulated to justify the maintenance of US global power. A typical product of this effort was the Project for an American Century in 1998, signed by many of the people who were soon to take office in the Bush Administration.[1]

The unipolarity of the international system after the demise of the Soviet Union focused attention once again on the precise role of the United States and the kind of power it represents, and whether this power is best described as imperial or hegemonic. The term empire has never been a popular one in the United States. Ever since the revolutionary war which founded the new state and separated it permanently from the British Empire, the Americans have presented themselves as a modern nation that is anti-imperial and anti-monarchical, firmly opposed to the practices and institutions of old Europe. The dissolution of the colonial empires of the European powers became a key objective of the United States in the 20th century, for ideological as well as economic and political reasons. The US set itself against other powers having exclusive spheres of interest, and did so in the name of national self-determination and the freedom and independence of all nations. The universalism of the American message contrasted with the particularism of the Europeans, and allowed the Americans to take a high moral position and project an ideal of world order which envisioned the disappearance of exclusive spheres of influence, colonies and empires. Woodrow Wilson distilled this approach in a style and rhetoric which still resonates today.[2] It makes it difficult for any American leader consciously to embrace the language of empire to describe US power. The United States still claims to be an anti-colonial power and sets its face against permanent incorporation of new territory. The language of empire contradicts the fundamental idea the United States has formed of itself.

Nevertheless, historians have long pointed to the contrast between American practice and American rhetoric. The determination of many of the American revolutionaries was that the new state should be different from the European empires with elaborate checks and balances to ensure that the executive power remained limited, that the standing army was small, and the budgets modest. From the very beginning the United States was expansionist in North America itself, displacing native Americans from their lands, and using every means to push out European powers and push back its immediate neighbours, Mexico and Canada. Jefferson, one of the leading advocates of states' rights and an opponent of the creation of a strong federal government, proved one of the most effective proponents of American empire in this most traditional sense of the term – an expansionist power claiming exclusive jurisdiction over a particular territory. The successful colonisation of the bulk of the landmass of North America by the state created by the union of the original 13 colonies laid the foundation for the United States to become a great power, and a player in the international system. From an early stage too this state began to intervene abroad, developing its own sphere of influence in Latin America and the Caribbean, seeking to displace the influence of others. At the end of the 19th century a more active imperialist policy began with the war against Spain, and the wresting of the Philippines and Cuba from Spanish control. A strong realist strand in American thinking associated with Theodore Roosevelt, John Hay, Alfred Mahan and others now asserted itself, and new military doctrines and a new strategic awareness came to characterise an important part of the political class.[3]

US participation in two world wars, which firmly established it as a world power, was therefore based on an experience of seeking and controlling first a continental empire and secondly a growing sphere of influence. The United States was never an imperial power in the sense of possessing extensive overseas colonies which it directly administered, but it was not devoid of them either, and it played the great power game for spheres of influence as ruthlessly as its European counterparts. Following the Second World War the United States in its bid to contain the Soviet Union embarked on a far-reaching policy of containment which ultimately led to a permanent US presence overseas, with 750 bases, 1.5 million personnel, and huge budgets for military equipment, which locked major sectors of the US economy into the new industrial military complex.[4] For proponents of the thesis that the US is now an empire, and relates to the rest of the world as an empire, and indeed the only significant empire that still functions, the vast US military deployment is the surest evidence of it. The failure of the deployment to contract once the ostensible reason for it, the need to contain the Soviet Union and its allies, had disappeared is often cited as proof that the deployment has developed its own rationale, and is geared to maintaining US supremacy in every part of the globe.[5] It is the permanence of the bases that suggests an empire, by giving the US the ability to intervene or apply pressure wherever it wants.

If the term empire is restricted to direct control and administration of territory by the imperial power, then the US is no empire. It tends to administer other countries only for short periods, generally preferring to rule through governments it instals rather than to incur the expense of ruling directly. But this has also been a characteristic feature of many empires in the past, including the British. For many analysts of empire the crucial element which makes a relationship between two states imperial is the direct coercion or threat of coercion which the imperial power can exert to achieve the objectives it seeks. Empire in this sense refers to the power of a state to expand and incorporate new spheres and territories by direct or indirect means. It is measured by the capacities of the imperial state and its spatial reach, which is normally regional, but in the last 200 years can also be global. The United States is the first empire which, following its defeat of the Soviet Union, has secured a true global reach, even establishing bases in many of the former satellites and component parts of the Soviet Union, particularly the states of central Asia.[6]

The extent of US power is so apparent, and the means to sustain it appear so similar to many previous empires, that an increasing number of the contemporary advocates of US power are quite happy for the term empire to be employed, and there are others who urge the US to become conscious of its position as an empire, on the grounds that it needs an ideology of empire and a consciousness of empire if it is to make full use of the opportunities which its position of supremacy confers on it. Niall Ferguson has called on the US to learn from the example of the British Empire and be prepared to govern territories for long periods, installing good government and good administration directly rather than ruling through proxies.[7] His call has been echoed by others, and there has emerged a widespread view that the position the US finds itself in at the start of the 21st century has certain similarities to Britain in the 19th. British imperialism, which was once so scorned and derided by the Americans as part of the old world and the old politics that they had risen above, now seems to be making a partial comeback.

The comeback is only partial of course, and most of the American political class, including both George Bush and Barack Obama, remains firm, claiming that to say the United States is an empire is a contradiction in terms.[8] The United States cannot be an empire and remain true to itself, and its anti-imperial heritage, and the proof that it remains true is that the United

States does not annex territories. It invades them, sometimes administers them, but never holds on to them for very long. The Americans always go home (although they rarely, voluntarily, give up a military base). Whether they will in Iraq remains to be seen.

There is however another line of argument which disputes that the United States is an empire, or at least disputes that it is primarily an empire. The basic facts of US power are not doubted, but it is suggested that the term which best characterises US power is hegemony. US power is hegemonic rather than imperial in two senses, which correspond to two of the main ways that hegemony has been developed as a concept; firstly because the US has acquired a structural position of dominance in the global economy, in the global international state system, and in the global culture; and secondly that the US has developed a conscious governing strategy in relation to its role in all three. Hegemony in this sense is used to refer to the exercise of power which does not involve direct territorial control. It draws on the distinction between formal and informal empire.[9] In the context of studies of imperialism hegemony was still regarded as a form of empire, but of informal rather than formal empire.

Contemporary theorists of hegemony in the international state system have developed this idea. John Ikenberry, for example, has distinguished between two logics of order, a unipolar order organised around liberal characteristics involving shared rule, and a unipolar order organised around imperial characteristics, involving self-rule.[10] For Ikenberry the US has always been more than a superpower; it is hegemonic because it produces a particular kind of world order, an order which is open and rule-based. The key difference between empire and hegemony is that the leading state is prepared to operate within multilateral rules and institutions. Ikenberry does not dispute that the US is often imperial in its relationship with many states. It pursues an imperial logic in its policies, particularly towards Latin America and the Middle East, but a hegemonic logic towards Europe, Japan, Russia and China. The classic instance of this exercise of hegemony has been the relationship between the United States and Europe since 1945. The nations of Western Europe willingly accepted the leadership of the United States in return for admittance as full members of the American world order, and the recognition and safeguarding of their key economic and security interests through the creation of a range of multilateral institutions. Since the end of the Cold War this relationship has come under strain, leading to a questioning on both sides of where their fundamental interests lie.

Europe and America

Europe and the United States have long been regarded as pillars of the West, but the order of priority has been reversed. At one time the West meant primarily Europe. But during the 20th century the West came to mean

Europe and North America, with the United States coming to play at first an equal and then a leading role. This reached its high point in the conception of the Atlantic partnership during the Second World War, after which the United States emerged as the unchallenged leader of the West, and Atlantic partnership was continued into the post-war period in the form of NATO. During this period the West attained its clearest expression, since it became embodied in a military alliance and crystallised in a set of values and principles, the formulation of a Western ideology to counter the ideology of communism.

The end of the Cold War and the collapse of communism in Europe was the moment at which much greater rifts began to appear between Europe and the United States. It accelerated after 9/11, with the identification by the United States government of a new enemy which the West as a whole, including Europe, should mobilise to confront, namely radical Islam. This perception was at best only weakly shared in Europe. This dissonance came to a head with the disagreements over the Iraq war and how to prosecute the wider war on terror, particularly with issues such as the legitimacy of the dentention camp in Guantanamo Bay and the CIA practice of extraordinary rendition, apparently violating the national sovereignty of many European states, as well as the civil and human rights of the detainees. The rejection by many in Europe of America's call to arms to combat the new enemy of radical Islam shook the Atlantic partnership, and made some like Robert Kagan question whether it was possible to revive it in its old form.[11] Events since 1991 also threw into sharp focus how the underlying premise of 'The West' that so dominated the 50 years after 1941 was that it was not just an Atlantic partnership but an Anglo-American partnership. At the heart of the version of the West and the Western ideology that triumphed was an Anglo-American understanding. During the ups and downs of the 'special relationship' in the 1940s and 1950s this was harder to perceive, especially with the priority that the United States gave to Germany and the EU after 1960.[12] But beginning in the 1980s with the special rapport Reagan and Thatcher enjoyed in launching the new Cold War, and then still more strikingly in the period after the collapse of communism and the proclamation of a new world order, the relationships of Tony Blair first with Clinton and then with Bush, revealed still more starkly the Anglo-American core of the alliance.[13] Some neo-conservatives in this period even revived some of the much earlier notions of Anglo-American partnership that had been part of the project of Greater Britain and its successors at the end of the 19th century through to the 1950s.[14] Their new name for it was the Anglosphere, which is defined as including the United States, Great Britain, Canada, Australia, New Zealand and Ireland (now forgiven for its Catholicism). Other nations, if they are English-speaking, such as some of the Caribbean states, some African states, and India, are admitted to a second tier of membership. Even Japan is allowed honorary membership. This leaves out certain countries, notably Germany, France and the rest of the European

Union, Russia, all of Latin America, China, all Islamic countries and most of Africa.

This notion of the West, current in the Bush years, was a long way from the idea of a partnership between America and Europe. Most of Europe was indeed excluded. Instead, the Anglosphere was presented as a group of nations whose shared language, culture, institutions and values made it the latest and truest embodiment of the West, which other nations should emulate if they wanted to achieve both freedom and prosperity. But beyond this there was a still more exclusive notion of the West which occasionally surfaced. This was the idea that only the United States truly represented the West, and though it might at times have allies, including the nations of the Anglosphere, they were not to be relied on. America no longer sought to build alliances but to assemble 'coalitions of the willing' which as the name suggested, were likely to be temporary and shifting, very vulnerable to changes in domestic circumstances. On this view only America understood the burdens of leadership and was prepared to bear the costs and make the necessary sacrifices.[15] Specifically, Robert Kagan maintained that in the 21st century only America, and in a much more limited sense, Britain, was prepared to defend the Western project and the Western ideology through the use of military power. The other great European powers had abdicated that role, and no longer sought to defend that notion of the West. By taking this position and defining the West so that it now excluded most of Europe, the Western ideology became synonymous with the American creed.[16] In itself this could be made to seem a natural development, since the American creed was a unique synthesis of Enlightenment and Christian values, with a range and resonance that British liberalism, for example, never matched, and which demonstrated its appeal throughout the 20th century. Other ideologies, like German nationalism, were anti-Western and sought to reject the Enlightenment version of modernity,[17] and those like Russian Communism, which were pro-Western and accepted it but tried to go beyond it, have been discredited, and mostly discarded.

Because America became the embodiment of modernity in the 20th century, alternative versions of the West were displaced, sometimes only after a prolonged struggle. Many of them, even when they had originated within the heart of the West and the Western ideology of modernity, were deemed anti-Western. America in particular was strongly opposed from its very beginnings to the *anciens regimes* of Europe, and to the values of hierarchy, tradition, authority and inequality which they embodied. But it came to be equally opposed to new ideologies such as socialism and communism which sought to go beyond liberal versions of the Western ideology of modernity, as well as those ideologies such as Nazism and fascism which rejected some of its core values. During the 20th century America was twice drawn into a global war and fought against German and Japanese militarism, Nazism and communism, in the course of which it was obliged to set out and defend its own conception of a liberal and democratic world order, and seek to realise it through the establishment of international bodies, first the League of Nations, and then after 1945 the United Nations.[18] By the middle of the 20th century every power in Western Europe that might have been a rival to the United States and an alternative centre for the West had either been defeated or subordinated to America. By the end of the 20th century the collapse of communism meant that for the time being there was also no power outside Europe that could contest the dominance of America.

It is against this background that the different attitudes within the political elites of the European Union towards the United States emerged. The relationship with the United States has been and remains a crucial relationship for all the members of the European Union. All can be said to have a 'special relationship' with the United States, but the substance of this relationship and the perception of it amongst different national elites and national electorates is very different. The position is further complicated by the existence of the European Union, and the different degrees of importance which states give to dealing with the United States collectively, through the European Union or bilaterally.

Security

During the Bush years divisions between the European Union and the United States became most marked in the security field. The triumph of the West so loudly celebrated after the fall of the Berlin Wall in 1989 has also been blamed as the cause of the fracturing of the West, since with the principal enemy removed, the unity of the West was harder to maintain. The strategic rationale for the close co-operation between Europe and America was weakened. The starkest characterisation of this new relationship was that of Robert Kagan with his depiction of America as the new Mars, mired in history, seeking to discharge its global obligations to maintain an open, liberal world order.[19] Europe, by contrast, he portrayed as the new Venus which, longing for Kant's perpetual peace, wished to avoid conflict and illegality, and insisted on conducting all international relations within a framework of law and human rights, relying for its security not on its own strength but on the goodwill of the United States. Kagan suggested that the European position was essentially false, and confirmed the continued subordination of the European Union to the United States because it was only possible given the willingness of the United States to continue to confront the enemies of the West and maintain the security of the liberal world order from which the Europeans derived such enormous benefit. He doubted that the Europeans would ever change their attitude. With the threat from the Soviet Union now in the past, the Europeans could afford to indulge their fantasies of peace and spontaneous harmony.

Kagan judged that the Europeans would no longer stand alongside the Americans in defending the liberal order, and were drifting by degrees ever further away from America. His largely unspoken fear was that without more support from those that so obviously benefited from the role America plays in the world, the Americans would grow tired of their global role, and look to withdraw once more to the Western hemisphere, leaving the rest of the world to cope as best it could. Kagan did not believe the European Union would ever emerge as a serious great power rival to the United States; its military budgets remained miniscule, and the willingness of European populations to support interventions for traditional realpolitik reasons would continue to dwindle, and was even weak, he argued, where major human rights violations were involved, as first Kosovo and then Iraq demonstrated. In one sense American policy had succeeded all too well. No part of Europe was a threat to the United States, and for the moment at least the European Union was not developing into a United States of Europe, which might have made it a threat at some stage. The problem for the Americans was that the Europeans did not want to fight, they did not want to pay, and they did not want to support the Americans in doing what had to be done. America still had a number of governments in the European Union on which it could count, particularly among the former communist states in the East. But the populations of Europe were increasingly hostile to the exercise of American power. The row over extraordinary rendition made Kagan's point. During the Cold War such illegal operations undertaken for reasons of state would have been criticised but also condoned by a large section of European public opinion. But it no longer seemed so.

Kagan's explanation of the deteriorating relationship between Europe and America was that these two former partners in the project of the West no longer shared the same view of power or of the essential nature of the international system. This was making cooperation increasingly difficult between them. His view can be contrasted with two other perspectives from the same period of why the West was in disarray. Niall Ferguson agreed with Kagan that the problem was about perceptions of power and the nature of the international order, but argued that the problem was not just on Europe's side. America needed to shed the conception of power it had long held, and embrace the older European perspective of the nature of the international system. America had more and more the trappings and the responsibilities of an imperial power, but refused to acknowledge it openly, and so constantly failed to act as an imperial power, with serious consequences, both for itself and the rest of the world. Ferguson's advice was that America should overcome its scruples and learn from the Europeans, governing its far-flung empire in the way that Britain and France used to rule their dominions. This would mean that America would have to be prepared to rule certain parts of the world for long periods, and would have to build domestic and international support to permit this to happen. The pattern of short campaigns using overwhelming firepower, followed by brief occupations and then rapid pull-outs, would be replaced by a more considered strategy of long-term occupation and reconstruction of failed states. Making the world safe for democracy would no longer be a matter of granting self-determination and expecting democratic institutions to take root spontaneously and flourish. America would have to be in for the long haul.[20]

Ferguson's ideas won some support among neo-conservatives, but many others, including Kagan, rejected them. For America to abandon the Woodrow Wilson approach to global leadership would be a major shift in thinking and in strategy, which most Americans were far from ready to take. It would be extremely hard to justify inside the United States, and it would be just as hard, if not harder, to justify in Europe, for all the reasons Kagan listed. If the Europeans were unhappy with assertions of unilateral American leadership in the cause of preserving the conditions for a liberal world order, they were unlikely to warm to steps to formalise American dominance as a new American empire, however much it might remind them of their own history. What Ferguson was clear about was the need for American leadership, of the need for a continuing role for the West. His dispute with Kagan was over the best form this role could take. In one way it was a conscious revival of the older argument between the British and the Americans, with the British sure that they understood much better than the Americans how to maintain order throughout the world and safeguard the liberal world economy. What was common to both Kagan and Ferguson was that they wrote off the rest of Europe as having a significant part to play in the maintenance of global security, yet were aware of how crucial Europe remained in legitimating the leadership of the United States.

A quite different position from either Kagan's or Ferguson's was taken by Samuel Huntington, and echoed in different ways by voices across the American political spectrum, from Patrick Buchanan to Gore Vidal. They all wanted America to disengage from its project of world leadership of the West which it had pursued for most of the 20th century, cut Europe and the rest of the world adrift, and instead focus on America itself, and its own national interest and tradition. Vidal argued that the American Empire had been a costly mistake and had gradually poisoned American democracy and the American republic;[21] while Buchanan denounced the neo-conservatives who had abandoned true conservatism and involved America in foreign wars and entanglements.[22] Huntington came to a similar position through his exploration of the nature of American identity, and his belief that the world was dividing up into civilisations.[23] For Huntington the key issue was not that America should remain the leader of the West in close touch with Europe, but that it should remain America. It needed to hang on to its Anglo-Protestant culture and ensure that all immigrants continued to assimilate into American society by adhering to its tenets. What Huntington advanced in effect was a new version of the much older notion of American exceptionalism, which set the United States apart from the other nations of the world, including the Europe from which it first came.

With his emphasis on Anglo-Protestant culture as the essence of America, Huntington might also have embraced the notion of the Anglosphere as the basis of a project for a new West, shorn of false friends in Europe. But he showed little interest. There was an important inheritance, he acknowledged, from Britain, but America was increasingly divergent from Europe, Britain included. In cultural terms Americans in his theory should have more in common with Europeans, and especially with the English, Welsh and Scots, than with other civilisations. But he clearly did not expect relations to be particularly close, or requiring the kind of orchestration which it received during the Cold War. America should concentrate on its own security and not provide guarantees for others. It should return to the simple maxims of the founding fathers and avoid foreign entanglements.

Amidst the swirl of arguments about America's future the Wilsonians remain in the ascendancy, as they have been more or less uninterruptedly since the 1940s, despite the many setbacks to American policy, and the growth of anti-American sentiment in many countries around the world. But as a result of recent events a curious inversion has taken place in the role that America and Europe occupy. For the first hundred years of its existence America had come to represent the new world of innocence, high ideals and moral values, and Europe the old world, corrupt and dominated by amoral power politics. In the course of the 20th century America entered international politics, but on its own terms. As a result of its military prowess, and its huge economic and cultural resources, it emerged as the unchallenged global leader in the West. There were growing criticisms of the direction and assumptions of American policy, and many of its results. But this criticism was held in check by the security threat to Europe and other countries. In the last 15 years, however, with the decline in this external threat, it was now Europe that emerged to reclaim the position of principle and morality, and America that was cast as the corrupt old world, mired in history, still engaged in managing the global polity and dealing with the problems the Europeans did not wish to confront. The Europeans' relative abandonment of power politics, and the Americans embrace of it during the Bush years, was a striking reversal of roles, and one that pushed America and Europe apart in security terms, but it was easy to exaggerate the gulf between them, and also to ignore he fact that Europe itself was far from unified, with different nations displaying very different attitudes to security.

These divisions were highlighted at the time of the Iraq war, when a number of European countries, including Britain, Spain and Italy, as well as several of the new member states in Eastern Europe, such as Poland, joined the coalition of the willing in supporting the United States' invasion of Iraq. Donald Rumsfeld memorably characterised the division as one between old and new Europe: 'You're thinking of Europe as Germany and France. I don't.

That's old Europe...but you look at the vast numbers of other countries in Europe. They're not with France and Germany on this, they're with the United States.' How Britain and Spain fitted into the category of new Europe was not explained.

With the election of Barack Obama a new phase opens in this relationship, with early indications that Obama will seek to emphasise multilateral relationships and the hegemonic role of the United States rather than unilateral relationships and the imperial role. The enthusiasm for him in Europe and in other parts of the world gives him a rare opportunity to remake American leadership, and repair bridges. The stridency of the Bush years may be over. Obama will still be faced with tough choices, however, and American capacities in several key respects are weaker than before. His presidency will be defined by his response to major events in his first two years in office. That will show how far he is able to restore the relationship between the United States and Europe.

Modernity

Another revealing set of contrasts between Europe and the United States concerns modernity. In the past much debate has centred on the question of whether America or Europe represents the most advanced form of modernity.[24] The impact of the revolutions of modernity upon perceptions of time and space brought with it an understanding of all societies as involved in a constant process of change and development. The leader in one stage might come to be seen as backward in the next. One persistent theme has been whether modern society is a single phenomenon in the sense that all societies are destined to evolve in the same direction and reach the same destination, or whether it is a multiple phenomenon, allowing a diversity of different experiences and paths of development within a common framework. As Offe argues, both Tocqueville and Weber were convinced that there was one dominant pattern, although they had very different ideas as to what that was. This viewpoint was widely shared in the 19th century.[25]

What constituted the essential aspects of modernity, however, were disputed. Tocqueville regarded the democratic revolution which he observed on his travels in the United States as providing a new and different model of civil society from the one familiar in Europe. It was the egalitarianism of American society which so struck him, the source of its dynamism, its restlessness and its conformity. Its natural counterpart was the spread of market relations, and the tendency to express all social relationships as commercial relationships. In this way an egalitarian civil society was the foundation for American capitalism with its emphasis on mass markets and mass production, which was eventually to sweep the world. Formal political equality was accompanied by widening economic inequality. This American model of civil society, capitalism and culture eventually became the leading model in the

20th century, and America became regarded as the most modern society, the standard that others aspired to. Americanisation was seen as the fate of all societies if they wished to be modern.

A very different view of modernity was set out by Max Weber, writing at the end of the 19th century during the great surge of German industrialisation. The German model, with its emphasis on science and technology, on organisation, on bureaucracy and concentration and centralisation of production, appeared to Weber the inevitable path of development for all societies. He was dismissive of the dreams of socialists that they could take control of the wealth and productivity of this great industrial engine and use it to build a society of simple cooperation and substantive equality. But he was also dismissive of the Anglo-American alternative, which he regarded as a pre-modern form of social organisation. Its voluntarism and decentralisation, he predicted, would have to give way to the imperatives of organisation and bureaucracy. In this way Europe, and in particular Germany, showed the way both to England and to America. If they wanted to compete with Germany they would have to adopt its methods.

Germany's defeat in two world wars meant that it was the American model rather that the German model that triumphed, although many of the traits of the German model were incorporated into the American, in particular the emphasis upon science and technology to drive innovation and productivity. But, contrary to Weber's expectations, many aspects of the American model were not abandoned, in particular the relatively decentralised and voluntaristic character of its civil society. For much of the 20th century the question of modernity was posed differently, through the debate on the rival claims of capitalism and socialism, and whether the socialist models of Russia and China offered a more advanced form of modernity to which the rest of the world would have to adapt.[26] When the unity of the West was at its height in the 1950s and 1960s the Western model was the American free-market model, to be defended against the communist model of central planning. But as the appeal of the communist model began to fade when its inability to compete politically, economically or culturally became clear, so there was a revival of debate about alternative capitalist models. In the 1980s this reached a peak when the apparent troubles of the US economy sparked speculation about American decline,[27] and about the supposed superiority of European and East Asian models of capitalism. These models were regarded as superior because of their better organisation, their ability to initiate and sustain long-term investment and their industrial relations, all of which produced higher productivity and greater social cohesion.

After 1991 the debate changed, and attention switched to the extraordinary position of dominance that the United States now occupied. The stagnation of German and Japanese economies through the 1990s and the relative success of the American and British economies revived speculation that it was still the American economy which was the leading world economy, and the success of other models had been due to special circumstances during the Cold War. America was still the leading capitalist power, and its model was still the one that was dominant. With the emergence of the IT revolution and the knowledge economy, the adapability and continuing dynamism of American civil society, and in particular the prowess of its educational institutions, now began to be compared to the relative stagnation and sclerosis of other capitalist societies. The new language of the Washington consensus emphasised flexibility, deregulation and privatisation, and the American model was once more promoted as the model that others needed to copy.

During the neo-liberal era there were observers on both left and right who believed that the American model would prove increasingly irresistible, and that there might once again be one Western economic model, one model of what an advanced modernity looks like. David Coates argued that the alternative models of capitalism that had flourished in different parts of the world in earlier decades looked increasingly fragile in the neo-liberal global economy.[28] This view was contested by others who argued that the foundations of the global economy remained national and regional, and that national models were becoming more divergent, not less.[29] In Europe the American model had long been contested, even in Britain, by variants of the European social model, which had a very different approach to welfare, corporate governance and labour markets to that found in the United States.[30] Varied institutional patterns supported by the authority of national governments are still pervasive, despite the pressure of competition and the opportunities for policy transfer. There might no longer be a serious alternative to the capitalist model, but the variety of capitalisms on offer was striking, and that increased the sense of a divide between Europe and America.

The global crash in 2008 both confirmed and went against some of these arguments. The speed with which the global crash came to affect all parts of the global economy, including Europe, and the way in which the problems of the British and American banks quickly became the problems of the European banks, supported the argument that the same neo-liberal logic had come to govern all capitalist economies. On the other hand the crash also signalled the wreckage of the neo-liberal model, and made it more likely rather than less that different models would emerge in different parts of the global economy as countries struggled to respond to the downturn.[31]

Ideology

There have been signs too of increasing ideological divergence between Europe and the United States. The unity which existed for a time when America was accepted as the leader of the West in the face of a common danger from Soviet communism has been fractured. In place of the pluralist Western tradition and the Western ideology of modernity, which had always embraced both different ideologies and alternative modernities, the Western ideology of modernity now became identified much more closely with one strand of the Western tradition, the American creed, which was treated increasingly as the most advanced and true statement of it. The current dominant version of the Western ideology is tied in with the idea of America, and specifically with the role assumed by the United States as global hegemon and leader of the West, the promulgator of a set of universal values which accurately distil the tradition of Western civilisation, and which have vanquished all alternatives.[32]

Even at the height of American influence and legitimacy during the early period of the Cold War, the Western ideology was not monolithic. A range of ideas was thought compatible with it, even moderate forms of social democracy. But in the past two decades it has perceptibly narrowed, and its dominant expression has become the twin doctrines of neo-liberalism and neo-conservatism. Like previous Western ideologies, neo-liberalism claims to be not one ideology among others, but to possess both rationality and objectivity, and therefore universality. This universality arises because neo-liberalism claims to understand the nature of modernity, which means there can be no serious or viable alternative to it.[33] Neo-liberalism is not the first or the only version of the Western ideology to make such claims, but after two centuries of ideological strife between different claimants to being the true version of the Western ideology, it has emerged as the dominant one. Many of its claims are contested, both within liberalism, and by other Western ideologies, as well as by traditions of thought outside the Western ideology and Western experience altogether.

This identification of America as the bearer of universalism is contested, not least within America itself. As Huntington notes, there has always been a conflict between three different ideas of America nationalism – the universal nation, the Western nation, and the exceptional nation.[34] As a universal nation America claims to embody universal values, valid at all times and in all places. As a Western nation America claims to be the inheritor and exemplar of European civilisation. As an exceptional nation America claims to be unique, neither universal nor Western, simply American. All three conceptions have been present from the beginning of the Republic, but all three are recognisable aspects of the American creed.

The narrow formulation of the Western ideology favoured by neo-liberals and neo-conservatives is widely rejected in Europe, where doctrines of social democracy and Christian democracy are still in the ascendancy and support a notion of social citizenship quite different from neo-liberal conceptions.[35] The virulence of American nationalism has been strongly criticised. This puts another question mark against the legitimacy of the Unites States as the leader of the West. Many Europeans do not any longer regard the United States as an effective guardian of many aspects of the Western tradition, and have ceased to believe in the possibility of one path of modernity, embracing instead the notion of many modernities. Some see a danger if some of the universal aspects of the Western ideology become a cloak for United States policy, rather than part of the structure of multilateral governance of world order, supplying universal norms and standards for the conduct of world affairs, such as are found in the key documents formulating the idea of universal human rights, such as the 1967 UN Conventions on Human Rights.[36] Many of the rules and standards and international law which have emerged have done so because of the commitment of Western ideologies to ideas such as the rule of law. But there has always been a tension between a rule-based international regime, and the willingness of all the participants to subject themselves to it.

One of the difficulties of thinking about ideology in security terms is that it ignores the extent to which ideas and ideological conflicts cut across national boundaries. There are not really two distinct spaces – Europe and America – as a single space, Euro-America, within which many different ideas contend for supremacy. The notion that there is a single 'American' perspective and a single 'European' perspective cannot be sustained. Nevertheless the differences encountered between European and American perceptions is now striking.

Territorial scenarios

The future of the relationship between Europe and America has been imagined in a variety of ways, in which territorial, multilateral and cosmopolitan perspectives all feature.

Territorial scenarios think in terms of blocs, empires, civilisations and nations. George Orwell's compelling vision in 1984 imagined a world divided between three blocs – Oceania, Eastasia and Eurasia. Each bloc claimed its own sphere of influence, and acted always to further its interests and maximise its power, making impossible the idea of One World, the unification of the whole world within one civilisation and set of values. Orwell's gloomy forebodings were based on a projection of what the world had actually looked like in the 1930s, although in the 1930s the struggle for supremacy between Germany and Russia for control of Eurasia was yet to take place, and the relationship between the United States and Britain in Oceania still had some way to run, while Japan was consolidating its control of East Asia. The outcomes of the Second World War left for a time only two blocs – those based around the United States and around the Soviet Union. Japan was destroyed as a military power, while China was yet to emerge. Orwell conceived these blocs as engaged in a perpetual military and economic struggle, each eternally seeking to mobilise its people against the external threat posed by the others. With the collapse of the Soviet Union, an unprecedented unipolar world was created, which for a time made it seem that the United States could achieve whatever it wanted because it faced no resistance. This unilateralist temptation, cutting free from multilateralist entanglements, was urged on the United States by neo-conservatives. It has become clear, however, that the more the United States acts unilaterally, the greater the erosion of its position in the multilateral system, which was the basis of the postwar idea of the West, and the more likely too the possibility of new powers arising in time to challenge US supremacy. The security community is already speculating about a new bipolar world, split between the United States and China. But in this scenario it is not clear where Europe would be.

One of the difficulties of a world divided into blocs, empires or civilisations is that there seem to be as many dividing lines within the blocs and the civilisations as between them. The relationship between America and Europe is a prime example. Opponents of the West certainly still speak of a Western civilisation and often treat Europe and America as though they were both equally part of 'the West'. But as noted above, many observers see Europe and America drifting apart, and reject the older claim that there are common evolutionary trends in all modern societies that will make them increasingly like one another.[37] If this is the case then the idea that the world is dividing into three or four mega-civilisations is unlikely. It is more probable that it will fragment into a much large number of cultural groupings. The separation of Europe from America, and indeed resistance to convergence and uniformity within Europe itself, become part of this much bigger pattern of multicultural differentiation and cross-cutting allegiances. To the extent, however, that some pattern of blocs or civilisations does impose itself, the question of whether America and Europe will be two blocs or one, one civilisation or none, becomes important. Many observers on both sides of the Atlantic see no basis for reuniting the West. Robert Kagan urges the Europeans to open their eyes and see that America is doing important work that someone has to do if the West and the civilisation it represents are to survive. But as he acknowledges, increasing numbers of Europeans do not see it like that, and want to define Europe as something quite distinct from America. Many Americans are beginning to feel the same way. Whether Obama can reverse that drift remains to be seen.

Isolationists take the territorial logic to its conclusion. If America cannot unite the West, and if the rest of the world is increasingly hostile to American values and goals, then it might be better for America to forget the 'West', and concentrate on America. Samuel Huntington conceives the struggle between civilisations as a clash of different values and institutions, but not necessarily involving military or economic competition. He argues that Western rationalism and many other Western values are specific to Western civilisation, and cannot be made universal. Attempts to force them upon non-Western cultures are doomed to failure, and may threaten their preservation at home. All nationalisms have within them a yearning to withdraw into themselves, into a world where only members of the nation or the group belong, and from which the rest of the world can be excluded. Dreams of isolation are often illusory, but that does not diminish their power or their appeal. Plans for a security shield, for halting immigration, for stopping trade and cultural exchange constantly recur. The decision of the Tokugawa Shogunate in Japan at the beginning of the 16th century to close the country to foreigners was an extreme measure, but it lasted three centuries. This kind of isolationism is unattainable for most contemporary nationalists, although there are still some states, such as Burma, which attempt a version of it.

Despite the occasional talk of isolationist America or Fortress Europe, no-one thinks either is remotely achievable in contemporary circumstances. Nevertheless what this scenario points to is a potential direction of travel, a gradual shutting down of external links, a disinclination to co-operate and a slow turning inwards. The appeal of this perspective will grow enormously because of the global crash in 2008 and the global recession that has followed it. Optimists have pointed in the past to the counter-tendencies of globalisation, but it is not enough to argue that the pressures of globalisation oblige every nation to become more cosmopolitan and open to the rest of the world. In this as in so much else the impact of globalisation is uneven, and in a global recession even more so. It creates, for example, information technology networks which are highly cosmopolitan, but many other groups, even while they utilise the new technologies and new opportunities that globalisation creates, remain resolutely fixed in very narrow ethnic, religious and national identities.[38]

Multilateralist scenarios

Multilateralist scenarios are committed to a very different idea of the relationship between Europe and America, one that is inclusive and outward-looking, even though they still regard the international state system as the basis of world order. The degree of interdependence in the international system in so many different spheres makes co-operative and multilateral solutions essential for maintaining the kind of order which, for all its failings, has been painstakingly constructed since the end of the Second World War. Rebuilding the partnership between America and Europe is a necessary first step towards this. The multilateral approach believes that America can still give leadership to the world, but only if it moves back from the kind of unilateralism favoured by neo-conservatives, with its ad hoc coalitions of the willing, and instead puts time and effort once again into long-term building of institutions and policies to combat common problems.[39] Francis Fukuyama, for example, now rejects the arguments for unilateralism made by neo-conservatives, and their naïve optimism about the ability of America to spread democracy to areas such as the Middle East, and counsels a return to what he calls 'realistic Wilsonianism', rebuilding alliances and restoring American legitimacy.[40] This is very much the stance that both Obama and McCain took in the 2008 presidential campaign.

Much of the case for a return to multilateralism rests on the argument that the alternatives (of blocs, empires, spheres of influence) either will not work, or will lead to very undesirable outcomes. America lacks both the will and the capacity to transform its dominance into an empire, or the staying-power needed for long-term nation-building. As a result what some describe as America's 'empire' looks increasingly incoherent,[41] and its foundations insecure. America of all nations cannot formally adopt a language of empire to rationalise its role in the world. Its power has always been clothed in the universal language of human rights and human freedoms, and its presentation of the West not as another empire on old-Europe lines, but as the catalyst for a wider human emancipation.

Multilateralists have frequently pointed out that American power is in any case inherently limited.[42] Since 1991 the United States has enjoyed overwhelming and unprecedented military power, but the same is not true of economic power, still less of its capacity to influence a whole set of issues such as drugs, immigration, climate change, terrorism and infectious diseases. What multilateralists want to see is the United States again taking the lead in the search for multilateral solutions to some of these problems, making sacrifices and concessions where necessary to bring others on board, including the Europeans. The success that Europe has had in developing its own forms of soft power are often held up as examples, although it is easy to exaggerate. On WTO negotiations the EU can often appear less liberal and less open than the United States, and the setbacks to European integration caused by the rejection of the Constitution in France and the Netherlands raised questions about the viability of the European model, now that membership has reached 27 member states.[43]

At the end of the Bush era it was unclear how far Europe and America could find new ways to deepen their co-operation in the future, committing themselves to extending the rule-based order into new areas, and beginning to tackle some of the problems that have grown up. The attitudes in the European capitals and in Washington were against that, but much of that was due to the Bush presidency itself, and to recent events. The renewal of democratic leadership does offer a chance for new perspectives, and for new understandings to emerge, such as have often occurred in the past. The Obama presidency starts with great goodwill. But the obstacles are formidable, partly because some of the misunderstandings have gone so deep on both sides. There is unlikely ever to be a return to the kind of unity the West exhibited during the early phase of the Cold War. But under Obama's leadership there is very likely to be a renewed commitment to make the multilateral regime work better.

Cosmopolitan scenarios

A third, more visionary, set of perspectives on the relationship between Europe and America are cosmopolitan scenarios, which come in a variety of forms. They are often discounted. But the increasing interconnectedness of all parts of the world through the global economy gives cosmopolitan solutions a growing influence, even if some of the practical obstacles to their implementation remain severe. What is common to all of them is that they do not rely on the state or the existing international system, believing that other forces are more fundamental in shaping the world order. One of the best known cosmopolitan solutions, originating initially in Europe, is the idea of the global market, and the benign effects of allowing a spontaneous market order to determine relations between the peoples of the world. Its champions have included Richard Cobden and Friedrich Hayek, as well as contemporary business gurus of hyperglobalisation. The creation of such an order and the removal of obstacles to its proper working are seen as the main objectives at which the leaders of both Europe and America should aim.

A second cosmopolitan scenario puts the emphasis less on global markets than on global civil society and on cosmopolitan democracy, focusing on the way in which new global organisations, global pressure groups, and global campaigns have begun emerging,[44] and the incremental steps through which the creation of a global polity from the bottom might be created. New global public forums to allow the voices of all peoples of the world, all civilisations, to be heard and recognised, new kinds of association, a new global politics would recognise universal human rights and allow for the first time the representation of all peoples and interests in the governance of the world. For many advocates of cosmopolitan democracy their programme is the antidote to the neo-liberal vision of the cosmopolitan advocates of the global market.[45] They argue that the movement for cosmopolitan democracy is in its very early stages, but will grow, and will reinforce the pressure for multilateralism, but will also go beyond multilateralism. This is a vision of the West in which its historical origins, in particular national and religious traditions, will be transcended through the creation of a universalist, rule-based order which, although inspired by much from Western experience, no longer discriminates in favour of particular regions, particular nations, particular ideologies, or particular traditions, but instead permits multiple modernities to flourish. Europe and America would have a major role in bringing such a world about, but the test of their success would be the much diminished role they would then occupy in the world's affairs. It is not a vision that commands much favour among the elites on either side of the Atlantic.

The global financial crash of 2008 has already begun to redraw the map of world politics. The era of triumphalist neo-liberalism is over, and the global economy faces an uncertain future. After two decades of hubris the Anglo-American model has been tarnished, and will not easily recover its former élan. The crisis revealed the limitations of global markets and the indispensability of governments to any kind of functioning capitalism. It greatly strengthened the arguments for a reconstruction not just of the international financial architecture but also of world governance. It may also come to be seen in retrospect as one of the decisive moments in the rebalancing of the international state system, the decline of the United States and the rise of China. It took time for the depth of the crisis to be understood, and there is a possibility that it may bring forth a coordinated response, unlike the situation in 1929. Whether this unity can be maintained and whether it will lead to lasting changes in the way the world is governed, and the way in which the international community responds to other challenges which it faces, remains to be seen.

Notes and References

1. *The Project for an American Century*: www.newamericancentury.org
2. Lloyd C. Gardner, *Safe for Democracy: The Anglo-American Response to Revolution, 1913–1923,* Oxford and New York: Oxford University Press, 1984; Lloyd C. Gardner, *A Covenant with Power: America and World Order from Wilson to Reagan,* London: Macmillan, 1984.
3. Christopher Hitchens, *Blood, Class and Empire: The Enduring Anglo-American Relationship,* New York: Nation Books, 2004.
4. Chalmers Johnson, *The Sorrows of Empire,* London: Verso, 2006.
5. David Rapkin, 'Empire and its Discontents', *New Political Economy*, 10 (3), 2005, 389–412.
6. Johnson, op. cit.
7. Niall Ferguson, *Colossus,* London: Allen Lane, 2004.
8. Rapkin, op. cit.
9. John Gallagher and Ronald Robinson, 'The Imperialism of Free Trade', *Economic History Review*, 2nd Series, 6, 1953, 1–15.
10. John Ikenberry, 'Liberalism and Empire: Logics of Order in the American Unipolar Age', *Review of International Studies*, 30, 2004, 609–30.
11. Robert Kagan, *Paradise and Power: America and Europe in the New World Order,* London: Atlantic Books, 2003.
12. The special relationship between the US and Britain has received most attention, but the US has had 'special relationships' with many other states, including within Europe, Germany and France. The relationship with France is particularly interesting for understanding the wider relationship between Europe and America.
13. Andrew Gamble, *Between Europe and America: The Future of British Politics,* Basingstoke: Palgrave Macmillan, 2003.
14. James Bennett, *The Anglosphere Challenge,* New York: Rowman & Littlefield, 2004; Robert Conquest, *Reflections on a Ravaged Century,* London: John Murray, 1999; Duncan Bell, *The Idea of a Greater Britain: Empire and the Future of World Order,* Princeton: Princeton University Press, 2007.
15. Kagan, op. cit.
16. On the American creed see Samuel Huntington, *Who Are We?,* New York: Simon and Schuster, 2004; Anatol Lieven, *America Right or Wrong,* London: HarperCollins, 2004. The term was used by Gunnar Myrdal in *An American Dilemma: The Negro Problem and Modern Democracy,* New York: Harper, 1962.
17. Ian Buruma and Avishai Margalit, *Occidentalism: The West in the Eyes of Its Enemies,* London: Penguin, 2005.
18. Gardner, *A Covenant with Power,* op. cit.
19. Kagan, op. cit.
20. Ferguson, op. cit.

21. Gore Vidal, *Imperial America: Reflections on the United States of Amnesia*, New York: Nation Books, 2004.
22. Patrick Buchanan, *Where the Right Went Wrong*, New York: Thomas Dunne, 2004.
23. Huntington, op. cit.
24. Claus Offe, *Reflections on America: Tocqueville, Weber and Adorno in the United States*, Cambridge: Polity, 2005.
25. Marx, for example, claimed in the first edition of *Capital* that 'the country that is more developed industrially only shows to the less developed the image of its own future'. The Germans might mock the English for their apparent subservience to industry and their abandonment of a heroic, spiritual life, but he warned them 'de te fabula narratur'. They could not escape modernity and the consequences of becoming modern.
26. Using a framework derived from Weber, this was the prediction which Joseph Schumpeter made in *Capitalism, Socialism and Democracy*, London: Allen and Unwin, 1943.
27. Paul Kennedy, *The Rise and Fall of the Great Powers*, London: Unwin Hyman, 1988.
28. David Coates, *Models of Capitalism*, Cambridge: Polity, 2000.
29. Paul Hirst and Grahame Thompson, *Globalisation in Question*, Cambridge: Polity, 1996; John Gray, *False Dawn*, London: Granta, 1998.
30. Howard Wilensky, *Rich Democracies: Political Economy, Public Policy, and Performance*, Berkeley: University of California Press, 2002.
31. Andrew Gamble, *The Spectre at the Feast*, Basingstoke: Palgrave Macmillan, 2009.
32. Francis Fukuyama, 'The End of History', *The National Interest*, 16 (Summer 1989), 3–18.
33. Andrew Gamble, *Politics and Fate*, Cambridge: Polity, 2000.
34. Huntington, op. cit.
35. Thomas Meyer and Lew Hinchman, *Theory of Social Democracy*, Cambridge: Polity, 2007.
36. The International Covenant on Civil and Political Rights and the International Covenant on Economic, Cultural and Social Rights. In an interesting mark of the divergence between Europe and America the USA has signed both, but has yet to ratify the second.
37. Offe, op. cit.
38. John Gray, *Al Qaeda and What It Means To Be Modern*, London: Faber, 2003.
39. John Ikenberry, 'Liberalism and Empire: Logics of Order in the American Unipolar Age', *Review of International Studies* 30 (4), 2004, 609–30.
40. Francis Fukuyama, *After the Neocons*, New York: Profile Books, 2006.
41. Michael Mann, *Incoherent Empire*, London: Verso, 2003.
42. Joseph Nye, *The Paradox of American Power*, New York: Oxford University Press, 2002.
43. Andrew Gamble, 'The European Disunion', *British Journal of Politics and International Relations*, 8 (1), 2006, 34–49.
44. Jan Aart Scholte, *Globalisation*, Basingstoke: Palgrave Macmillan, 2005.
45. David Held, *Global Covenant: The Social Democratic Alternative to the Washington Consensus*, Cambridge: Polity, 2004.

2

The European Union: Divisions and Unity in European External Policies

Mario Telò

The EU's power: beyond a twofold misunderstanding

How to understand and conceptualise the EU regional and global role and its international political identity is a highly controversial research issue. Far from being the result of renouncing a serious political science approach, to identify the EU as an 'unprecedented' power may pave the way to a conceptual innovation in international relations, linking political economy with an updated analysis of the new stakes of world politics. What is needed is to go beyond the international literature which has accompanied the transatlantic rift of 2002–7 regarding the Iraqi war. The realist perspective focuses on the EU as a fragile and powerless entity unfit to cope responsibly with new threats and responsibilities (Venus-EU versus Mars-US), whereas the idealist one emphasises the emerging 'EU superpower' or civilising power within global governance.[1] At least as a starting point for an innovative research agenda, the notion of EU as an 'unprecedented power'[2] still appears to be more open and penetrating than the two above, in the process of conceptualising the *longue durée* evolution of a regional entity, which is also an international actor capable of changing the other's behaviour.

The word 'unprecedented' may recall at a first glance the critical remark made by Hedley Bull in the early 1980s about François Duchêne's definition of the European Community as a 'civilian power' as a 'contradiction in terms'. However, also unprecedented are the European Common Market (agreed in 1957, according to a new model of integration, far beyond the earlier German Zollverein), and the European currency without a state (established by the Treaty of 1992). Regarding the EU as a political power, what used to be definitely unrealistic in the context of the Cold War maybe is less absurd after the break-up of the bipolar system and the end of the nuclear confrontation between East and West.

However, the concept of 'civilian power' should be freed from idealistic misunderstandings as well. It is a matter of fact that it is often confused with 'civilising' or 'gentle power', or even with 'normative empire'.[3] Even the more understated concept of the EU as a 'normative power'[4], thought to be much more sophisticated in terms of internal complexity and analytical background, covers only a very partial side of EU external relations, namely the norm-setting action based on values and principles: in relevant policy fields such as the protection of human rights and the fight against climate change, the EU has developed a leading norm-setting role.

The influence of the EU as the largest world market and a democratic polity, and the external implications of its internal policies, are perhaps the most relevant aspects of EU influence and power. In other words, a concept of civilian power fits both the internal context of polity/policies and the external context of world politics. Analysing the contradictory dimension of EU foreign relations, between multilateralism, interregionalism and bilateralism, may also offer very interesting case studies as far as the external impact of internal divisions is concerned.

The dominant idealistic conceptualisation of 'civilian power Europe' has three major weaknesses:

1. They misunderstand the significance of the turning point of 2001–2. In the 1990s, the EU internal multilevel governance was often seen as both a model and a microcosm of what Andrew Gamble calls the 'liberal peace', or of a decentralised, peaceful multilevel (neo-medievalist) kind of global governance. This was shattered by 9/11.
2. They neglect the huge gap between EU normative power and the external Westphalian world. Methodologically, it is a throwback to the previous epoch of mainly inward-looking European integration studies, which lack an updated and comprehensive understanding of an increasingly conflict-ridden globalisation and the heterogeneous world politics of the post-Cold War era.
3. They ignore the structural character and the weight of internal socio-economic and political divisions – both at elite and public level – on external relations. In some cases, they deal with the EU as a united actor, a 'nice Leviathan'. Meanwhile its decentralised polity, its multiple internal components (states, organised interests, lobbying), its decentralised and non-hierarchical supranational institutional system, make of the EU a horizontally and vertically fragmented actor, unable to act as a united and rational actor like other states.

The end of illusions of the 1990s and the return of world politics

The attacks on the World Trade Center (2001) and the subsequent new US security agenda (2002), which led to the Afghan and Iraqi wars, brought to an end not only the immediate post-Cold-War period, marked by James Baker and George Bush Senior's short-lived designs for a 'new world order', but also the multilateral external policy of the entire Clinton era. Why did the 1990s appear for many observers as a new era of international relations? Decreased military spending, a 50 per cent fall in international arms trading[5] and the peace dividend that flanked the reduction in inter-state violence were all accompanied not only by greatly increased interdependence, but also by the prevailing discourse of a globalisation beneficial to all[6] that would provide the basis for a more democratic, peaceful, cybernetically self-governed and efficient type of global governance.[7]

The 1990s represent the cradle of 'global governance' research. The concept of 'multilevel global governance' goes beyond the mere description of a network of regimes and international organisations set in the context of the triumph of the market economy and democracy, the growth of complex interdependence and the development of globalisation and the information revolutions, the rise of multinational companies and transnational socio-cultural phenomena. Several authors contrasted the concepts of 'governance' and 'government', emphasising the greater inclusiveness of the former. Beyond the institutionalised and formalised types of regulatory power linked to the state (and considered to be in decline), 'governance' includes complex forms and levels of authority that can be public, private, pluralistic and informal (neither institutionalised nor hierarchical), decentralised and devolved in a polycentric, subnational and transnational system of variable geometry.[8] However, two problems quickly emerged. First, this understanding of multilevel global governance was conceived as an evolutionary and peaceful framework, replacing hierarchical and power relations. Second, the internal EU system looked to many to be a microcosm of global multilevel governance. In this context, some accounts of this important trend in the social sciences emphasised the end of the state and government and went so far as to predict the demise of the state and politics itself as a consequence of globalisation.

Andrew Gamble is the author of a penetrating and comprehensive critical analysis of those schools of thought:[9] the 'hyper-globalisers',[10] who foresee the complete absorption of the state and politics by a globalised economy; 'trans-governmentalists',[11] who envisage the success of the trend towards the creation of international agencies designed to deliver technocratic solutions to common problems (such as the definition of standards by antitrust and inter-banking agencies); and neo-medievalists.[12] These borrow the pre-modern medieval metaphor to emphasise how the emergence of new technologies, transnational processes and the proliferation of non-governmental actors have given rise to partially overlapping forms of authority, post-modern politics and non-state feelings of identity within a multilevel global system that is increasingly without centre, hegemony or power.

Although they may take significant empirical elements into consideration,[13] such interpretations of the global governance system in the post-Cold War era not only ignore the asymmetries of power and the challenges relating to political economy and international security; they also continue to marginalise the political implications of economic changes and the Weberian importance of state political power, which can legitimately use force to uphold the law and achieve social and economic objectives. Moreover, the crises of 1997–8 in South East Asia and in Latin America exposed the lack of transparency, democracy and justice in the system of 'multilevel global governance'. When underpinned by pure economic, functionalist and post-modern illusions, theories of global governance will neither investigate 'who governs the governance system', nor whether the objectives of such governance are peace or mere technocratic efficiency.

In the 1990s the social contradictions and geopolitical limits of the globalisation process – which are some of the causes of the following 'globalisation malaise' – were seriously underestimated. Interdependence is not always a positive-sum game and creates conflicts as well as new forms of vulnerability, including within Europe. Growing differences have emerged between regions of the world which demonstrate differing reactions to the asymmetric distribution of the advantages of globalisation. The aforementioned schools of thought forget that the deep roots of state durability also lie in the 'implementation deficit' of the institutions of global governance, as well as in the lack of societal and economic compliance in relation to soft forms of informal governance.[14]

While useful in focusing on societal trends, these analytical approaches have been radically called into question by two international changes: the repeated failures of the WTO Round and the 'globalisation malaise' on the one hand, and, on the other, the terrorist attacks in 2001 followed by the wars in 2002–8, and in general by the increasing uncertainties of the world order. International hierarchies of power and the territorial dimension of authority had been forgotten in favour of the mere functional dimension of governance. The military and economic primacy of post-hegemonic US power was thus inevitably overlooked, when the focus was directed at soft power alone.

However, it would be simplistic to argue that the EU's distinctive international identity collapsed because of this radical change of the international context: the picture of a multidimensional internal division is more accurate. On the one hand, no EU institution (European Council, Council of Ministers, Parliament, Commission) welcomed the 'preventive war' doctrine and practice, while cooperation in Justice and Home Affairs has been even enhanced at the European level. On the other hand, the vertical consistency between EU institutions (namely the Common Foreign and Security Policy – CFSP) and several important member states was weakened by the conflicting political stances. This political divide has been improperly defined by Donald Rumsfeld as a rift between 'new Europe' and 'old Europe', a consequence of the Eastern enlargement of 2004, while in fact it was a new political cleavage affecting public opinion and a serious division of national elites within every country, including the pro-US UK, and the swing states – the Iberians and Italy.

'Globalisation malaise' signifies both serious troubles within global organisations and emerging domestic pressures for protectionist policies. The WTO crisis emerged at the Seattle (2000) and Cancún summits (2003), and was confirmed by the deadlock of the Doha-Development Agenda. It increasingly left the EU without an updated strategy of global governance, capable of coping with the efficiency and legitimacy gaps of the global network. For example, the open crisis in 2003 of the Prodi/Lamy Commission's strategy, to assert the primacy of global over regional and interregional arrangements, put the EU for some years in a situation of confusion and disarray, with overlapping bilateral, global and interregional trade policies.[15]

The EU risks missing an opportunity to shape globalisation and rescue political multilateralism. Its controversial performance was the convergent effect of internal and external factors. The external factors were the return of a hard systemic constraint, namely a security agenda at the global level set by the United States, and the 'globalisation malaise'. The internal factor which mostly mattered was, and still is, the political relevance of the cleavages between member states and between internal organised interests.

The international literature about the EU as a civilian power: three main streams

Two decades of European and international studies make it possible to look beyond two opposed oversimplified pictures: on the one hand realists forecasting the coming revival of the worst phantoms of European history and the collapse of the EC; on the other hand, idealists presenting the EU as having become a post-modern power within a world of expanding free markets and democracy. Realists underestimated the institutional dynamics of inter-state cooperation and the increasing convergence of interests which were transforming the EC into the EU in the new regional and global context. The idealist scenario simply overlooks the external and internal impact of power politics.[16]

What happened to the EU, faced by the wars in the former Yugoslavia and the 'war on terror', cannot be simply considered as a simple gap between discourse and implementation. This idealistic understanding of the EU is in daily conflict with the empirical analysis of real EU behaviour. Immanuel Kant, in his famous article of 1793, showed how it is misleading to focus on contradictions between theory and practice without addressing the true question[17]: if a theory is clearly opposed to empirical evidence, it means that we need more theory – the existing theory has to be radically revised.

There are three main strands in the open and pluralistic debate about the EU as a civilian power:

1. *Seeing the EC as a civilian power in idealistic terms*, not only in its goals and international message, but also in its means and its internal democratic legitimacy procedures. During the Cold War these bottom-up approaches to the external world (the EC providing the example of peace and democracy) would however have been inconceivable without US nuclear protection, a point already argued by Hedley Bull in 1980. The post-Cold War EU has been presented either as a 'civilian power' or as a 'normative power'. It is expected only to act according to values and principles. That would mean simply renouncing not only any military means, but any kind of coercion as well, while strictly limiting its external action to diplomatic persuasion, cultural influence, regime-building, norm-setting, assertion of principles, and so on. The ideal-type of civilian power adopts civilian means to achieve civilian objectives and is based on democratic procedures of internal legitimacy.

   The problem is that no political actor will ever be able to satisfy these criteria within the actual and foreseeable international system. It is a very easy game to show that the practical behaviour of the EU on a regular basis enters into conflict with every criterion above. For instance, as far as the means are concerned, it is obvious that whatever their degree of danger, the European peace-keeping and peace-enforcing soldiers or police officers engaged in missions abroad necessarily act as 'tertium' or the third actor in conflict situations where a certain degree of potential coercion, including military coercion, is essential to being recognised as a credible player. It proves necessary to combine peaceful means and moderate use of force in a credible way, of course within the strict limits of the provisions, well-known as 'Petersburg Tasks' (humanitarian mission, peacekeeping and peace enforcing missions)[18] set by the Amsterdam Treaty in 1997. Oscillations, compromises with internal and external power politics, and inconsistencies are obvious within the heterogeneous world politics of the post-Cold War era.

   For example, the peace missions in Macedonia, Kosovo, Congo, Lebanon (and the missed missions in Sudan, Myanmar and others) cannot be correctly analysed without situating them within the framework of the complex interplay between an unprecedented power and world politics. Interplay is a two-way process, whether based on cooperation or competition. The EU as a transforming power interacts with international power politics and hierarchies, including internal division among member states and between organised interests. The EU itself is transformed by external uncertainties, while it transforms the external environment.

   Secondly, an idealised civilian power should satisfy high standards of internal democratic legitimacy and accountability. It is evident that according to the treaties, the CFSP does not benefit from the co-decision power of the most democratic institution of the EU, the European Parliament (EP). However, the High Representative will 'consult the EP on the main aspects and basis choices' in Common Foreign Security Policy and ESDP, including the new European External Action Service (according to the Lisbon Treaty). Furthermore, the Council is composed of democratically elected governments (submitted to national scrutiny procedures) and the EU supranational democratic deficit is much less pronounced as far as civilian external relations are concerned. What is interesting for research is to examine the peculiar balance, evolving at the EU level, between the democratic scrutiny of foreign policy and external relations by the EP, the role of public opinion and national parliaments, and the impact of transnational lobbying and social movements, particularly active on the issues of globalisation and peace.

Even major realist scholars critically present the concept of 'civilian power' as totally opposed to power politics not only in values and aims, but also where means and internal legitimacy are concerned. However, since such a 'Candide power' will never exist in world politics, particularly as an isolated case, this approach risks discrediting other studies of the EU's 'unprecedented power'. Opposing the idealistic concept of the EU as a civilian power to the actual practice is not very helpful, nor is treating the EU as nothing but a conventional kind of power. What is interesting from a comparative politics point of view is precisely the opposite; what makes the EU something distinct, different from a classical kind of power, notably a global actor different from the USA?

2. *The EU as an example of soft power.* Notwithstanding its US-centred character, Joseph Nye's concept of 'soft power' is often transferred to EU foreign policy analysis. According to Nye, the large array of tools which he summarises as 'soft power' is much more efficient than hard power in ensuring the successful US role in the world.[19] However, that is not a completely new notion of international power, but the nice side of an international actor whose second side is still hard power. That is not very far from the famous cover for the first edition of Hobbes' *Leviathan* (1651) showing a long sword in his right hand and a symbol of spiritual authority in his left hand. The concept of 'hegemonic power'[20] combines domination and cultural influence, material coercion and a series of tools, institutions and policies, making the acceptance of allies and of dominated states possible. In Nye's understanding, depending upon which US administration is in office at the time, the balance of the two tools may significantly change over time. The 'modern' combination of two diverse and complementary powers is out of the question. The problem is that the EU is not (and will not be in the foreseeable future) provided with such a complementary 'military power', which makes it very different from the US and the classical hegemonic powers.

Table 2.1:   Summary of the three concepts of the EU as a civilian power

Concept	Authors	Reference	Context	Definition
Soft power	J. Nye	USA	Post-Cold War	Power by persuasion and a large array of instruments, complementary to hard power
Civilian power 1	F. Duchêne	EC	Bipolar world	Collective action by civilian means and towards civilian ends as expression of a democratic polity, however protected by US security policy
Civilian power 2: normative	I. Manners	EU foreign policy	Post-bipolar world	Collective capacity of influencing international relations by values, principles and norm setting rather than by material and military means
National Civilian power 3	H. Maull P. Lagrou	Germany and Japan	Bipolar and post-bipolar world	Action of a nation state, whose foreign policy, values, forms of influence and international objectives largely depend upon various national experiences of defeat (in the world wars, colonial wars)

3. *Civilian power studies could be more helpful for a distinctive European research agenda.* The EU was born out a history of defeats, military defeats in the Second World War (Germany and Italy) as well as the defeats for the imperial and colonial powers (France, UK, Portugal, Belgium, Netherlands). In only 15 years after 1945 these powers lost their empires and colonies, and in the end none of them found a better alternative than to support the joint European enterprise. The step-by-step construction of the EU in the future as a collective civilian power will need to be underpinned by the continuous evolution of the largest number of member states as national civilian powers.

The interplay of internal divisions with external relations

When applied to the EU political system, the idealistic versions of the concept of civilian power clearly underestimate the nature and consequences of internal socio-economic and political divisions due to the weight of interests and power politics. Given that the famous Chinese wall between inside and outside is even less relevant for the EU than for states, the external impact of internal cleavages is becoming a fundamental issue of European studies. For decades various literatures of international relations have been drawing attention to the internal cleavages and dividing factors shaping the foreign policy and external relations of every state, notably the USA.[21] This background is of even greater utility when analysing the multilevel polity and decision-making process which is unique to the EU. Compared with the USA, the EU is a much more decentralised and complex polity, where the balance between the plurality of interests and aims and the central decision-making in foreign policy is much more affected by continuous-negotiation and consensual-democracy paths. To draw attention to such non-state features of the European supranational political system is essential for our demonstration, because they well explain not only why for the EU as such it is impossible to act as a classical political-military power, but also why it cannot become a kind of united and totally coherent and consistent post-modern and gentle actor, shaping world politics by its good message of peace and its norms.

Three kinds of internal divisions are important. Some of them are very much linked with the external environment. Others have mere domestic origins and still others combine both factors.

1. *Divisions regarding low politics, notably the relations between the EU and globalisation.* They are, on the one hand due to the politicisation of organised interests and the hostile perception of globalisation by national public opinion. What seems apparently astonishing is that the record of EU institutional centralisation regarding trade policy (through the 'community method' invented by Jean Monnet, providing the EU Commission with negotiating power on behalf of the 27 member states) is the highest one, second only to the EU's monetary policy (centralised by the European Central Bank, an independent authority). Whereas the ECB looks able to resist opposite pressures regarding interest-rate policy within an extremely unstable international financial system so far, the EU approach to globalisation is a perennial source of internal controversies.

   Trade policy is part of an internal negotiation complex which interplays with multiple policies (CAP, structural funds, budgetary policy, co-ordination of national policies within the Lisbon modernisation agenda set for 2000–10) depending either upon national authorities, or upon the EU's competence. The divisions among internal organised interests are only the first part of the problem. It is not just a cleavage between protectionist and free-trade-oriented elites: transnational interest networks interplay with national perceptions recorded by public opinion polls. For both historical and recent reasons, France and the Netherlands represent, according to Eurobarometer, the two extremes of a large array of hostile popular perceptions of globalisation within the EU (from largely shared pessimistic fears to enthusiasm for openness) supporting protection or free trade. The second is the complex institutional system, mixing various competences and voting procedures. The consequence is that external-relations deficits are becoming evident. For example, the EU is one of the main causes of the delays to the Doha-Round agreement and of oscillations in inter-regional arrangements as well. All in all, while it looks able to defend and update its distinctive socio-economic model, the EU appears not yet able to act as a united regional player shaping globalisation though enhanced regulation,

2. *Divisions regarding world politics.* The US unified its foreign and security policy in the very first years after its independence. On the contrary, for the EU, the more the external issues at stake are sensitive to international politics, the more internal divisions matter. However, when looking deeper, starting with the less political external policy up to the most sensitive rifts regarding world politics, the political dimension of foreign affairs reveals an even more complex balance between divisions and consensus, and coherence among national interests across the EU's foreign policies, which are hardly framed by the desired internal 'solidarity' and consistency.[22]

3. *Divisions regarding the policy of co-operation with developing countries* are relevant both between the EU and member states, and among individual member states. Colonial legacies are still an extremely important factor as far the Western member states are concerned. The African policies are obviously affected, as at the controversial preparation of the December 2007 Lisbon summit. In that case, the strength of the institutional dynamics supported by Council and Commission proved stronger than national criticisms (over Zimbabwe), whether well-grounded or not. As a counter-example, the new member states' cooperation policy has not significantly changed as far as its priorities are concerned (Balkans, former communist countries), whereas situating their national policy (notably exporting expertise) in the EU framework fosters an enhanced consistency with the policies financed by the community budget.[23]

4. *The European neighbourhood policy (ENP) is not only fragmented because of the external differentiation between Eastern and Southern EU partners.* Internal divisions of various kinds appear to challenge the EU institutional system itself. Note, for example, the recent crisis of the 'Barcelona process' and the vertical division between France and Germany regarding the Mediterranean Union project launched in 2007 by President Sarkozy. It demonstrates that historical ties, geographic proximity and domestic political imperatives are still capable of provoking serious internal cleavages within the widening EU; they may affect immigration policy, energy policy, human rights policy and so on. However, the compromises

approved by the EU Council of March 2008 and the July 2008 Conference provide evidence of the dynamics of the EU institutional system in their framing of internal conflicts in a balanced way, notably when bilateral, multilateral and community relations are under threat.

5. *In Central and Eastern Europe, the EU institutional settlement looks able to frame historical conflicts consensually to a large extent*: for example, with the border conflicts and the minority problems within Eastern/Central Europe (Hungarian minorities in Romania and Slovakia) and between CEECs and Western European states (Oder-Neisse, Sudet mountains) as it had done between Western European states (Germany and France; Austria and Italy; Ireland and the UK). However, internal divisions matter, notably in relation to the economic and political relationship with a declining Russia. Recent episodes offer evidence of a mix of continuity and discontinuity as far as the new member states' post-2004 Russian policy is concerned: the Latvian crisis of 2007, the antimissile system controversy in the Czech Republic and Poland, and the multiple tensions between Poland and Russia.

6. *For particularly sensitive political issues, such as state-recognising and state-building, reaching internal unity is a harder issue.* In explaining the political division over the Kosovo Declaration of Independence between the majority of EU member states, including the four largest ones, and Spain, Greece and Cyprus, many factors matter: historical differences in nation-state building, the degree of threat of internal secession, and the Atlantic Alliance. However, this very relevant controversy has been balanced by two institutional tools: the unanimous vote of the Council in favour of the largest civilian mission ever sent abroad by the EU (Eulex) and by the common enlargement policy fostering the Serbian association agreement as a step towards full membership.

7. *Divisions between member states regarding the controversial relations with the main ally, the United States, were and still are the most relevant internal cleavage within uncertain post-Cold War world politics.* Certainly, they have historical roots within the EC-9, and seemed to be supported by the USA as a long-term internal cleavage after the enlargement of 2004 even beyond the transatlantic rift regarding the Iraqi crisis of 2002–6. However, as in the past, the Constitutional Treaty of 2004 and, after its demise in 2005, the Reform Treaty signed in Lisbon in 2007 were eventually able to take advantage of this crisis as an opportunity to move towards deeper provisions strengthening coherence and consistency.

8. *Divisions within the EU political system itself, and between the European institutions matter as well*; what is notably relevant within a hyper-institutionalised international and transnational polity, as the EU

intrinsically is, is that negotiations, conflicts and consensus all occur within a rule-based legal system. External relations depend upon two centres of authority, the Council (regarding the CFSP and EDSP) and the Commission (regarding trade, cooperation and humanitarian aid policies). The first one is one-tenth the size of the second, in terms of both its budget and the number of public servants; however, its political weight is increasingly relevant.

The problem is that these two centres of authority not only imply different decision-making procedures as far the 'pillars' are concerned (unanimity is required in the second, while QMV procedure applies in the first), but also different approaches to external relations: the Council emphasises the primacy of classical diplomatic relations and foreign policy, while the Commission focuses on low politics and comprehensive external relations. However, a tendency has recently emerged which stresses the need for enhanced coherence between internal and external policies, and high and low political partnerships; for example, the Commission's Communications of 2006 and 2008, both regarding external relations. The European Parliament is no longer marginal and limited to a mere 'declaratory' foreign policy as it used to be: its enhanced budgetary and political role, combined with new instruments of external relations (inter-parliamentarian dialogue with partners abroad, such as the Mediterranean, Latin America and so on) are about to strengthen its role in foreign affairs, which will make the EU's external relations both more political and more complex.

9. *Last but not least, who is leading the institutional consensus-making process?* Even within the problematic Nice Treaty framework (including the weak system of rotating Presidency) the European Council Presidency is openly expected to play a major leading role by fostering strategy innovation and internal convergence. Note, for example, the multiple papers provided by the Portuguese Presidency of 2007, namely the innovative 'Declaration on Globalisation' of 14 December, originally combining the aforementioned traditional Commission and Council approaches.[24] However, the ongoing reform is strengthening four major figures, whose reciprocal borders are still controversial as far as the leading role in external relations is concerned: the standing President of the European Council, the rotating Presidency of the Council of Ministers, the High Representative for Foreign Policy, and the President of the European Commission.

A second interesting example of 'would be' convergence between Commission and Council is the ongoing revision of the European Security Strategy of 2003 (the so-called 'Solana Paper') towards a more comprehensive concept of security. Beyond the classical diplomatic approach, and the pleas in favour of 'effective multilateralism', the new paper links political multilateralism and global governance, including the main global issues, notably climate change (Climate Change and Security, March 2008), which is analysed in all its implications for stability and security. Discursive institutionalism may offer penetrating explanations of the potential relevance of this ideational renewal and of its impact on the policy-making process.[25]

In summary, internal divisions, in contrast to federal states such as the US,

- are traditionally more relevant for high-politics international issues, and also because of the deeper institutional EU settlement regarding low politics. The bottom-up politicisation of the EC/EU is expanding the internal consensus-making mechanisms to external new policy fields, but not according to a state model;
- are not limited to intergovernmental ones between member states, but often overlap with transnational cleavages, including organised interests and pluralist networks. Moreover, they are not only a matter of elite conflicts but also of popular resentment, as shown by Eurobarometer;
- do not mainly involve old and new member states being in opposition, at least as far as external policies are concerned. We are rather witnessing a combination of historical legacies, national interests, transnational networks and external pressures, on the one hand, and their impact on the common institutional framework on the other.

EU external action is affected by internal divisions to various degrees and with diverse results. Far from behaving as a supranational post-modern entity, above member states' authority, the EU plays its external role in a variety of ways, depending on internal pressures, various procedures and policy fields. The resulting external profile is contradictory: it can be defined sometimes as an incipient civilian power shaping globalisation, sometimes as a divided regional entity, sometimes as a defensive fortress, while it always acts and interacts within a heterogeneous international system which is conditioned by various Westphalian tendencies, including fragmentation, multipolarism, and unipolarism.

A new research agenda regarding a 'civilian power EU'?

In this chapter I have argued first that the securitisation of the international agenda after 2001–2 makes it impossible for an isolated post-Westphalian actor to emerge; second, that the normative and idealistic concepts of civilian power are not fit to cope with the complexity of external challenges. Third, the institutional system appears able to limit and overcome internal tensions and divisions only to a certain extent and not according to a classical state model. Finally, we realised that internal divisions of various types and impacts are necessarily part of a new and deeper notion of civilian power. A further and more comprehensive multidisciplinary research agenda is needed.[26] The external challenges and the complex interplay within world politics in the early 21st century – that is, with more traditional global actors – fosters the inclusion of external variables as an essential part of the research agenda.[27] This is summarised in Table 2.2.

What would it mean in this framework to specify the notion of 'unprecedented power' as a 'civilian power'? The first point that has to be made is that the EU, contrary to its picture as a marginal 'Venus' or a naïf 'Candide', is a power indeed, that is, an actor capable of changing other actors' behaviour; and that its power, as a second global actor after the US, has to be correctly evaluated:

- Regarding the GDP of the wider EU member states, by 2007 it had grown beyond that of the United States (to about €12.5 billion), which makes access to the EU market an appealing carrot and the competition policy an internal/international instrument for setting standards and regulation;
- The EU-widening process from 6 to 27 member states and the ongoing negotiation for further enlargement are unanimously considered a success in stabilising a quasi-continental area and expanding democracy and prosperity in the near abroad. Though its member states represent just 7 per cent of the world's population, the EU boasts 450 million inhabitants, surrounded by 500 million neighbours, which are both a potential market and a source of immigrants. If correctly managed, migration may balance

Table 2.2:   A new research agenda regarding the EU as a civilian power

Concept	Author	Reference	Context	Definition
Civilian power	J. Howorth M. Telò, A. Sapir, and others	EU and other regional actors	Post-bipolar and post-hegemonic world, considered as a gradual revision of the Westphalian paradigm	Collective capacity of asserting external influence and power, mainly as a 'model' and by persuasion, but also through external pressures, according to the various partners and policy fields (including political conditionality, use of limited military means, by peace-enforcing and peacekeeping missions). Such unprecedented features depend upon the interaction with both a Westphalian world on the one hand, and, on the other, the internal two-level polity.

negative demographic trends in many member states and guarantee the sustainability of the welfare-state system.

- As far as the trade of goods is concerned the EU is the largest global actor, the largest exporter and the second largest importer of goods with around 20 per cent of global imports and exports.
- The euro has not only provided the EU with regional exchange stability within an unbalanced global financial system, but is about to become the second reserve currency fostering global stability; the strength of the euro is partially balancing the rising costs of oil and food, as well as serious energy dependency.
- Even if its efficiency is controversial (and the new China-African policy is a new and unresolved challenge) the EU development policy is still the largest and the most comprehensive in the world in terms of budget and scope.
- Even if its middle-range credibility depends upon the internal problematic-implementation records, the EU is recognised after the conferences of Kyoto and Bali as a world leader in environmental policy and the fight against climate change.
- Even if criticised as corresponding to a hub-and-spoke model, the EU benefits from the largest network of bilateral, multilateral and interregional agreements with near and far partners.

Such a rapid growth of external influence and action as a civilian kind of power is going to have some effect in terms of global power redistribution. For example, EU civilian power is inevitably reducing US power.

Two main reasons explain why this definition of the EU as a civilian power is so controversial. First, as a consequence of its political weight and the growing international responsibility the EU is more and more committed to peacekeeping and peace-enforcing missions and a literature is focusing on the 'normalisation' of EU power,[28] or even asserting inflammatory concepts such as 'EU Empire' or 'EU hegemonic power'. By contrast, a second and larger part of the international literature asserts that US primacy as a military power is now not only unchallenged and getting stronger than at the end of the 20th century, but is fitter to cope with the current global challenges.

Asserting the thesis of a long-term US decline does not in any way mean that a comparable rival EU hegemony is about to emerge, at least in the previously introduced theoretical understanding of 'hegemony' as a combination of cultural influence and domination, of two complementary hard and soft powers. Hard-power relations at an international level are increasingly in favour of the US, which spends more than the next 10 states combined on its defence budget. The military capacities of the EU are still so limited that the capacities-expectations gap remains a distinctive profile of the EU, which looks like a kind of civilian power by default.

On the basis of this emphasis on the military gap between the first and the second global actor, a large amount of scholarship looks at rethinking the structural background of the civilian features of the European power. First, why is military action so small a part of the EU external influence? And why are the limits to rearmament so deeply rooted? The low profile of defence budgets of member states is a structural feature of the EU, because the legacy of the national welfare state is alive and still plays a central role in domestic politics. This is an important internal reason why the practice of low-profile civilian power has solid roots, not only in the history of the defeat of several member states, but also in the preferences of European citizens. Regardless of the political orientation of national governments, seriously raising a military budget is not an option. These subjective factors (popular perceptions of external threats; long-term priorities in domestic preferences; weight of the *mémoires* of the world wars and colonial wars) make an unfavourable environment in which the EU can 'normalise' its international power.

Such 'civilian power by default' looks limited in its scope and ambitions. To be able to cope with the civilian challenges of the 21st century the EU needs to grow up as a collective and transforming power: the notion of 'collective power' may underpin a more ambitious understanding of civilian power by linking inside and outside. Could the internal experience of deep cooperation among dozens of states and societies support the spreading of the European kind of multilateralism[29] within a wider context?

The practice of internal multilateralism at the scale of six to 27 states explains the EU political commitment to multilateral cooperation, both in the economic and political fields. In spite of oscillations and shortcomings, this identity marker may have increasing implications on world politics. For example, the opposition of the EU multilaterally shared sovereignty to US neo-sovereign power[30] means not only that the EU is unable to develop a crucial feature of a classical political power (the *jus ad bellum*, the political capacity to declare war), but that it is intrinsically oriented to multilateral cooperation.

The EU's multilevel multilateralism and the contradictory impact of the international context

Is the EU always consistent in its multilateral approach? In the European Union understanding, multilateralism is not only an ad hoc instrument for international cooperation, but much more. The EU discourse about world politics has been rooted since the Maastricht treaty (1992) on the explicit principle of multilateralism which has to do with values and identity (TEU art. 11, European Security Strategy ...) and, what is more relevant, the internal experience of the EC/EU. And, after the 2004–7 enlargement, the EU looks to many less like a federal state in the making and more like a regional multilateral (and trans-national) grouping of neighbouring states and societies.[31]

However, the wider-regional-entity EU cannot further develop as a civilian power without at least a partial, corresponding, evolution of the international context towards a new multilevel multilateralism.

A relevant feature of an increasingly multilateral world is, from the EU point of view, the consolidation and the politicisation of emerging regional actors abroad. Why does a post-hegemonic multilateral agenda necessarily entail regional arrangements and new civilian actors like the EU as essential pillars?[32] Because the strengthening of regional associations of states, like MERCOSUR, UNASUR, ASEAN, SAARC, SADC, ECOWAS and AU, may provide global multilateral governance with enhanced efficiency and legitimacy, despite the declining support of the United States. Regionalism is not a panacea and the idea of regional cooperation underpinning a bottom-up global multiregional system, not only as an emergent feature of a post-hegemonic global order, but also a consistent and comprehensive reform of the international organisations, is probably utopian. However, in the market of political ideas regarding future world order, there is not very much that is both more attractive and realistic. Multidimensional regionalism looks to be a structural and irreversible feature of global governance indeed. Furthermore, comparative studies agree that we will have more regionalism in the 21st than in 20th century.[33]

Regional cooperation proved resilient enough as a structural feature of global governance, notwithstanding recent financial crises, political challenges and external obstacles. It continues providing regions and global governance with some concrete benefits: implementing conflict prevention, conflict resolution, post-conflict reconstruction; ensuring regional financial stability and welfare; limiting distributive problems (addressing the challenge of the knowledge society); enhancing compliance to global rules (regional implementation of WTO provisions and CAP reform); defending the UN's reputation and, to a certain extent, fostering the creation of new regimes (Kyoto protocol, ICC, human rights protection); paving the way towards interorganisational cooperation and supranational coordination about convergent standards; and managing national diversities towards regional convergence.

In conclusion, more regional multilateral cooperation, provided that it avoids the Scylla and Charybdis of regional fortress or mere free-trade areas, limits anarchy and fragmentation, and may help frame a multipolar agenda which limits unilateral and bilateral tendencies. Since its foundation in the 1950s, EC regional multilateralism has gone far beyond the borders of the GATT article XXIV, by developing the multidimensional side of regional cooperation (common market, common commercial policy, common agricultural policy, political cooperation). As mentioned, multilateralism as a kind of EU flag in world politics has been diffused through the external action supporting multilateral cooperation at a global level and among neighbouring countries, including previous enemies, in other continents.

Furthermore, it has been asserted by the EU institutions, Commission, Parliament and Council (which does not mean by every member state) during the transatlantic rift of 2002–6 against US unilateralism.

However, the complementarities of the European regional model with global multilateral regulation are no longer to be taken for granted in the current context of 'globalisation malaise'. The EU looks to many partners as increasingly becoming an actor defending its particular interests (and the ones of its largest member states) within a controversial global economy and a hierarchical world order. The possible discrepancy within the multilevel governance system, namely between regional cooperation, bilateral partnerships and global regulation, risks causing a kind of twofold and contradictory 'mirror effect'. On the one hand, as an established regional entity, interested in region-to-region dialogue, the EU has been sponsoring regional and inter-regional cooperation (for example: ASEM, with East Asia, started in 1996; the 'Rio de Janeiro process' commenced in 1999; ACP). On the other hand, the EU increasingly acts as a quasi-state, fostering individual 'strategic partnership' with major powers (Japan, Russia, China, India, Canada, the US and, in 2007, Brazil) or individual Preferential Cooperation Agreements with ACP countries and Mediterranean partners.

While for decades the EU actively supported regional cooperation abroad as a distinctive feature of global governance, more recently it was working less as a regional 'model' and consistent inter-regional actor. It could have been seen as almost a provocation against both traditional power politics and the classical economic free-trade understanding of multilateralism (as intrinsically global and inclusive). However, it has been seriously challenged during the first decade of the new century.

Conclusions

What about the future of these contradictions? The apparently opposite caricatures of the EU as 'Empire of good' or as 'imperialist power' are both reviving traditional Eurocentric thought, and are not appropriate at all for the EU's role within a world politics shifting eastward to the Pacific.

One of the main and most challenging contradictions the EU is facing in its development as an incipient power is between its nature as a regional multilateral entity and the need for partnerships with old and new powers, namely the US and the newly emerging powers. Most of them are fostering shifts of the EU from global/interregional to bilateral relations, provoking a kind of 'Zelig syndrome'. Secondly, the competition with the US and China for bilateral trade policies, notably with weaker (not only African) states, is negatively affecting the previous coexistence of regional cooperation and development policy.[34]

As a middle-range power the EU has little choice but to look towards developing a strategic regionalism,[35] that is, inter-regional partnerships and global cooperation through an understated but distinctive international role. It can only look for a collective leadership within a revised multi-level, multilateral governance. The issue at stake over the next decade, by implementing new forms of governance of its external relations, by revising treaties, and rewriting the European Security Strategy, is for the EU to assert a new strategic combination of global, regional and interregional multilateralism. Interregional relations remain an irreplaceable tool linking globalism and bilateralism. A kind of new multilateral politics is possibly emerging between fragmentation and international hierarchies. Moreso than in the past, the internal EU's institutional solutions are interplaying with external governance at the regional and global level.

Notes and References

1. For the first approach see among others, see R. Kagan, *Paradise and Power: America and Europe in the New World Order*, London: Atlantic Books, 2003. For the second one, see R. G. Whitman, *From Civilian Power to Superpower? The International Identity of the European Union*, London: Macmillan, 1998; U. Beck, *Das kosmopolitische Europa*, Frankfurt a.M: Suhrkamp, 2004; J. McCormick, *The European Superpower*, Basingstoke: Palgrave Macmillan, 2007 and, in journalistic format, M. Leonard, *Why Europe Will Run the 21st Century*, London, Fourth Estate, 2005.

2. Among others, M. Telò, *Europe: a Civilian Power?*, Basingstoke: Palgrave Macmillan 2005, and J. Howorth, *Defence Policy in the European Union*, Basingstoke: Palgrave Macmillan, 2007.

3. T. Padoa-Schioppa, *Europe as a Civil Power*, London: Federal Trust, 2004 and Z. Laïdi, *Norms over Force: The Enigma of European Power*, Basingstoke: Palgrave Macmillan, 2008.

4. J. Manners and S. Lucarelli, *Values and Principles in European Foreign Policy*, London: Routledge, 2007, and also J. Manners, 'Normative Power Europe: a Contradiction in Terms?', *Journal of Common Market Studies*, 40 (2), 2002, 235–58.

5. From an average of US$45bn between 1983 and 1988 to one of US$20–25bn between 1991 and 1999 (statistics from SIPRI). Inter-state conflict decreased from 39 (1979) to 29 (2001); nuclear warheads from 65,000 to 20,000. The military budget decreased from US$1.3bn in 1987 to US$750 million in 1997 (and has since gone back up to US$1.3bn in 2007 mainly due to the US defence budget growth in 2002–7).

6. F. Bergsten, 'Globalizing Free Trade', *Foreign Affairs*, 3, 1996, 105–20. See also the observations on the socio-political contradictions of globalisation in the 1990s in P. Hirst and G. Thompson, *Globalization in Question*, Cambridge: Polity Press, 1996; S. Sassen, *Globalization and Its Discontents: Essays on the New Mobility of People and Money*, New York: New Press, 1998; Z. Bauman, *Globalization: The Human Consequences*, New York: Columbia University Press, 1998; I. Clark *Globalization and Fragmentation: International Relations in the Twentieth Century*, Oxford: Oxford University Press, 1997 and R. Gilpin, *The Challenge of Global Capitalism: The World Economy in the Twenty-first Century*, Princeton: Princeton University Press, 2000.

7. Francis Fukuyama (who largely contributed to this American ideology in the 1990s with his 1993 article in *Foreign Affairs* and the book *The End of History and the Last*

Man, New York: Free Press, 1992), admitted after September 11 in *Le Monde* and elsewhere that such an historic event necessitated a new periodisation.

8. James Rosenau, the clearest interpreter of this concept, increasingly insists on the notion of a 'bifurcated system' comprising two worlds of global governance and world politics. See E. O. Czempiel and J. Rosenau (eds), *Governance without Government: Order and Change in World Politics,* Cambridge and New York: Cambridge University Press, 1992, and 'Governance in a New Global Order', in D. Held and A. G. McGrew (eds), *Governing Globalization. Power, Authority and Global Governance,* Cambridge: Polity Press, 2002, 70–86.

9. A. Gamble, 'Regional Blocs, World Order and New Medievalism', in M. Telò (ed.), *The European Union and New Regionalism: Regional Actors and Global Governance in a Post-Hegemonic Era,* Farnham: Ashgate, 2007, 21–35.

10. K. Ohmae, *The End of the Nation State: The Rise of Regional Economies,* London: HarperCollins, 1995.

11. See also W. Reinicke, *Global Public Policy. Governing without Government?,* Washington DC: Brookings Institute, 1989.

12. The theoretical reference is to H. Bull, *The Anarchical Society,* London: Macmillan, 1977 and A. Tanaka, *A New Medievalism,* Tokyo: Nihon Keirai, 1996.

13. For example, international conferences and the exponential increase in the number of NGOs – estimated to be approximately 30,000 at the turn of the century – and their influence on governments.

14. R. Gilpin, 'A Realist Perspective on International Governance', in Held and McGrew (eds), *Governing Globalization,* op. cit., 237–49.

15. For example, the last-minute pressures to reach an inter-regional substitute, namely a free-trade agreement with Latin America and MERCOSUR in 2004, failed as well. It was realistically too late, despite the decline of the two main competing US inter-regional and bipartisan projects, APEC and FTAA, which started in the 1990s and came to a deadlock in the first decade of the new century.

16. The first application of system theory to IR, by Morton Kaplan, *System and Process in International Relations,* is from 1957.

17. I. Kant, *Théorie et pratique,* Paris: Librairie philosophique Vrin, 1972.

18. European Union, Treaty of European Union (revision by the Amsterdam Treaty, 1997), art. 11 and 17.

19. J. Nye, *The Paradox of American Power: Why the World's Only Superpower Can't Go It Alone,* New York: Oxford University Press, 2002, and J. Nye, *Soft Power. The Means to Success in World Politics,* New York: PublicAffairs, 2005.

20. A. Gramsci, *Quaderni del carcere,* Torino: Einaudi, 1975; he has inspired the Canadian school of International relations, namely Robert W. Cox, Stephen Gill and others.

21. G. T. Allison focuses on the crucial weight of internal negotiation among pluralist institutional actors (*The Essence of Decision,* 1971); Th. Löwy classifies external policy decisions of a state along three main degrees of fragmentation/polyarchy/concentration, according to more or less sensitive issues and policy fields (in *World Politics,* 2, 1964). J. Rosenau (*New Directions of the Study of Foreign Policy,* Boston: Allen and Unwin, 1987), R. O. Keohane, and H. V. Milner (*Interests, Institutions, and Information: Domestic Politics and International Relations,* Princeton: Princeton University Press, 1997) combine foreign policy analysis, system-theory and socio-political research regarding public opinion, internal interests, decision-making procedures, institutional divisions, and other domestic factors shaping the state's external relations.

22. C. Hill and K. Smith, *International Relations and the European Union*, London: Routledge, 2006. See Declaration n13 of the IGC 2007 regarding the CFSP, which should not 'affect the current responsibilities of MS for the formulation and conduct of their foreign policy and ... their national representation in third countries and international organizations', notably the UN Security Council. And Declaration n14 which claims that the 'CFSP will not affect the existing legal basis, responsibilities and powers of each MS in relation to its own foreign policy'.

23. Maria Francesca Vencato, *The Development Policy of the CEECs: The EU Political Rationale between the Fight Against Poverty and the Near Abroad*, PhD thesis, Katholieke Universiteit Leuven, 2007.

24. Gabineite do Premeiro Ministro, Presidency of the EU 2007, 'Developing the External Action of the EU. New Instruments and Global Players', including expert papers, proceedings of meetings with Chinese, Russian, Indian and Brazilian partners, joint official statements and the final paper, 'Declaration on Globalization', Lisbon, 2008.

25. V. A. Schmidt, 'Comparative Institutional Analysis', in T. Landmann and N. Robinson (eds), *Handbook of Comparative Politics*, London: Sage, 2008.

26. K. Nicolaydis and R. Howse, 'This is my Utopia', in J. H. H. Weiler, I. Begg and J. Peterson (eds), *Integration in an Expanding European Union. Reassessing the Fundamentals*, Oxford: Blackwell, 2002, 341–65. See also the excellent paper by Robert Keohane, 'Realist and Institutionalist Theory After 9.11', for the Advisory Group in Social Science and Humanities for the European Research Area, EU Commission DG Research, December 2004.

27. Transnational research networks are necessary to cope with such a complex analytical and theoretical challenge, a key issue for the development of a European vision of international relations and world politics. For example, the two following networks are financed by the 6th FP of the EU Commission (2005 to 2010): 'Garnet (Global Governance, Globalization and Regulation. The Role of the EU)', an NoE among 41 Universities (www.garnet-eu.org); and 'Nesca', a network between five European universities and five East Asian higher education institutions focusing on regional cooperation and inter-regional relations.

28. Thomas Diez, 'Constructing the Self and Changing Others: Reconsidering "Normative Power Europe"', *Millennium*, 33 (3), 2005, 613. Some concrete argument in favour of this thesis is provided by 'Reform Treaty' provisions stressing the commitment to the progressive improvement of military capabilities and committing civilian and military capabilities of all member states. See A. Duff, *Opinion of the Committee of Foreign Affairs for the Committee on Constitutional Affairs on the Reform Treaty*, 22 January 2008.

29. Multilateralism is an 'institutionalized collective action by an inclusively determined set of independent states'; it is also defined as 'persistent sets of rules that constrain activity, shape expectations and prescribe roles' (Keohane, 'Realist and Institutionalist Theory After 9.11', op. cit.). 'Multilateralism is an institutional form that coordinates relations among three or more states on the basis of generalized principles of conduct' (J. G. Ruggie, *Multilateralism Matters: The Theory and Praxis of an Institutional Form*, New York: Columbia University Press, 1993, 11). By European 'multilateralism' we understand a deeper form of collective transnational action and co-operation amongst states. It implies generalised principles of conduct and diffused reciprocity, and, in its European understanding, includes several degrees – regional, transnational and global – and various types of institutionalisation, from arrangements and regimes to international organizations.

30. R. O. Keohane, 'The Ironies of Sovereignty', in J. H. H. Weiler, I. Begg and J. Peterson (eds), *Integration in an Expanding European Union: Reassessing the Fundamentals*, Oxford: Blackwell, 1993.

31. This is why a large international literature has emerged over the past 15 years comparing EU with ASEAN, MERCOSUR and other regional groupings of neighbouring states; Louise Fawcett and Andrew Hurrell, *Regionalism in World Politics: Regional Organization and International Order*, Oxford: Oxford University Press, 1995; Edward D. Mansfield and Helen V. Milner, *The Political Economy of Regionalism*, New York: Columbia University Press, 1997; Bjorn Hettne, *National Perspectives on the New Regionalism in the South* (with Andras Inotai and Osvaldo Sunkel), New York: St Martin's Press, 2000, and *Global Politics of Regionalism: Theory and Practice* (with Mary Farrell and Luk Langenhove), London: Pluto Press, 2004; R. Higgott, *Democratisation, Governance and Regionalism in East and Southeast Asia*, London: Routledge, 2006; F. Laursen, *Comparative Regional Integration: Theoretical Perspectives*, Aldershot: Ashgate, 2004; M. Telò, *The European Union and New Regionalism*, op. cit.

32. Why do we propose the concept of 'new multilateralism'? Compared with the multilateral legacy of the UK-centred multilateral system, and with the US-centred system of Bretton Woods, the new multilateral tendencies are more binding and able to cope with a demanding transnational public opinion, focusing on fair trade, the fight against poverty, the environment, and human-rights protection. However, contrary to post-modern expectations, states still matter, even if they cannot be seen as the sole actors of multilevel global governance, which increasingly includes regional entities, private actors, civil society, and international organizations.

33. See the chapters by R. Higgott, A. Gamble and others in Telò, *The European Union and New Regionalism*, op. cit.

34. See the ACP-Cotonou Convention of 2000.

35. By 'strategic regionalism', we mean an incipient civilian power, consciously and consistently playing as international catalyst of a better regulated and more legitimate globalisation and a less unstable world politics. See M.Telò, 'Global Challenges and the Political Dimension of the EU External Action: the Key Issues', paper for the Lisbon Agenda Group, Gulbenkian Foundation Lisbon, in the framework of the Portuguese Presidency, 2007.

3
Russia's Transition to Capitalism: The Rise of a World Power?

David Lane

Russia enters the world system

One of the major policies underpinning reforms in, and later the transformation of, the USSR was a movement to, and participation in, the world economic system and its acceptance as a political power in the political order of the West. Gorbachev's intention was for the USSR to 'rejoin its European home'. Boris Yeltsin's objective was to ensure that Russia would be a full and accepted member of the economically advanced capitalist nations.

Initially, in the early 1990s, after gaining the Presidency of Russia, to demonstrate its commitment to international political cooperation and distance itself from the previous Soviet confrontational stance, Yeltsin's policy accepted American leadership. Russia supported American policy in Libya and Iraq, and UN sanctions against Yugoslavia. Russia joined the IMF and other international organisations, such as the Council of Europe. However, Yeltsin's stance was not reciprocated in the West. While the Treaty of Rome provided that any European country could apply for membership of the European Economic Community (and later the European Union which defined conditions for membership), it became clear that the Central European States as well as the former Soviet republics in the Baltic were favoured to become members, while Russia was not. Russia was regarded as an unstable political state, only partially economically 'reformed' and with military potential which spurred its former allies in Central Europe to join NATO.

Yeltsin's foreign policies met with internal opposition, on the grounds that he had capitulated to the West, and from 1992 even he took a more challenging line against the USA. The seeds were being sown for a more Eurasianist foreign policy. However, Russia's feeble economic position and vacillating political leadership led to its marginalisation by the leading Western states. Russia had lost its sphere of influence in Central and Eastern Europe and had little political clout in the Third World. Its opposition to NATO's position over Kosovo, to the eastward expansion of NATO, and to US plans to extend their missile defence system, was ignored. By the time Putin came to power in 1999, Russia was faced by a much enlarged political and economic block of the European Union and a military alliance of NATO stretching to its own (Kaliningrad) borders with Poland to the West, the Baltic states to the northwest, and another NATO member and EU candidate, Turkey, in the south.

Not only had Russia's position in foreign affairs deteriorated, the domestic situation was worse. When Boris Yeltsin took power in 1991, he had considerable backing for radical political and economic reforms. He presided over a political elite-led redistribution of property rights. He moved swiftly, at least initially, in the direction of an Anglo-American type of market capitalism and a formally polyarchic competitive political system. But earlier expectations were not met: the much-hoped-for financial aid of the magnitude of a new Marshall plan did not materialise, while conditionalities of the IMF and EU for trade and aid were linked to levels of marketisation, privatisation and 'civil society' issues which created internal problems. Capital flight, enabled by the freedom to transfer assets, severely impoverished the country at the expense of the new capitalist class – 'oligarchs' – often based abroad. Economic management was discredited when, in 1998, the government defaulted on the repayment of debt.

The economy declined rapidly in a major transition recession – the loss in Russian GDP was comparable to that of the USSR during the Great Patriotic War of 1941 to 1944. Mass unemployment, significant levels of poverty, a major population decline resulting from a declining birth rate, emigration and a dramatic rise in the death rate, and internal strife in the republics and regions of the Russian Federation led to political instability. Moreover, the effects of policy led to considerable internal opposition. In autumn 1993, Yeltsin had illegally dissolved the country's legislature and subsequently used troops and artillery to destroy the Duma building to dispatch the elected representatives. This policy, and his re-election victory against the communist contender, Zyuganov, was backed financially and politically by the West, as well as Russia's own liberal reformers, who saw Yeltsin as the best insurance against a reversion to a state-centred society.

Yeltsin had presided over a systemic decline of the Russian Federation. While under the Soviet regime Russia's ranking in the world social development indicators (a composite index of GDP, educational levels and health conditions) was in the high social development category (the USSR was ranked 25th, compared to the USA, which was ranked 18th), by 2000, when Putin came to power, it had fallen to 60th and by 2006 to 65th place – just below Libya. In 2004, it ranked in terms of life expectancy at 115, just below Grenada.[1] Soviet Russia had been a relatively equalitarian society, but the results of the privatisation of property had led to the rise of a small superwealthy bourgeois class, led by 'oligarchs' who had plundered much of the previously state-owned natural wealth. Moscow, and to some extent St Petersburg and Ekaterinburg – thanks to Western involvement – had maintained their previous economic and civil infrastructure, whereas in the rest of the country de-population, unemployment and poverty were rife.

Moreover, serious problems were associated with the new Russian state: legitimated by a pluralist ideology, regional authorities claimed control of their areas while negotiating 'treaties' with the central authorities (later affirmatively dubbed by Western commentators as 'asymmetric federalism'). The central government had considerable difficulty in enforcing federal laws in the localities, and was unable to collect taxes; not only did regional authorities refuse to pay them but so did leading companies. Yeltsin conceded major political influence to the emerging economic elites with which he was entwined, especially those having assets in Russia's rich minerals industry, and there were also related conflicts between the federal centre and the regions which in turn were also linked to business interests. Tight budgetary controls, insisted on by the IMF, together with a tax deficit, led to restriction of the money supply and consequently employees and pensioners were left unpaid and social welfare services rapidly deteriorated. In the early transition period, hyper-inflation wiped out people's savings, and the privatisation of state assets led to enormous benefits for very few. While the population had expected the transformation to lead to significant improvement in well-being, the result was economic decline, growing inequality and moral decay. Russia was widely regarded, domestically as well as abroad, as a failed state.

When Vladimir Putin came to power as President in 2000, the economic, political, international and moral standing of the Russian Federation could not have been lower. Russia had neither the economic basis, political will, military resources nor the moral confidence or leadership to exert much influence in international affairs. However, there remained elements from the Soviet period that defined the country as a world power. Russia remained a nuclear power – though there had occurred some decommissioning, more than 3000 strategic nuclear warheads remained. Russia had inherited the Soviet Union's position as a permanent member of the United Nations Security Council. It has the largest land mass of any country in the world and is richly endowed with natural resources.

Putin's policies

Putin sought to change Russian policy both internally and in foreign affairs. His vision was to re-establish Russia as a major world power. To do this he adopted a number of interrelated objectives: to establish the authority of the federal government in Russia over the regions and over the political and economic elites; to create a new moral ethos and political ideology which would legitimate a politically led economy; to rebuild the economy through the transfer of energy wealth to strategic industries, science and research; and to restore the Russian Federation as a world power in foreign affairs. This involved a realignment of Russia with respect to the USA, European states and other powers (particularly China and India). This chapter addresses the question of whether these changes have made Russia a 'world power' and whether this power poses a threat to the West.

To achieve these goals, Russia's policies under Putin and his successor, Dmitry Medvedev,[2] have involved, economically, the establishment of state control over the leading Russian companies and their 'oligarchic' owners, renationalisation of some strategic energy companies; a renegotiation of energy contracts with foreign companies; greater state leadership of Russian companies and strategic appointments to the boards of public, private and semi-private companies. Politically, Putin has sought to make an elite 'contract' or 'pact' with other independent sources of power (industrial leaders and the media in particular) and has asserted his authority over political competitors and economic interests. He has sought to introduce a law-governed state derived from Presidential power. Internationally, he has portrayed, and sought to secure recognition for Russia as a great world power. Ideologically, he has legitimated state politics in terms of sovereignty and democracy. On taking power, as acting President, in 1999,[3] he declared that 'Russia was and will remain a great power, preconditioned by the inseparable characteristics of its geopolitical, economic and cultural existence'.[4]

The foreign policy of the Russian Federation is spelled out in the Foreign Policy Concept of the Russian Federation, approved by the President on 28 June 2000. Its objectives were:

> To ensure reliable security of the country, to preserve and strengthen its sovereignty and territorial integrity, to achieve firm and prestigious positions in the world community, most fully consistent with the interests of the Russian Federation as a great power, as one of the most influential centres of the modern world, and which are necessary for the growth of its political, economic, intellectual and spiritual potential [...]
>
> At the same time, new challenges and threats to the national interests of Russia are emerging in the international sphere. There is a growing trend towards the establishment of a unipolar structure of the world with the economic and power domination of the United States. In solving principal questions of international security, the stakes are being placed on western institutions and forums of limited composition, and on weakening the role of the UN Security Council.[5]

The thrust of the policy statement is to claim greater recognition of Russia's position in world politics, to emphasise the importance of state sovereignty, which was being eroded by international institutions, to call for strengthening the United Nations, and to criticise the domination of the United States and the operations of NATO. There was little on the European Union, though Putin has reiterated Gorbachev's claim that Russia first of all is a 'powerful European nation', ideologically and culturally.[6] Politically, however,

Russia has emphasised the importance of European contacts at the state level, particularly with France, Germany, Britain and Italy. The objective of policy is to move from a unipolar world, dominated by the USA, to a multipolar one, in which Russia would have influence. The Russian National Security Concept (2000), identified the 'attempts to create an international relations structure based on domination by developed Western countries in the international community, under US leadership and designed for uni-lateral solutions (including the use of military force) to key issues in world politics in circumvention of the fundamental rules of international law'.[7]

While the Russian Federation was weak when Putin took power, by 2008 Russia's position has changed. Its rate of economic growth has averaged around 6.5 per cent per annum since 1998 (in 2007, Goskomstat claimed an 8.1 per cent rate of growth),[8] it has amassed $430 billion in currency reserves and has established a $120 billion Stabilisation Fund. Levels of inequality and poverty have fallen: in January 2001, there were 9.1 million unemployed and 39 million people (27 per cent of the population) were living below the min-imum official subsistence level. By 2007, the latter had fallen to 15 per cent of the population,[9] and the number of unemployed was some 4.5 million (a considerable decline though both figures greatly underestimate the real level of unemployment).[10] Despite the progress that has been made, the Russian population remains one of the poorest in Europe, its birth rate is shrinking and emigration is high: the average wage in November 2007 was only $560 per month.[11] The economic advances, on balance, have been positive, but income distribution remains highly polarised: some have done exception-ally well but most people are not much better off than during the time of the Soviet Union and a large number of people, especially among the old, are much worse off. The world financial crisis of 2008–9 has led to a sig-nificant decline of the price of energy which in turn will severely diminish Russia's currency earnings. Its financial reserves have fallen, though they are still considerable.

Russia as a New World Power

Despite these shortcomings, Western writers in assessing Putin's Russia have labelled the country as a 'Re-emerging Great Power'.[12] Nikita A. Lomagin writes: 'In the early 1990s some foreign affairs experts in the United States warned that the Soviet threat would reappear in a revived nationalistic, authoritarian Russia, with the natural resources, people and nuclear weapons again to challenge American principles and threaten American security. It seems that by 2006 this prognosis has become a reality'.[13] Russia's assertive-ness, indicated in the Foreign Policy Concept, led to alarm among Western academics and media which, at best, regarded Russia as claiming a responsi-ble place among the world's powers and, at worst, saw its leaders as autocrats seeking to inaugurate a Russian empire.

While Yeltsin had been an agent in the destruction of the Soviet Union, Putin recognised the damaging consequences of its demise for Russia. Putin has been widely reported in acknowledging that '… the collapse of the Soviet Union was a major geopolitical disaster of the century'.[14] Western writers have conflated Putin's remarks about the consequences of collapse with the desire to perpetuate empire.[15] But what Putin was complaining about (not unreasonably) was the consequences for Russia of the fall of the Soviet Union.[16] For many writers, Russia is not just a political empire, but an economic imperial empire. One might concede the 'nostalgia', but there is very little evidence that the Russian Federation has any serious policy for reconstructing the USSR; and even claims that it is an 'empire' are empirically very weak. (A bizarre example, sometimes cited in support of this view, is the planting of a Russian flag on the North Pole.) The claim made against the Russian invasion of Georgia that it illustrates Russian expansionist intentions is again hyperbole: Russia did not occupy Georgia, did not even capture its capital, and left its buffer zone after a few weeks; the 'prize' of diplomatic recognition of South Ossetia – a province in 2008 of some 50,000 people[17] which had declared its independence from Georgia in 1991 – does not make an empire.

Putin has received a hostile portrayal in the Western media, which has strongly coloured public opinion. On 13 December 2006, the cover of *The Economist* contained a picture of a trilbyed Vladimir Putin toting a petrol pump as a light machine gun, with the caption, 'Don't Mess with Russia'. In 2008, the magazine's Central and Eastern Europe correspondent, Edward Lucas, published *The New Cold War* which, according to its blurb, purports to show 'how the Kremlin menaces Russia and the West'. Mass media accounts in quality publications such as *The Economist* and *The Financial Times*, portray Russia under Putin as moving towards authoritarianism and even fascism.[18]

These journalistic accounts, however, lack any kind of underpinning political theory, and appeal to distant legacies in Russian history or the personal role of Putin, Medvedev and their immediate associates.

For other scholars, the crucial defining element for Russia's newly found political power is not its military capacity, but the utilisation of its oil and gas wealth to 'assert [its] geo-strategic interests'.[19] The most detailed and influential version of the rise of Russia as a global power has been developed by Marshall Goldman[20] in his book *Petrostate: Putin, Power and the New Russia*.[21] Though I believe this point of view to be flawed, Goldman's argument is that Russia is 'again a superpower… an *energy* superpower'.[22] While others have pointed to the importance of Russia's material resources, Goldman's contention is that 'Gazprom, and by extension, the Russian government, are already beginning to enjoy a power over their European neighbours far beyond the dreams of the former Romanov Czars or the Communist Party Secretaries. Today President Vladimir Putin, with his control of Gazprom, as well as another state-owned company Rosneft, has become a real-life Dr No – an archetypal James Bond villain, complete with yacht and retinue'.[23] There has arisen a new assertive Russia.[24] The potential for Russia's political power, Goldman points out, was recognised during the Cold War when the Reagan administration sought to weaken the USSR by denying Western technology and also by lowering the price of oil (to reduce the value of Soviet exports).

Writers critical of contemporary Russia contend that, unlike Western companies which enjoy the ownership and control of resources and act autonomously as economic agents, Russian companies operate internationally as political actors. Russia's power is derived from its *state* control over resources. This is a theme which underpins a great deal of the implicit ideology in much of Western concern about the real or supposed power of the Russian government. It informs the widespread interpretation of Russia as 'undemocratic and authoritarian'. The Western concept of democracy is based on the presence of autonomous associations and institutions (crucially, business firms). State-owned and/or controlled companies lacking autonomy are thus antithetical to democracy. Hence 'democracy' is *defined* in the terms of a particular type of pluralistic capitalist society – in the image of the USA – and I shall return to this subject later.

The Russian government, under Putin, reinstated state ownership in petroleum, metal and manufacturing companies. The role of the state over other privately (or partially privately) owned companies, which operate in a formally capitalistic and market economy, has been strengthened. Here Putin has devised a policy of raising 'national champions' and considers that, regardless of ownership, the state has the right to regulate the process of development in the interests of society as a whole. In this respect, he is not unlike Western governments which, in 2008, took control of banks to provide economic (and political) stability. The difference is that the Putin-Medvedev administration considers such control to be a necessary and long-term commitment.

Russia's critics, however, regard the natural gas and oil pipelines to Europe as giving Russia 'unchecked powers and influence that in a real sense exceed the military power and influence [the USSR] had in the Cold War'. This, it is contended, is evident by the action of Gazprom in stopping the supply of gas to Ukraine in January 2006 and again in January 2009. Russia's critics contend that the strategy is not that of an economic actor (as would be that of a profit-maximising private company) but that of a political one. By legitimating the concept of *national* resources, and changing the political elite configuration,[25] Putin was able to achieve a policy of moving Russia in the direction of a world power.

In 2006 the Polish government, led by President Lech Kaczynski, adopted a similar political and ideological stance and proposed the setting up of an 'Energy NATO' as a component in the proposed European Energy Security Treaty, which could use force against any country that threatened energy supplies to NATO and other associated countries, such as Ukraine.[26] It is certainly true that European countries are dependent on external supplies of energy, and particularly from Russia. But the argument is one-sided as it grossly exaggerates the power of the Russian government in relation to its energy exports and reserves. All governments defend their own countries' companies.[27] There is nothing particularly perverse in seeking oversight over companies in which the state has an interest. No doubt Gazprom was influenced by the Russian government in its dispute with Ukraine. But it does not seem unreasonable, in the context of free-market economics, to secure a market price for one's product.[28] The upshot of the confrontation of January 2009 is that Ukraine has agreed to pay a comparable price to that of other Western governments.[29] Western governments act in support of their own companies when confronted with countries which threaten their interests.[30] Russia's main European customers, Germany and Italy, have never had cause to doubt the reliability of Russian supply. Rather than Russia being a supply risk, the truth is that Ukraine is a transit risk. Russia's policy in 2009 has been to procure some EU participation in securing transit of its energy.

It is true that Russian companies seek markets and affiliates abroad and receive assistance from the Russian government to pursue this aim. As we shall see in the next section, Western companies, to a much greater extent than Russian ones, extend their sphere of activities globally. This is not something novel to the Putin regime.[31]

Finally, one may question why the Russian government would want to cut off its energy supplies to the West. Energy exports are Russia's greatest income earner. Gazprom lost $100 million per day during the gas dispute with Ukraine in 2009.[32] It is not practical to export the gas to the Far East (to China) as there is no pipeline and it would take several years to build one. It is in their economic and political interest to maintain reliable export of fuel. Ironically, perhaps, it is transit countries such as Ukraine that have more incentive to use pressure to cut off supply, as they have less to lose than the producer or purchaser further along the pipeline. Yet Ukraine was framed by the West as a victim of Russia rather than a cause of the shortfall (as a consequence of the theft) of deliveries.

Despite the potential provided by the supply of energy, Russia is far from a world economic power. Saudi Arabia, on the periphery of the world political system, illustrates the political and economic limitations of a world major energy supplier. In the remainder of the paper, I will show that Russia has not been able to turn its energy wealth into a viable competitive economy: it lags considerably behind the Western countries and is outstripped by China. But, as is clear from the foregoing discussion, Russia is seen as a political threat. My contention is that the cause is not solely apprehension about its economic power, but has to do with an alternative politics and ideology which provide a challenge to the neo-liberal policies guiding Western powers and to the form that globalisation is taking under the hegemony of the USA.

Russia's place in the world economic system

The 'power' of a country in international affairs may be assessed from a number of points of view: its military capacity, which in turn is derived, in great part, from its economic strength; its human and social capital – the size and quality (level of health and education) of its population, and finally, its moral and ideological values. To discuss the extent to which Russia is a world power, I consider its economic capacity and research effort and the ideology of the Putin/Medvedev administration. I outline the economic strength of Russia's companies and make comparisons with China, the USA and the UK. I shall show that, despite its energy wealth, Russia is not a major world economic power. I then address the question of why Russia's power in international affairs is exaggerated and why it is considered a 'threat'.

The economic power of capitalist companies is evaluated in two ways: by measuring their revenue and by their market valuation. On the basis of these measures, the post-socialist countries have very low rankings. *Fortune* magazine publishes a list which is based on revenue[33] which has the advantage of including companies not quoted on the stock exchange (and therefore having no market valuation). In the July 2008 edition (data for March 2008) of Fortune 500 top global companies, the United States has 153 companies, followed by Japan with 64; France and Germany had a significant number. The only post-socialist country to have any significant companies is China with 29; Russia had only five companies, four in the energy sector and one bank, as shown in Table 3.1. The total revenue and profits of these companies is relatively small in comparison with the top Western corporations. Gazprom, the highest post-communist earner, had a smaller profit than Exxon Mobil, though profit constituted a much higher proportion of its revenues in 2008.

Table 3.1:   Russian companies in world rankings of Top 500, 2008 (by revenue)

World Ranked Company	Revenue ($m)	Profit ($m)
World Top Two:		
1. Wal-Mart Stores	378,799.0	12,731
2. Exxon Mobil	372,824.0	40,610
Russian Top Five:		
47. Gazprom	98,642	19,269
90. Lukoil	67,205	9,511
203. Rosneft Oil	36,184	12,862
357. Surgutneftegas	23,302	3,466
406. Sberbank	20,785	4,164

Source: Fortune, Top Hundred Companies, issue for 21 July 2008, available at: http://money.cnn.com/magazines/fortune/global500/2008/countries/Russia.html

The sum of revenues earned and market value[34] of the top 500 global companies located in China, Russia, Britain and the USA is shown in Figure 3.1. Data here illustrate the enormous gap between the USA, and Russia and China. In terms of revenue earned, the companies in the United States earned 41.7 times more than Russian ones and the comparable statistic for total market value was 16.46 times. Russia and China are on the same economic level as Canada, Switzerland or Spain and are considerably behind the leading European countries such as Britain, Germany and France.

A wider survey of the top 2000 companies has been constructed by *Forbes* and this gives a good indication of the strength of economic diversity in each country. Each company has an index derived from four major commercial components: sales, profits, assets and market value. Again an element of caution is necessary as wholly state corporations and others with no publicly available accounts are excluded. Russia has only 20 companies in the list. The sector breakdown of data shows that for Russia the largest group of companies was composed of oil and gas (eight companies) followed by materials (iron, steel, aluminium, gold, nickel) with seven companies; in addition, there were two banks, two telecom companies and one utility (UES).[35] China not only has twice as many companies (44) but also the firms are much more diversified by sector. In 2007, the most numerous were in banks (nine), followed by materials (eight), transportation (seven), insurance (three), utilities (three); oil and gas, capital goods, technology and hardware and equipment,

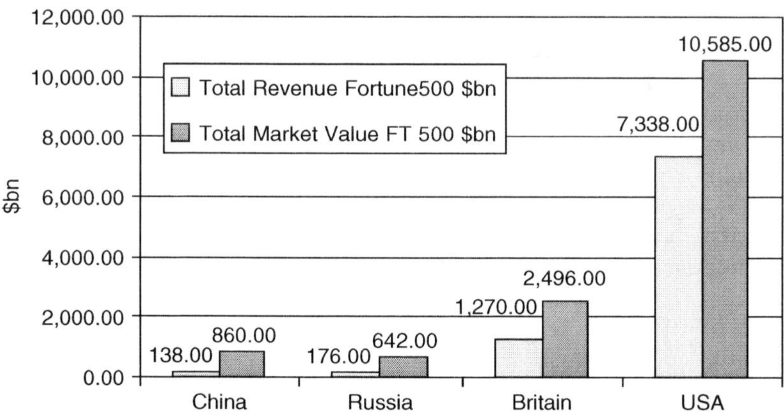

Figure 3.1:   Total revenue and market value Top 500 companies: USA, Britain, Russia and China 2007

Source: *Fortune*, Top Hundred Companies, issue for 21 July 2008 (as in Table 3.1); FT Global 500, 2007; www.FT.Com/Global500_2007_by_country, updated 29 June 2007, accessed 19 October 2007.

Data for China here excludes Hong Kong which had eight companies valued at $393,079.8m.

consumer durables, food and drink – all with two firms; finally there were single companies from telecoms, construction, diversified finances and trading companies.

Even with the reservations noted about the omissions in the data sets, the data show quite conclusively that the economic power of Russia and China, as measured by the presence of their major corporations, is qualitatively at a lower level than the advanced Western states – particularly the USA. China has a rather wider range of companies in terms of economic sectors, but Russia is limited to companies in the primary sectors – oil and gas and materials and is particularly lacking in high-tech industries. While Russia may have considerable cash and gold reserves, it does not qualify as a 'financial power-house'.

Export profiles

We noted above the writers who stress the significance of the role of energy exports as a source of Russia's wealth. In a wider context of export dependency, however, this is not a strength. Just how important energy exports are in relation to other countries and to other types of exports is illustrated in Figure 3.2 which presents the types of exports of the Russian Federation next to those of three leading Western capitalist states. Not only is Russia's

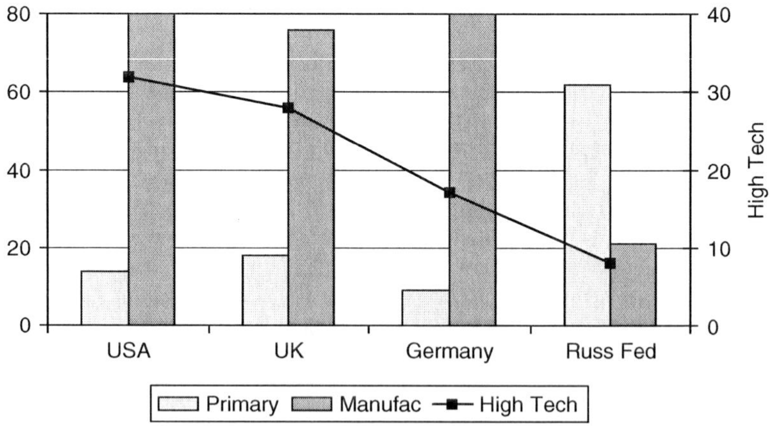

Figure 3.2:   Structures of exports: USA, UK, Germany, Russian Federation, by primary, manufacture and high-tech components, 2004–5
Note: Primary and manufacturing (2004) measured on left axis (per cent), high-tech exports (per cent of manufactured exports) (2005) measured on right axis.
Sources: UNDP, *Human Development Report*, New York: Palgrave Macmillan, 2006, 339. World Bank, *2007 World Development Indicators*, Washington DC: World Bank, 2007, 308–10.

manufacturing at a much lower level, but also the 'high-tech' component in manufactured exports is extremely low.[36]

Russia has a particularly skewed distribution of exports, with energy-sector exports accounting for 62 per cent of merchandise exports in 2004.[37] Figure 3.2 brings out the asymmetric relationship of the type of exports between the post-communist countries and the UK and the USA. The top five traded products for Russia (value traded 2002–3) were: crude petroleum (27 per cent), natural gas (14 per cent), 'special transactions' (arms) (12 per cent), petroleum products (11 per cent) and aluminium (3 per cent). The United States had its top exports in: transistors (6.5 per cent), aircraft (6 per cent), motor vehicle parts (4 per cent), special transactions (3.2 per cent), and passenger motors (3.1 per cent) (the low figures indicate a much more diverse range of export products); for the UK, the leading exports were passenger motor vehicles (5.6 per cent), pharmaceutical products (5.6 per cent), telecom equipment (5 per cent), crude petroleum (5 per cent), and engines and motors (3.7 per cent). Russia provided 9 per cent of the world's crude petroleum, and 18 per cent of the world's gas. The USA's production was concentrated in high-tech products: 17 per cent of the world's transistors and valves and 36 per cent of aircraft; the UK produced 4.7 per cent of the world's passenger vehicles and 9 per cent of its pharmaceutical products.[38] The only major economic power in the post-socialist world is China. Eight per cent of her exports are in automatic data-processing equipment, 6.3 per cent in telecom equipment, 4.5 per cent in office machinery, 3.53 per cent in toys and sporting goods and 3.3 per cent in footwear. Importantly, its share of automatic data-processing equipment came to 15.56 per cent of world exports, and telecom equipment 11 per cent.[39]

The conclusion to be drawn from this analysis is that, with the exception of China and Hungary (the latter is not discussed here), the post-socialist societies have entered the global system, but they are low in value-added and are competitive only in low-technology products. In this context, Russia would appear to be an economically weak country, not a leading economic power. China would seem to be a better candidate, though it is still in a qualitatively different league from the USA.

One of the reasons for this is its minimal level of research and innovation. As illustrated in Figure 3.3, the USA, followed by the industrialised capital-ist states, greatly outranks the remainder. The USA and Japan have a much higher absolute expenditure on R&D, and Japan has a much greater relative research effort than any other country. China and Russia are in a completely different league to the Western major powers. To bring home the signifi-cance of the differences: the Ford Motor Company spends 7.2 billion dollars on research and development, while the total for the Russian Federation is 4.3 billion – the same as for Volkswagen.[40] As the largest companies are located in the Western countries, it follows that they will dominate the R&D out-lays. Of the 700 largest R&D spending firms, 296 are located in the USA and

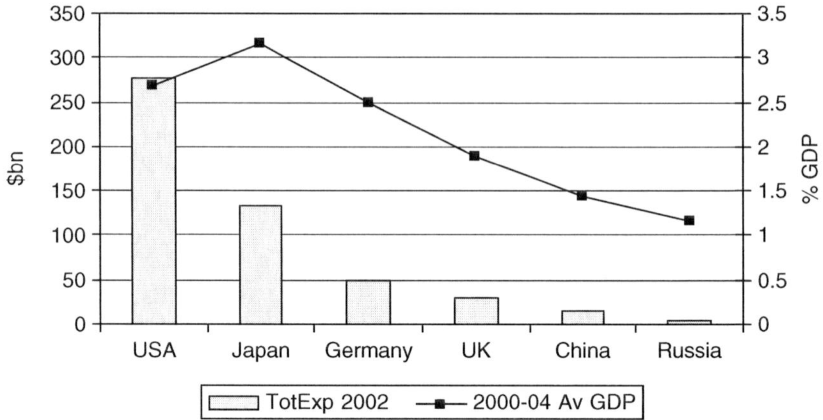

Figure 3.3:   Research and development: USA, Japan, Germany, UK, China and Russia
Sources: Total expenditure on research and development, Unctad, *World Investment Report 2005*, Geneva and New York: United Nations, 2005, 105.
Per cent of GDP, World Bank, *2007 World Development Indicators*, Washington DC: World Bank, 2007, 308–10.

account for 42 per cent of the spending, followed by Japan (22 per cent), and Germany 7.6 per cent. China accounts for only 0.3 per cent (Russia's expenditure is so small that it does not appear in the table).[41] If one takes other measures of innovation, such as patents and research, or the world ranking of universities, Russia also is found to be in a much lower league than the advanced Western countries. (Details cannot be elaborated here.)

Russia in the world system: a weak hybrid economy

This analysis shows that the post-communist countries have moved into the world capitalist economic system; the central and eastern European countries, now members of the EU, are particularly well integrated. In Russia, the globalisation of companies and the role of transnational companies have been limited. Russia is becoming a hybrid economy with a large primary exporting sector, and a declining manufacturing one; there has been considerable deindustrialisation. The Russian energy sector is integrated into the world economy and significant transnational companies are emerging. The former state socialist countries, particularly Russia, have a low component of high-tech industries in their export profiles. The more successful post-communist countries now in the European Union attract manufacturing industry at the lower end of the production chain, but remain at a qualitatively lower level of research and industrial innovation than the core Western countries.

Russia's place in the world economic system is limited to a small number of energy companies. However, unlike the majority of the new (ex-socialist) states in the EU, in many respects Russia is not incorporated into the world system, as its economy has a high level of state ownership and control, and foreign companies have little penetration. (Its transnationality index is below the average for developed and developing economies.) Russia's military and political elites (not discussed in this paper) are not integrated into those of the Western hegemonic states. The inclusion of the elites of the post-communist states in the European Union and NATO has strengthened the cohesion of these states (as represented by their elites) with the West, though not in the case of Russia.

An assumption of many advocates of entry into the world economy, both before and after the fall of state socialism, is that participation benefits all. What is lacking in these accounts is recognition that the world economy is composed of rich and poor states, economically advanced and economically backward, militarily powerful and weak. Evidence suggests that the core countries extend their lead and keep to themselves research, design and development, finance, and ownership of intellectual and physical property. Their economic power is a necessary condition of their political hegemony. The quality and quantity of their weapons of mass destruction cannot be matched. The peripheral states act as manufacturing subcontractors, as well as providing primary and secondary products, and they experience an outflow of profits and labour in return for FDI and manufactured products.

Many nations on the periphery, when confronted with the economic, political and military power of the core states, have little alternative than to accede to their policies. But some countries (Brazil, India, Russia and China) of the 'semi-periphery' may have more options than assumed by world system theorists and those who envisage a 'one-world' economy regulated by hegemonic American capitalism. There are divergences as well as convergence in the world economy.[42] The 'semi-periphery' may lead to the rise of alternative groupings of states which interact with the core but are not part of it – in the same way as the state socialist societies did before their collapse. The economies of many countries have production which is local in character, and regional companies and political actors have considerable scope for action independently of the global economy.

In this context, the Russian Federation has a limited number of choices. Membership of the EU, as an alternative regional bloc sustaining political and economic networks, is not on the agenda. Russia has to trade as best it can on the world market and meet the conditions of global institutions such as the WTO. Concurrent with pursuing economic exchange with other actors in the world economy (the EU, the USA, Japan, China, India), it has opportunities as part of a wider CIS. Russia has an option for a type of national state-led capitalism[43] as an alternative to participation in the global economy on the terms of neo-liberalism. Statist China rather than the neo-liberal West is a model for Russia to copy.

Russia's state-led capitalist 'Sovereign Democracy'

The articulation of a national state-led model of development is the key to understanding why Putin's policy is distorted and opposed in the West, particularly by the neo-liberal press. Russia does not have the economic power to pose an economic or military 'threat' to the West. What it does pose is an articulated form of opposition to the hegemony of the USA and its neo-liberal order. Unlike the early reformers, such as Gorbachev and Yeltsin, who sought to develop a positive image of 'the West', Putin has defined the USA and its hegemony as 'the other', as something not to be associated with, to be resisted – not militarily, but economically, politically and morally. *Edinaya Rossiya*'s standpoint, which reflects Putin's policy perspective, provides an empowering ideology to those who oppose the West's hegemony. The current political leadership (Putin and Medvedev) offers a critique and an alternative, phrased in terms of a corporate economy, democracy, self-determination and sovereignty.

A corporate state involves a market economy with partnership between state and private ownership, in which the state is the major instrument of coordination. In distinction from the West, Putin has emphasised the collectivist and corporatist nature of Russia:

> The [Russian] public looks forward to the restoration of the guiding and regulating role of the state to a degree which is necessary, proceeding from the traditions and present state of the country. [...] It is a fact that a striving for corporative forms of activity has always prevailed over individualism. Paternalistic sentiments have struck deep roots in Russian society. The majority of Russians are used to connecting improvements in their own condition more with the aid and support of the state and society than with their own efforts, initiative and flair for business ... (Speech, 30 December 1999).[44]

His successful pursuit of a statist policy is one of the reasons for Putin's immense popularity in Russia.

The Federal Administration has utilised economic rents, and earned from materials-export industries, for social support, innovation and renewal. In terms of world politics, Putin and Medvedev oppose the 'unipolar world' dominated by the USA. The presidential spokesman, Vladislav Surkov, advocates 'democracy and sovereignty' as legitimating concepts for Putin's power.[45] For Surkov 'sovereignty is a synonym for political competitiveness' (*konkurentosposobnost*').[46] Unlike the Soviet Union, and taking its cue from China, Russia continues to participate in the world system, as exclusion would weaken it. However, the country must retain its 'sovereignty', which is threatened by the neo-liberal global order. In Surkov's view, state sovereignty is a necessary condition for 'competing' in the international political and economic system. Achieving sovereignty entails countering foreign influences within Russia's borders, whether they be transnational corporations or ideologically foreign-inspired and financed civil society organisations which might undermine the state (the 'coloured' revolutions are one such manifestation).

Hence Putin, to achieve what he has called 'real democracy' and 'real sovereignty', adopted two interrelated measures to assert the power of the state against systemic opposition. First, internally, he sought to reduce the power of the 'oligarchs', and second, he sought to curb the external threat, represented by 'global democracy'. These policies, viewed from a Russian perspective, have worked against Western interests and, I would claim, explain why Putin's policy is so vehemently opposed in the West.

Surkov, like Putin, views 'democracy' in rather a different way to that modelled on the institutions promoting 'electoral democracy' which have been exported to, and copied by, the post-communist European Union countries. This latter version of democracy excludes the conditions entailed by 'maximalist' definitions of democracy which focus on socio-economic equality and the societal *outcomes* of politics.[47] While the defining conditions of 'liberal democracy' vary between different writers, they share a common perspective. In Larry Diamond's terms, ' ... most scholarly and policy uses of the term *democracy* today refer to a purely political conception of the term'.[48] Philippe Schmitter and Terry Karl, for example, define it as a 'system of governance'.[49] Archie Brown's 'ten requirements' for democracy are conditions of the *political* system.[50] This version of Western liberal democracy considers 'democracy' in terms of a political regime supporting free, fair and open electoral competition for the people's vote – and the subsequent acceptance of the results.[51] However, the socio-economic base of democratic regimes (market, private property, law and autonomous association making up civil society) are part of the conditionalities insisted on by Western governments furthering the transformation process. What needs to be added to the political democracy concept of writers such as Fish, Diamond, Schmitter and Karl is that it is dependent on a certain type of social and economic infrastructure for it to function. These practitioners define democracy to fit their own interests (and the people to whom they relate). This is reflected in calls, made by Western politicians, for Russia to 'return to democracy' which usually means to adopt policies which weaken the state and strengthen Western economic and political interests.

The current Russian political leadership views 'democracy' not as conditions of democratic electoral processes but in terms of the social outcomes of politics and their acceptability. 'Democracy' is regarded as the state functioning 'with the consent of the people' and promoting their welfare. Surkov, for example, refers to 'democratic institutions' fighting terrorism, extremism and corruption. Poverty, also, he maintains, is a negative feature of democracy – 'Our democracy must show its effectiveness' in combating poverty.[52]

A democratic society is one which promotes the peoples' interests and well-being, with their consent. Consent is indicated by the election/endorsement of the President. For the Presidential administration, 'sovereign democracy' in Russia will ensure development, 'economic prosperity', 'political stability' and a high cultural level.[53] There is a major difference here in what the concept of democracy means for the Presidential administration and for Western writers. Schmitter and Karl, for example, make it clear that by 'attaining democracy' a society will not necessarily resolve its political, economic, social, administrative and cultural problems.[54] They opine that 'democratization will not necessarily bring in its wake economic growth, social peace, administrative efficiency, political harmony, free markets or "the end of ideology"'.[55] The point is also clearly put by Samuel Huntington: 'Democracy is only one public virtue, not the only one, and the relation of democracy to other public virtues and vices can only be understood if democracy is clearly distinguished from the other characteristics of political systems.'[56] In political science terms, what Surkov refers to is not the strictly political 'democratic' electoral credentials of the system (where Russia is clearly lacking in some important respects), but other politically desirable outputs – the conditions necessary to the making of a 'good life', including the provision of adequate public and private services for the population. This is not so different from Western socialist ideas about 'real democracy' rather than electoral democracy. The Presidential administration would contend that the pro-government bias in the media of communications is not 'undemocratic' if the President is acting with the 'people's consent' (which public opinion polls and electoral results would seem to confirm), and if he enjoys electoral support. Clearly, Surkov, Putin and Medvedev seek to define the Russian system as 'democratic' in their own terms, as 'democracy' is the only politically acceptable global ideology. In this respect they are no different from other contemporary political leaders. Democracy is a legitimating ideology, which can take different forms. However, the Presidential administration does share some common ideological values in common with the Western conception, particularly those of rule by consent and an electoral process.

Russia is portrayed as an economic and military threat to the West and it is my contention that these views have no substantive basis. Why Putin and his associates are regarded so disapprovingly is because they challenge the universality of the version of 'democracy', as advocated academically and pursued politically by the agents of the West in their extension of the global system. 'Sovereign democracy' is an ideological and political challenge to the Western notion of 'global democracy'. Just as the Soviet Union provided an alternative culture, political institutions and value system, Western interests fear that Russia's possession of energy resources will make its conception of politics an alternative, a model which might have a resonance with, and could be copied by, countries such as India and Latin American nations, and adopted by China. It might also appeal to others in the West seeking to retain more powers for the nation-state – as a depository of democracy, which is widely regarded as being undermined by the forces leading political and economic globalisation.

Notes and References

1. UNDP, *Human Development Report 1990,* New York and Oxford: Oxford University Press, 1990. The USSR included many economically backward republics of central Asia, making Russia much higher than 25th. The GDR at this time was ranked 20th, for example. For later data see the *Human Development Report* for 2000. Data for 2004 and 2006 taken from http://hdr.undp.org/hdr2006/statistics. Accessed February 2008.
2. In May 2008, Dmitry Medvedev became President and Putin moved to become Prime Minister.
3. He was subsequently elected President and inaugurated in May 2000.
4. Cited by Ingmar Oldberg, 'Russia's Great Power Ambitions and Policy under Putin', in Roger E. Kanet, *Russia: Re-Emerging Great Power*, Basingstoke and New York: Palgrave Macmillan, 2007, 13.
5. Foreign Policy of the Russian Federation, at: www.russiaeurope.mid.ru/Russia Europe/concept.html (accessed January 2008).
6. This is made clear in his speech of 25 April 2005. Printed in Aleksay Chadaev, *Putin. Ego Ideologiya*, Moscow: Evropa, 2006. See 188.
7. Russian National Security Concept at: www.russiaeurope.mid.ru/russiastrat2000. html (accessed January 2008).
8. See detailed data on the VTB Press Release, February 2008. VTB's own estimate for 2007 is a more modest 6.2 per cent.
9. www.statrus.info/catalog/readbook.jsp?issue=701736 (website of the Russian statistical office, accessed February 2008).
10. www.statrus.info/catalog/readbook.jsp?issue=159551 (accessed February 2008).
11. Ibid.
12. Kanet, op. cit.
13. Nikita A. Lomagin, 'Forming a New Security Identity Under Vladimir Putin', in ibid., 33.
14. Speech to the Federal Assembly on 25 April 2005 at: www.kremlin.ru/eng/speeches/ 2005/04/25/2031_type70029type82912_87086.shtml (website of the Presidential administration of the Russian Federation, accessed 28 Jan 2008).
15. See, for example, Mark R. Beissinger, 'The Persistence of Empire', *NewsNet* (Boston, MA, AAASS), 48 (1), Jan 2008, 3.
16. This is clear in the continuation of his speech: 'As for the Russian nation, it became a genuine drama. Tens of millions of our co-citizens and compatriots found themselves outside Russian territory. Moreover, the epidemic of disintegration infected Russia itself. Individual savings were depreciated, and old ideals destroyed. Many institutions were disbanded or reformed carelessly. Terrorist intervention and the Khasavyurt capitulation that followed damaged the country's integrity. Oligarchic groups – possessing absolute control over information channels – served exclusively their own corporate interests. Mass poverty began to be seen as the norm. And all this was happening against the backdrop of a dramatic economic downturn, unstable finances and the paralysis of the social sphere.' Speech to the Federal Assembly, op. cit. (footnote 14).

17. This is an estimate as the census was unable to take place in 2002. In the 1989 census the country had 99,000 people.
18. E. Lucas, *The New Cold War*, London: Bloomsbury, 2008; 'A murder, a grudge, deportations and what they say about Russia's worrying political direction. Is it time to use the f-word?' *The Economist*, 12 October 2006.
19. Beissinger, op. cit., 6.
20. Marshall Goldman is the former Director of the Davis Russian Research Center, Harvard University and an influential economist with many publications on the USSR and Russia.
21. New York: Oxford University Press, 2008.
22. Italics in original. Marshall Goldman, *Petrostate: Putin, Power and the New Russia*, Oxford and New York: Oxford University Press, 2008, 14.
23. Ibid., 3.
24. See the discussion in ibid., 207.
25. The work of Kryshtanovskaya and White is often cited as showing the placement of people from the power ministries (police, security and army) to effect a power elite. See O. Kryshtanovskaya and S. White, 'Putin's Militocracy', *Post-Soviet Affairs*, 19 (4), 2003, 294.
26. The upshot, however, was that the proposal was not supported by other leading European countries such as Germany. I am indebted to Mattias Roth for bringing this to my attention.
27. The British Conservative government, under the influence of Michael Heseltine, prevented Ford from buying out the British firm, Rover. The European Union has decreed conditions for foreign ownership of energy companies in its territory. The French government places its representatives on the boards of companies in which it has a stake, as did the British government when it had significant shares in British Petroleum.
28. Ukraine held Russia (and its customers further along the pipe chain) to ransom over the supply of oil to Western Europe. When Gazprom started negotiations with Ukraine to raise prices in March 2005, its price to Ukraine was five times less than to neighbours Turkey, and Ukraine's customers were paying less for fuel than were Russian consumers. In the agreement that followed the curtailment of supplies, Ukraine was able to offset the price rise by increasing considerably the transit costs to the West. Price increases also followed for Belarus (a less pro-EU market economy) in 2006; and, even under supposedly pro-Russian Prime Minister Yanukovich, Gazprom again raised its prices to Ukraine in 2007.
29. Part of the problem is negotiating a price, taking into account the transit fees charged by Ukraine. For details of the 2009 crisis see *Russian Analytical Digest*, www.laender-analysen.de/russland, accessed 31 January 2009. There is a particularly good account by Simon Pirani, *The Russo-Ukrainian Gas Dispute*, 2009: available at: www.quintessential.org.uk/SimonPirani/
30. They boycotted the purchase of Iran's oil, for example, when (democratically elected) Mohammed Mossadeq nationalised the Anglo-Persian oil company (predecessor of BP); the British and Americans also funded a coup which brought down Mossadeq. If the purpose of the 'American-led' task force in Iraq was to secure the West's energy supplies, it is here that one should look to the use of force to secure economic interests. While much has been made of the gas dispute between Russia and Ukraine, it was resolved in three days (between 1 and 4 January 2006); by comparison, Mossadeq was imprisoned for three years and then kept under house arrest until his death.

31. See Peter Rutland for a similar argument related to the 1990s. Peter Rutland, 'Oil Politics and Foreign Policy', in David Lane, *The Political Economy of Russian Oil*, New York: Rowman & Littlefield, 1999, 185.
32. Pirani, op. cit.
33. The data include companies that 'publish financial data and report part or all of their figures to a government agency'.
34. The FT index for market value includes companies which have at least 15 per cent of shares in 'free float'; it therefore may underestimate some corporations which have very large state or family holdings. The FT allocates companies to a parent country on the basis of 'incorporation, stock market listing and market perception'. Data for 30 March 2007, published 29 June at FT.com/global_500_2007. Accessed 19 October 2007.
35. The Global 2000, Forbes.com. Data for 29 March 2007. Accessed 21 October 2007.
36. The low share of a high-tech component in exports also applies to the EU post-communist member states, with the exception of Hungary. UNCTAD, *Handbook of Statistics*, New York and Geneva: United Nations, 2005, 168.
37. This may understate energy products, as enterprises will often classify goods derived from oil and gas as part of another sector where tax is lower.
38. UNCTAD, *Handbook of Statistics*, op. cit.
39. Ibid., 163.
40. UNCTAD, *World Investment Report 2005*, Geneva and New York: United Nations, 2005, 120.
41. Ibid., 121.
42. For further discussion see H. Kitschelt, P. Lange, G. Marks and J. D. Stephens, 'Convergence and Divergence in Advanced Capitalist Democracies', in H. Kitschelt, P. Lange, G. Marks and J. D. Stephens (eds), *Continuity and Change in Contemporary Capitalism*, Cambridge: Cambridge University Press, 1999, 427–60.
43. I use the term 'state-led' to mean that the political powers either directly or indirectly ensure collaboration with privately (or partly privately) owned business to further some national ideology. 'Corporatist' is sometimes used in this paper interchangeably with 'state-led capitalism', though 'corporatism' usually includes organised labour as a stakeholder, which is not the case in Russia. Putin and others use the term corporatism rather than state-led capitalism.
44. www.geocities.com/capitolhill/parliament/3005/poutine.html. This source is from an American site. I have searched Putin's speeches on the Kremlin website, with no success.
45. V. Yu. Surkov, *Osnovnye tendentsii I perspektivy razvitiya sovremennoy Rossii*, Moscow: Sovremennaya gumanitarnaya akademiya, 2006, 13–16. See also *Grani globalizatsii*, Moscow, 2003, esp. Chapter 9.
46. Ibid., 14.
47. This distinction is well made by M. Steven Fish, *Democracy Derailed in Russia: The Failure of Open Politics*, Cambridge and New York: Cambridge University Press, 2005. See 17–19.
48. Larry Diamond, *Deepening Democracy: Toward Consolidation*, Baltimore: Johns Hopkins University Press, 1999, 8; as cited by Fish, 19. Italics in original.
49. P. C. Schmitter and Terry Lynn Karl, 'What Democracy Is ... and Is Not', in Larry Diamond and Marc F. Plattner (eds), *The Global Resurgence of Democracy*, Baltimore: Johns Hopkins University Press, 1993, 50.
50. Archie Brown, 'Russia and Democratization', *Problems of Post-Communism*, 46 (5), September 1999, 3–13. He includes freedom of association, expression, right

to vote, eligibility for public office, alternative sources of information, fair and free elections, dependence on public voting, political accountability and the rule of law.

51. Most American and British political scientists currently take this approach which is derived from Joseph Schumpeter who defines democracy as 'that institutional arrangement for arriving at political decisions in which individuals acquire the power to decide by means of a competitive struggle for the people's vote'; *Capitalism, Socialism and Democracy*, London: Allen and Unwin, 1943, 269. This is positively quoted and developed by Schmitter and Karl, op. cit., 49–62, quotation 61, fn 3.

52. Surkov, *Osnovye tendentsii...* loc. cit.

53. Ibid.

54. Schmitter and Karl, op. cit., 59.

55. Ibid., 61.

56. Samuel P. Huntington, *The Third Wave: Democratization in the Late Twentieth Century*, Norman: University of Oklahoma Press, 1991, 9–10.

4
The Implications of the Rise of China[1]

Martin Jacques

The rise of China has taken place with stunning speed. At the time of 9/11 and subsequently the invasion of Iraq in 2003, Western discourse was dominated by the idea of the United States as the sole superpower: China was still very much an afterthought. China began to impinge, in dramatic fashion, on the global consciousness from around 2004, as its exports became ubiquitous around the world and then its demand for commodities began to drive up primary prices. From Europe to Japan, Africa to the United States, its impact has been worldwide. There are two factors that lend China's rise a special character: first, an extremely high growth rate since 1978 and second, an enormous population of 1.3 billion people. Together they mean that the speed of China's rise, by historical standards, is unprecedented and likewise its global effect. One example of this is the use of terms like 'China goods' and 'China prices' in the early 2000s in response to the dramatic growth of Chinese exports in a multitude of markets: similarly, we might use the term 'China speed' to describe the greatly foreshortened sense of time that is involved in every aspect of China's progress and impact. When considering how China's rise is likely to affect Europe it is important to bear this in mind: what might lie in the far future in the context of other countries is more likely to lie in the near future in the case of China.

China and East Asia

If we want to understand what the rise of China might mean, and the sheer speed of that process, the best vantage point is not Europe, even though the effects are clearly and increasingly being felt in myriad ways on that continent, but East Asia. The latter is far from being some kind of backwater. On the contrary, it is already the largest economic region in the world, exceeding North America and Europe, and home to around one-third of the world's population. Until the late 19th century, China was the centre of the East Asian economy. That state of affairs is now fast being restored. Until the 1990s, China remained relatively isolated in East Asia, not least because it firmly resisted being drawn into any multilateral arrangements. Over the course of that decade, however, it began to shift its position, helping to establish what became known as the Shanghai Co-operation Organisation and, even more importantly, in a profound change from its previous approach, becoming closely involved with the Organisation of South East Asian Nations (ASEAN) embracing around half a billion people. In the past, China had stood aloof from its neighbours, adopting a rather superior and haughty attitude, but now it not only sought closer relations with ASEAN, but also did it on what were largely the latter's terms. The result was a series of bilateral free trade agreements, an agreement to establish a China-ASEAN free-trade zone, the largest in the world, and an agreement by China not to use force in order to pursue its claim on the Spratly and Paracel islands in the South China Sea. The rapprochement between China and ASEAN, within much less than a decade, not only transformed their relationship but also entirely reshaped the political dynamics of the East Asian region. Taiwan feared being left out. South Korea followed the Chinese lead. Most importantly of all, Japan, the previous regional hegemon and China's greatest rival, found itself on the back foot and has since been rather anxiously trying to make up the lost ground. China's dramatic diplomacy with ASEAN redrew the political and economic map of the region.

Behind this reconfiguration, of course, lies China's growing economic power. Whereas Japan has exercised its economic influence over the region largely by virtue of foreign direct investment and exports by its international firms, while at the same time keeping its own market relatively closed to exports from East Asia, China has pursued a very different strategy. It now has one of the most open economies in the world and, as China has grown, it has become increasingly important as a destination for the exports of other countries in the region such that, in a handful of years, it could emerge as the largest market for every country in the region. For the ASEAN countries, the Chinese market is now three times the size of Japan's. No country – not even Japan, whose trade with China has recently overtaken that with the United States – can afford to ignore the Chinese market, or, as a consequence, China. Since 2000, China's imports from ASEAN have increased at an annual rate of 30 to 40 per cent. China, for example, accounted for 13.2 per cent of Singapore's exports in 2001, compared to 2.5 per cent in 1993, 18.5 per cent of South Korea's exports in 2001, compared to 6 per cent in 1993, and 9.2 per cent of Australia's exports in 2000, compared to 6 per cent in 1994. At the same time, Chinese overseas investment is increasing rapidly, the majority of it directed to East Asia, which, in the case of South East Asia, has compensated for the decline in Western investment. East Asia thus appears to be returning rather rapidly to an earlier era when China was the epicentre of the regional economy.

What will China's growing clout mean in broader political and security terms? It is interesting to observe that, contrary to much expectation, East

Asia has been notably peaceful since the end of the Cold War, far more peaceful, in fact, than it was during the Cold War.[2] The rise of China has not been accompanied by growing tension in the region. There has been no serious attempt by countries in the region, with the important exception of Japan, and the distinct case of Taiwan, to try and hedge with the United States in order to counter the rise of China. On the contrary, the overwhelming tendency has been to bandwagon with China and to seek a closer relationship with it.[3] This has even been the case with countries like Singapore and the Philippines which have a military relationship with the USA. In other words, the economic reconfiguration is being accompanied by the beginnings of a broader political reconfiguration around and towards China. In fact, what has been striking over the last decade is the extent to which the United States – which, following the departure of Britain and France in the post-1945 period, has enjoyed hegemony in the region through its military presence and bilateral alliances – has found its influence in East Asia in rapid decline. The most important exception to this is Japan, which enjoys an intimate military relationship with the USA. In addition, the United States, of course, still remains fundamental to Taiwan's existence. But even South Korea, a long-established military ally of the USA, has moved away from it towards China. Increasingly the USA's influence in the region rests on its military power, which for the most part is essentially naval and offshore.

How should we explain the post-Cold War stability of the region and the relative equanimity with which other states have responded to China's rise? Prior to China's decline after the Opium Wars, the region enjoyed a very long period of relative peace and fundamental to this, arguably, was the huge imbalance of power between China and the other countries in the region.[4] Whereas Europe was dominated for many centuries by constant war between relatively evenly matched states, East Asia was characterised by peace resting on massive disparity. The peace that the region has experienced since the end of the Cold War may, thus, represent the beginnings of a return to a much older tradition based on disproportionate Chinese power. The nature of the arrangements that defined China's position and power in the region during its heyday is worth exploring in more detail for the light that it might throw on future Chinese behaviour. Prior to the late 19th century, the East Asian regional order was based on the tributary system, which lasted for many centuries, rather than the later Westphalian system, which only arrived with European imperialism. The latter, with its notions of national sovereignty, de jure equality, and 'one system, many countries', was only introduced into the region following the Opium Wars from the mid-19th century, and even at the end of that century the tributary system still remained influential. The tributary system rested on the following main propositions: that China was the centre of the region, the guarantor of its peace and stability; enjoyed a superior culture to that of other countries; and that countries showed their respect to China by sending regular tribute to the Emperor. Within these ground rules, the countries were allowed considerable latitude. It was a hierarchical and paternalistic system, a country's place in the hierarchy depending, broadly speaking, on its distance from the Forbidden City.

It is not unreasonable to ask whether, as China restores its position at the centre of East Asia, we are likely to witness a return – at least in a partial form – to the tributary system. The European powers may have introduced the Westphalian system to the region, but they have long since departed, while their successor, the United States, is experiencing a rapid decline in its regional influence and authority. It was the decline of Chinese power, furthermore, that led to the demise of the tributary system and this is now in the process of being restored. There is a further reason why this might be a plausible scenario. In a sense the tributary system never completely disappeared but rather the Westphalian system was superimposed on it, so that in effect there has been a hybrid system, mainly Westphalian (because of Western dominance) but also tributary (by virtue of tradition and custom). Perhaps the most likely outcome is a continuing hybrid, given the persistence of the Westphalian system globally, but, with the rise of China, one in which tributary principles are increasingly pronounced.[5]

This argument has important implications with regard to how China might impact on Europe, or more accurately, the European-made world in which we still largely live. First, the rise of China has already made East Asia a more important economic region than Europe (and North America) and this process is likely to continue apace. Second, China is once again becoming the epicentre of the region, thereby returning it to its pre-European configuration. Third, the inter-state system that developed as a result of European hegemony in the region is now in decline. What may be involved, therefore, is not just a shift in power but also, potentially, a shift in the concepts and principles on which regional inter-state relations are based. If this were to be the case, it would mean the decline of the European-designed world and the rise of an increasingly Chinese-designed world, at least in East Asia.

What does the rise of China mean?

The overwhelming majority of the attention paid to China's rise, hitherto, has centred on its actual and potential global economic impact. I will not seek to repeat that in detail here. It will suffice to suggest the following. If China should, broadly speaking, continue its remarkable economic growth of the last 30 years then, according to the most recent Goldman Sachs forecast, it will overtake the United States in 2027 to become the largest economy in the world measured by GDP (based on exchange rates), although, it will still be much poorer than the US in terms of per capita GDP.[6] These projections are based on the assumption that China's growth rate over time will decline. In the extremely long term, it is worth noting that, given that China's population is more than four times that of the USA, then, on the assumption that China and the USA enjoyed the same per capita GDP, then the Chinese economy would be approximately four times the size of that of the USA. This gives some idea of China's potential as far as the distant future is concerned. While China's greatest resource is its huge population – whence the size of its potential market and massive labour force – it is, at the same time, also relatively bereft of natural resources, with the consequence that China's development also translates into a huge global demand for primary products, including oil, wood, metals and food. China's growth was responsible for reversing the long decline in commodity prices followed, in the last few years, by their rapid rise. The potential ramifications of China's appetite for the world's resources are, of course, enormous, from growing geopolitical rivalry over resources on the one hand to its implications for climate change on the other.

There is, notwithstanding this, a strong tendency to underestimate what the rise of China might mean for the world. There are several reasons for this. First, China's rise has overwhelmingly been seen in the West in narrowly economic terms, with very little attention paid to what it might mean politically or culturally. The most obvious exceptions to this are the occasional warnings, mainly emanating from the United States, concerning China's growing military prowess: but the effect of these is, by and large, not to emphasise the novelty of China's rise but rather to inculcate a sense of déjà vu, that the Chinese Communist regime threatens a return to the days of the Cold War. Second, the main reason for this economic preoccupation is what might be described as the Fukuyama 'End of History' syndrome: that, ever since the defeat of communism, the whole world is headed in the same direction, namely, towards Western-style societies based on free markets and democracy. The heyday of this thinking was the 1990s when the United States was in triumphalist mood, globalisation was overwhelmingly seen as a process of Westernisation, and political and cultural difference was largely perceived as a transient phenomenon in the onward march of Westernisation. Although weakened by the failure of neo-conservatism, the ills of the American economy and the rise of China, this way of thinking still remains largely dominant in the West and certainly influences perceptions about what China will be like. Third, China has sought to portray its rise in extremely reassuring terms, arguing and acting in a manner that seeks to demonstrate that it wants to be a responsible member of the international community, that it acquiesces in the present international system, and that it constitutes no threat to it. This makes a great deal of sense on China's part. Unlike the Soviet Union, it has tried ever since 1978 to become part of the international system (as illustrated by its long pursuit of WTO membership), and sought the support of the USA to this end, in the belief that this would create the most favourable conditions for its economic growth, which has been its overriding priority for the last 30 years and to which all other considerations have been subordinated. Such has been the success of this strategy that arguably China has been the greatest single beneficiary of globalisation, more so even than the United States, which was its primary architect.

It would be wrong, however, to confuse this phase of China's development, and accompanying policy assumptions, with the longer term. This is not to suggest that China is insincere, but rather that the exigencies of the present phase are specific to this stage of its development. As China becomes steadily more powerful and prosperous then inevitably its priorities and attitudes will change. The phase of Westernisation, of absorption and adaptation, will in time be superseded by the opposite tendency, namely a desire to project and convey Chinese attitudes and values to others. China is likely in time to become increasingly proud and assertive of its history, traditions and culture. Indeed, the beginnings of this shift can already be observed. Far from China becoming a Western clone, Chinese modernity will be highly distinct, a hybrid that draws above all on its Chinese roots but also borrows from the West and East Asia. Given that a country's modernity is shaped by culture and history as much as economics and technology, this is hardly surprising. Contrary to the prevailing Western commonsense, we are moving into a world of multiple modernities rather than a singular Western modernity. Hitherto, the main example of this has been Japan, but with the rise of China and India, this will soon become abundantly clear. This, of course, has far-reaching implications for the West. For over two centuries, the West – in the form of Europe, then latterly the United States – has provided, and enforced, the template for the world. The modern world has seen the domination of two great global powers, first Britain and then the United States: the only country that has enjoyed a significant global presence over the last two centuries which was not wholly or partly a product of Western culture is Japan and its role has, for various reasons, been relatively peripheral. The rise of China marks the arrival of a country which comes from an entirely different set of coordinates to the West. As such it also prefigures the beginning of the end of Western hegemony. Combined with the rise of India, the growing power of China will mean that the global polity is no longer dominated – to the virtual exclusion, or marginalisation, of all others – by Western values and assumptions.

At present there is an underlying assumption in the West, which in some measure is also more widely shared, that the world is essentially Western – that its values define the global discourse, that civilised values are synonymous with those of the West, that the 'international community' is composed of Western countries, supplemented by others as and when, that global institutions are essentially Western institutions (G8, IMF, World Bank et al.: indeed, the only serious exception to this is the United Nations), that its language – namely English – is the lingua franca, that Western history is the defining story of (to the point of being almost coterminous with) global history, that white skin colour and Caucasian physical characteristics are the global norm. One could go on. There is, in other words, still a huge presumption of Western universalism, and this is by no means confined to the political right or the United States, but still largely informs Europe, including much of the left. Essentially this view holds that Western values, for example those of the Enlightenment, are both a desirable and also a necessary condition for the progress of the non-Western world.[7] The rise of China, however, suggests that this will become an increasingly untenable position. In this context, China's rise is quite different from the challenge posed by the Islamic world: the latter remains largely the voice of the globally excluded and marginalised, whereas China is destined to become a major global power, ultimately perhaps *the* major global power. As a consequence, it will be impossible to ignore either its voice or its example. The rise of China, in other words, relativises the world and thereby spells the end of Western universalism. It is difficult to underestimate the political, cultural and psychological consequences of this for the West, Europe not least.[8] The West is so accustomed to enjoying a position of overwhelming global hegemony that it has long since become an unquestioned assumption – not just by governing elites, but also by the ordinary citizen.

Let us consider some of the ways in which the rise of China might relativise what have previously been fundamental tenets of Western universalism. The first example is that which I have already discussed, namely the possible revival of the tributary system in East Asia. There seems little likelihood of this happening outside East Asia (with the possible exception of South and Central Asia), especially as historically it was always confined to East Asia. But East Asia alone constitutes one-third of the world's population (and if one includes South Asia and central Asia as well – very unlikely but not entirely inconceivable – then one is talking about over half the world's population). The possibility that the Westphalian system – the invention of the European nation-state system – might no longer hold sway in East Asia, certainly in its purist form, not only immediately relativises it, but also inevitably affects the global system of inter-state relations. In other words, if a latter-day version of the tributary system becomes predominant in East Asia, or even simply part of a more hybrid system that combines both Westphalian and tributary principles, then the effects will be felt throughout the world.

The second example concerns the ubiquity of the nation-state. This is the status and identity shared by all politically independent territories and continues to be the aspiration of those peoples that think they should be independent. In the postwar period, there has been an enormous expansion in their number: never has the popularity of the nation-state been greater. China, for its part, describes itself as a nation-state and has done so for around a century. Given its extremely long history, however, which stretches back around two millennia in roughly its present form, its self-identity as a nation-state is, in historical terms, an extremely recent phenomenon. The great majority of what the Chinese see as defining their identity – customs, language, food, the state, ancestral worship, the family, Confucianism, its borders – long predates China's emergence as a nation-state. For most of its history, China was a civilisation-state rather than a nation-state, constituted not by the characteristics of the latter, but by what might be described as the slow expansion and evolution of Chinese civilisation.[9] It was only when China became embroiled with the European powers from the mid-19th century that it was obliged to entertain the idea of considering itself as a nation-state with, for example, defined borders and a relationship of de jure equality with other nation-states. Until then, it had regarded itself as the Middle Kingdom, the centre of the world, a universe in its own right, superior to all other states, not even vaguely comparable with them, and therefore not required to have a name or fixed borders. China's status as a nation-state is not only extremely recent – certainly in Chinese terms – but was also forced upon it. Given all this, China's nation-state status remains an awkward fit, notwithstanding the fact that China now invariably describes and defines itself as such. In fact, in its attitudes and structure, China still remains essentially a civilisation-state, with its nation-state identity not really describing what it is or what in practice animates it.

For the time being this is not an issue. China is presently preoccupied with its modernisation and, towards that end, its desire to be accepted as a responsible member of the international community. But as it acquires growing power and self-confidence then it seems likely that it will behave increasingly according to what it is and has been rather than to what it purports to be because of the exigencies of its present circumstances. In other words, it will tend to see itself as a civilisation-state rather than a nation-state. In truth, of course, the nation-state system, though resting on de jure equality, has always been, in reality, highly unequal; a formal legal equality concealing huge discrepancies in actual power. As China becomes a major global power, this is bound to have the effect of transforming the present system of international relations, including the concepts that underpin it. If China comes to regard itself as a civilisation-state at least as much as a nation-state – probably linked to the re-emergence of patterns of the tributary system in East Asia – then the nation-state, a European creation, would no longer be dominant in the way that it has been for well over a century, if not longer.

The third example concerns the nature of politics. The difference between Western democracy and the absence of it in China is usually explained in terms of the attitude of its Communist government. This fails to recognise that the roots of the present polity, rather than being aberrant, lie deep in Chinese history. For around a millennium, the Chinese state, unlike the European state, has never been forced or obliged to share power with other elites, such as the church or the merchant class.[10] Politics was and remains exclusively a matter for government. Constructed around Confucian tenets, the state was not regarded as answerable to the people – apart from in extremis, when the people were in widespread revolt, and it was deemed that the mandate of Heaven had been withdrawn from the emperor[11] – but instead was measured by its ability to live up to the moral principles of Confucianism. In retrospect, China's state system was remarkably successful, capable of extraordinary feats – from holding such a huge country together for long periods of time, to large-scale public works projects such as the building of the canals. Within the Chinese tradition, the state occupies a far more pivotal position than in the vast majority of other political cultures. It is seen as the expression and quintessence of China, its legitimacy rooted in China's long existence as a civilisation-state. Although the Communist regime has been viewed as some kind of deviation from the historical norm, there are powerful lines of continuity between the communist and Confucian traditions,[12] not least with regard to the role and nature of the Chinese state. China has an extremely distinct and sophisticated polity whose nature and dynamics is very different from the European tradition. It therefore seems highly unlikely that China will conform to Western norms but instead will remain highly distinctive and, as it emerges as a global power, will offer an alternative model to that of the West.

The fourth example concerns a stark and defining difference with Europe, namely China's unity. While, after the decline of the Roman Empire, Europe splintered into many different units and ultimately into numerous nation-states, China, at more or less the same historical time, was moving in the opposite direction, with the steady unification of the country after the Warring States period, the key moment being 221BC and the creation of the Qin Empire.[13] For at least half the period since, China has been divided and for the other half united: since 221BC its borders have, broadly speaking, been similar to those of today, with the exception of most of the territories conquered during the Qing dynasty. The Chinese attach a huge priority to the importance of unity, which is regarded as the state's first duty and responsibility. The legitimacy of the Maoist regime, above all, derived from the fact that it succeeded in restoring the country's unity after a century of disunity and divided sovereignty. That same instinct animates China's attitudes towards the 'lost territories' and in particular the recovery of Taiwan: it would be wrong to believe that this is primarily a governmental concern, for popular sentiments, if anything, run even stronger. The highly distinctive Chinese attitudes towards race are also shaped to an important extent by the idea of Chinese unity. The Han Chinese, who constitute around 92 per cent of the population, believe they are of one race. This, of course, is an illusion – in reality, they are derived from countless races – but it is part of the Chinese commonsense. The roots of this mentality stem from the fact that over thousands of years there has been a long process of melding and assimilation, together with an ideology of affinity whose origins lie in the civilisation-state as well as, more recently, in the nation-state.[14]

Whereas European nation-states have spent many centuries at war with each other, China, in contrast, has invested similar energies in seeking a means by which to stay united as one country, a task which has been hugely difficult. Although this is usually underestimated, China is an extremely diverse country which, though united, is also highly decentralised. In many respects the provinces resemble nation-states, enjoying different standards of living, cultures and economies.[15] This is as true today as it has always been. This, indeed, is an important characteristic of the civilisation-state: within its borders, unlike a nation-state, there are many different systems that co-exist alongside each other. A classic contemporary example of this is the 'one country, two systems' solution in Hong Kong, which is entirely alien to European notions of sovereignty but is a typical feature of China as a civilisation-state. The latter, in fact, might be described as 'one civilisation, many systems'.[16]

The emergence of China as a major global player means that there will now be an alternative to the European model of governance, in both an historical and contemporary context. Europe, in other words, will no longer be the global template for governance, whether in the form of the nation-state or, as in more recent times, a political union. The European Union has been widely seen as a model for others to emulate, a means by which small-medium-sized nation-states can share some aspects of their sovereignty and thereby concert their strength and effectiveness. China offers an entirely different model and, in population terms, on twice the scale. Rather than an agglomeration of nation-states, China is what can only be described as a mega-state whose cohesion and sense of shared identity lies in its roots and reality as a civilisation-state. If we look beyond China, moreover, it is clear that we are moving into a world that will be increasingly dominated by mega-states: according to a Goldman Sachs projection, by 2050 the three largest states in the world as measured by GDP (exchange rates) will be China, the United States and India respectively (see below).[17] Diverse as they are, these mega-states are likely to increasingly dominate global affairs in the second half of the 21st century. Furthermore, the Goldman Sachs projections also indicate just how relatively insignificant the major European economies are likely to be in comparison.

China's arrival on the world scene provides a stark contrast to Europe in a host of different ways. If Europe has provided the dominant global paradigm (to the point where its experience was regarded as universal) for the last two centuries, and in some respects very much longer, the emergence of China suggests an entirely different kind of paradigm. While Europe remains divided into many different nation-states, China, in population and land mass, is the size of a continent. While Europe developed a highly aggressive culture as a result of constant inter-state warring, which then translated itself into the conquest of overseas empires by means of its overwhelming naval power, China in contrast devoted its energies to seeking to stay united and adding to its territory by a steady process of continental expansion. While Europe spoke many different languages, China enjoyed a common written language. The rise of China, thus, represents, at least for Europe, a dramatic

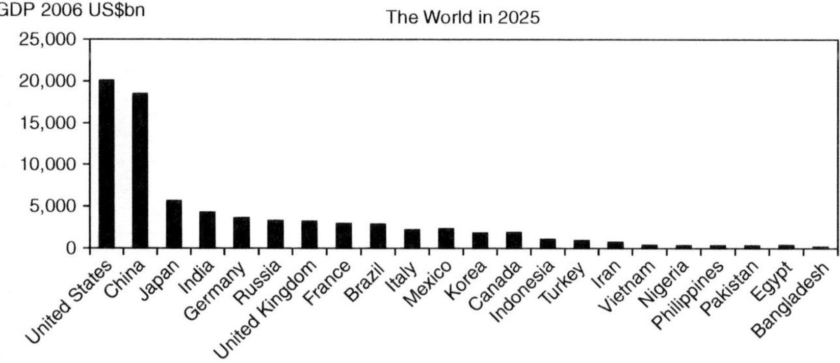

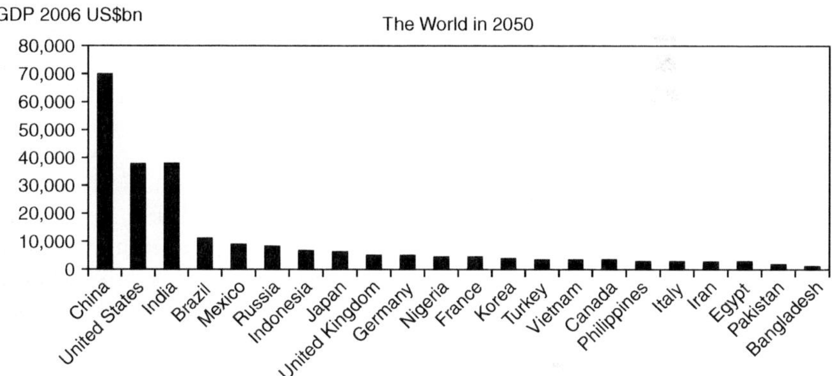

Figure 4.1:   World scenarios 2025 and 2050
Source: Goldman Sachs (see Note 17).

changing of the global guard in a way that the earlier rise of the United States did not. The latter was and remains in many respects a European transplant. In racial, ethnic, intellectual, cultural, political and religious terms it shares much with Europe. China most certainly does not: it is a product of entirely different civilisational co-ordinates.

China and Europe

While China's relations with the United States have been an intermittent source of controversy, this has not been true of Europe's relationship with China. There are several reasons for this. First, China's trade with the United States, until very recently, has been on a far greater scale. Second, Europe's balance of payments deficit with China has also been rather smaller, although it has been growing rapidly. Together with the value of the RMB (*renminbi,* the Chinese currency), these have been the key sources of economic tension between China and the United States. Third, as a disparate union rather than a nation-state, the EU speaks with a weaker voice than the US.[18] Fourth, the United States clearly perceives China as a long-term threat to its position as sole superpower; hence, for example, the regular Pentagon statements about China's military spending. As Europe does not consider itself to be a major military power, it does not feel concerned about China in the same kind of way. Fifth, the United States has the most powerful military presence in East Asia of any country. It also has military pacts with Japan, Taiwan and South Korea, amongst others. Its military power in the region clearly bears upon China, although for the most part relations between the two have, since the beginning of their rapprochement in 1971–2, been relatively harmonious and conflict-free. In contrast, Europe, since the handover of Hong Kong in 1997 and Macau in 1999, has had no significant interests in the region other than economic ones, and even these former colonial territories were of relatively minor importance: in other words, ever since the loss of their East Asian colonies in the early postwar period, the European powers have enjoyed no real influence in the region, having ceded it to the United States. Given that East Asia is the most powerful economic region in the world, nothing more clearly illustrates the decline of Europe as a global force and influence.

How are European-Chinese relations likely to evolve? There are five key components to this question. The first concerns the economic relationship between Europe and China. The second comprises the broader bilateral relationship between the EU and China. The third is the extent to which European and Chinese relations might be affected by their respective interests in other regions, for example, Africa. The fourth consists of the likely path of the China-American relationship and how this might bear upon Europe as a US ally. The fifth might be described as the existential dimension: how Europe might be affected by and react to the rise of a non-Western power to the point where it becomes one of the two major global powers and perhaps ultimately the world's most powerful state.

The economic relationship between China and Europe has grown very rapidly. Essentially it consists of the import of consumer goods made in China – in the majority of cases by American, European, Japanese, Korean and Taiwanese firms – and the export to China of high-technology products, especially from Germany. Although the trade deficit between the EU and China is now very large, this has so far had relatively little political impact, even at the level of the individual member state, where it is most likely to be felt and expressed. It is true that the EU-China economic relationship is becoming more strained – for example, over the value of the RMB and intellectual property – but this should not be exaggerated.[19] So far, the rise of China has had a largely positive impact on Europe. It has significantly lowered the price of many manufactured consumer goods, which has clearly been beneficial for the average European household. Of course, the displacement of jobs to China has had a negative effect on those workers who have been made redundant as a consequence, but so far the number of winners greatly outweighs the number of losers, as is also the case in the United States. Moreover, those nations that compete most directly with cheap Chinese goods are the new entrants from Eastern and Central Europe, plus Portugal and Greece, which were the weakest countries in the unexpanded European Union.[20] The fact that the rise of China has resulted in a sharp increase in the prices of commodities, most notably oil, but also food, is clearly having an increasingly negative effect on European consumers, but this might be considered a more exogenous political factor in that it lies outside the bilateral economic relationship.

What would transform European attitudes towards China is if the latter began to move rapidly up the value chain and threaten more mainstream areas of European production, resulting in a very large increase in the number of losers. So far there has been relatively little evidence of this. China for the most part still specialises in low- and medium-technology products, with a very weak presence at the high end: this is reflected in the fact that China's trading relationships are largely orientated towards the developing rather than the developed world. Likewise, the majority of its overseas investment is directed towards East Asia, and to a much lesser extent Africa and Latin America, rather than North America and Europe.[21] It would be wrong, however, to believe that China is destined to remain at the lower end of manufactured products. On the contrary, it is making strenuous efforts to rise up the technological ladder, with, for example, growing sums being spent on R&D, increasing numbers of overseas Chinese scientists being persuaded to live and work in China, and Chinese universities producing huge numbers of science and technology graduates. It will, of course, take time – albeit rather less, one suspects, than people think, given the prodigious rate of change demonstrated so far – but, in a similar manner to Japan and South Korea, China sooner or later will become a major competitor in more high-tech products. Furthermore, given its sheer size, the scale of Chinese competition in these areas is likely to resemble its performance at the lower end. The emergence of China as a high-end player will transform the political dynamics of the relationship between Europe and China, with the number of losers exceeding the number of winners. In such circumstances, trade with China is likely to become a major political issue in Europe and calls for protectionism could become irresistible.

The second issue concerns the broader bilateral relationship between China and the European Union. There are many aspects of this, from migration to arms. Here I want to concentrate on the latter. After Tiananmen Square, Europe imposed an embargo on the supply of arms to China. The Chinese, largely dependent on Russia for their weapons, lobbied hard to persuade the EU to lift the ban, and finally, at the end of 2004, they met with some success when, after much argument, the EU agreed to end the embargo. The

United States then put intense pressure on EU to reverse the decision, making it, in effect, into an issue of confidence in the Western alliance.[22] The EU eventually bowed to American pressure. The Chinese are certainly keen to develop an independent relationship with the EU, which is illustrated by their growing bilateral ties. Since the 1990s, the Chinese have shown growing interest in both the EU as an institution and also in European societies, in contrast to the early reform period when the Chinese looked overwhelmingly towards the United States as a model. Hu Jintao, China's current leader, has been particularly associated with this shift. The Chinese are also interested in exploring the extent to which Europe can be persuaded to act independently of the United States. After initial encouragement, the arms embargo experience was ultimately discouraging.

The third aspect concerns relations between China and Europe in 'third-party' regions (that is, outside East Asia and Europe) where both have significant interests. Hitherto, Chinese involvement outside East Asia has been extremely restricted so this has not really been a matter of particular interest or concern. But since the turn of the century and the unveiling of China's 'Going Abroad' policy, China's involvement elsewhere has increased greatly, albeit from an extremely low base. The strategy has been directed overwhelmingly towards the developing world, above all those countries which are rich in the raw materials that China needs to fuel its economic growth. The most dramatic example is Africa, where Chinese interests have, in just several years, increased enormously. Africa, of course, is a continent in which the British and French have extensive interests. So far, there has been little sign of any resulting conflict, but it is conceivable that Africa could become a source of friction between China and Europe, though it is perhaps rather more likely that the Americans will become embroiled. The other major area of Chinese involvement has been Latin America, but apart from connections with Spain, this is not a region where there is a strong European interest. Although the Chinese interest in the Middle East has grown considerably, especially with Saudi Arabia and above all Iran, the Chinese have accepted that the Middle East is an American sphere of influence and have therefore acted with great caution. Nonetheless, China's relationship with Iran is a difficult balancing act which could bring it into conflict with the United States and also with European powers acting in concert with the USA.

The fourth issue concerns the relationship between the United States and China and how this might impact on the Europe-China relationship. This seems to be by far the most likely cause of conflict between Europe and China, aside from their economic relationship. As China becomes an increasingly important global power, it seems likely that its expanding interests will bring it into growing conflict with the United States. With the exception of the decline of Britain and the rise of the United States during the 20th century, which for various reasons involved relatively little acrimony, the decline of an established global power and the rise of its would-be successor have normally been marked by considerable conflict; and it is difficult to imagine that China's rise will represent a departure from this pattern. It would be wrong to think that the US-China relationship will become a simple rerun of the Cold War – China, after all, has pursued a very different strategy to that of the Soviet Union – but it seems likely that their relationship will, nonetheless, become increasingly fraught and conflictual. How will Europe react to such a situation? The Iraqi war suggested that Europe – or, more accurately, Germany and France in particular, but European public opinion more generally – feels a declining affinity with the United States, certainly in the context of the latter's shift to a more nationalist and unilateralist position under the Bush administration. There are many imponderables here. To what extent will that unilateralist stance continue under future administrations? How will European countries react to the United States if it does? Was the schism over Iraq an isolated issue or a harbinger of deeper trends? In the event of growing US-China tension, however, it seems unlikely that Europe will adopt a semi-detached attitude towards the United States. The United States and Europe have long shared a close relationship whose roots are historical, geographical, cultural and, above all, racial and ethnic. They have been close allies ever since the Second World War. They also overwhelmingly constitute the developed world with the shared interests and attitudes that this implies. In contrast, China and Europe have precious little in common. They come from entirely different cultural and historical roots. They are of very different racial origins. They have never been allies. The European powers colonised parts of China and were the cause – along with Japan – of its 'century of humiliation'.

This brings us to the fifth issue, namely the existential question of how Europe is likely to react to the rise of such a different kind of country and people to a position of global pre-eminence. Earlier I tried to trace what this might mean in terms of the slow but steady deconstruction of the European-made world of the last two centuries and the undermining of Western universalism. Western Europe has experienced its decline over the postwar period as a long-running trauma. This has especially been true of the two major colonial powers, Britain and France, but its consequences have been more widely felt, as the examples of Belgium and Italy illustrate. It is extremely difficult for countries and peoples that are used to being at the centre of global affairs and, in effect, 'bossing the world', to adjust to a constantly diminishing role. The impact of national decline, of course, has been partially cushioned by the European Union and the fact that the United States was one of the two dominant global powers during the Cold War, embracing Western Europe as its closest ally. The very notion of the West – and the historical, cultural and racial bonds that this implied – allowed Europe to feel it was still at the centre of things. There will be no such compensations with the rise of China: Europe will experience a process of dramatic displacement in the world order, with the inevitable and consequent painful sense of loss.

Notes and References

1. This paper is based on Martin Jacques, *When China Rules the World*, London: Penguin, 2009.
2. David C. Kang, 'Getting Asia Wrong: The Need for New Analytical Frameworks', *International Security*, 27 (4), Spring 2003, 61–6.
3. Ibid., 178.
4. Ibid., 79.
5. For an interesting discussion of these issues, see Wang Gungwu, 'Early Ming Relations with Southeast Asia: A Background Essay', in John King Fairbank (ed.), *The Chinese World Order: Traditional China's Foreign Relations*, Cambridge MA: Harvard University Press, 1968, 60–2.
6. Dominic Wilson and Anna Stupnytska, 'The N-11: More Than an Acronym', Goldman Sachs Global Economics Paper No 153, 28 March 2007, 8.
7. For example, Will Hutton, *The Writing on the Wall: China and the West in the 21st Century*, London: Little, Brown, 2007, x–xi.
8. Paul A. Cohen, *Discovering History in China: American Historical Writing on the Recent Chinese Past*, New York: Columbia University Press, 1984, 95.
9. William A. Callahan, *Contingent States: Greater China and Transnational Relations*, Minneapolis: University of Minnesota Press, 2004, 81, 109; Shi Anbin, 'Mediating Chinese-ness: Identity Politics and Media Culture in Contemporary China', in Anthony Reid and Zheng Yangwen (eds), *Unequal Siblings: China's Place in an Asymmetric Asia*, Cambridge MA: Harvard University Press, forthcoming, 13.
10. R. bin Wong, *China Transformed: Historical Change and the Limits of European Experience*, Ithaca: Cornell University Press, 2000, 92.
11. Karel Van Wolferen, *The Enigma of Japanese Power: People and Politics in a Stateless Nation*, New York: Vintage, 1990, 241–2.
12. bin Wong, op. cit., 70, 194–7, 205.
13. Ibid, 76.
14. Suisheng Zhao, *A Nation-State by Construction: Dynamics of Modern Chinese Nationalism*, Stanford: Stanford University Press, 2004, 39, 40, 166–7.
15. David S. G. Goodman and Gerald Segal, *China Rising: Nationalism and Interdependence*, London: Routledge, 1997, 31–2, 44–5.
16. Callahan, op. cit., 88–9.
17. Wilson and Stupnytska, op. cit., 8–9.
18. Katinka Barysch with Charles Grant and Mark Leonard, *Embracing the Dragon – the EU's Partnership with China*, London: Centre for European Reform, 2005, 77.
19. Patrick Messerlin and Razeen Sally, 'Why It Is Dangerous for Europe to Bash China', *Financial Times*, 13 December 2007.
20. European Commission, 'The Challenge to the EU of a Rising China', *European Competitiveness Report*, Brussels, 2004.
21. 'Reaching for a Renaissance', A Special Report on China and Its Region, *The Economist*, 31 March 2007, 6.
22. Barysch, Grant and Leonard, op cit., 60–5.

Part II
Divisions within Europe

5
Divisions between Elites

György Lengyel

The paper investigates whether there is an East-West divide among European elites in regard to identity, visions about EU goals and supporting integration. If the divide does exist, is it greater than the one between founding and accessing countries? Are these attitudes – concerning identity, the goals and integration – consistent? What differences can be discerned among the newly integrated East European countries?

Concerning pro-integration attitudes, an earlier study by Inglehart highlighted the importance of cognitive mobilisation.[1] He stressed that in explaining attitudes, the cultural and social resources at individual level ought to be considered. Gabel tested the relevance of five theories: cognitive mobilisation, post-materialist values, utilitarianism, partisanship and the attitude towards the given government. He has found that as regards the founding states, the model has explanatory force, while the attitude of the populace of New Member States (NMSs) is more strongly influenced by utilitarianism, as well as by variables of their affinities to parties and the government.[2] In his pilot research Bruter argues that it is worth differentiating the general, civic and cultural aspects of European identity, which – though interrelated – are also distinct from one another. European identity and the support of European integration are also two different things: though related to each other, the degree of correlation does not suggest a deterministic relation.[3] Hooghe and Marks have also investigated whether it is identity or economic rationality that influence people's attitude to integration more profoundly. They have found that identity has a more powerful explanatory force than the individual or contextual variables of economic rationality.[4]

In accessing countries it has been studied which social groups expected advantages/disadvantages of integration, and what social factors influenced the symbolic and pragmatic aspects of their attitude to integration. It has been found that those in a better material and cultural position expected advantages to a greater extent, but the counterpart of this connection was untrue: instead of the socially most handicapped social strata, it was the middle social layers (for example, the entrepreneurs along the western frontier) that expected the most disadvantages. The disadvantaged social groups were either just as optimistic as the average or were overrepresented among those who had no opinions. Cultural resources more powerfully influenced both the symbolic aspects (identity) and the material aspects (evaluation of EU redistribution) than the material resources.[5]

The conceptual frames of this paper are similar to the above works but the focus is different. The investigation shifts the focus from the population to the elites. European integrative processes are often described as an elite-controlled top-down phenomenon.[6] If this holds true, it is particularly important to examine how homogeneous the European elites' opinions are on the key factors of integration. Critical analyses often presume that, unlike the public, there is a homogeneous elite opinion and a consistent elite interest. However, the concept of the elite has remained vague in many investigations. We study two representative groups of national elites: political and economic. Other, sometimes also important, segments of national elites and supranational elites are not included due to lack of information. The paper is based on the INTUNE elite research project. The fieldwork was carried out in February-May 2007 in 18 European countries. (The case of Serbia – not being a member state yet – is excluded from the current analysis.) According to the design 80 MPs and 40 top business leaders were to be interviewed in each country by standardised questionnaire during a face-to-face or computer-assisted telephone interview (CATI). The design presupposes that the weight of representatives' opinion doubles that of the business leaders and the weight of the different national elites is equal. No further weighting according to countries or elite groups was applied. As for the actual numbers in some countries there were deviations from the design, but the difference proved to be statistically insignificant. All in all the sample consists of 1335 political and 690 economic elite members. Unless otherwise mentioned the data are from this survey. The goal of this paper is not to test theories but to explore the specific features of East European elites concerning European integration. It does not break down identity to its constituents, but examines what individual and contextual factors influence supranational attachment. The question is not whether it is identity or economic rationality that influences the attitude to integration more strongly, but

- whether Eastern and Western elites differ on this issue;
- whether the elites of the founding and accessing member states diverge in judging identity, economic rationality and support of integration;
- and whether there are considerable differences among the East European elites in this regard.

To put it in more abstract terms: the aim is to see how the attitudes of the European elites concerning the EU are distributed in the dimensions of social space and time.

Dependent variables: identity, aims and support of integration

Territorial attachments – as parts of individuals' identity – could be conceived as mutually exclusive, or alternatively, as inclusive or overlapping feelings.[7] There are people who think that it is very important for them to belong to the country or to their town, but not at all important to belong to Europe. There are others whose territorial attachments are not excluding but coexisting. Recent literature has clarified that exclusive national identity is not necessarily the dominant type in Europe, thus coexisting territorial attachments are more frequent than excluding ones.[8]

This is the situation in the case of the elites that we studied. The vast majority of the European elites feel attached to Europe, as noted in Figure 5.1.

There is a positive correlation between supranational and national (or European and local) identities. It is not the case that strong attachment to the nation, region or locality would contradict European identity. Since we deal with elites of nations belonging to the EU, we interpret European attachment as a territorial aspect of supranational, or EU, identity. Perhaps this identification is not without problems, but the important point here is that national and subnational identities are positively correlated with supranational attachment. What has been pointed out as a general tendency for the population proved to be true in the case of the elites as well: national and subnational identities do not hamper, but rather facilitate, positive feelings

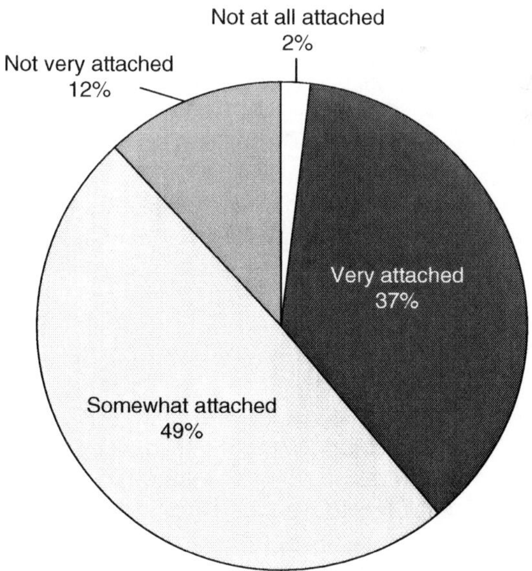

Figure 5.1:   Attachment to Europe

Table 5.1:   Attachment to country and attachment to Europe (per cent)

Country	Europe				
	Very attached	**Somewhat attached**	**Not very attached**	**Not at all attached**	**N**
Very attached	44.1	46.6	7.9	1.4	1434
Somewhat attached	15.8	59.0	22.3	2.9	449
Not very attached	26.0	34.2	31.5	8.2	73
Not at all attached	27.6	31.0	27.6	13.8	29
Total	36.8	48.7	12.3	2.2	1985

Cramer's V = .19****

towards Europe and the EU. There is an especially strong correlation between the two subnational identities that can practically substitute for each other. Strong attachment to Europe is overrepresented within the categories of those who are very attached to their nation, region or settlement. On the other hand, among those who are just somewhat attached or not attached to their country, it is significantly lower than the average.

Ninety per cent of those who are strongly attached to their countries are to some extent also attached to Europe, whilst this proportion is below 60 per cent among those who are not attached to their country. The correlations between subnational, national and supranational attachment are even stronger if we investigate them inside the Eastern bloc of countries, except for the connection between European and national identity.

As for the visions concerning the major aims, half of the national political and economic elites of the EU think that the main aim of the EU should be to make the European economy more competitive in world markets as against providing better social security for all its citizens.

Slightly more than a quarter preferred improving social security and slightly more than one-fifth opted for both competitiveness and security. (Fieldwork experience – especially among economic elites – did show that some interviewees explained competitiveness as a precondition for better social security.) The evaluation of unification shows that support for further unification is much higher than scepticism among European elites. Roughly three out of five definitely supported further unification while the proportion of those who think that unification has already gone too far is one in ten.

The formulation of the question used the issue of unification as if it were interchangeable with integration. For those who support both, the distinction is superficial, and they usually think that unification is a necessary

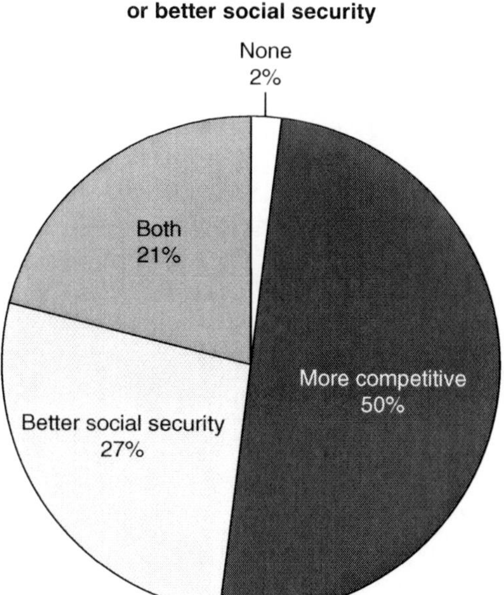

Figure 5.2:   Visions about the major goal of the EU

regulatory institution and driving force of transformation. Indeed, unification is a form of integration but not the only form. There are others who think that integration is acceptable and might be useful, but unification contradicts their aims and undermines their institutions. Surveys are usually not very sensitive towards such semantic nuances, but it is worth keeping in mind that the question addressed the attitudes toward a certain form of integration. Since we deal with elites, it is a realistic supposition that they were more sensitive concerning attitudes toward supranational institutions than the interviewees in a general population survey.

Taxation and the use of force are two exclusive functions of a state. European national elites would feel it would be fair to redistribute €17 tax income out of €100 on the supranational level, with half of the rest on the national and the remainder on the subnational level. A detailed analysis clarifies that interviewees most frequently would distribute between 10 and 20 per cent on the EU level. Only 5 per cent would not spend a euro on the supranational level.

Thirty per cent of European elites prefer a single European army, and roughly the same proportion is opposed to any form of supranational integration of armed forces. Two out of five elite members think that a combined national and supranational solution would be useful. It means that the

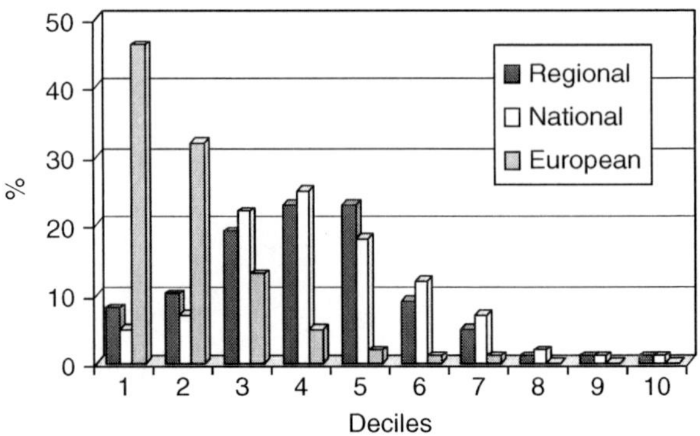

Figure 5.3:   Level of tax redistribution

Table 5.2:   Connections between identity, goals and support of integration (Cramer's V/Phi)

	Vision: competition vs. social security	Unification	Tax redistribution	Army
Attachment to Europe	.088****	.225****	.115****	.09***
Vision		.1****	Ns	.073*
Unification			.186****	.208****
Tax redistribution				.182****

majority of European elites support a certain degree of integration of armed military forces, and within this a minority would give up a national army. A closer look at the options of either supranational or entirely national armed forces shows that the national version was mostly supported in countries that were occupied or attacked by central powers during the Second World War, while the single European solution was overrepresented among countries with totalitarian historical experiences.

Three variables – identity, vision on goals and support of supranational institutions – display unambiguous correlations. Support for unification, preference for EU taxation and a single EU army – that is, the criteria of the integration of supranational institutions selected here – have internal logical connections. There is a similarly close and positive correlation between supranational identity and support for unification. The vision of a competitive EU is in loose negative correlation with symbolic supranational identity and with the consolidation of unification, and it is only loosely connected to EU taxation and an EU army. It is especially noteworthy here that the relative majority of the European elite prefers market competitiveness, and they are overrepresented in the group of little symbolic attachment. A quarter of the elite would prefer greater social security, distributed more or less evenly among the identity categories. Those who emphasise both aims are slightly overrepresented among those with strong European attachment. In the very small minority rejecting European attachment the social security and the combined versions are unpopular.

The independent variables and what they explain

1   The East-West divide and the length of EU experience

A basic description of the East-West division of the elite is that those of the post-socialist countries are less attached to the EU, and they are less committed to unification and to the strengthening of the supranational institutions than the average. By contrast, the supporters of the liberal EU – preferring market competition against regulated capitalism emphasising the social security of the citizen – are overrepresented among them. It must be borne in mind that half of the European elites are committed to competition and only a quarter would give priority to social security. Therefore, the EU concept as regards varieties of capitalism should be refined. If we accept that the EU is an elite project – as it is often claimed – it must be realised that the European elites are closer to a competitive EU vision. This needs to be stressed because institution-based typologies often contrast the American and European economic models, claiming that the latter embody regulated capitalism as against the liberal Anglo-Saxon model. It must be made clear that the European national political and economic elites prefer the competitive model and in this respect the elites of East European countries are more strongly committed to competition than the average.

As to differences between political and economic elites, nearly three-quarters of the economic elite consider the most important goal of the EU to be the strengthening of competition, as compared to only one-third of the political elite. This is the strongest divide manifested in the dimensions we studied.

According to the statistics in Table 5.3, the deepest gap between Eastern and Western European member countries is in the extent of support for the studied dimensions of integration. The divergence is systematic and can be demonstrated in regard to unification and the role of institutional actors. The East European elites support supranational unification and a common EU army to a smaller extent and they regard smaller EU redistribution more desirable than their colleagues.

Table 5.3: Connections between attitudes and elite-divisions (Cramer's V/Phi)

	East-West	Founding+-Accessing	Political-Economic elite	GDP
European identity	.063***	.124****	Ns	.049*
Goal: competition	.193****	.052*	.331****	.187****
UNIF2: unification should be strengthened	.213****	.131****	Ns	.205****
EUREDIS2: above-average support of supranational tax-redistribution	.167****	.096****	Ns	.138****
EUARMY2: single EU army vs. any other solutions	.196****	.167****	.105****	.185****

+ 'Founding member' countries in the sample are Belgium, France, Germany and Italy, 'Accessing members' are Austria, Great Britain, Greece, Portugal, Spain plus the East European countries.

Legend
**** level of significance = .0001
*** Level of significance = .001
** Level of significance = .01
* Level of significance = .05
Ns = not significant

Table 5.4: Preferred EU goals of the political and economic elites: to strengthen competitiveness on the world market or to provide better social security to citizens (per cent)

	More competitive	Better social security	Both	None/can't say	Total/N/Phi = .346
Political elite	38.0	36.3	23.9	1.8	100(1301)
Economic elite	72.5	9.5	16.4	1.6	100(685)
Together	49.9	27.0	21.2	1.7	100(1986)

Concerning goals – the support for competition as opposed to social security – three-fifths of the Eastern elites supported competition as against two-fifths of the Western elites. On this issue, as we have seen, there is a wider gap between political and economic elites – the latter obviously stress the priority of competition more. However, this functional difference referring to the division of labour between the elites is insignificant or weakly explanatory in all other regards.

The divide between founders (Belgium, France, Germany, Italy) and accessing members (East European countries plus Austria, the UK, Greece, Portugal,

Spain) in the sample proved significant concerning the interpretation of identity. There was a strong correlation in GDP in all aspects, but it was not as strong as in the East-West divide. Consequently, the East-West differences imply more than just the differences of material conditions.

Along most dimensions, the East-West divide appears to have greater explanatory force than the difference between the elites of founders and new member states. The only aspect on which length of EU membership has a more significant influence is that of identity. The elites of the founding members are far more attached to the EU than the elites of the later-accessing countries: half of the founder elites expressed great attachment to the EU as against a third of the elites of the later members.

2   The explanatory power of the East-West division checked by logistic regression models

In the binary logistic regression models, the socio-demographic variables (age, gender and birthplace), the cultural indicators (level and type of education, foreign studies and career) and the social resources (foreign contacts during work, living experience abroad) were also studied. Political orientation on the basis of the self-reported left-right scale, as well as the interviewee's (political or economic) elite position have been included. At first two model families were built: one with the dichotomy of the East-West division as the contextual explanatory variable and the other with the accessing vs. founding member states dichotomy. In both families, per capita GDP was also used as a contextual explanatory variable. Dependent variables were the dichotomised variants of attachment, vision about the major aim of the EU, attitudes toward unification, redistribution, and the formation of an EU army. (Where the measurement level of dependent variables allowed – in the field of supporting redistribution and unification – linear regression models were run as well.)

The most important factors influencing European identity ('very attached to Europe' answers) with similar force in a positive direction were university education, older age, intensity of foreign experiences and contacts during work. Thus, supranational identity appears to be positively influenced by cultural resources and international social experiences in addition to age. By contrast, being born in a large city acted against supranational identity. It is therefore a more complex question and we cannot be satisfied with the usual explanation which associates metropolitan life with cosmopolitanism and with more intense international orientation. As we have seen, East European elites displayed below-average attachment to supranational identity, but in the model this connection was not found significant. What appeared significant in the cross tabulation proved to have been caused by the impact of other factors, and this effect could be eliminated by the involvement of these factors.

Table 5.5:   Logistic regression model for goals (COMPETITION2)

Variables in the equation	B	Wald	Exp (B)	Sign
MALE	0.4	5.8	1.4	.016
LEFT	−1.3	113.0	0.3	.000
LEADER	0.3	8.5	1.4	.003
ECEL	1.1	80.2	3.1	.000
GDP2	−1.1	96.3	0.3	.000
Constant	0.1	0.2	1.1	.741

Legend
N = 1808; Forward stepwise method, cut point: 0.5
Cox&Schnell = .2; Nagelkerke = .3; correct = 71.1
Variables not in the equation: EW, CONTACT, UNIV, BIRTHPL, DEGREE_FIELD, STUDY_ABROAD, SECTOR, ABROAD, AGE2;
Where COMPETITION2 is 1 if s/he prefers competition (vs. social security, both or none); AGE2 is 1 if s/he is 50+ years old; UNIV is 1 if s/he has an MA or higher degree; CONTACT is 1 if s/he had at least monthly foreign contacts during work in the last year; EW is 1 if s/he is from an East European member state; ECEL 1 = economic elite (vs. political elite position); MALE 1 = male; BIRTHPL 1 = large town, capital;
LEFT 1 = 0-3 on a left-right scale (0 = 4-10); GDP2 1 >= 17001 Euro pps GPD/cap.; DEGREE_FIELD 1 = business, engineering; STUDY_ABROAD 1 = had foreign study experience; LEADER 1 = previous occupation: leader; SECTOR 1 = previous sector of occupation: private; ABROAD 1 = did live abroad.

The model with the most vigorous explanatory force illuminates the goals of the EU.[9] Those who envisage the enhancement of market competitiveness as the main goal of the EU were significantly underrepresented among leftists, while economic elite members identified with this goal many times more than the average. Elite members with managerial experience (filling leading positions earlier) and males supported more intense competition than the average, which was a more powerful effect than the East-West divide. A single contextual variable – per capita GDP – contributed to this significant aspect, clarifying the attitude to the alternative goals of the EU, and exerting a significant negative effect on the attitude to competition. The elites of more affluent countries identified with the model of regulated capitalism far more than those of poorer countries. The elites of the richer countries did not prefer competitiveness and this factor was more important than the East-West divide as well.

The strengthening of unification was principally influenced by the East-West difference: elites of Western countries apparently regard the reinforcement of European unification as a much more significant goal than East European elites do. The explanatory force of GDP remained about the same as above, though it largely overlaps with the East-West division (therefore, the significance level of GDP is low). The elites of richer countries were more in favour of strengthening unification.

Other factors that considerably increased support for unification included leftist political affiliation and the factors of cultural and social resources (university qualifications, foreign studies, intense working contacts abroad). The economic elites were more strongly in favour of unification than the national political elites, and this effect remained significant despite several control variables.

To predict the attitude to redistribution, the linear regression model brings in the East-West divide, leftist affinities and the economic elite: members of the economic elite and leftists would like to see significantly more centralised taxes compared to East Europeans as a whole. Logistic regression produced similar results for the East-West divide, with the only other significantly influential factor – in a negative direction – being age.

Preference for a unified EU army was far more typical of Western than of Eastern elites, of leftists and of economic elite members. The model revealed a moderate response over the issue of redistribution. Leftist political attitudes particularly strongly influenced preference for a supranational army over pure national or mixed alternatives.

It seems from the models that when direct effects were further refined by the inclusion of variables referring to the position of elite members, their socio-demographic, cultural and social characteristics and the country's level of development, the East-West divide did not show significant connection to responses regarding identity and visions about EU goals. However in relation to attitudes related to institution-building – unification, supranational redistribution and a unified EU army – it had a significant explanatory effect.

A preliminary conclusion at this point might be that the East-West divide has no role in explaining the symbolic aspects – EU identity and goals – of integration, whereas it has considerable explanatory power in regard to the pragmatic aspects of integration. East European elites support the strengthening of supranational institutions to a significantly lower extent than their Western counterparts.

The differences between the economic and political elites also proved significant in most of these pragmatic aspects (unification and common army). However, their decisive significance was found in explaining the EU goals: this difference influenced more than any other factor the views elite members expressed on competition and social security as the envisioned EU goals.

At this juncture, another three questions can be raised:

- Is the length of membership a better explanatory variable than the East-West divide?
- How do the models change if the dependent attitude variables are included in explaining one another?
- Do these explanations remain valid even if one of the crucial factors (the East-West divide) is eliminated, and what factors assume importance when the correlations are tested within the East European elites?

3   Models testing the effect of length of membership

The year of accession (more precisely: the dichotomy between founders and accessing member states – AMSs) explains the intensity of EU identity slightly more powerfully than the East-West divide. This suggests that among the elites of the AMSs there are more sceptical partners than in the East European elites, too. Indeed, the date of accession exerted an important negative impact on EU identity: the elites of AMSs are significantly underrepresented among those who claimed to be 'very attached to the EU' compared to those of founder states. The former include, for example, the British in addition to East European countries. In terms of individual traits, age and the accumulation of cultural and international social resources (foreign contacts and first-hand experience abroad) have a significant positive effect on EU identity.

As regards goals, the explanatory power of the two models testing spatial and temporal distances is equally strong, but like the East-West divide, the year of accession had no role. This is the strongest explanatory model in this model-family, which diagnosed very strong commitment to competition by the economic elite, men, and elitemembers with former managerial experience, while GDP as the contextual variable had a very powerful negative effect. Against this, leftists were opposed to competition as the high-priority EU goal as strongly and significantly as the economic elite supported it.

In the model using the year of accession, slightly different factors made the support of unification more likely. The difference between founders and later joiners did not prove significant, while the East-West divide did. In this model, cultural resources had smaller, whilst social resources had greater, explanatory force: unlike in the examination of the East-West divide, university qualifications and foreign studies had no explanatory effect in this case. In addition to foreign contacts, the experience of living abroad had the greatest explanatory force. Despite the differences in the involved variables, the explanatory power of the models is similar, and so is the rate of correctly classified cases. GDP had a greater explanatory force than in the case of the East-West divide, and richer countries urged unification to a greater extent.

In the logistic regression model of redistribution the founder vs. later admitted states dichotomy had no explanatory force. Both age and higher qualifications had a negative impact on supporting EU-level redistribution. By contrast, the elites of richer countries were more likely to support EU redistribution.

As for the common EU army, the year of accession had a weaker explanatory force than the East-West divide. In the model by year of accession, GDP also played a role (elites of richer countries preferred the idea of the single army more strongly); further positive impacts came from belonging to the economic elite, to the left and to younger age groups.

4   Models including the other attitude variables into the explanation of each other

In the model where supranational identity was the dependent variable, it was closely linked to the support of unification and EU redistribution. Age, university qualifications and intensity of international work connections had positive impacts on supranational identity. The explanatory power of the model doubled with the inclusion of attitude variables concerning the support for central institutions. Place of birth and life experiences abroad proved to be secondary in comparison to these attitudes. The aims were not included in the explanation of identity, which means that identity seems to be formed by separate social and cognitive factors.

Strengthening competition as the major aim of the EU is very strongly explained by social characteristics, but the support for this aim is independent from identity and support of integration. The most important impacts were that the interviewee was male, a member of the economic elite and had a managerial career; these positively influenced the vision of competition as a major aim. On the other hand, elites from countries with high GDP, and those with a left political orientation opposed the competition aim. The inclusion of the other attitude variables did not enhance the explanatory power of the model.

The model explaining support for unification included many variables. It included attitudes toward redistribution and an army, as well as a positive orientation to identity. Elites of rich countries, those with a left orientation and with foreign study experiences expressed above-average support for unification. EU identity and attitudes toward EU redistribution and an EU army proved to be more important than East-West divide, university degree and foreign work experiences.

The model of EU redistribution improved significantly with the introduction of attitude variables. Views on redistribution were strongly and positively connected with support for unification and supranational identity. The impact of the East-West divide remained important, since East European elites supported EU redistribution far less the Western elites. The same held for both older and highly educated elites.

Support for the idea of a single EU army was strongly connected with the other two attitude variables concerning EU integration. East European elites were much more against it, whilst economic elites everywhere in Europe were much more in support of a single army. Leftist elites and – as a newly included variable - those with previous work experiences in private companies showed above-average support for the single army. This means that not only economic elites, but those MEPs who have had experiences in the business world appear to be supportive of integrated solutions, at least as far as centralised defence is concerned. The model's explanatory power was doubled with the inclusion of the earlier-investigated EU attitudes.

Table 5.6:   Blocs and countries: Cramer's V/Phi values

	East-West (incl. Med)	Visegrád 4-rest of East-West (incl. Med)	Visegrád4-rest of East-West-Med	Visegrád4-Baltic-Balkan-West-Med	Seven East-European countries and the rest
European identity	.063***	.17****	.171 ****	.171****	.225****
Support for competition	.193****	.229****	.245****	.261****	.240****
Support for unification	.213****	.216****	.234****	.237****	.279****
Support for EU-redist.	.167****	.167****	.173****	.174****	.177****
Support for single army	.196****	.21****	.21****	.214****	.263****

Legend: ****level of significance is .0000 *** level of significance = .000

5   Differences within Eastern Europe

In the case of symbolic aspects – identity and goals – the refinement of blocs of countries considerably strengthened explanatory connections, while in the case of pragmatic issues – support for unification, redistribution and a single army – the improvements in explanatory power were much more moderate and country differences within East European countries were more relevant.

As regards European identity, connection to a Visegrád country rather than to the East and/or West overall had considerably more impact than the simple East-West divide, but neither the more detailed Western nor the more elaborate Eastern blocs increased the explanatory power. However, the differences in supranational identity among East European countries proved significant.

It can be seen in Table 5.7 that underlying the moderate difference between the East and West European member countries in regard to supranational identity, there were very marked differences from country to country. The average two-thirds 'very attached to Europe' response of the East European bloc as a whole conceals considerable fluctuation country by country. Those with below-average European identity included Bulgarian, Czech, Estonian and Lithuanian elites, while Polish and Hungarian elites produced markedly above-average levels.

To this it can be added that the attachment of the majority of West European elites to Europe is around average, with two considerable deviations: 10 per cent of the British elite and 60 per cent of the French elite felt they were strongly attached to the supranational European entity.

When we interpret these findings, the first thing to be considered is the nature of elite consensus upon which European attachment depends. To what

Table 5.7: East European countries by attachment to Europe (per cent)

	Attachment to Europe		Total
	Not very attached	**Very attached**	
West (incl. Med)	60.5	39.5	100.0
East	66.7	33.3	100.0
Bulgaria	83.1	16.9	100.0
Czech R	75.2	24.8	100.0
Estonia	78.9	21.1	100.0
Hungary	49.6	50.4	100.0
Lithuania	80.4	19.6	100.0
Poland	37.7	62.3	100.0
Slovakia	65.0	35.0	100.0
Total N = 1987	63.1	36.9	100.0

extent is European attachment part of the elite consensus and to what extent and in what tone is it involved in elite conflicts? It appears that in Poland, Hungary and France there is a tacit elite consensus on positive European attachment in spite of the fact that elite consensus in general is undergoing a particular crisis in all three countries.

The Hungarian and Polish elites have arrived at a crossroad where they have to decide between consolidating and stimulating democracy (as has been explicated in more detail elsewhere).[10] Concerning the French case, there has emerged a wide gap between the elite and public opinion, as the outcome of the referendum on the EU Constitution demonstrated. Indeed, only one-fifth of the adult population in France and less than a quarter of those in Poland expressed strong attachment to Europe. The Hungarian case is different again: nearly half the population is strongly attached to Europe – hence there is no significant divergence between the elite and the public in this regard. The general tendency in relation to European identity of the elite and the public there is that the elite professes a slightly but not considerably stronger attachment to Europe than does the general public. The proportions broadly match the rates in higher-qualified strata and groups with higher occupational status within the population sample as a whole.

As regards the attitudes towards EU aims, the inclusion of blocs sheds light on important differences, whereas the differences among East European

Table 5.8:   Visegrád and other countries by the major aim of the EU (per cent)

Competition or social security should be the major aim of the EU			Total
Social security	**Competition**		
Visegrád-4	32.7	67.3	100.0
Baltic	40.9	59.1	100.0
Balkan	63.3	36.7	100.0
West	52.9	47.1	100.0
Mediterranean	67.2	32.8	100.0
Total N = 2025	51.0	49.0	100.0

countries prove as significant as the divergences between Western and Mediterranean countries.

The Visegrád and Baltic elites have adopted the liberal capitalist model more extensively than the elites of the Mediterranean and Balkan states. The divergences between these blocs are statistically far more marked than the differences between individual countries, though some specific cases of countries can also be illuminated here; 70 per cent of the Polish and Slovakian elites profess as the primary goal of the EU the strengthening of competitiveness, as against less than one-third of the Bulgarian elite. The pro-competition segment of the French elite is also underrepresented, but there are even fewer in the Greek elite – 14 per cent – who support competition as the main goal of the EU. The Greek elite also expressed moderate identification with the EU. There is considerable difference between the Spanish and Portuguese elites, the former rejecting and the latter supporting competition to an above-average degree.

Comparing these data with the opinion of the public, it must be realised that the opinion of the Visegrád and Baltic elites on competition differs markedly from the opinion of their respective populations. About a third of the population in general prefer the competition model and two-thirds support the social security model: the ratio is exactly the inverse of that of the elites. By contrast, the opinions of the elites and the public in the Mediterranean and Balkan states are better harmonised. In what appears a special case, the French public appears more competition-minded than the French elite.

As for the strengthening of unification, the differences between both the East and West blocs and among East European countries proved considerable.

Table 5.9:   East European countries and the West ranked by support for 'unification should be strengthened' (per cent)

Unification should be strengthened (0–10)			Total
	Up to 6	**7 and over**	
West (incl. Med)	31.4	68.6	100.0
East	52.5	47.5	100.0
Bulgaria	49.6	50.4	100.0
Czech R	61.5	38.5	100.0
Estonia	80.4	19.6	100.0
Hungary	38.3	61.7	100.0
Lithuania	39.2	60.8	100.0
Poland	44.3	55.7	100.0
Slovakia	56.3	43.7	100.0
Total N = 1968	40.3	59.7	100.0

Three-fifths of the elites strongly support unification, but this derives from the opinions of fewer than half the East European elites and three-quarters of the Mediterranean elites.

Deviations between countries demand attention since in both the Visegrád group and among the Baltic countries there is an elite that is very sceptical about unification: they are the Czech and especially the Estonian elites. (Only the British elite expresses as low support for unification as the Estonians. This suggests that the average opinion of Western elites also conceals a wide scatter.) Let me note that the question may have a semantic aspect: the synonymous use of unification and integration may not be acceptable in some cases and evident in others. It alludes to problems of interpretation in some countries such as Estonia, Hungary and Bulgaria where the 'I don't know' answers had a high rate, sometimes in excess of 10 per cent.

There are significant divergences in judging attitudes to EU redistribution, but the differences between blocs and among East European countries do not deviate considerably from those related to the East-West divide.

The main gap in opinions about EU redistribution is between the East European and Mediterranean elites. The former would like to see redistribution far below the average, the latter far above the average. There was smaller scatter among the East European elites in this respect, while the mean of the

Table 5.10: Out of €100 of tax a citizen pays,
how much should be allocated on the EU level?

	Mean	**Std. Deviation**
West	17,9357	13.71093
Mediterranean	20.1829	11.05602
East	14.6250	8.90577
Bulgaria	14.5175	7.15348
Czech R	14.9749	10.07697
Estonia	12.5714	7.87254
Hungary	16.1102	9.22444
Lithuania	15.2394	11.49935
Poland	13.6870	7.76206
Slovakia	15.2783	8.17414
Total	17.0452	11.34339

Western, at around €18 (close to the all-European average), shows a far greater scatter.

In regard to the single European army, the differences between East European countries are noteworthy. There is below-average sympathy among East European elites and above-average sympathy among West and South European elites for a single army. There are, however, extreme differences among East European elites: just one out of 20 Polish and Estonian elite members supported the single army, while two out of five of Hungarian elite members would opt for this possibility.

The majority of the Estonian and Czech elites supported the maintenance of national armies. Most of the Mediterranean and East European elites would prefer the mixed solution. In addition to the Hungarians, the German, Italian, Spanish and Belgian elites supported the single European army to an above-average degree. The British and Danish elites were similar to the Czech and Estonian elites in supporting the national army alternative. Above-average rates of Polish, Bulgarian and Slovakian, as well as French, Greek and Italian, elites believed in a combined solution. One has to keep in mind that the idea of a single EU army is more popular among the elites than among the general population.

Table 5.11: Single European army and other solutions in blocs and countries (per cent)

	Single European army or keep a national army				Total
	National army	**European army**	**Both national and European**	**Neither/ nor**	
West	27.8	38.1	31.0	3.1	100.0
Med.	15.8	36.5	44.6	3.1	100.0
East	34.1	19.0	44.7	2.2	100.0
Bulgaria	24.1	19.0	56.0	0.9	100.0
Czech R	51.2	15.7	31.4	1.7	100.0
Estonia	51.5	3.9	43.7	1.0	100.0
Hungary	18.5	42.0	36.1	3.4	100.0
Lithuania	41.5	15.3	43.2	0.0	100.0
Poland	38.3	5.8	51.7	4.2	100.0
Slovakia	15.3	29.7	50.8	4.2	100.0
Total N = 1969	27.3	29.8	40.2	2.7	100.0

Conclusion

The tacit presupposition of the above analysis is that the weight of each national elite group's opinion is identical. This presupposition is refuted by everyday experience and it is denied by elites themselves; therefore further efforts are needed in measuring elites' influence. Within these conceptual and methodological constraints the questions addressed in this paper were the following: is there a difference between East and West European elites in identity, vision of goals and the support for integration? How consistent are these attitudes, are there important differences between founding and accessing member states, and are there notable differences among East European elites?

At first sight, the statistics reveal significant differences along the East-West divide in relation to identity, goals and support for integration. The East European elites show less support for supranational identity, support the institutions of integration to a lesser degree and see competition as the main aim of the EU. However, examinations using more elaborate regression models show that the East-West divide only mediates the impact of other explanatory factors. The East-West divide ceased to be influential in the symbolic – theoretical or ideological – aspects in defining identity and goals. Supranational identity is mostly influenced by the elite members' education and social resources. Generally the differences between founding and accessing member countries were less important in explaining the attitudes than was the East-West divide. The only exception was the question of European identity: there was a greater difference in professing supranational identity between the elites of the founding states and those of the accessing member states than between Eastern and Western elites even after checking this effect against cultural and social factors. On the other side, the explanatory effect of the East-West divide retained its explanatory power in the field of pragmatic viewpoints: the East European elites remained moderate supporters of unification and supranational institutions even if this outcome was controlled with cultural, social and other differences.

As for the choice between competition and social security, the main effects were found in the dimension of the economic vs. political elites and the financial standing of the country as contextual variables: the elites of richer countries laid greater stress on better social security, and hence on the model of regulated capitalism. In this respect differences were apparent not only among countries but also among blocs of countries: the Visegrád elites advocated the goal of competitiveness to an above-average degree, while the Mediterranean and Balkan elites supported it to a below-average extent.

To respond to the second question – how consistent these EU-related attitudes are – it can be concluded that views on goals did not correlate with identity or support for integration. Thus, the choice between competitive market economy vs. regulated capitalism ensuring greater social security was not influenced by the views on identity and integration (nor was it influenced by the East-West divide, according to the models). By contrast, most dimensions of identity and the support for integration correlated even under the impact of control variables.

As to the third question – divergences among East European states – marked differences were found between countries in EU attitudes and these proved more important than the East-West divide. Estonian and Czech elites were highly sceptical about EU identity, while the Polish and Hungarian elites appeared most enthusiastic. As for the pragmatic aspects, this picture acquired subtler shades along the individual variables, but it seems that Estonian and Czech elites were still on the sceptical side while the Hungarian elite remained on the supportive side in relation to supranational institutions. However, there were divergences in the Western elite group as well: between the British and French elites, to cite an extreme case.

Notes and References

1. Ronald Inglehart, 'Cognitive Mobilization and European Identity', *Comparative Politics*, 3 (1), 1970, 45–70.
2. Mathew Gabel, 'Public Support for European Integration: An Empirical Test of Five Theories', *Journal of Politics*, 60 (2), 1998, 333–54.
3. Michael Bruter, *Citizens of Europe? The Emergence of a Mass European Identity*, Basingstoke: Palgrave Macmillan, 2005.
4. Liesbet Hooghe and Gary Marks, 'Does Identity or Economic Rationality Drive Public Opinion on European Integration?', PSOnline, July 2004, at: www.apsanet.org

5. György Lengyel and Zsuzsa Blaskó, 'Kik félnek az európai integrációtól?' ['Who is afraid of European integration?'], in *Társadalmi Riport*, TÁRKI; György Lengyel and Borbála Göncz, 'Symbolic and Pragmatic Aspects of European Identity', *Sociologija*, 18 (1), 2006, 1–17.

6. Michael Bruter, 'Civic and Cultural Components of European Identity: A Pilot Model of Measurement of Citizens' Level of European Identity', in Richard K. Hermann, Thomas Risse and Marilyn B. Brewer (eds), *Transnational Identities: Becoming European in the EU*, Oxford: Rowman & Littlefield, 2004, 186–213; Max Haller, 'Economic Elites and Their Role in European Integration and Enlargement', in David Lane, György Lengyel and Jochen Tholen (eds), *Restructuring of the Economic Elites after State Socialism. Recruitment, Institutions and Attitudes*, Stuttgart: ibidem Verlag, 2007, 317–46; Liesbet Hooghe and Gary Marks, *Multi-Level Governance and European Integration*, Lanham: Rowman & Littlefield, 2001.

7. Benedict Anderson, *Imagined Communities: Reflections on the Origin and Spread of Nationalism*, London: Verso, 1991.

8. Hermann, Risse and Brewer, op. cit.

9. Due to lack of space we include only this model in the text. The rest of the models are available from the author on request.

10. Gabriella Ilonszki and Gyorgy Lengyel, 'Democratic Elitism in Hungary. Between Consolidated and Simulated Democracy'; Jacek Wasilewski, 'Democratic Elitism's Troubles in Poland'. Both in J. Higley and H. Best (eds), *Democratic Elitism Reconsidered*, Leiden: Brill, 2008.

6
Divisions in Europe between Elites and Citizens[1]

Max Haller

In the negative outcomes of the 2000 referenda on the European Constitution in France and the Netherlands, a deep split has arisen between elites and citizens about European integration. This fact, recognised by the elites themselves, is highly challenging from the scientific point of view. How can we explain the fact that such a historically unique, seemingly successful process is pursued enthusiastically by the political, economic and bureaucratic elites, and seen as a model for the world among some social analysts,[2] but accompanied by much more sober, sceptical and critical attitudes among the citizens? Is it true that citizens do not recognise the achievements of integration, as the political elites argue? Or is it simply false that integration has brought with it all the blessings that are ascribed to it? This division is highly problematic also from the viewpoint of the legitimacy of the European Union. Even a huge new political community such as the EU is based on feet of clay if it is not supported by a clear majority of citizens. Both its stability and its capacity to act will be seriously undermined if it does not posses an adequate degree of identity, that is, a consensus on its basic characteristics and its ultimate aims.

In this chapter, these questions shall be investigated in three steps: first, the growing division between the elites and citizens is documented; second, the interests of the different elites – political and professional, economic, and bureaucratic – are investigated in order to understand their enthusiasm for integration; third, it will be investigated if 'output legitimacy' can provide a substitute for 'input legitimacy'.

The increasing division between elites and citizens over European integration

Already in the referenda about the Maastricht treaty in the early 1990s, a split had emerged between elites' and citizens' evaluation of the integration process. This treaty was accepted by only small margins of the French and rejected by the Danes. Later on, only small majorities of the Swedes and Finns voted for joining the EU and the Norwegians and Swiss rejected membership altogether, in spite of the fact that their elites had also supported it strongly.

The signing of the Constitution for Europe in October 2004 was rightly seen as a significant step forward in European integration. In France, President Chirac decided that a popular referendum should be held about the Constitution. After this announcement, a very vivid debate unfolded in France. The constitution itself and books about it appeared in millions, and in the printed media and TV a very vivid discussion went on. A very high turnout rate (70 per cent) characterised the referendum itself. The Constitution was rejected by a clear majority of 54.8 per cent of voters – in spite of the fact that all large and governing parties and politicians had supported it. Only three days later, the Dutch people rejected the constitution, with an even larger majority, 61.6 per cent. Also in this country, the ruling economic and political elites had advocated its acceptation unanimously. In two other popular referenda, the Constitution was accepted, however: in Spain with 76.2 per cent and in Luxembourg with 56.5 per cent. However, the latter proportion was surprisingly low, given the wholehearted support for integration in this small country. In both Spain and Luxembourg, subsequent parliamentary votes were held about the Constitution. Results were: 94.2 per cent and 97.4 per cent in Spain (parliament/senate), and 100 per cent in Luxembourg.

In these referenda, three characteristics emerged which are typical of the two dozen popular referenda and the preceding or successive parliamentary votes about important steps in European integration which have been held since the early 1970s.

First, a much higher level of endorsement came out in the parliaments than in the popular referenda. To give just a few examples: in Norway, joining the EU was endorsed in 1992 by the parliament with a 67 per cent vote; in 1994, citizens rejected it again (they had already done so on 1972) with a 52.2 per cent vote; in Switzerland, participation in the European Economic Area was supported by 85 per cent/62 per cent of the parliaments (Council of States/National Council) in 1992, but the citizens rejected it (50.3 per cent); the French Congress accepted the Maastricht Treaty in 1992 with a majority of 89 per cent, citizens did so with only 51.1 per cent. In the new member states in central east Europe, the referenda usually brought out high percentages of 'yes' voters (about 66 per cent in the Baltic states and up to 90 per cent in Slovakia and Slovenia); in the parliaments, the result usually was 100 per cent.

Second, there exists a significant correlation between the level of turnout and the outcome of the referenda: the higher the turnout, the lower the proportion voting 'yes'. High proportions of 'yes'-votes but low levels of turnout were characteristic for the post-communist new member countries, low levels of 'yes'-votes but high levels of turnout for the smaller western and northern European countries (Norway, Sweden, Denmark and Switzerland). Analyses of these referenda have shown, in addition, that particularly in those countries where the decision was highly contested, at the time of the referendum the voters were quite well informed about the issues.

Third, referenda about the integration process were held more frequently in countries with a longer democratic experience and well-established democratic institutions. In all those countries which had experienced fascist periods in the 20th century (Italy, Germany, Greece, Portugal), the citizens never or only recently (Spain) got a possibility to co-decide about this extremely important process which transferred significant competences from the level of nation-states to the EU and thus changed all national constitutions in a significant way. Also in the two post-communist countries with the least democratic experience during the 20th century, Bulgaria and Romania, citizens were not asked about their consent.

Furthermore, several surveys carried out both among political elites and citizens show a deep split in the attitudes to European integration. In the late 1990s, British and German political scientists investigated attitudes toward integration among members of the European Parliament, members of national parliaments and citizens in the 15 EU member states.[3] It turned out that the first two groups, but particularly Members of the European Parliament (MEPs), had much more positive views of integration than citizens. Pride in Europe, for instance, was very high among 75 per cent of the first, 68 per cent of the second, but only 55 per cent of the voters. The authors concluded: 'One might wonder whether the governments and politicians responsible for the Maastricht Treaty were living in the same European world as the people they were supposed to represent.'[4] In 1996, EOS Gallup Europe made a survey on behalf of the EU Commission among 3778 top decision-makers in the 15 member states.[5] The sample included politicians, high civil servants, business leaders, top media persons, and cultural, academic and religious leaders. Some of the questions put to the elites were taken over from the Eurobarometer series; thus, they could be compared directly to citizens' opinions. Also here, there was a deep split between elites and citizens. The statement '(our country's) membership in the EU is a good thing/a bad thing/neither good nor bad' was answered as follows: elites 94 per cent good, 2 per cent bad, 4 per cent neither good nor bad; citizens 48 per cent good, 15 per cent bad, 28 per cent neither-nor.

A deep split between elites and citizens is also evident if we look at the views concerning the political role of the European Union in the world. The Centre for the Study of Political Change (CIRCaP) at the University of Siena (Italy) has carried out a survey[6] among the public in nine member countries of the EU, telephone interviews among MEPs and top officials of the EU Commission in Brussels. Table 6.1 shows that large majorities of MEPs and top EU officials were in favour of an active role of the EU in foreign politics and of the use of military force; the public, however, was much less sympathetic toward such a position and a majority opposed the use of military force altogether.

Table 6.1:   Attitudes toward the role of the EU in world politics among the public and among political and bureaucratic elites of the EU (per cent agree*)

	Public	MEPs	EU officials
The European Union should have its own foreign minister, even if (country) may not always agree with the positions taken	69	79	96
The European Union should strengthen its military power in order to play a larger role in the world	48	71	65
The European Union should concentrate on its economic power and not rely on its military power when dealing with international problems outside Europe	82	66	64

* Rest up to 100%: disagree
Source: CIRCaP, *European Elites Survey 2006*, Siena: Centre for the Study of Political Change, 2006. Available at: http://www.gips.unisi.it/circap/ees_overview; 8 March 2008. Survey method: computer-assisted telephone interviews, May–July 2006; Ns: 205 MEPs, 50 top-level officials of the EU Commission; public: representative population surveys in nine EU member countries.

How did this astonishing split come about? Three theses are proposed in this paper: 1) already the 'founding fathers' of the EEC/EU exhibited an elitist stance which is typical of many European politicians up to the present day; 2) the elites themselves benefit from the integration process in a significant way; and 3) the benefits for the populations at large are much more modest than those claimed by the elites. In the next section, we shall substantiate these theses.

Interests of the elites in the process of European integration

In recent decades, there has been a proliferation of integration theories. Functional and neo-functional theories hold that integration between hitherto separate units emerges because this leads to gains in economic productivity and welfare. Once integration has been initiated in one sector, it spills over to others, and from the economic to the social and political sphere. Thus, integration processes acquire a logic of their own and reinforce themselves with increasing exchange and division of labour between the members of the Union. The final stage will be a highly integrated economic and political community.[7] Intergovernmental theories see integration as a strategy pursued by national governments in order to gain security in a changed international situation, and to enable them to come to grips with the forces of globalisation. Integration strengthens the position of national governments both within their own state and at the international level.[8] However, both these theories contain serious flaws.

First, the distinction between the normative and the empirical-analytical perspective is blurred. Functionalist theory, which holds that integration begins in the economic sector and then spills over to other sectors, 'was imbued from the outset with pro-integration assumptions'.[9] This is also true for intergovernmentalism and in particular federalism, where integration is seen as the outcome of deliberate actions of governments, and which expects that its final state will be the United States of Europe.[10] Second, citizens do not play a significant role in both theories. They focus on general, abstract 'laws' of integration, but neglect the specific social interests and forces that lie behind them. Third, social and political values, ideas and visions connected with integration are neglected.

Both postulate more or less homogeneous 'national interests' which in reality do not exist. Interests often diverge considerably between different groups within a nation-state, and also between elites and citizens. As a consequence, they cannot explain the increasing split between elites and citizens over European integration.

Democratic elite theory – a sociological approach to European integration

The basis of the following analysis is democratic elite theory.[11] Within this theory, two perspectives can be distinguished. The empirical-analytical perspective tries to explain the actions of the elites and their consequences. From this point of view, elites are seen as those relatively small groups in any society which dispose of disproportionate power; this power originates from the fact that they occupy specific power-conferring positions or dispose of particularly useful resources.[12] It is not assumed here – as in early elite theory (Pareto, Mosca, Michels) – that elites are per se power-driven, egoistic, ruthless or even corrupt. However, elites are not inherently efficient and do not work in the common interest as much as they themselves would have it.

The basic assumption of normative democratic theory is that the power, the aims and the actions of elites must be monitored and controlled continuously. These include the values and goals of the elites (which often are not declared openly), the functional differentiation and the network structures between the elites, the patterns of elite recruitment, and the forms of their recognition and remuneration.

The role of the different elites in the successive stages of European integration

The first thesis proposed in this paper relates to the role of different elites in the process of integration. European integration as a whole is a discontinuous process in which moments of dynamic integration are followed by periods of stagnation and crisis. The political elites are the force of acceleration, but also of slowdown of the integration process; the economic elites and the new European bureaucratic and professional elites are the forces continually furthering integration. As a consequence of the interaction of these different forces, the speed and direction of integration is often quite erratic, contradictory and produces problematic results. However, it is also going on continuously, even in periods of political stagnation and 'eurosclersosis'. In such periods, the integration process is furthered particularly by the Eurocracy and the professional-juridical elites in the European Court of Justice (ECJ). By and large, we can say that in the first phase of European integration, from the early 1950s up to the mid-1960s, the political elites were the driving force. Between the end of the 1960s and of the 1980s, the economic and the new European bureaucratic-professional elites (the members of the EU Commission and of the ECJ) took matters into their own hands. During and after the period of the breakdown of the state-socialist systems in Eastern Europe, however, the political elites again became proactive. Let us look here shortly at the decisive postwar period when the process of European integration was initiated. Three facts must be considered in order to understand the successful takeoff of the process of integration after the Second World War, and the form which it adopted later.

The new international situation is the first crucial factor. Federations between nation-states, from ancient Greece up to postwar Europe, have been initiated in situations of foreign threat; the aim was to gain security by uniting against a strong external, often despotic, power.[13] Such a situation existed also in postwar Europe. The United States and the Soviet Union emerged as new world powers from the Second World War, and all former large European states were relegated to second-order political and military powers on the world scene.[14]

Second, France and Germany, the two main proponents of integration, found themselves in a situation of profound internal weakness. Germany was devastated economically, divided into two parts, and morally compromised due to its connection with national socialism and the Holocaust, and its responsibility for the Second World War. Participating actively in European integration was seen – and is still seen today – as an undisputed strategy of its political elites to regain political autonomy and international respect. However, France also found itself in a weak situation; it was a defeated nation, with a poor economy and a damaged moral reputation due to the collaboration of many of its leaders with the Vichy regime.[15]

Third, the values, strategies and actions of the decisive political actors who initiated integration in the postwar period made a crucial and long-lasting imprint on this process. These were the French Foreign Minister Robert Schuman, the German Chancellor Konrad Adenauer and the Italian Prime Minister Alcide De Gasperi. They shared four characteristics. First, they all had been born in the 1880s, and thus were of prime adult age when fascism came to power in Italy and Germany. Their resistance to fascism awarded them a high personal charisma after the Second World War. The lack of such charisma is one among the characteristics of political personalities at the end of the 20th century, which has contributed to the decreasing trust in politics in general and the European Union in particular. Second, they all were devout Roman Catholics. Catholicism was important for European integration for two reasons. Due to its universalistic orientation, it was sympathetic to European integration. But Catholicism is also characterised by a focus on tradition and dogma, hierarchy and authority.[16] A third common characteristic of Adenauer and De Gasperi was their elitist and autocratic attitude and behaviour. Adenauer was frequently criticised because of his autocratic style of governing.[17] Both Adenauer and De Gasperi shared a related, fourth characteristic, a fervent anti-communism. Adenauer continued the traditional German anti-communism, and saw to it that the Communist Party of Germany (KPD), re-established in the four occupied zones, was forbidden by the German constitutional court in 1956. De Gasperi was able to achieve a large share of the votes in the 1948 national elections not least because of a rather aggressive and spiteful election campaign in which the Italian Communist Party (PCI) was slandered as paving the way for a Soviet-style communist regime.[18] Thereby, the foundation was laid for the political dominance of the Democrazia Cristiana (DC) for decades, a reign that ended abruptly in 1992 when its deep involvement in clientelism and corruption was uncovered.

This elitist stance was also a very decisive characteristic of the most important 'spin doctor' of European integration, Jean Monnet (1888–1979). His political thinking and behaviour exhibited several characteristics which are typical of the European Union even today: the realisation of new ideas and plans 'from above' with no involvement of citizens and parliaments; the use of the strategy of persuasion, that is, the continuous replication and propagation of a few simple and seemingly true ideas to the public; a high degree of flexibility and inventiveness in developing new plans for cooperation and integration; and a focus on the restricted and seemingly politically 'neutral' area of economic integration.[19]

Let us now look at the specific interests of the different groups of elites in the process of European integration.

The political elites

At first sight, it seems difficult to comprehend why the governing political elites in Western Europe were and still are ready to give up a considerable part of their autonomy and power to the new EU institutions. Established theories of integration assume that integration was and is in the interest of the member states.[20] Membership of the EU also provides the possibility of pursuing national political goals at the world level whose implementation would be difficult even for the very largest member states alone. In addition, membership of the EU provides the possibility of accomplishing political goals that national politicians would have been unable or unwilling to pursue in their home countries, using decisions of the EU (in which they have participated) as a pretense.

However, political elites are all the time also pursuing their own individual interests, as the economic theory of democracy has argued convincingly.[21] The first interest that politicians have – as with any other professional group – is to improve their job and income opportunities. European integration supports this interest strongly.[22] First, the EU has created myriad new political jobs and careers in the institutions of the European Parliament (EP), the European Commission and the European Court of Justice (ECJ), to mention only the most important. These are quite large numbers. MEPs get significantly higher salaries than members of national parliaments,[23] as well as generous allowances for personal expenses and a considerable sum (up to €15.000 monthly) for a secretariat and assistants. In addition to the MEPs, about 4000 persons are employed by the European Parliament, among them 1400 accredited personal assistants to the MEPs.[24] Another new career avenue is the European Commission where every member state has its political representative; this is particularly attractive for national politicians who have held top positions in their home country. All these new political jobs open up the possibility for national politicians to prolong their political careers after having been relegated from their political offices at home or after having been defeated in national elections. In this way, their chances of getting generous pensions later on are also increased significantly.

A second area where European integration has created individual gains for national politicians is the possibility it provides to participate in collective decisions at the level of the EU. This provides all heads and members of national governments with an additional source of prestige. The taking over of high offices (such as president of the European Council), the carrying through of the related manifold organisational activities on behalf of the EU, and the participation in the many festive summits and other public rituals provide immediate gratification, publicity and prestige.[25] This is particularly the case if a proposal of the presiding country is accepted by all other members. This is also one of the mechanisms which keep the process of integration running; every country and government that takes over the half-year presidency of the Council is eager to develop an ambitious programme of further integration.

The economic elites

The economy was a central element of European integration from the beginning. Integration started as a coordinated administration of a few basic industries, extended into a free-trade area, and still today – even if called a 'Union' – it is characterised in the first instance as a huge common market. This market is dominated increasingly by large, multinational 'European corporations'. About 40 per cent of the 100 largest corporations in the world belong to the EU.[26] But other economic interests, such as those of agriculture, have also played an important role in the process of integration. The economic elites have played highly significant roles in all stages of the European integration process. The exertion of this influence mostly occurred unrecognised in public and by scientific observers but has led to a rising public scepticism and distrust of large corporations and of the economic-political system of the EU among the general public.

Economic elites have several interests. Besides that of attaining an adequate income and profit, they also strive for security, power and prestige. In this regard, the interests of large European enterprises coincide with those of large member states. A widely established thesis holds that neo-liberalistic economic theories were dominant in the process of integration. The thesis proposed here is, however, that the dominant integration ideology has never been that of unconditional (neo-)liberalism. Rather, from the beginning both the leaders of the industrial corporations and the political elites were aiming toward establishing the EU and its large enterprises as 'big players' on the world scene. This motive was present already in the foundation of the European Coal and Steel Community in 1952. However, this 'Monnet-myth' does not withstand closer examination. The formal cooperation between the French and German steel and coal industry initiated by the ECSC was consistent with postwar efforts of many other French politicians of the time. The Nazi period and the Second World War had not destroyed earlier, close cooperation. Throughout this period, the big German coal and steel producers preserved the close and friendly relationship with the French, Belgian and other enterprises that they had been close to previously; in this way, the German type of 'organised capitalism' had been expanded to the occupied territories. Postwar, the French politicians' intent was to reintegrate Germany into Europe under similarly 'organised', but French, conditions and to subject Ruhr industry to 'organic control'.[27]

Business interests were also highly influential in later stages of the integration process. The postwar boom in Western Europe was associated with a strong process of industrial concentration. With the expansion of financial markets, a separation of ownership and management took place; ownership itself was transposed into a commodity. The process of European integration has contributed significantly to the emergence of this shareholder capitalism in Europe.[28] The basics for this process were laid by the internal market programme, activated to a large degree by the European Round Table of Industrialists (ERT) in the 1980s.[29] In this process, leading industrialists, such as the Swede Pehr Gyllenhammar and the Dutchman Wisse Dekker, played a significant role. They were able to establish the ERT as an informal, yet well organised and highly influential group of leading European businessmen. From 1983 to 1985, this group developed a comprehensive plan ('Europe 1990') whose aim was to create the fully integrated market and to concentrate efforts to strengthen strategic sectors of industry and research in Europe. Their ideas were taken over by Jacques Delors and formally established in the Single European Act and the Maastricht Treaty. This aim led to a 'strategic industry and trade policy' which is used by the EU to support 'European champions', even if this runs counter to the preservation of competition.[30]

In the second half of the 1990s, this project was furthered by initiatives to create a single financial market, for instance, through the Financial Services Action Plan. The 2003 action plan for 'Modernising Company Law and Enhancing Corporate Governance' further extends this policy. A milestone was the earlier establishment of the European Monetary Union (EMU) and the euro. Since then, the EU Commission has attributed great importance to cross-border mergers. In spite of its official policy of a strict control of such mergers, there was only a very low number of cases in which the Commission was involved. In the period 1991–2004 about 152,000 mergers occurred in the EU, but only 1.7 per cent were notified to the Commission; of these, only about 5 per cent raised serious competition issues that could not be resolved in the first phase of the procedure. This means that, all in all, only the tiniest proportion of all M&A activities were seen as problematic by the Commission.[31] An important issue in this regard concerns the relation between business interest groups and the political and bureaucratic elites. Brussels has attracted thousands of lobby and interest groups who are in continuous close contact with the EU offices and representatives responsible for the enactment of new laws and regulations. These lobbies and their activities are considered as quite positive not only by the representatives of business but also by EU officials. Quite different are the perceptions of the public throughout Europe: they consider these activities with a high degree of suspicion and believe that large enterprises, farmers and the like have much more influence than workers, employees and 'normal' citizens.[32]

Agriculture is another area where business interests played a central role. The Common Agricultural Policy (CAP), one of the basic pillars of European integration, is also an area where the preponderance of sectional interests, the collusion between the interests of economic, political and bureaucratic elites at the expense of those of citizens, but also the ideological appeal to certain ideals and values, masking particular interests, can be demonstrated very clearly. The majority of experts consider this policy, in spite of partial successes, as an overall failure.[33] In spite of its self-proclaimed aim: 'Investment in growth and better jobs ... building a foundation for the future', the bulk (54.8 per cent) of the EU budget of €121 billion still goes to the agricultural sector (2006). At the same time, the importance of this sector for employment has declined to less than 5 per cent in most member states, and it contributes only about 1 to 3 per cent to the gross national product. The agricultural policy has been extended into a highly refined system of import and export regulations and tariffs, and domestic market regimes; a staff of 5000 Eurocrats in Brussels administrates the highly complex procedures.

A third period and process where economic interests played a central role in integration was the transition of the former state-socialist countries to market economies and their access to the EU. Following neo-liberal American economists, in many post-communist East European countries (most notably in Poland) a vigorous privatisation programme was carried out, the state sector was constricted in its activities, the unions were disempowered, and a restrictive monetary policy was established. The consequence was hyper-inflation, an expropriation of savers, a drastic reduction in industrial output, an explosion in unemployment, massive losses in real income of workers and employees, and a deterioration of the living standards of the entire population, expressed in a strong reduction of life expectancy and general decline in quality of life. Today, even leading Western economists (such as Joseph Stiglitz) admit that this form of transition, a kind of 'peaceful annexation'[34] was a failure.[35] One further consequence of this enforced process of transition was a political destabilisation of post-communist Eastern Europe.[36] The EU supported the accession of these countries by specific financial programmes, and even by public relations campaigns, before referenda about accession were carried out. Western capital, however, was extremely interested in the possibilities of investment in this region. Already since the early 1990s, a real 'buyout fight' for enterprises was setting in. The expected (and later on realised) high profitability of investments in these countries was enhanced by the fact that these countries provided formidable tax oases for Western capital. Today a considerable share (up to one third) of the large private enterprises in Eastern Europe is owned by Western capital, especially in the strategic banking sector; the income from these investments is significantly higher than from comparable investments in Western Europe.

The new Eurocratic elites

There is a third group of elites that is one of the most important driving motors of integration, whose personal interests, strategies and actions, however, are much less visible and publically discussed than those of the political and economic elites. This is the new EU bureaucracy in Brussels and in the member states.

At first sight, it may seem surprising to consider the EU administration in Brussels as representative of a new and powerful bureaucracy. Two arguments are frequently brought forward in this regard: first, size; with about 40,000 employees it is rather small, compared with those of the member states. Second, it seems it works in a much less 'bureaucratic' and more efficient way than national bureaucracies. It portrays itself and is seen by many analysts as being less hierarchically structured, less bent on documenting every decision on paper, and more flexible and cosmopolitan-oriented, not least because of its multinational and multicultural composition.[37] However, all of these assertions are highly questionable.[38] Four arguments and facts are relevant in this regard.

First, as in any bureaucracy,[39] the EU Commission and its bureaucratic apparatus are instruments of power and domination. This is true even more strongly than for national bureaucracies. The EU Commission has a right that no national bureaucracy possesses, namely, to initiate legislation. The use of this extraordinary right is supported by the fact that the EU Commission in Brussels is remote from national capitals and, thereby, much less under the scrutiny of a critical public than are national bureaucracies. The effectiveness of the law-producing capacity of the Commission is enhanced by its impersonal and collective nature: the members of the Commission are appointed, not elected, to their offices; and the Commission is responsible only as a whole for its decisions. Even if a Commission contains many mediocre personalities, there are always some energetic members who continually propose far-reaching steps of integration which usually are accepted by the Commission as a whole and transformed into proposals for new regulations. Also, the top EU bureaucrats, the Directors General, are very powerful.[40] Benefiting from lifetime appointments, they are highly educated and often experienced politically. Their roles include developing a global mission and strategy for their Directorate, organising the work of their staff and establishing relations with the outside world. They have been compared to 'medieval barons'.[41]

The European Commission is no less bureaucraticised than national bureaucracies. Its formal structure is articulated closely along the hierarchy of educational degrees; Eurocrats enjoy a high level of job security (lifetime tenure). The Eurocracy continuously enacts new laws and regulations. In the decade 1970–80, the EU enacted about 9000 legislative and regulative acts, in 1991–2000 nearly 24,000.[42] These activities are seen more and more as being detrimental to entrepreneurial activity and economic growth in Europe, even by high-level EU representatives (see, for example, the former Commissioner Günter Verheugen) and by national political leaders (such as the German chancellors Helmut Kohl and Angela Merkel).

Finally, the thesis that the new Eurocracy is a comparatively slim apparatus is highly misleading in three regards. First, it overlooks the fact that this bureaucracy is mainly concerned with the enactment of laws and regulations; this corresponds to the fact that the majority of EU officials are highly educated (about half of them are academics), polyglot and efficient. Second, the EU is a young institution, and so is its bureaucracy, compared with the bureaucracies of established nation-states in Western Europe. If one looks at the dynamics of development of this bureaucracy, a wholly different picture emerges (see Figure 6.1): Since 1968, the number of EU employees has grown

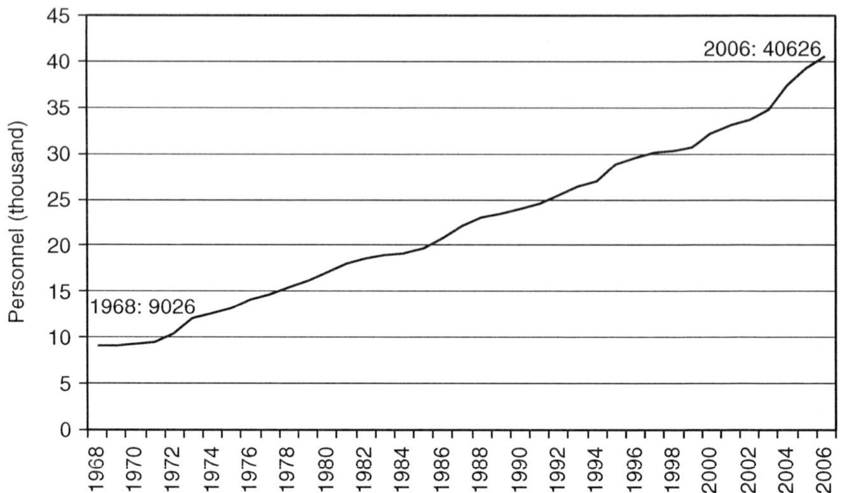

Figure 6.1:   The development of EC/EU employees*, 1968–2006 (absolute numbers)
*In all institutions, including decentralised units and officials with fixed-term contracts
Source: Data from Eurostat/European Statistical Data Support (ESDS).

in a continuous manner; in 2006, their number was four times that of 1968. No deceleration of this trend is in sight.

A third fact is significant in this regard: since the EU is mainly a legislative body, in each member state an 'EU substitute bureaucracy' exists, which is concerned with the enactment of EU regulations, the administration of subsidies and so forth. An extrapolation of the size of this EU substitute bureaucracy from pilot studies in four member states resulted in a figure which is comparable to the number of employed officials in Brussels.[43]

The power of the Eurocracy is also confirmed by the fact that its members are highly privileged in terms of security of employment, income levels and fringe benefits: 'EU officials are reputedly among the most privileged public officials in the world'[44], and a position in the EU civil service has been called 'a bureaucrat's paradise'.[45]

Achievements of European integration and their perception by citizens

The foregoing section has shown that the political, economic and new European bureaucratic elites have massive interests in furthering integration. Their enthusiasm for the process of integration is hardly surprising from this point of view. This fact per se, however, is no argument against integration. If this process works in the interests of the citizens and peoples involved, a generous remuneration of the elites that have initiated and furthered this process may well be accepted.[46] We must also investigate objectively, therefore, what the achievements of European integration have been and how they have been and are perceived by citizens.

How did the member states of the EU perform economically in the past decades? Is it true that European integration has been so successful? How do citizens throughout Europe perceive the achievements of the EU? It is well known that many citizens are quite critical in this regard. Political elites and some social scientists[47] argue that the population does not recognise the true achievements of integration. In order to get a comprehensive view of this situation, we have to look both at objective developments and their subjective perception by the populations.

Looking at objective developments in some important socio-economic indicators in the decade 1994–2005 and comparing the EU15 as a whole with its three main 'rivals', the USA and Japan, the following situation emerges: in terms of economic growth, the EU and Japan were far behind the USA; in terms of unemployment, development in the EU was a failure, with the worst figures in all of the ten years; only in terms of inflation did the EU perform quite well, but not as well as Japan. Within the EU, the countries of Euroland performed significantly worse than those outside of it (Denmark, Sweden, UK). However, the younger southern European members and Ireland were more successful. In these countries, EU membership may have contributed to economic growth, although in a moderate way.[48]

Let us now look at the perception and evaluation of these trends among the citizens. Asked about the role and success of the EU in several areas of politics, it turns out the negative evaluations overbalance the positive ones in five important indicators: 43 per cent said that 'the EU plays a negative role' in the area of unemployment (24 per cent see a positive role), 51 per cent in inflation (23 per cent a positive), and 29 per cent in social standards (22 per cent a positive).[49] Only in two areas (economic growth and the fight against crime) were positive evaluations somewhat more frequent than the negative ones. People in countries with objective positive developments saw things more positively, while those in countries with negative developments were more critical and negative.

Thus, in the perceptions of citizens the achievements of the EU were not very noteworthy. In addition, quite high proportions – between 40 and 80 per cent – had concrete 'fears about the building of Europe' (see Table 6.2). Among the six achievements mentioned, the majority saw a positive effect in only one area, namely the perceived influence of one's own country in the EU. In two regards, the negative evaluations far outweighed the positive ones. One was the over-proportional influence of the big member states, the other was personal influence in the EU; 76 per cent of the respondents in the 15 EU member states felt that 'the biggest countries have the most power in the EU'; but only 32 per cent felt that 'my own voice counts in the European

Table 6.2:   Perceived achievements of the EU and fears about the building of Europe, 2004

Perceived achievements		Tend to agree	Tend to disagree*
I feel I am safer because (our country) is a member of the European Union	%	43.0	46.6
I feel we are more stable economically	%	43.7	45.7
I feel we are more stable politically	%	40.0	47.7
My voice counts in the EU	%	31.8	55.0
(Our country's) voice counts in the EU	%	62.8	26.9
The biggest countries have the most power in the EU	%	76.0	14.3
Fears about integration			
A loss of power for smaller member states	%	49.4	42.0
An increase in drug trafficking and international organised crime	%	68.2	27.2
Our language being used less and less	%	39.7	55.7
Our country paying more and more to the EU	%	64.4	26.5
The loss of social benefits	%	53.6	38.5
The loss of national identity and culture	%	42.2	52.3
An economic crisis	%	47.7	42.5
The transfer of jobs to other member countries which have lower production costs	%	74.1	19.9
More difficulties for (nationality) farmers	%	62.2	26.2

* Percentages missing up to 100% are 'don't know'
Source: Eurobarometer 61 (Spring 2004). Questions 12 and 15; N = 16216.

Union'. An even more negative picture comes out if we look at the fears that the respondents associated with the EU. In four dimensions – job transfer to other member countries, drug trafficking, national payments to the EU, and difficulties for farmers – large majorities (between 62 and 74 per cent) had fears in connection with European integration.

Conclusion

Since the adoption of the treaty about the European Union in Maastricht in 1991, an increasing division is emerging between elites and citizens over European integration. While the political, economic and new European bureaucratic elites are zealous about this process and use all means to further it, citizens throughout Europe are accepting it just as a matter of fact, and large groups in many countries are critical about it. In this paper, it has been shown that elites hold clear interests in integration that may well explain their enthusiasm. However, there are also structural reasons for the increasing split between elites and citizens. On the one side, citizens throughout

Europe are becoming more educated and critical; on the other side, the EU has taken over more and more competencies from the nation-states. The latter trend clashes sharply with the fact that the European Union exhibits a serious democratic deficit.[50] Citizens can only very indirectly co-determine politics at the level of the EU; the directly elected European Parliament still does not have the crucial competences of a democratic parliament, that is, the autonomous proposal of laws and the election and de-selection of a government. This situation is all the more problematic because the thesis that the EU can refer to a high level of output legitimacy did not come true. Contrary to the assertions of politicians and some social scientists, the record of the EU in central matters of socio-economic policy – economic growth, employment, inflation, internal security – is rather modest compared to other large and advanced nation-states such as the USA and Japan. Citizens are well aware of these deficits.

The Lisbon Treaty, which takes over 95 per cent of the Constitution for Europe, improves the democratic accountability and effectiveness of EU institutions. The measures proposed (for instance, the strengthening the role of the European and the national parliaments, and the introduction of the right of initiative by EU citizens), however, are far from resolving the problem of democratic deficit. Three issues stand out as most pressing at present, and they offer a challenge to critical social science and politics alike:

1. The discussion and definition of the fundamental values, goals and visions of the Union;
2. The (re-)definition of the competencies of the Union, *vis-à-vis* the nation states; a clarification of this task would also be the first step toward a solution of the democratic deficit; and
3. The solution of the dilemma between market liberalisation and the preservation of the positive elements of the European welfare states.

Notes and References

1. An extended exposition of the main arguments of this paper can be found in my book, *European Integration as an Elite Process. The Failure of a Dream?*, New York and London: Routledge, 2008; German version: *Europäische Integration als Elitenprozess. Das Ende eines Traums?*, Wiesbaden: VS Verlag für Sozialwissenschaften.
2. Ulrich Beck and Edgar Grande, *Das kosmopolitische Europa. Gesellschaft und Politik in der zweiten Moderne*, Frankfurt/Main: Suhrkamp, 2004; Jeremy Rifkin, *The European Dream*, New York: Jeremy P. Tarcher/Penguin, 2004.
3. Hermann Schmitt and Jacques Thomassen (eds), *Political Representation and Legitimacy in the European Union*, Oxford: Oxford University Press, 1999.
4. Ibid., 4.
5. *The European Union. A View from the Top.* Report prepared by Jacqueline Spence, conducted by EOS Gallup Europe, Wavre (Belgium). The report is also available online at: http://ec.europa.eu/public_opinion/archives/top/top.pdf

6. CIRCaP *European Elites Survey 2006*, Siena: Centre for the Study of Political Change, 2006. Available at: www.gips.unisi.it/circap/ees_overview; accessed 8 March 2008.

7. Ernst B. Haas, *The Uniting of Europe. Political, Social, and Economic Forces, 1950–1957*, Stanford: Stanford University Press, 1958; Philippe C. Schmitter, 'Neo-Neofunctionalism', in Antje Wiener and Thomas Diez (eds), *European Integration Theory*, Oxford: Oxford University Press, 2004, 45–74.

8. Alan Milward, *The European Rescue of the Nation State*, London: Routledge, 1992; Andrew Moravcsik, *The Choice for Europe. Social Purpose and State Power from Messina to Maastricht*, London: UCL Press, 1998; for reviews see Michael Burgess, 'Federalism and Federation', in Michelle Cini (ed.), *European Union Politics*, Oxford and New York: Oxford University Press, 2003, 65–79; Anne Faber, *Europäische Integration und politikwissenschaftliche Forschung. Neofunktionalismus und Intergouvermentalismus in der Analyse*, Wiesbaden: VS Verlag für Sozialwissenschaften, 2005, 86ff.

9. Carsten Stroby Jensen, 'Neo-functionalism', in Cini, op. cit., 80–92; see also Cini, op. cit., 6.

10. For critical reviews see Burgess, op. cit., 6; Mario Dehove (ed.), *Le nouvel état de l'Europe. Les idées-forces pour comprendre les nouveaux enjeux de l'Union*, Paris: La Découverte, 2004.

11. Eva Etzioni-Halévy, *The Elite Connection. Problems and Potentials of Western Democracy*, Cambridge: Polity Press, 1993.

12. See also Jacques Coenen-Huther, *Sociologie des élites*, Paris: Armand Colin, 2004; Michael Hartmann, *Elitesoziologie*, Frankfurt and New York: Campus, 2004.

13. Elisabeth Fix, 'Integration als "Vernunftehe" im Spannungsfeld zwischen, loyalty, "voice" und "exit" – Zu den Rahmenbedingungen der Genese und des Fortbestandes von Föderationen', in *Jahrbuch zur Staats- und Verwaltungswissenschaft*, vol. 6, Baden-Baden: Nomos, 1992–3, 113–161.

14. Karl W. Deutsch et al., *Political Community and the North Atlantic Area: International Organisation in the Light of Historical Experience*, Princeton: Princeton University Press, 1957; Wilfried Loth, *Der Weg nach Europa. Geschichte der europäischen Integration 1939–1957*, Göttingen: Vandenhoeck & Ruprecht, 1996.

15. Thierry Wolton, *Brève Psychoanalyse de France*, Paris: Plon, 2004.

16. Hans Maier, *Katholizismus und Demok*ratie, Freiburg/Basel/Vienna: Herder, 1983.

17. Karl Jaspers, *Wohin treibt die Bundesrepublik? Tatsachen, Gefahren, Chancen*, Munich: R. Piper, 1966.

18. Giuliano Procacci, *Geschichte Italiens und der Italiener*, Munich: C. H. Beck, 1983, 386ff.

19. See Jean Monnet, *Memoirs*, Garden City: Doubleday, 1978.

20. Milward, op. cit., 6.

21. Joseph A Schumpeter, *Capitalism, Socialism, and Democracy*, New York: Harper, 1962 [1950]; Anthony Downs, *Inside Bureaucracy*, Boston: Little, Brown, 1967.

22. Roland Vaubel, *The Centralisation of Western Europe. The Common Market, Political Integration and Democracy*, London: Institute of Economic Affairs (IEA), 1995, 16.

23. Hans Herbert von Arnim, *Das Europa-Komplott. Wie EU-Funktionäre unsere Demokratie verscherbeln*, Munich/Vienna: Carl Hanser, 2006.

24. See www.europarl.europa.eu/news/public/focus_page/008-2987-050-02-08-901-20070209FCS02971-19-02-2007-2007/default_de.htm

25. Randall Collins, *Interaction Ritual Chains*, Princeton: Princeton University Press, 2005.

26. See Forbes, *World's Business Leaders 2000*; www.forbes.com

27. John Gillingham, *Coal, Steel, and the Rebirth of Europe, 1945–1955: The Germans and French from Ruhr Conflict to Economic Community*, Cambridge and New York: Cambridge University Press, 2004.

28. Bastian van Apeldoorn, *Transnational European Capitalism and the Struggle over European Integration*, London and New York: Routledge, 2002; David Coen, 'The Evolution of the Large Firm as a Political Actor in the European Union', *Journal of European Public Policy*, 4, 1997, 91–108.

29. Volker Bornschier, *State-building in Europe. The Revitalization of Western European Integration*, Cambridge: Cambridge University Press, 2000.

30. Norbert Berthold and Jörg Hilpert, 'Wettbewerbspolitik, Industriepolitik und Handelspolitik in der EU', in R. Ohr (ed.), *Europäische Integration*, Stuttgart: Kohlhammer, 1996, 77–109.

31. Fabienne Ilzkovitz and Roderick Meiklejohn (eds), *European Merger Control. Do We Need an Efficiency Defence?*, Cheltenham and Northampton MA: Edward Elgar, 2006, 22ff.

32. Max Haller and Regina Ressler, *Wir da unten – die da oben. Die Europäische Union aus der Sicht von BürgerInnen und von Eliten*, Graz: Institut für Soziologie, Universität Graz, 2006.

33. Ali M. El Agraa (ed.), *The European Union. Economics and Policies*, Harlow: Pearson Education/Prentice Hall, 2004, 371ff.; Eve Fouilleux, 'The Common Agricultural Policy', in Cini, op. cit., 246–63.

34. Jörg Roesler, *Der Anschluss von Staaten in der modernen Geschichte. Eine Untersuchung aus aktuellem Anlass*, Frankfurt am Main: Peter Lang, 1999.

35. Barbara Ingham, *International Economics. A European Focus*, Harlow: Prentice Hall, 2004, 243.

36. Hannes Hofbauer, *Osterweiterung. Vom Drang nach Osten zur peripheren EU*, Vienna: Promedia, 2003.

37. Maurizio Bach, *Die Bürokratisierung Europas. Verwaltungseliten, Experten und politische Legitimation in Europa*, Frankfurt and New York: Campus, 1999.

38. Cris Shore, *Building Europe. The Cultural Politics of European Integration*, London and New York: Routledge, 2000.

39. Max Weber, *Economy and Society. An Outline of Interpretative Sociology*, ed. by G. Roth and C. Wittich, 2 vols, Berkeley, Los Angeles and London: University of California Press, 1978[1922]; Schumpeter (1962[1950]) op. cit., 10; Downs (1967) op. cit., 10; B. Guy Peters, *The Politics of Bureaucracy*, White Plains: Longman, 1995.

40. Keith Middlemas, *Orchestrating Europe. The Informal Politics of the European Union 1973–95*, London: Fontana Press, 1995, 242ff.; Morten Egeberg, 'The European Commission', in Cini, op. cit., 131–47.

41. A very informative survey of 33 Directors General has been carried out by the German Identity Foundation; available at: www.euro.de/europa/studie_eur_kommission/studie.htm.

42. Alberto Alesina, Ignazio Angeloni and Ludger Schuknecht, *What Does the European Union Do?*, NBER Working Paper 8647, Cambridge MA: National Bureau for Economic Research, 2001.

43. Max Haller, *European Integration as an Elite Process. The Failure of a Dream?*, New York and London: Routledge, 2008, 152ff.

44. Shore, op. cit., 15.

45. Edward C. Page and Linda Wouters, 'The Europeanization of the National Bureaucracies?', in Jon Pierre (ed.), *Bureaucracy in the Modern State*, Aldershot, Edward Elgar, 1995, 185–204; see also Desmond Dinan (1999), *Ever Closer Union. An*

Introduction to European Integration, 2nd ed., Basingstoke: Palgrave, 1999, 221; Vaubel, op. cit., 37.

46. Fritz Scharpf, *Governing in Europe: Effective and Democratic?*, Oxford: Oxford University Press, 1999.

47. Nicholas Moussis, *Access to the European Union. Law, Economics, Politics*, Rixensart: European Studies Service, 2006, 189f.

48. Volker Bornschier, Mark Herkenrath and Patrick Ziltener, 'Political and Economic Logic of Western European Integration. A Study of Convergence Comparing Member and Non-member States, 1980–98', *European Societies*, 6, 2004, 71–96.

49. Results from *Eurobarometer* 61.0, Spring 2004; N about 16.000.

50. Larry Siedentop, *Democracy in Europe*, New York: Columbia University Press, 2001.

7
European Elites and the Middle East

Rosemary Hollis

The intention here is to examine what contemporary European policies and engagements in the Middle East reveal about European elite assumptions, interests and intentions. Four facets or 'policy areas' of contemporary European relations with the Middle East are examined: two initiatives for the Mediterranean; the Iraq invasion crisis and the Middle East Peace Process. To varying degrees the policies adopted were intended to effect change in Europe's neighbourhood. All had to do with regional and Western security cooperation. Together they reveal a dichotomy between the advocacy and projection of assumed European values on the one hand and the dictates of European security interests and safeguarding of those values on the other.

Before proceeding to these case studies, however, it is necessary not only to define the elites of Europe, for the purposes of this discussion, but also to say something about the broader context of European relations with the Middle East in terms of geography, culture, history, economic interdependence and identity.

Examination of this context reveals that contemporary relations between Europe and the Middle East are but the latest phase in a saga dating back many centuries and that the emergence of a European identity in recent times cannot be understood in isolation from European interactions with neighbours in North Africa and the Middle East.

European elites

The definition of European elites adopted here mirrors that chosen and discussed by Max Haller in Chapter 5 of this book, with some additions. Included in the definition are both national or member-state elites and the relatively small number but nonetheless powerful elites operating at the collective EU level. The political elites are thus taken to mean national politicians, MEPs, EU commissioners and EC bureaucrats. Business elites are broadly defined to include those in the energy, finance and manufacturing sectors.

Of less significance for present purposes, but not to be forgotten, are also the senior echelons of the armed forces of member states. Also significant in policy formulation and presentation are the European media elites and interest groups, including NGOs and intellectuals in think tanks and academia. Religious leaders and spokesmen (or women) for ethnic minorities are not singled out specifically here, though the more religion and race feature in debates about European identity, migration and policies to combat terrorism they do deserve mention.

Clearly the interests and preoccupations of these different sector elites vary somewhat, both within member states and at the EU level. Yet, as documented in the other chapters, the most noteworthy distinctions are between elites at the national and EU levels and above all between the political and business elites on the one hand and the general public or national populations on the other.

For present purposes the focus will be on the intentions, assumptions and efficacy of the political and bureaucratic elites of Europe, both collective and national, as revealed in the case studies discussed below. They are assumed to be the main architects of European policies and interventions in the Middle East, informed by their interpretations of what public opinion and in particular the pressures of the media and interest groups will tolerate or demand.

Context: a shared and divided heritage

The European neighbourhood encompasses both states to the east of the EU and those to the south, around the eastern and southern shores of the Mediterranean. The latter includes the Arab states of North Africa (the Maghreb) as well as the Levant or Near East (including Israel). In EU parlance this grouping has been designated the Middle East and North Africa region, which includes Jordan but not the Arabian Peninsula states or Iran, except when referred to simply as 'the Middle East' or 'wider region'.

Europe and the Middle East, however subdivided, are adjacent geographically, economically interdependent and linked by a shared history. Cultural interchange, migrations, imperial conquests and wars between the two regions have informed their respective identities for centuries. Consequently, contemporary debates about the defining characteristics and boundaries of Europe are in many respects just the latest phase in a process that has involved the Middle East as a reference point for what distinguishes Europeans from others.

Successive empires – among them the Greek, Roman, Byzantine, Umayyad, Ottoman, French and British – have straddled the shores of the Mediterranean. The three great monotheistic faiths – Judaism, Christianity and Islam – originated in the Middle East and share the same prophets and heritage, while each has also evolved in distinction and sometimes conflict with the others.

As discussed by Montserrat Guibernau in this volume (Chapter 14), a Christian heritage does inform European identity but religion is not a sufficient basis upon which to distinguish Europe or 'the West' from 'the East' or the 'Orient'. On the contrary, the contemporary European identity emerged on the back of an attempt to link the European heritage to pre-Christian Greek democracy. More significant was the combination of state formation, the separation of church and state, property rights, industrialisation and capitalism. Thus, as depicted by Guibernau, it was the transformation of the Industrial Revolution that rendered Europe distinct from the non-industrialised East in the 19th century.

The same combination of factors drove European imperial expansion and competition in the 19th century, galvanised and justified no doubt by attendant assumptions of superiority over the peoples colonised. The contrasting imperial ethos and styles of the British, Dutch, Belgian, Italian and French also reveal the differing purposes served for the national myth of each imperial power by their respective colonies. The manner in which the British and French arrived and then departed in the Middle East and North Africa had as much to do with their respective theories about national identity and empire as conditions on the ground.

Whereas the British took control of Egypt in 1882 as a 'temporary' measure (and lingered on until 1952), the French made Algeria part of metropolitan France (until forced out in 1962). The British (using Indian troops) invaded Mesopotamia in 1914, claiming their mission was to liberate the peoples from Ottoman rule, and then stayed to suppress those who revolted against the government they installed. The French Mandatory powers in Syria presided over the separation of Lebanon from the remit of Damascus. The British Mandatory powers in Palestine helped the Zionists form a homeland for the Jews there and then tried to curtail the Zionist enterprise and eventually gave up in the face of both Jewish and Arab opposition.

Such experiences were as formative for the European imperialists as for the peoples over whom they presided in the 19th and 20th centuries, yet awareness of a shared history is more prevalent in the Middle East and North Africa today than it is across Europe. Various explanations for this contrast suggest themselves. In Europe the end of empire was accompanied by other developments: soul-searching and rebuilding after the Second World War; the Cold War; the spread of American cultural influence; and the formation of the European Community. Together these developments produced a reorientation in Europe which involved the rejection of the very idea of empire[1] and espousal of the values now associated with the EU (and discussed in other chapters), namely freedom, liberal democracy, respect for human rights, the rule of law, prosperity and progress.

In the Middle East, meanwhile, opposing colonial rule and/or control became the galvanising cause for separate Arab nationalist movements, the Iranians and the Zionists. Yet even as political independence was attained, the exploitation of oil by Western companies determined the shape of economic development in the region. It was not until the 1970s that the last vestiges of European imperialism were dismantled in the Persian Gulf and Arab oil producers and Iran finally gained full control of their energy industries. It should be no surprise, therefore, that the peoples of the Middle East remained more conscious of the imperial heritage than the Europeans.

The Cold War context

Even so, the Middle East might have shaken off the resentments and preoccupations of the imperial legacy in time had it not been for the continuation of the Arab-Israeli conflict and rise of US hegemony in the region. Since the early Zionists were mostly European Jews fleeing persecution and then the Holocaust, the Arabs came to see them and thence Israel as a Western implant and even a colonial enterprise. When the United States became the leading supporter of Israel after the 1967 war (in which Israel captured territories from the neighbouring Arab states) the Americans were assumed to be using Israel as a basis for controlling the region. The Soviet Union gave its support to Arab opponents of Israel, in particular the Baathist (national socialist) states of Syria and Iraq.

For the duration of the Cold War superpower rivalry provided a context within which Arab governments, Iran and Israel could count on the support of either the Americans or the Soviets in pursuit of their competition with each other. The effect was to enable the various regional states to consolidate around distinct roles and identities. In almost all cases, regime legitimacy was pinned on espousal of regional causes and external support. Only in Israel were citizenship rights and democratic accountability a source of government legitimacy.

European political elites dealt directly with regional governments and eschewed support for civil-society groups and sub-state movements and minorities for fear of encountering accusations of internal interference and old imperialist habits. The arms manufacturers of Britain and France capitalised on the growing market for weapons fuelled by Cold War confrontation and the oil wealth generated by the oil booms of the 1970s. The Arab oil boycott of 1973 against supporters of Israel also deterred most European states from challenging the broader Arab trade boycott on companies dealing directly with Israel.

The contemporary context

The end of the Cold War and collapse of the Soviet Union was not only transformative for Europe but also the Middle East. After this came the formation and expansion of the EU discussed in other chapters in this book, which paved the way for the development of new European initiatives for relations with Europe's Mediterranean neighbours discussed below. Meanwhile, in August 1990 Iraq invaded Kuwait. All the Europeans as well as Russia lined up behind the Americans to restore Kuwaiti sovereignty, defend international law and then support a new US-led multilateral effort to resolve the Arab-Israeli conflict.

However, the beginnings of a new transnational phenomenon emanating from the Middle East was also emerging. Radical Islamist movements were not new to the region but in the early 1990s they surfaced across North Africa. Arab governments allied to the United States held Washington partly responsible because the CIA had helped fund and train the mujahedin and Arab volunteers to defeat the Soviets in Afghanistan in the 1980s.[2] When that war was won the foreign fighters regrouped and went on to develop an anti-Western agenda to oust the US presence and allied governments in the Middle East.

The existence of migrant communities in Europe deriving from North Africa as well as asylum-seekers opposed to Arab regimes also posed a dilemma for European governments hoping that a new era of liberal democracy and human rights was the answer to all ills. Crucially, the sense that expansion of the EU was the best way to stabilise the newly independent Eastern European states and thence the Balkans appears to have contributed to a belief in the virtues and values represented by the EU, at least in the minds of the European elites. Such thinking also emerged in EU policies with respect to North Africa and the Middle East from the mid-1990s, discussed below.

Another problem became manifest in the wake of 9/11, as European governments and the Union introduced new measures to track and combat potential terrorists. The realisation that the threat was in part coming from within, from radicalised Muslim youth, generated a crisis that several governments interpreted as a failure of their 'multiculturalism' policies and forced a re-examination of assumptions previously made by European elites about universal values and identity.

Contrasting regional orientations

Contemporary European policies on the Middle East are multifaceted and encompass defence and security, migration, human rights and democracy promotion, trade, investment and energy security, as well as political and diplomatic initiatives and dialogues. In all respects the policies adopted are presented as benign in so far as they are not about territorial expansion, subjugation, dominance, coercion or expropriation. Indeed, European elites manifest a belief in peace, conflict resolution, human rights, shared prosperity, the rule of law, countering nuclear, chemical and biological weapons proliferation and combating terrorism as positive goods in their own right.

Such goals or values make sense in the internal context of the EU, where a return to inter-state war or imperialism has been disavowed by all the member states and membership of the Union means acceptance of democracy and human rights. In the context of the contemporary Middle East, however, these are all loaded concepts, in so far as pursuit of these goods for their own sake favour some players in the region above others.

Conflict resolution or peace – even saving lives – do not apparently constitute a compelling or urgent objective for its own sake for most of the key players in the region. That is because most of the key actors in the region are either too weak or too strong to want to settle for the status quo. Some are clearly on the ascendant and have more to gain from resisting compromise, or from one more round of conflict before making peace. Others are weak and fear institutionalising that weakness if they concede to any particular deal at present.

The Hamas leadership in Gaza, Hezbollah in Lebanon, and senior figures in Damascus and Tehran can all logically calculate that they have more to gain from avoiding a regional or even partial deal on the issues in contention today. By contrast, the Israeli and Palestinian Authority leaderships are both too threatened by Hamas and other opponents to agree a peace deal unless and until they have prevailed over their detractors and thence Hamas.

In the background, the Palestinian refugees who are spread around the region are weak and divided but also disinclined to embrace a peace deal at their expense. Even the Arab governments championing the peace offered to Israel known as the Arab Initiative (first launched in 2002 and revived in 2006) would risk exposure to public hostility if they accepted a deal that looked like a sell-out by the Palestinians, especially on the issue of Jerusalem. Even Washington has not wanted regional peace at any price. Hence the US administration adopted an agenda at the Annapolis conference of 2007 designed to reward the Palestinian president at the expense of Hamas and its reluctance to bargain with Damascus or Tehran.

On the Israeli-Palestinian front at least, there are players who do, more or less, want peace for its own sake. Among these are the governments of Jordan, Egypt, Saudi Arabia, the other Arab Gulf states, and the North African or Maghreb states. But while they are not in a position to deliver the main protagonists in the conflict, so those protagonists lack the strength to dictate the terms of peace to their satisfaction.

In the circumstances it is perhaps not surprising that the policies emanating from the European Union have been less than decisive or instrumental in effecting change in the region. By the same token, however, they reveal much about the orientations, preferences and constraints on those who make them.

Policy areas: four case studies

Examination of four specific European policy areas serves to illustrate and illuminate the assumptions, values, interests and intentions of European elites. They reveal contrasts between EU member states, between the EU and the United States and between European elites and their Middle Eastern counterparts. The cases in point are:

1. The Euro-Mediterranean Partnership (EMP) or Barcelona Process
2. The Iraq crisis of 2002–3
3. The European Neighbourhood Policy (ENP) with respect to the Middle East
4. The Middle East Peace Process (MEPP).

The Euro-Mediterranean Partnership (EMP)

The impetus behind the EMP initiative launched in Barcelona in November 1995 was revealing in itself. It came from the southern Europeans, France and Spain in particular, to match and counterbalance moves led by Germany to stabilise and embrace the central European states newly liberated from the Soviet Union. As such the EMP was designed to frame relations with all the EU's southern neighbours, irrespective of whether they would subsequently become candidate members or require separate provision – as was the case with Malta, Cyprus and Turkey.

The gathering in Barcelona in 1995 thus included the 15 member states of the EU at the time, together with Morocco, Algeria, Tunisia, Egypt, Israel, Jordan, Syria, Lebanon, Turkey, the Palestinian Authority, Cyprus and Malta. As embodied in the Barcelona Declaration,[3] the central objective was the creation of a Euro-Mediterranean Economic Area, to come into effect by 2010. The intention was to dismantle tariff and non-tariff barriers to trade in manufactured and some other products between the EU and Europe's southern neighbours.

It was the northern Europeans who championed the benefits of free trade as an attractive end in itself. Southern Europeans by contrast stood to lose if forced to open their agricultural sectors to competition from North African producers of citrus fruits, olives and olive oil. Yet for those North Africans the attractions of the EMP lay principally in gaining better access to the internal market for their main exports. To satisfy both therefore, the deal promised progressive liberalisation of trade in agricultural goods but retained some protection for the southern Europeans in the near term.

The interests of the Spanish, French, Italians and Greeks lay in promoting capital investment in North Africa as a vehicle for stimulating economic growth and thence job creation in the Maghreb. This, they envisaged, would serve to stem the tide of migrants seeking to enter Europe from the south. They also stood to gain from expansion of their manufacturing and service industries into the Maghreb.

Consequently, from its inception the EMP had built-in contradictions. The goal was free trade, but unlike in Europe, the free movement of some goods and capital was not to be accompanied by the free movement of labour. Instead, trade and capital flows were to be liberalised in order to prevent migration. It amounted to a leap of faith for all concerned and the North African governments could only hope that the outcome would prove beneficial in the long run as their economies adjusted to increased competition.

In addition, the EMP went beyond trade liberalisation to envisage political, cultural and security cooperation as well. Yet there was no expectation that such cooperation would involve political change in Europe – it was the southern partner states who were supposed to implement reforms to make them more like their European counterparts. In addition, the EU hoped to stimulate greater south–south economic cooperation and integration by allocating funds to promote new communication and trade links between the Maghreb and the Levant and by 2004 was spending about €1 billion a year on the programme.

Essentially, therefore, the EU hoped to turn its southern neighbourhood into a more politically open, self-sustaining and prosperous belt of economic activity, the better to relieve pressure on Europe itself. It was counted a notable achievement of the EMP that Syria and Lebanon were involved as well as Israel, notwithstanding the unresolved conflict between them. In any case, in the mid-1990s progress in Middle East peace-making through the Oslo process was expected to deliver an end to the conflict and the Barcelona initiative was intended both to complement and capitalise on that process, but not directly interact with it.

As it transpired, the EMP survived the demise of the Oslo process, but not without some stormy encounters at ministerial meetings of the participants, and the collapse of early efforts at security cooperation across the Arab–Israeli divide. Thus the EMP fell short of expectations by taking for granted that Middle East peace was in the offing and placing inflated hopes in the power of free trade (which was never truly free anyway) to stimulate peaceful cooperation.

A series of bilateral Association Agreements were concluded between the EU and Morocco, Algeria, Tunisia, Egypt, Jordan, Lebanon, Israel and the Palestinian Authority. Negotiations with Syria were held up in part because of a new requirement for partner states to renounce weapons of mass destruction. The Syrians resisted, arguing – not without reason – that the Europeans were using economic pressure to pursue their security agenda. Libya was initially excluded from the EMP, pending resolution of the Lockerbie issue and sanctions.

By 2003 the broad parameters and shortcomings of the EMP were apparent. Instead of an integrated region around the Mediterranean, what emerged was a hub and spokes arrangement, with the EU as the hub connected to each partner state by separate bilateral trade links or spokes.[4] The southern partner states discovered that they lacked the capacity to match the European Commission in managing the bureaucratic and technical complexities of the relationship. Thus the EU ended up setting the pace, at least in terms of trade relations, but not much more than that.

However, their early experiences with the Barcelona process did prompt Arab partner states to cooperate more among themselves. Conscious of their relative weakness in relation to the EU, Morocco, Tunisia, Egypt and Jordan decided to join forces in the Agadir Agreement of 2003, pledging to dismantle trade barriers between them and thence qualify for EU aid in support of south–south cooperation.

On the European side EU elites voiced disappointment that provisions in the Barcelona process to combat corruption, promote accountability and transparency and export European norms for human rights protection did not achieve the desired results. In fact, Arab elites proved adept at maintaining their relatively privileged positions in the partner states and governments resisted European efforts to support civil society, democracy and human rights movements on the grounds that such activities would interfere with indigenous culture and sovereignty.

The Iraq Crisis of 2002–3

When terrorists attacked the World Trade Centre and the Pentagon on 11 September 2001 (9/11) all Europe's leaders rallied in support of the Americans. NATO members pledged readiness to support Washington's plans to take on Al Qaeda and the Taliban in Afghanistan. However, in 2001 the US government was convinced of its capacity to take on its enemies unilaterally if need be and its allies were expected to fall into line. Consultation, multilateralism, international law and the United Nations were out of fashion in Washington.

For Europe's elites this posed a challenge that deepened as the possibility of a US invasion of Iraq loomed. For the Eastern Europeans, loyalty to America, the champion of the anti-Soviet cause in the Cold War, was paramount. Yet they were publicly rebuked by France and Germany for lacking solidarity with the rest of the EU. Among Western Europeans the Iraq crisis proved even more fraught. Most foreign policy civil servants revealed a prescient awareness of the likely fallout from a US invasion, with or without allied support, but for the politicians that was not the only consideration.

British Prime Minister Tony Blair proved exceptional in his belief in the correctness of the goal of toppling Saddam Hussein and his dismissal of expert advice on the probable consequences. President Jacques Chirac of France challenged Blair personally on the dangers of such an undertaking when the two met for an EU summit in late 2002. While Chirac's approach betrayed disdain for the younger politician's lack of awareness of the situation in Iraq and the region, for his part Tony Blair allegedly told aides that Chirac 'doesn't get it, does he?'.[5]

However, not just Iraq but the future of the Western alliance itself seemed to be at stake and as the possibility of a US invasion of Iraq gathered momentum, the Europeans split ranks principally over how best to handle the Bush administration. German Chancellor Gerhard Schroeder, running for re-election in 2002, played to German public antipathy to an invasion of Iraq by ruling out German participation even if UN backing for such a move proved forthcoming. In doing so Schroeder was breaking with Germany's own commitment to adhering to international law and UN Security Council decisions.

The French leadership, by contrast, proved determined to make the UN Security Council the ultimate arbiter and thereby counter US unilateralism. At the same time, Chirac was not prepared to short-circuit the weapons inspection process instigated in November 2002 under UNSC Resolution 1441. In early 2003 he even indicated that France would veto a new resolution sanctioning the use of force against Saddam Hussein at that point. Conceivably, therefore, France might have changed its position in the event that inspections had revealed evidence of a covert Iraqi weapons programme. At the time, however, the British government blamed the French for paralysing the Security Council.

European intelligence services apparently did concur with their American counterparts that Iraq was most probably in possession or actively seeking weapons of mass destruction. None were convinced by US claims of links between Al Qaeda and the regime of Saddam Hussein, though the British Prime Minister did apparently fear that in time such links could be forged.

In any case, once the prospect of a US invasion became irreversible, Europeans were deeply divided. Having sought UN cover in vain, the British government opted to join US forces in the invasion of March 2003 without UN endorsement. Opposition in parliament and among the British public was countered by government insinuations that to oppose the invasion was tantamount to anti-Americanism and support for Saddam Hussein.

European public opinion generally was largely opposed to the war, though Prime Ministers Berlusconi of Italy and Aznár of Spain sided with Bush and sent troops to Iraq following the invasion. After Aznár's handling of the terrorist bombings in Madrid lost him the subsequent election to Jose Luis Rodriguez Zapatero, the latter carried out his promise to withdraw Spanish troops from Iraq – incurring lasting antipathy to the Zapatero government in Washington. The governments of the Eastern European states, by contrast, maintained their military commitments in Iraq for longer, but except for the Poles, their numbers were comparatively small and constituted more of a gesture to Washington than an instrumental presence on the ground.

When the occupation met increasing Iraqi opposition in early 2004, fears of a spillover effect in the region gained momentum. Token European support for the rebuilding effort in Iraq also began to peel away as all foreign nationals there began to fear kidnap and some were executed by the newly emergent 'al-Qaeda in Iraq' and other extremists. After mass attacks on Iraqi civilians triggered sectarian warfare in 2006 the US military was left virtually alone to try to restore security.

Ultimately, the fallout from the Iraq crisis for European unity and EU expansion was damaging but not fatal. However, it did contribute to subsequent timidity in Europe over criticising Washington's policies in other parts of the Middle East. When Washington cold-shouldered those governments who had stood out against the Iraq invasion, European officials appeared to go out of their way to show that they could be cooperative in other areas – not least in their efforts to demonstrate determination and solidarity in the war against terrorism outside Iraq.

The European Neighbourhood Policy (ENP)

The origins of the European Neighbourhood Policy (ENP), like the EMP before it, had as much to do with Eastern Europe as the Mediterranean. In the wake of EU enlargement from 15 to 25 members, the EU needed a policy for non-candidate countries on the eastern periphery – notably Belarus and Ukraine. Meanwhile, the original line-up of partner states in the EMP had depleted, with Malta and (southern) Cyprus joining the EU and Turkey becoming a potential EU member. In this context, it was logical that a new formula – the ENP – should apply to all Europe's neighbours not destined for EU membership.

Furthermore, by 2003 the shortcomings of the EMP were apparent. Yet the need to promote economic growth and stability around Europe's perimeter remained a consideration on security grounds – especially in light of post-9/11 fears about terrorism and radicalisation spreading among Europe's migrant communities with links to North Africa and the Middle East. Meanwhile, the United States had become an advocate of political and economic reform in the region, prompting the Europeans to scramble to defend their own initiatives.

The new ENP was thus announced in the midst of the excitement generated by Washington's new initiative for economic and political reform in 'the Wider Middle East' (including Pakistan and Afghanistan) and G8 endorsement of such goals. The core concept of the ENP was a 'strategic partnership' with neighbours both in Eastern Europe and in North Africa and the Middle East, where it was intended to complement the EMP and potentially expand to embrace Iran and the Arabian Peninsula states as well.[6]

Unlike the EMP, however, which had been launched as a partnership at Barcelona in 1995, the application of the ENP to the Mediterranean was instigated solely by the Europeans. As subsequently refined and embellished in Brussels it was presented as a framework to provide a flexible and differentiated approach to bilateral relations with each of Europe's neighbours, taking account of the size and relative level of development of partner economies.

In detail the ENP was designed by bureaucrats in the EC as a technical instrument for achieving the goals not met through the EMP for political and governance as well as economic reform. Believing they could make it more viable and palatable by offering to assist with indigenously generated reform programmes, the EC officials also believed they could achieve measurable results this time by agreeing individual Action Plans with each of the partner governments. Assistance was to be based on achievement of agreed objectives, though the main benefit was supposedly to be derived from increased harmonisation of standards with those of the internal market and thence increased trade.

For all except Israel these promised benefits were essentially a chimera. To match European product standards required significant changes to existing practices in the partner states. In Jordan, for example, simply making manufacturers bear the penalties for failing to meet European standards would represent a shift from public- to private-sector responsibility. There could therefore be unforeseen political implications to introducing the proposed reforms. The bureaucracies in all the Arab partner countries also lacked the capacity to master all the technical requirements embodied in EC proposals and Action Plans.

Crucially, the EC bureaucrats failed to see the conceptual bias and technical drawbacks in the initiative they were trying to sell to Europe's Arab neighbours. Governments in the Mediterranean partner countries did not necessarily see the ENP as a logical progression from the EMP. They saw the latter as a partnership and the former as an EU reform initiative. In the Arab world it was well understood that the purpose of the initiative was more about making them better neighbours for Europe than responding to their judgements of their own priorities.

In agreeing an Action Plan partner states were expected to choose from a menu of measures developed in the EU for would-be member states, without any expectation of the assumed benefits of membership. Furthermore, choice was not really the operative word because, as seen from the region, the Europeans were insisting that certain items be included in the mix of measures in the Action Plans, irrespective of whether the partner state thought these were needed or appropriate.

Fundamentally the ENP initiative embodied a set of assumptions made in Europe about the essential ingredients of liberal economic and political development that was more culture-specific than EC elites realised. They apparently thought that all the values embodied in the EU laws and regulations were desirable and beneficial in the interests of economic development and the public good, irrespective of culture and context. In the Arab states, by contrast, the measures they proposed represented a threat to government and other vested interests.

In Egypt, if the government is determined to do something, it will happen. However, Egyptian government enthusiasm for economic and administrative reform has not been matched by an appetite for political reform. In Lebanon there is some appetite for political and economic reform. However, politicians have been unable to take any significant initiatives pending resolution of the country's political difficulties with Syria. In Jordan social stability is underpinned by a tribal and patronage system that cannot be dismantled without upset and resistance. A culture change is called for by the proponents of reform but they lack the power to deliver this without the King using his patronage and authority to help them. In the context of the occupation of Iraq and the 'war on terror' that leadership on reform has not been forthcoming.

In sum, the ENP has not necessarily been received as it was intended to be by its architects in the EU. Were it not for the sudden rush of reform initiatives from various quarters, including the US and G8 in recent years, the ENP might have proceeded quietly. But as it was, Arab publics have been led to understand that Western initiatives are about countering Islamist extremism. So their ability to agree and embrace the logic of reform has been tempered by the sympathies of some for Islamist causes and the perception of others that it is US, British and to some extent all European policies which are primarily responsible for terrorism.

Europe and the Middle East Peace Process

Individually and collectively, the Europeans have held to the view that the land-for-peace formula embodied in UN Security Council Resolutions 242 (1967) and 338 (1973) is the best approach to resolving the Arab–Israeli conflict. Resolution 242 was passed in the aftermath of the 1967 war in which Israel captured the Sinai Peninsula (and Gaza Strip) from Egypt, the West Bank from Jordan and the Golan Heights from Syria. Resolution 338 was passed following the 1973 war in which Egyptian forces managed to restore some semblance of their national pride previously shattered in the defeat of 1967. With US mediation thereafter Egypt made peace with Israel in 1979.

Since that time Washington has taken the lead on peacemaking in the Middle East and the Europeans have been relegated the role of supporter and latterly banker for efforts to resolve the Israeli–Palestinian dimension of the conflict. In 1980 the European Community demonstrated both unity and prescience when it issued the Venice Declaration[7] calling for the Palestinian people to be able 'to exercise fully their right to self-determination' and stating that the Palestine Liberation Organisation (PLO) would have to be involved in peace negotiations.

At the time neither the United States nor the Israelis were prepared to countenance either proposition, but by the 1990s both had gained acceptance in Washington, at the UN and among key states in the region.

Under the so-called 'Oslo process' in the 1990s the EU became the largest single donor to the Palestinian Authority (PA). In the late 1990s the European

Commission funded a major inquiry into the functioning of the PA, identified sources of corruption, questionable procedures and overlapping mandates, and initiated measures for reform.[8] The US administration kept to itself management of actual peace negotiations, but acknowledged that the whole process was facilitated by the EU role. For their part, the Europeans remained critical of some Israeli policies, but worked more to support than to impede US mediation efforts.

Latterly, Europeans have echoed the views of some Israeli commentators that the continued occupation of Palestinian land by the Israelis is counter-productive for the long-term security of both sides. Yet in the United States and Israel the view still prevails that terrorism is the core problem and unless and until the Palestinian leadership can prevent acts of terrorism against Israelis they cannot be a partner for peace.[9] In any case, residual suspicion of the Europeans in Israel, dating from the Holocaust, has inclined Israelis to resist any European advice or peace proposals not led by Washington.

When the Oslo process collapsed in 2000, the United States held the Palestinians responsible for the ensuing violence and horrendous suicide bombings, while the Europeans were equally critical of Israel for the continued occupation and settlement expansion in the West Bank. The EU did not support the decision of the Bush administration to boycott and sideline PLO Chairman Yasser Arafat, and emergency aid from the EU kept the Palestinian Authority afloat, when US assistance was suspended.

However, since 9/11 and increased fears of Islamist-inspired terrorism in the West, the Europeans have proved reluctant to confront the Israelis over the measures they have adopted, including the construction of a 'security barrier' in and around the West Bank to fend off the dangers they have faced from Palestinian terrorists. Consequently, the Europeans have increasingly accommodated to American and Israeli demands for the Palestinians to reform their political and security arrangements to prevent more terrorist incidents as a prelude to peacemaking.

For their part, the Americans have become advocates of a 'two-state' solution to the conflict, with, as President Bush envisioned in 2002, a Palestinian state living 'in peace and security' alongside Israel. Responding pragmatically to Bush's endorsement of a two-state solution in Spring 2002, the EU worked through the mechanism of 'the Quartet' (the EU, US, UN and Russia) to produce the 'Road Map', formally launched in 2003, spelling out steps to reach that goal. However, like other peace plans, the Road Map languished while the protagonists continued their struggle and the 'facts on the ground' began to render the prospect of Palestinian statehood ever more improbable.

In 2005 the Israelis unilaterally evacuated settlements from the Gaza Strip but proceeded to consolidate their hold on the West Bank. As the Europeans persisted with their efforts to bolster the PA they were increasingly accused by the Palestinians of enabling the continued occupation rather than helping to end it. EU and member state officials became mired in the minutiae of arguments with the Israelis over checkpoints, travel permits and other security issues, losing sight of the big picture.

Then came a major turning point in European involvement in the peace process. In January 2006 the Palestinians went to the polls to elect a new legislature, with the EU providing organisational support, funds and monitors. Contrary to expectations in Europe and Washington, the Palestinian Islamist movement Hamas won a clear victory over its Fatah rivals and in the process presented the EU with a diplomatic and political headache. As part of Europe's strategy to demonstrate solidarity and determination in the 'war on terror' the EU had included Hamas in its official list of terrorist organisations and EU law prevented Brussels from funding such groups.

Meeting in crisis mode, the members of the Quartet decided to withhold financial support to the Palestinian Authority pending acknowledgement by Hamas of three principles – renunciation of violence, acceptance of agreements previously reached by the Palestinian leadership, and recognition of Israel. In the meantime, Brussels introduced a temporary mechanism to funnel aid to vital service personnel in the West Bank and Gaza. Having tried and failed to form a unity government, in 2007 Hamas and Fatah clashed in Gaza, leaving Hamas in sole control there, while Fatah leader and Palestinian President Mahmoud Abbas formed a new administration in the West Bank that was again accorded direct EU support.

The consequences of this turn of events were deeply damaging for Europe's standing in the Middle East. The EU had stood for and preached democratisation and the rule of law, yet refused to recognise the winners of a free and fair election in Palestine which the EU itself had funded and monitored. The emergency government formed by Abbas was unconstitutional under Palestinian law, yet the EU accorded it funds at the expense of those elected to power. When the Gaza Strip was deemed 'a hostile entity' by the Israelis in 2007 and placed under a strict blockade, the Europeans proved incapable of rectifying the situation and ordinary Gazans suffered the consequences.

Behind the scenes some EU member states and the Norwegians expressed doubts about the efficacy and morality of the official policy on Hamas and its consequences – but the political will to change the policy proved absent. Washington and the Israelis were apparently adamant that there could be no reprieve for Hamas, only humanitarian measures to alleviate some of the suffering of the Gazans. Whether for fear of openly crossing the Israelis or the Americans or both, the Europeans proved unable or unwilling to take a different stance.

Conclusions

The case studies examined above reveal much about European elite commitment to the ideals of the EU. Free trade is advocated provided it does not damage key constituencies inside the EU such as the agricultural sector.

The free flow of goods, labour, capital and services are to be encouraged within the EU and make sense as a coherent package, but when introduced selectively in the European neighbourhood they only reinforce dependency on Europe and do not generate prosperity except in pockets. Thus, by attempting to export EU values piecemeal rather than comprehensively the European policy elites have demonstrated a curious disregard for the lessons of their own experience in Europe. With the EMP and the ENP they thought that a little of what has proved beneficial inside the EU would be beneficial outside, disregarding the absence of other necessary conditions.

In promoting the ENP Action Plans the European elites also seem not to have realised how the actions proposed would affect political arrangements as well as economic and governance practices in the partner states. A paternalistic, tribal social system such as that in Jordan and the pervasive statist system in Egypt cannot be transformed incrementally by technical measures. The governments concerned must embrace and lead comprehensive change if the population is to endure the disruptions of transition. In EU candidate states such leadership has been present and populations can be induced to accept pain in return for the promise of belonging to the EU with all its benefits in the long run.

Eastern Europeans eager to assert their independence from the former Soviet bloc were ready ideologically to embrace European-ness as a goal in itself, embodied in EU membership. However, Arab states do not have the same goal of asserting a European identity – on the contrary, they want to preserve their independent Arab character and norms and thereby resist 'Westernisation' or 'Europeanisation'. History has also taught them to be suspicious of European motives and the European elites seem not to have realised that however benign and well meaning they may perceive themselves to be, they are not thus perceived.

By resisting real partnership and integration around the Mediterranean the Europeans also revealed their desire to maintain their own distinct heritage and identity. The prospect of increased migration from Africa and the Middle East represents a positive danger to social cohesion in Europe, and one to be resisted. Indeed the nature and depth of European security concerns are demonstrated in all the case studies.

Fear of Islamist extremism appears to be at the heart of recent European policy decisions and possibly runs deeper than fear of terrorism per se. Conceivably, fear of a backlash against European Muslims if migration threatens jobs and social stability inside Europe is interconnected with the fear of Islamist extremism at the elite level. In other words, European publics cannot be trusted to embrace diversity, multiculturalism and integration with the neighbourhood if their relative comfort and lifestyles are at stake. Hence the elites have taken it upon themselves to place protection of their perceived identity and values within ahead of spreading such values abroad.

Notes and References

1. E. Said, *Culture and Imperialism*, London: Random House, 1993.
2. George Joffe, 'The European Union, Democracy and Counter-Terrorism in the Maghreb', *Journal of Contemporary Mediterranean Studies*, 46 (1), 2008, 147–71.
3. Barcelona Declaration, 28 November 1995, at: http://europa.eu.int/en/comm/dg1b/en/den-barc.htm
4. See D. Xenaksis and D. Chryssochoou, *The Emerging Euro-Mediterranean System*, Manchester and New York: Manchester University Press, 2001.
5. *The Blair Years*, BBC Documentary, Episode 2, 2007.
6. See the 'Interim Report on an EU Strategic Partnership with the Mediterranean and the Middle East', *Euromed Report*, Issue No 73, 23 March 2004, at: http://europa.eu.int/comm/eexternal_relations/euromed/publications.htm
7. Venice Declaration 1980, *Bulletin of the EC*, 6–1980: 10–11, point 1.1.6.
8. Council on Foreign Relations, Task Force Report, 'Strengthening Palestinian Public Institutions', at: www.cfr.org/public/pubs/palinstfull.html
9. See D. Allin and S. Simon, 'The Moral Psychology of US Support for Israel', *Survival*, 45 (3), 2003, 123–44.

Part III
Political Economy of Europe

8
European Deregulation and National Re-Regulation: National Response Strategies Revisited

Georg Menz

Recent debates in comparative political economy have focused on the implication of economic liberalisation in Europe, variously associated with domestic factors engendering the embrace of neo-liberal ideology or more general tectonic shifts often attributed to globalisation and European integration.[1] More recent contributions, especially those informed by the 'varieties of capitalism' approach, contest that earlier pessimistic predictions of convergence on a minimalist liberal Anglo-American model of capitalism are inaccurate, suggesting instead a taxonomy that encapsulates coordinated market economies (CMEs) and liberal market economies (LMEs), while recent contributions also suggest categories encompassing Central and Eastern European emerging market economies (EMEs) and Mediterranean mixed market economies (MMEs).[2]

Though the number of categories and indeed their very nature are contested as well,[3] such recent strides reject dire predictions of neo-liberal convergence. One obvious point of weakness in the attempt to sketch alternative capitalist models that are seen as robust enough to sustain liberalising shocks is the ongoing steadily proceeding liberalisation of these very models, due to the 'internalization of globalization'.[4] Therefore, surviving institutions of politico-economic governance may serve radically different macroeconomic policy goals and their very existence ought not to be interpreted as evidence of a truly alternative model of capitalism.[5]

A major external pressure that remains somewhat bereft of the scholarly attention it merits is the European Union (EU) Single Market Programme (SMP). The deregulatory liberal nature of the SMP clashes with and in some cases directly undermines the pillars of European politico-economic governance models by interfering with national authority over labour-market regulation. 'Negative integration', as one analyst refers to it,[6] weakens and distorts national regimes of wage-setting and labour-market standard and access control regulation.

Recently, the European Commission has undertaken sustained attempts to revive relatively neglected aspects of the SMP, especially regarding service

Table 8.1:   Average hourly wages in the European construction sector (2006, except where otherwise noted)

*Latvia	3.23
*Hungary	4.36
*Lithuania	4.56
*Slovakia	4.79
* Poland	5.37
*Estonia	5.69
Malta	5.78
*Czech Republic	6.50
Portugal	8.94
Greece	8.94 (2003)
*Slovenia	10.37
Spain	14.22
*Cyprus	14.75
Ireland	16.60 (2000)
Italy	17.67 (2004)
Luxembourg	19.91
Germany	21.10
Finland	24.93
United Kingdom	25.04 (2005)
Austria	25.17
France	25.91
Netherlands	27.80 (2005)
Sweden	28.05
Denmark	29.61 (2005)
Belgium	30.07

Notes: All wage levels are denominated in euros. * denotes countries that joined the EU in 2004.
Source: Eurostat 2006.

provision. The Bolkestein directive sought to curtail national market-access regulation and promote trans-European service provision. Simultaneously, clever entrepreneurs are availing themselves of new opportunities for outsourcing and subcontracting by seconding employees transnationally, exploiting significant gaps in wages and social standards across Europe. By formally registering corporate headquarters in low-cost Latvia or Cyprus, significant savings can be realised and the obligation to pay Irish or Swedish wages can be legally avoided. A number of recent European Court of Justice decisions undermine national regulations governing transnational service provision.

Though warmly welcomed by economic liberals, any such liberalisation of service provision (LSP) was bound to prove highly politically contested. It evokes legitimate fears of promoting social dumping in the context of significant wage and income gaps (see Table 8.1). Flying cheap flags of convenience has, of course, become standard practice in international shipping, but doing so legally within the EU by exploiting wage gaps raises concerns over a deregulatory race to the bottom. Temporary secondment of service sectors appears like less of a legitimate exploitation of Ricardian comparative advantages in wage levels because Romanian or Latvian wages do not reflect the true cost of living for such posted workers in high-cost north-western European countries. Just how pivotal this theme became is evident in the rejection of the European Constitution in referenda in the Netherlands and France, at least partially influenced by concerns over a neo-liberal bias in this document, embodied in the home country principle for wages and working conditions applicable to any posted workers that the Bolkestein directive sought to introduce.

While a clash between the liberal-minded architects of deeper economic integration and advocates of national sovereignty in these policy domains appears inevitable, the argument submitted in this chapter is that the outcome of this conflict is strongly conditioned by institutional elements of the respective models of capitalism. The study of this conflict also affords a dynamic, rather than static, analysis of the viability, internal organisational structure and capacity to formulate and defend national response strategies. Building on earlier work,[7] I argue that these national response strategies will be shaped by the organisational-institutional characteristics of relevant domestic actor coalitions who can respond to top-down Europeanisation pre-emptively or reactively in formulating re-regulatory national response strategies. The institutional characteristics of trade unions and employer associations as well as the quality of their access channels to relevant national ministries condition the overall nature of such national response strategies.

Governments are in essence involved in two-level game negotiations.[8] The national interest position is conditioned by the interaction of labour-market interest associations and their relative success in exporting their interests and successfully shaping the agenda.[9] Different varieties of capitalism thus generate different responses to a common EU-led impetus. This obviously also implies that not all such attempts at formulating a national response strategy will be equally successful. In emphasising *institutional* characteristics, I situate this argument within the neo-institutionalist framework.[10] Empirically, the paper examines the repercussions and attempts at re-regulation with regards to more recent attempts at EU LSP, especially the so-called Bolkestein directive.

The organisational power of unions and employers in shaping responses to Europe

Recent advances in the Europeanisation literature have highlighted that the process is hardly 'passively encountered', but rather actively conditioned by national-level actors and can therefore result in a great variety of outcomes.[11]

The exact interactive effects between top-down Europeanisation and national actors' activities remain somewhat underspecified. Are advocacy coalitions ad hoc in nature, is their emergence contingent on certain variables, do veto players emerge spontaneously or do sceptics of liberalism manage to sustain more long-term coalition-building? By insisting on a radical interpretation of mutual recognition[12] and the country of origin principle, the European Commission could expect to face powerful reactions both by unions and employers. Similarly, the emergence of national-level liberalising initiatives based on the LSP provoked national re-regulation, generally led by the unions. A strong interactive effect between the European and the national level in labour-market policy can be expected. Powerful and often strongly positioned interest associations face governmental actors and are keen to modify, influence or in some cases impede the liberalising EU impetus. National governments can ill afford to ignore the activities of labour-market interest associations and, given close contacts and superb access channels enjoyed by unions and employers, are unlikely to do so.

The idiosyncratic institutional embeddedness of actors in socio-economic policy thus conditions the degree of policy influence they can hope to exert in shaping national re-regulation and negotiating adaptation to change induced by the European integration process. The response strategy reflects the preference of the strongest actor. Organisational strength is conceptualised as a combination of degree of organisational centralisation, internal coherence, and representation among their clientele. A pivotal fourth variable is access to government.

In order to maximise variance among different politico-economic models of governance, this paper examines responses to the EU liberalisation of service provision (LSP) in different varieties of the coordinated market economy category (Austria, Germany and Sweden), a case of a mixed market economy (France) and a liberal market economy (Ireland). They are thus 'most different' cases along key dimensions of politico-economic governance.[13]

In *France*, the trade unions are impeded by a low level of representation among their clientele, underdeveloped internal coherence and problems in exercising control over the rank and file, ideological and organisational fragmentation and underdeveloped links with the government. The employer association Medef represents major French business, but also organises a significant number of small and medium-sized enterprises. Its internal coherence and centralisation is much more strongly developed and its hierarchical top-down organisation offers additional advantages. However, recent change seems to have undermined organisational coherence. Common socialisation patterns facilitate access to governmental actors.[14]

In *Austria*, the union movement represents a very high number of its constituents and internal coherence and centralisation are strongly developed. Despite the recent decline in importance of the social partnership, formal and informal channels of influence-seeking still exist. The employer association

WKÖ boasts a 100 per cent membership rate, as membership is compulsory. It is highly hierarchical and centralised and also gains access to government through longstanding formal and informal consultation mechanisms.[15]

In *Germany*, the union movement is no longer as encompassing, internally coherent or centralised as is often assumed.[16] In the 'union of parts',[17] sectoral unions, especially the powerful metalworker union IG METALL and the service sector union ver.di command strong power. Access to government is secured through informal ties to the Social Democratic Party and formal hearings during legislative deliberations.

The employer association BDA is organisationally similarly subdivided along sectoral and regional lines but their representation levels are superior, recent trends towards atrophy notwithstanding.[18] The employers rely on strong sectoral members, especially in the metal section, and make use of informal contacts with the ministry of labour and social affairs.

In *Ireland*, the trade union movement organises a medium level of employees, but most union members are concentrated in the public sector. It is organisationally subdivided and hampered by persistent sectoral subdivisions. However, the institutionalisation of various social-partnership agreements has created new pathways for informal consultation with the government.[19]

The employer association IBEC commands a weaker membership base but is organisationally strong. Like the unions, it is regularly consulted by the apposite ministries and plays an active role in the framework of the social partnership.

In *Sweden*, the trade union movement has been traditionally very strong and continues to organise large sections of the workforce, institutional characteristics remain robust, but access to the government is no longer as strongly pronounced as has been the case historically.

The employer federation Svenskt Näringsliv is characterised by a medium-level degree of coverage and organisational coherence.[20]

In sum, the organisational characteristics of labour unions and employer associations in the five countries included here afford them different opportunities for affecting the national response strategies to EU LSP. Thus, we would expect a particularly strong position for French and Irish employers, a potential stand-off and compromise solution in Austria and Sweden and a somewhat stronger position for German employers.

New initiatives reinforcing the Liberalisation of Service Provision (LSP)

Though originally already contained in Art. 59–66 of the Treaty of Rome and one of the 'four freedoms', considerable legal uncertainty clouded trans-European service provision and it remained of little practical significance well into the 1980s. Historically relatively homogenous wage levels meant that

Table 8.2:   Union and employer organisation density (per cent)

	Employers	Unions
France	75	8
Germany	73	23
Ireland	38	35
Sweden	54	78
Austria	100	37

Notes: Employer organisation data refers to density in terms of employees within the organisation's domain for 1991–3 (source: F. Traxler, S. Blaschke and B. Kittel, *National Labour Relations in Internationalized Markets*, Oxford, Oxford University Press, 2000; Union density according to OECD data, cited in B. Ebbinghaus, 'Ever Larger Unions: Organisational Restructuring and Its Impact on Union Confederations', *Industrial Relations Journal*, 34(5), 2003, 446–60.

Table 8.3:   A comparison of the relative power of labour-market interest associations

Internal power index	Austria	Germany (Employers-Unions)	France	Ireland	Sweden
Centralisation	strong-strong	medium-medium	weak-medium	weak-medium	strong-strong
Internal cohesion	strong-strong	medium-medium	medium-medium	weak-medium	strong-strong
Representation among clientele	strong-strong	medium-strong	medium-medium	medium-weak	strong-medium
Access to government	strong-strong	medium-medium	weak-medium	medium-medium	medium-strong
Comparison	strong-strong	medium-strong	weak-medium	weak-medium	strong-strong

transnational service provision was limited to instances of highly specialised niche providers. De facto, European service sectors remained well within the legal remit of national regulatory authorities and the often highly technical nature of applicable regulation deterred transnational service provision. The EU's activity largely focused on banking and financial services, as with the 1977 and 1989 banking directives, establishing a 'passport' for financial service providers. Somewhat vague wording in the Treaty of Rome permitted protection of public service domains. The ECJ ruled favorably in regards to the French government funding the postal service provider La Poste in 1997, along with the similar 1993 Corbeau and the 1994 Almelo cases.[21] The court referred to Article 86.2 of the Treaty of Rome (ex 90.2), which details that member states have special rights regarding certain economic sectors and that a restriction of standard competition rules can be accepted in services deemed in the general interest.

The Commission grew increasingly frustrated with this state of affairs. At the same time, the 1990s had witnessed a massive increase in transnational service provision, especially in the construction sector. Table 8.1 illustrates the substantial wage gaps across Europe in this sector, which were first exploited by a Portuguese subcontractor for the French construction conglomerate Bouygues in 1986 and reached epic proportions in booming Berlin in the mid-1990s.

Such transnationally active service provision, spawning 'posted workers' from low-wage countries such as Portugal and Greece to high-wage destinations in northern Europe, were welcomed by economic liberals, while critics perceived the emergence of islands of foreign law that imported Portuguese wages into Germany as a neo-liberal nightmare entailing minimal wages and employee rights.

A 1990 ECJ decision (Société Rush Portuguesa Lda vs. Office National d'Immigration 27 March 1990; C-118/89) opened up the way to national response strategies. National re-regulatory strategies were particularly powerful in France and Austria, much more liberal in the Netherlands, occasioned protracted battles in Germany, and based on 'Scandinavian gentlemen's agreements' in the Nordic countries, including Finland.[22]

However, EU eastward enlargements in 2004 and 2007 re-ignited this *problématique*. Despite the imposition of temporary bans on labour mobility and service provision in all but three of the EU–15, the potential for competition via the wage factor re-emerged.

Political debates focusing on social dumping very quickly were met by a number of practical developments that juxtaposed national regulatory regimes in wages and working conditions with European deregulatory tendencies. Companies availed themselves of new opportunities for transnational service provision with the explicit aim of lowering wages. In some cases, this entrepreneurial exploitation of wage gaps generated legal battles, but generally a predictable conflict between profit-driven companies and trade unions concerned with wage dumping and a downward spiral in remuneration and social protection levels ensued.

In Ireland, the shipping company Irish Ferries incorporated a Cypriot subcontractor, replacing existing employees with new staff from Latvia, remunerated at Latvian wage levels. In Sweden, a Latvian construction company active in Växholm applied its home-country regime in terms of wages and working conditions offered to posted employees in Sweden. In Germany, meat-processing plants and construction companies found enterprising avenues for circumventing the temporary ban on service provision by employing nominally self-employed workers from Central and Eastern Europe (CEE) remunerated also at home-country levels. In the absence of a statutory minimum wage, it proved possible to circumvent standard German wages, legally applicable only to businesses with membership in the German employer association.

Finally, and most controversially perhaps, the Commission issued a draft directive that would have enshrined the home-country principle for transnational service provision, while forcing member states to open up significant segments of their economies to foreign competition, including areas traditionally regarded as public services, such as health and education. While economic liberals, notably the EU Trade Commissioner Peter Mandelson, warmly welcomed the 2004 draft directive named after former Commissioner Frits Bolkestein,[23] critics perceived the 'Frankenstein' directive as an incarnation of runaway neo-liberalisation, undermining fair wages and working conditions and pushing forward the doctrine of privatisation by stealth. Such fears were nourished by the practical implications of the home-country principle for host-country wages, setting in motion a downward spiral.

Ireland

Concerned about increasingly ferocious competition pressures arising from the emergence of low-cost airlines, the ferry operator Irish Ferries announced in late 2005 that it was re-flagging its fleet, outsourcing management to Cypriot subcontractor Dobson and replacing its workforce with Eastern European, predominantly Latvian, agency crew. This proved a shrewd manoeuvre, as the temporary restrictions on service provision did not apply to Cyprus and Malta, while the company claimed that Latvian wages (average hourly wages of €3.60, but an hourly minimum wage of €0.71 per hour in 2004) should be legally applicable to these ostensibly temporarily posted workers. The sectoral trade unions Services Industrial Professional and Technical Union (SIPTU) and the Seamen's Union of Ireland (SUI) responded immediately and robustly with industrial action. Management deployed security guards to assist the introduction of agency crew, leading to a number of violent confrontations and the blocking of vessels in Irish and Welsh ports in December 2005. A major nationwide demonstration organised by the union on 9 December 2005 attracted a turnout of 100,000, widely viewed as a considerable demonstration of strength.[24] However, despite the considerable negative publicity the company was courting, its management seemed unwilling to budge, arguing that outsourcing would save it €3.4 million, while the union's suggested reforms proposal entailed savings of only €2.4 million, including government assistance offered.[25]

The conflict had commenced on the Rosslare-Cherbourg service as early as 2004, when the company had flagged out its vessel Normandy to the Bahamas, announcing subsequently a layoff of 700 employees[26] and locking out SIPTU-organised seafarers to apply additional pressure. With the 2003 Employment Permits Act the government had demonstrated a more restrictive stance regarding the administration of employment permits, as it sensed that previous exemptions from work-permit requirements for temporary postings for up to three years had opened up channels for massive deployment of often low-skilled migrants. It acted without the standard consultation of the social partners, much to the dismay of the employer association IBEC.[27]

IBEC initially supported the company, arguing that greater flexibility for the Irish labour market and new transnational corporate strategies were desirable. The Irish Congress of Trade Unions was equally adamant about its rejection of management actions in this case, arguing that the outsourcing strategy was indicative of broader trends towards systematic undercutting of wages and exploitation of migrant workers.[28] Over the course of 2005, its irritation grew, culminating in the temporary refusal to negotiate the new sixth social-partnership agreement, following the expiration of the 2003–5 framework 'Sustaining Progress'.

Following intensive negotiations at the Labour Relations Commission and intervention of the National Implementation Body, itself established within the neocorporatist Social Partnership framework, a compromise agreement was eventually found in late 2005. The agreement entailed the continuation of outsourcing as planned, but safeguarded the existing wages and working conditions for Irish crew members. Crucial for acceptance by the union was the concession to pay all employees the Irish statutory minimum wage of €7.65 per hour and €18,615 per annum and thus accept host-country conditions. Though ostensibly an agreement that ended undercutting of wages, the overall conflict resolution is employer-friendly, as it permitted the effective de-unionisation of a formerly state-owned enterprise, significant wage cuts and the outsourcing to a company incorporated abroad.

The overall response strategy is thus business-friendly and can be categorised as liberal and voluntarist, merely entailing the application of minimum wages, but not more exacting standards on companies posting employees to Ireland.

Sweden

When the Swedish town of Växholm invited tenders for a school-renovation project in 2004, it received a highly attractive offer from the Latvian construction company Laval & Partneri, a vehicle established to carry out construction work in Sweden using Latvian employees. Construction commenced in 2004, with 14 employees posted directly from Latvia. A conflict over pay quickly ensued between the sectoral construction union Svenska Byggnadsarbetareförbundet and the company, as no collective wage agreement had been signed and the company paid its workers an hourly wage of SEK 80, thus exceeding standard Latvian wages, but still falling well short of local sectoral hourly wages of SEK 130 to 145. The union justified its blockade of the building site on 2 November 2004 by reference to the 1991 Lex Britannica, according to which non-Swedish collective agreements, such as the Latvian one applicable here, do not have to be recognised in Sweden. The Swedish electricians' union (Svensk Eletrikerförbundet) supported the blockade. The company demonstrated willingness to raise the hourly wage to SEK 105, but refused to be bound by standard wages or sign a Swedish collective wage agreement. Work on the site continued for a few days longer regardless, but eventually came to a halt on 14 December, after the company had exhausted cement supplies from non-unionised suppliers.

Unable to complete a June 2005 deadline, the company withdrew from the site and took legal action against the union in the Swedish labour court (Arbetsdomstolen). For the first time since the posted workers' controversy of the 1990s, the Scandinavian gentleman's agreement, enshrined in the 1991 modification to the Swedish Law on Co-determination, was put to a serious practical test in Sweden. There had been a brief episode in the mid-1990s during which an Italian company in Copenhagen sought to pay its posted workers Italian wages, but eventually succumbed to union pressure and paid Danish wages. The intriguing question was whether the key component of this agreement – the right to impose a blockade to ensure the payment of Swedish wages – was consistent with EU law and whether the hourly wage of SEK 109 was a de facto minimum wage. Also, if a Latvian collective agreement existed, the blockade would have been illegal under existing Swedish legislation (Lex Britannica). The Swedish labour court referred the case to the ECJ.

The ECJ 18 December 2007 Laval decision (C-341/05) ruled that industrial action can not be allowed

> where the negotiations on pay, which that action seeks to require an undertaking established in another Member State to enter into, form part of a national context characterised by a lack of provisions, of any kind, which are sufficiently precise and accessible that they do not render it impossible or excessively difficult in practice for such an undertaking to determine the obligations with which it is required to comply as regards minimum pay.

Industrial action was ruled unlawful as it sought to attain higher than minimum conditions for the posted workers. Unsurprisingly, Swedish business cheered the result, while the union was exasperated.[29] As Sweden does not have statutory minimum wages, as many other countries do, in the absence of any legislative applicable instrument, obvious strategies for outsourcing and undercutting of wages emerge.

Germany

Given that the original German national response strategy to the EU LSP had only ever been limited to the construction sector in the broadest sense (including installation work and building-cleaning services), the possibilities for succesful undercutting of wages through the exploitation of the wage gap with CEE seemed extraordinary. The Schroeder government had responded to considerable popular discontent over EU eastward enlargement by introducing a seven-year ban both on labour mobility and transnational service provision from the eight new Eastern members. A particular Achilles heel was the absence of a national minimum wage. Sectoral wage agreements are drawn up as the result of regional collective bargaining between unions and employer associations. Given the recent trend of businesses leaving employer associations to avoid the legal obligations such agreements entail, certain service sectors, especially private security, gastronomy and private personal services including hairdressing, witness truly minimal sectoral wages. In certain sectors, notably meat-processing, there is no recognised employer association and henceforth no applicable and legally binding sectoral minimum wage. Consequently, from 2004 onwards the posted worker syndrome re-emerged, this time focused primarily on the meat-processing sector. German companies dismissed regular employees and replaced them with more than 15,000 posted workers from Eastern European subcontractors. The sectoral union Nahrung-Genuss-Gaststätten (NGG) claimed 26,000 job losses as a consequence of the deployment of Eastern European subcontractors, especially from Romania.[30] Remunerated at hourly wage levels of €3 to €5 and thus well below standard wage levels, the posting of workers offered the additional advantage of circumventing laws regarding holiday payment, sick payment and contributions to health-insurance and social-insurance schemes.

The sectoral subdivision of the union movement impaired attempts at responding in a timely and robust fashion in the way the Irish and Swedish unions had. It pursued a two-pronged strategy, lobbying both for a statutory minimum wage and the extension of the existing legislative national response strategy to additional sectors. This so-called Posted Workers Act had been amended in 1999 to enable the Ministry for Labour and Social Affairs to declare universally applicable wages and working conditions even in the absence of employer consent. The construction sector union IG BAU successfully lobbied for construction-related trades to be covered, including building cleaning, painting, demolition and roofing, while the metalworking union IG METALL secured coverage of electricians.[31] Somewhat more controversial was the creation of a sectoral wage in postal services, as the main company in the sectoral employer association Deutsche Post is majority government-owned, attracting criticism from the employer association BDA of undue union influence and political manoeuvring to outflank private competitors.[32]

But not all sectoral employer associations agreed to rendering their sectoral minimum wage universally applicable and the umbrella association BDA remained staunchly opposed on ideological grounds to accepting the introduction of a statutory minimum wage in Germany.[33] Between 2007 and 2008, a major political battle between unions and employers ensued, which was represented respectively by the Social Democratic Minister for Labour Olaf Scholz and the Christian Social Minister for Economic Affairs Michael Glos within the Grand Coalition. Both camps used their political access channels to the major two political party blocs to lobby actively in this matter.[34] The Social Democrats championed the issue to accommodate the significant popular discontent over the Red-Green government's cuts in social assistance and labour-market deregulation. Only a few sectoral employer associations agreed to the legally sanctioned universal applicability of sectoral minimum wages, notably in construction and related fields.[35]

Though an initial compromise seemed to appear during the summer of 2007, it took until July 2008 for a legislative response strategy to emerge. This consisted of two components: firstly, the existing national response strategy, the modified 1996 Posted Workers Act, was to be amended to permit sectoral minimum wages to be declared universally applicable if at least 50 per cent of employees in the sector in question are covered by existing wage agreements and both sectoral unions and employers agree to such measures. Interestingly, such universal applicability can be decreed by government fiat, a notable legal instrument for government intervention. Secondly, a modification of the 1952 Act on Minimum Working Conditions was to permit the creation of sectoral minimum wages even in sectors in which employer associations either do not exist or possess very low levels of membership. No agreement could be found on whether or not to permit such sectoral minimum wages for the sector of temporary work agencies, where the sectoral employer association remains fiercely opposed.[36]

In the meantime, the advocacy position of the unions had improved somewhat due to the remarkable ECJ Rüffert ruling, which struck down the obligation imposed on companies tendering for public bids in the *Land* of Lower Saxony to pay standard regional wages (*Tariftreue*). In its very liberal ruling, the court found that 'to impose to the service providers established in another Member State, where the standards of minimal wages are lower, an additional economic load that is likely to prohibit, to obstruct or make less attractive the execution of their services in the Member State of reception [...] is likely to constitute a restriction within the meaning of Article 49 EC'.[37]

This ruling effectively undermined regional laws aimed at impeding wage dumping in the construction sector and thus rendered the need for a national minimum wage more pressing, considering it a legitimate component of the *ordre public* in the way the French minimum wage, SMIC, is.

After long-winded political battles and considerable lobbying activity by both sides, the amended legislative acts present a revamped version of the German national response strategy, enabling the government to create sectoral minimum wages based on the recommendations of a bipartisan expert commission on low wages. This creates fairly powerful legislative tools to introduce sectoral minimum wage regulations in sectors affected by transnational service provision.

The Bolkestein directive

In 1999, the Dutch politician Frits Bolkestein, an adviser to the secretive neo-liberal think tank the Mont Perin Society, became Commissoner of Internal Market and Services. Perhaps inspired by Art. 49 of the Rome Treaty,[38] but certainly by the Lisbon Agenda of promoting economic growth through neo-liberal deregulation, the DG MARKT presented its draft directive on service deregulation on 13 January 2004, drawing on an internal study identifying remaining 'barriers' to services.[39] Very little external consulting of stakeholders had been conducted and the European union umbrella association ETUC had simply been ignored altogether. The directive's remit was extremely broad. Article Art. 2: 4 (1) clarified that 'any self-employed economic activity, as provided for by Art. 50 of the Treaty, consisting of the provision of a service against consideration' was covered, including management consultancy, certification and testing, maintenance, facilities management and security, advertising services, recruitment services, including the services of temporary employment agencies, services provided by commercial agents, legal or tax consultancy, property services, such as those provided by estate agencies, construction services, architectural services, distributive trades, organisation of trade fairs and exhibitions, car-hire, security services, tourist services, including travel agencies and tourist guides, audiovisual services, sports centres and amusement parks, leisure services, and health services and personal domestic services, such as assistance for old people. Excluded from the remit of the directive were non-economic activities and activities performed by the state as part of its social, cultural, educational and judicial functions where there is no element of remuneration. This obviously implies that public services that do involve a small service charge, including, for example, municipal libraries or swimming pools, could be covered. Also not included were financial or transportation services, to the extent that they were covered elsewhere in the treaty.

The section containing the most political dynamite was Art. 16, containing the 'country of origin' principle regarding applicable contract law. In essence, the host country was limited in enforcing its own laws to instances in which a very narrowly defined range of issues involving the *ordre public*, public health and public safety were at stake. Articles 14 (3) and especially 24 of the draft, the latter of which regulated the division of labour in administrative terms betweeen country of origin and host country, outlawed existing practices of obliging posted workers to carry appropriate documents detailing wages and working conditions and the requirement to appoint a national representative. Worse yet, any new administrative requirement introduced by national governments would become subject to approval by the Commission (Art. 15 (6)). Art. 15 further sought to abolish restrictions regarding quantitative, regional or financial restrictions. It is no exaggeration to characterise the original Bolkestein directive as the single most aggressive deliberate act of assault on the structure of European society and economy.

While a number of neo-liberal governments, including usual suspects such as that of the British Prime Minister Tony Blair, rushed to the defence of the draft directive, substantial political controversy ensued. On 22 November 2004, Irishman Charles McCreevy took over DG MARKT from Bolkestein, admitting in early 2005 that this directive did not have a 'snowball's chance in hell of getting through either the Council of Ministers or the European Parliament'.

At the national level, the Bolkestein directive spawned vociferous political debates and conflicts. In France, the response of the employer organisation Medef was somewhat lacklustre. In its 6 April 2005 summary of the draft directive, the employers acknowledged the potential for social dumping and expressed concern over the abolition of documentation requirements for posted workers. During the first half of 2005, a vociferous public debate over the merits of the European Constitution unfolded, during which the Bolkestein directive was often invoked as representative of the neo-liberal fundamentalism informing the European project. The trade unions strongly opposed the directive, expressing their concerns to the government.[40]

In Austria, the union movement was very active in coordinating street demonstrations and political lobbying aimed at blocking the first draft of the directive in general and removing the home-country principle in particular.[41] The employer association generally welcomed a less bureaucratic and more transparent process for transnational service provision, but shared some of the concerns over potential social dumping.[42] The government thus responded by assuming a moderate stance and embracing a compromise solution. During the Austrian EU presidency in early 2006, the much-revised directive, notably no longer containing the country of origin principle, was accepted by national governments across Europe and eventually passed in the Council of Ministers in late July 2006.

In Sweden, the trade unions developed a very clear and active position from early on, insisting on an abolition of the country of origin principle and Swedish standards of wages and working conditions for posted workers.[43] Their lobbying activities at the national level proved quite successful, with the Swedish government assuming a very reserved stance. The employer organisation Svenskt Näringsliv dismissed the social dumping argument as an 'unfounded concern' and strongly supported the directive, yet did not insist on maintaining its more controversial components.[44]

In Ireland, the government assumed a broadly supportive stance, partly informed by employer positions. The liberalisation of services was broadly characterised as potentially beneficial for Irish companies. However, the con-current Irish Ferries case, which attracted so much public attention, demonstrated starkly the potential negative ramifications for wages. The trade unions were very strongly opposed to the directive, perceiving it as a 'Frankenstein directive' that would set into motion a downward spiral in wages and working conditions.[45] The employer association IBEC, by contrast, supported the directive, as it considered 'further reduction of red tape and unnecessary restrictions for companies' as desirable goals and regarded the fears over social dumping to be largely inflated.[46] The Department of Enterprise, Trade and Employment organised a number of consultation exercises with the social partners, receiving the positions of both unions and employers.[47] Despite the strongly expressed reservations about the country of origin principle and the concurrent Irish Ferries industrial action, the overall Irish position was broadly favourable towards the directive, with the government being strongly favourably inclined towards the employer position.

In Germany, the trade unions vehemently opposed the directive and the country of origin principle in particular. The head of DGB, Michael Sommer, referred to the project in a speech during a demonstration in Berlin on 11 February 2006 as 'madness'.[48] The trade union also very strongly lobbied against the end to national enforcement of local labour standards, against the coverage of temporary work agencies in the directive as well as broader exemptions from its remit for public services, especially health and education. The German government proved quite open to these concerns and assumed a deeply sceptical stance. Even the employers were concerned about possible negative ramifications regarding national labour and health standards[49] and accepted that although the general impetus of the directive was desirable, certain 'contradictions' regarding the rights of posted workers seemed to exist and needed to be 'clarified'.[50]

The principle of origin, which attracted pronounced criticism throughout Europe, was directly criticised by the Austrian, German, Swedish and French governments and contributed to the negative results in the 29 May 2005 French referendum on the European Constitution. During the debates in the European Parliament it was this point again that led to the most heated exchanges, with an eventual compromise between the major two groupings consisting of substituting the expression with the term 'freedom to provide services'. The compromise was of high political significance, essentially signalling an end to the original goal of home-country rules. The amended proposal was presented by the Commission on 4 April 2006, containing thousands of minor amendments, notably reinstating the right to conduct national controls over working conditions and wages. The final result is the Directive on the Single Market (2006/EC/123) to be implemented into national law by 28 December 2009.

Implications

LSP proves politically contentious because it is perceived by some as undermining national sovereignty, creating islands of foreign law, promoting wage and social dumping and unfair competition between companies posting workers temporarily to high-wage destinations paying home country wages and those bound by local standards. The nightmarish vision of a downward spiral and a neo-liberal Europe in which shell companies registered in Lithuania post workers to Copenhagen, Stockholm or London was invoked by the unions during the long-winded political battle surrounding the Bolkestein directive.

Employer associations generally welcomed the new services directive, but many expressed concerns over a distorted and unfair competition from low-wage locales and, with the exception of Ireland, henceforth did not attempt to defend the home-country principle originally embedded in the Bolkestein directive. In Ireland, a slightly organisationally superior employer association managed to shape the official position towards the directive.

At the national level, the LSP has also unleashed a number of political conflicts, undermining existing arrangements and national response strategies. The EU liberalising impetus and recent ECJ rulings on LSP therefore undermine national labour-market regulation and politico-economic governance. However, in subsequent attempts at national re-regulation, new equilibria could be created, as in Germany and Ireland. In these instances, organisational characteristics and access to government are crucial variables in accounting for the different policy outcomes. In the Irish case, a business-friendly compromise emerged, which proves face-saving for the unions and avoids the wholesale import of foreign wage levels and working conditions. In Germany, currently planned legislation will permit sectoral minimum wages, nominally requiring the consent of both employers and unions, but permitting an override by the ministry in select instances. As such, it is a true compromise solution, with the political colour of future governments likely affecting any such override. Far from leading to convergence, European-induced liberalisation thus interacts with different national-level institutionalised political economies in Europe. In analysing these interactive effects, such differences create varying outcomes. The effects of a generally liberalising impetus are thus far from uniform on the ground.

Notes and References

1. Colin Crouch and Wolfgang Streeck (eds), *The Political Economy of Modern Capitalism*, London: Sage, 1997; David Stark and Laszlo Bruszt, 'One Way or Multiple Paths? For a Comparative Sociology of East European Capitalism', *American Journal of Sociology*, 106 (94), 2001, 1129–37; Vivien Schmidt, *The Futures of European Capitalism*. Oxford and New York: Oxford University Press, 2002; Wolfgang Streeck and Martin Höpner (eds), *Alle Macht dem Markt? Fallstudien zur Abwicklung der Deutschland AG*, Frankfurt: Campus, 2003; Wolfgang Streeck and Anke Hassel, 'The Crumbling Pillars of Social Partnership', in Herbert Kitschelt and Wolfgang Streeck (eds), *Germany: Beyond the Stable State*, London, Frank Cass, 2004, 101–24;

David Lane, 'Emerging Varieties of Capitalism in Former State Socialist Societies', *Competition and Change*, 9 (3), September 2005, 221–41.

2. Bruno Amable, *The Diversity of Modern Capitalism*, Oxford: Oxford University Press, 2003; Bob Hancké, Martin Rhodes and Mark Thatcher, *Beyond Varieties of Capitalism: Conflict, Contradictions and Complementarities in the European Economy*, Oxford: Oxford University Press, 2007; David Soskice, 'Varieties of Capitalism and Macroeconomic Institutions', in Hancké, Rhodes and Thatcher, ibid.

3. Matthew Watson, 'Ricardian Political Economy and the "Varieties of Capitalism" Approach: Specialization, Trade and Comparative Institutional Advantage', *Comparative European Politics*, 1 (2), 2003, 227–40; Jonas Pontusson, 'Varieties and Commonalities of Capitalism', in David Coates (ed.), *Varieties of Capitalism, Varieties of Approaches*, Basingstoke: Palgrave Macmillan, 2005, 163–88; Colin Hay, 'Two Can Play at that Game … or Can They?', in ibid., 106–21.

4. Susanne Soederberg, Georg Menz and Philip Cerny (eds), *Internalizing Globalization: The Rise of Neo-liberalism and the Decline of National Varieties of Capitalism*, New York and Basingstoke: Palgrave Macmillan, 2005.

5. Georg Menz, *Europeanization and Varieties of Capitalism: National Response Strategies to the Single European Market*, Oxford and New York: Oxford University Press, 2005; Georg Menz, 'Old Bottles and New Wine? The New Dynamics of Industrial Relations', in Kenneth Dyson and Stephan Padgett (eds), *The Politics of Economic Reform in Germany, German Politics*, 14 (2), Special Issue, June 2005.

6. E. Scharpf, 'Negative and Positive Integration in the Political Economy of European Welfare States', in G. Marks, F. Scharpf, P. Schmitter and W. Streeck (eds), *Governance in the European Union*, London: Sage, 1996, 1–14.

7. Georg Menz, 'Auf Wiedersehen, Rhineland Model: The Internalization of Neo-liberalism in Germany', in Susanne Soederberg, Georg Menz and Philip Cerny (eds), *Internalizing Globalization: The Rise of Neo-liberalism and the Decline of National Varieties of Capitalism*, New York and Basingstoke: Palgrave Macmillan, 2005, 33–48.

8. See R. D. Putnam, 'Diplomacy and Domestic Politics: The Logic of Two-level Games', *International Organization*, 42 (3), 1988, 427–60.

9. Helen V. Milner, *Interests, Institutions and Information: Domestic Politics and International Relations*, Princeton: Princeton University Press, 1997; Orfeos Fioretos, 'The Domestic Sources of Multilateral Preferences: Varieties of Capitalism in the European Community', in Peter Hall and David Soskice (eds), *Varieties of Capitalism: The Institutional Foundations of Comparative Advantage*, Oxford and New York: Oxford University Press, 2001, 213–46.

10. S. Steinmo, K. Thelen and F. Longstreth, *Structuring Politics: Historical Institutionalism in Comparative Analysis*, Cambridge: Cambridge University Press, 1992; Wolfgang Streeck and Kathleen Thelen (eds), *Beyond Continuity: Institutional Change in Advanced Political Economies*, Oxford: Oxford University Press, 2005.

11. Christoph Knill and Dirk Lehmkuhl, 'How Europe Matters: Different Mechanisms of Europeanization', *European Integration Papers*, 3 (7), 1999, at: eiop.or.at/eiop/texte/1999-007a.htm; Helen Wallace, 'Europeanisation and Globalisation', *New Political Economy*, 5 (3), 2000, 369–82; Claudio Radaelli, 'The Europeanization of Public Policy', in Kenneth Featherstone and Claudio Radaelli (eds), *The Politics of Europeanization*, Oxford and New York: Oxford University Press, 2003, 27–56; Paolo Graziano and Maarten Vink (eds), *Europeanization: New Research Agendas*, Basingstoke: Palgrave Macmillan, 2007.

12. Nikolaidis Kalypso and Susanne Schmidt, 'Mutual Recognition "On Trial": The Long Road to Services Liberalization', *Journal of European Public Policy*, 14 (5), 2007, 717–34.

13. B. Guy Peters, *Comparative Politics: Theory and Methods*, Basingstoke: Macmillan, 1998.

14. Peter Hall, *Governing the Economy: The Politics of State Intervention in Britain and France*, Cambridge: Polity Press, 1986; Bob Hancké, *Large Firms and Institutional Change: Industrial Renewal and Economic Restructuring in France*, Oxford and New York: Oxford University Press, 2002; Pepper Culpepper, 'Employers' Associations, Public Policy and the Politics of Decentralized Coordination in Germany and France', in Peter Hall and David Soskice (eds), *Varieties of Capitalism: The Institutional Foundations of Comparative Advantage*, Oxford, Oxford University Press, 2002, 275–306; Pepper Culpepper, 'Capitalism, Coordination and Economic Change: The French Political Economy since 1985', in Pepper Culpepper, Peter Hall and Bruno Palier (eds), *The Politics that Markets Make*, Basingstoke: Palgrave Macmillan, 2006, 29–49; Cornelia Woll, 'National Business Associations under Stress: Lessons from the French Case', *West European Politics*, 29 (3), 2006, 489–512.

15. Bernhard Ebbinghaus and Jelle Visser, *Trade Unions in Western Europe since 1945*, Basingstoke: Palgrave Macmillan, 2002; Franz Traxler, Sabine Blaschke and Bernhard Kittel, *National Labour Relations in Internationalized Markets: A Comparative Study of Institutions, Change and Performance*, Oxford: Oxford University Press, 2001.

16. Stephen Silvia, 'Every Which Way But Loose: German Industrial Relations since 1980', in Andrew Martin and George Ross (eds), *The Brave New World of European Labor*, New York and Oxford: Berghahn Books, 1999, 75–124; Anke Hassel, 'The Erosion of the German System of Industrial Relations', *British Journal of Industrial Relations* 37 (3), 1999, 484–505; Anke Hassel, 'The Curse of Institutional Security: The Erosion of German Trade Unionism', *Industrielle Beziehungen*, 14 (2), 2007, 176–91.

17. Kathleen Thelen, 'Varieties of Labor Politics in the Developed Democracies', in Peter Hall and David Soskice (eds), *Varieties of Capitalism: The Institutional Foundations of Comparative Advantage*, Oxford, Oxford University Press, 2001, 71–103.

18. Daniel Kinderman, 'Pressure from Without, Subversion from Within: The Two-Pronged German Employer Offensive', *Comparative European Politics*, 3, 2001, 432–63.

19. Niamh Hardiman, 'Economic Governance and Political Innovation in Ireland', *West European Politics*, 25 (4), October 2002, 1–24.

20. Peter Swenson, 'Bringing Capital Back In, or Social Democracy Reconsidered: Employer Power, Cross-Class Alliances, and Centralization of Industrial Relations in Denmark and Sweden', *World Politics* (43) 4, 1991, 513–44; Peter Swenson and Jonas Pontusson, 'The Swedish Employer Offensive Against Centralized Wage Bargaining', in Torben Iverson, Jonas Pontuson and David Soskice (eds), *Unions, Employers, and Central Banks: Macroeconomic Coordination and Institutional Change in Social Market Economies*, Cambridge and New York: Cambridge University Press, 2000, 77–107.

21. Adrienne Héritier, 'Market Integration and Social Cohesion: The Politics of Public Services in European Regulation', *Journal of European Public Policy*, 8 (5), 2001, 825–52.

22. Menz, 'Auf Wiedersehen, Rhineland Model', op. cit.

23. Commission of the European Communities, *Directive of the European Parliament and of the Council on Services in the Internal Market*, COM (2004) 2 final/3.
24. *Irish Independent*, 10 December 2005.
25. SIPTU, 13 December 2004, at: www.siptu.ie/PressRoom/NewsReleases/2004/Name,1977,en.html
26. SIPTU, 8 December 2004, at: www.siptu.ie/PressRoom/NewsReleases/2004/Name,1981,en.html
27. IBEC, 2004, at: www.ibec.ie
28. ICTU, 2006, at: www.ictu.ie/html/news/2006%20talks/OPENING%20STATEMENT%20TO%20PARTNERSHIP%20NEGOTIATIONS.pdf
29. Svenskt Naerignsliv, 2007, at: www.svensktnaringsliv.se/english/article41232.ece; Byggnads, 2008, at: www.byggnads.se//byggnads/63815.cs
30. Lars Czommer and Georg Worthmann, *Von der Baustelle auf den Schlachthof: Zur Übertragbarkeit des Arbeitnehmer-Enstsendegesetzes auf die deutsche Fleischbranche*, IAT Report 2005/03, Duisburg: Institut für Arbeit und Technik; *Financial Times Deutschland*, 24 May 2007.
31. EIRO, 2007, at: www.eurofound.europa.eu/eiro/2007/10/articles/de07110019i.htm)
32. 'Arbeitgeberpräsident Hundt: Fall Post belegt, dass gesetzliche Branchenlöhne ein gefährlicher Irrweg sind!', Press Release 100/2007, Berlin: BDA, 30 November 2007.
33. 'Vorrang für Tarifautonomie'; interview with BDA President Dieter Hundt on radio station Deutschlandfunk on 17 July 2008, at: www.dradio.de/dlf/sendungen/interview_dlf/817854; 'Tarifautonomie statt Mindestlohn – 13 gute Gründe gegen einen gesetzlichen Mindestlohn', Berlin: BDA, 2008.
34. For the respective positions, see the two websites, established by the union and the employer association respectively: www.mindestlohn.de and www.mindestlohn-macht-arbeitslos.de
35. In an interview with the author, a representative of the employer association mentioned concerns over unfair wage competition, jeopardising a level playing field (interview Hauptverband der Deutschen Bauindustrie, Berlin, July 2008).
36. Personal communication to the author, 2 July 2008; see also *Financial Times Deutschland*, 16 July 2008; see also 'Beschluss: Präsidium der BDA: Stellunghnahme zu den Referentenentwürfen zum Arbeitnehmer-Entsendegesetz und zum Mindestarbeitesbedingungengesetz', Berlin: BDA, 28 January 2008.
37. In the original: 'imposer aux prestataires de services établis dans un autre État membre, où les taux de salaire minimal sont inférieurs, une charge économique supplémentaire qui est susceptible de prohiber, de gêner ou de rendre moins attrayante l'exécution de leurs prestations dans l'État membre d'accueil [...] est susceptible de constituer une restriction au sens de l'article 49 CE.'
38. 'Within the framework of the provisions set out below, restrictions on freedom to provide services within the Community shall be prohibited in respect of nationals of Member States who are established in a State of the Community other than that of the person for whom the services are intended.'
39. In a 2003 speech, Bolkestein declared: 'The mistake that is often made is to think that after ten years the Internal Market is completed. This is to misunderstand the Internal Market. [...] It is a continuous process that will require constant attention.'

In its consultative communication, the new Prodi Commission declared in 1999 that: 'Less progress has been made in the services' sector. The Community's objective must now be to eradicate any remaining obstacles to cross-border trade and to prevent the emergence of new barriers. Concrete work is now underway to address the problems identified in business surveys. These include: problems with the application of the mutual recognition principle; the additional costs incurred by business in conforming with national testing and approval procedure; inadequate access to national procurement markets; misuse of national rules protecting the "public good" in order to restrict unfairly the cross-border provision of services. Many of these weaknesses were identified in the Single Market Action Plan as needing further attention.'

The draft directive was European Commission 2004: 'Proposal for a Directive of the European Parliament and of the Council on Services in the Internal Market', 25 February, COM (2004) 2 final, 2.

40. CGT, 'Coup d'arrêt à la directive Bolkestein: un premier succès à mettre à l'actif de la mobilisation sociale', Paris: CGT, 28 July 2008.

41. ÖGB, 'Dienstleistungsrichtlinie: ÖGB weiter gegen Herkunftslandprinzip', 23 November 2005, at: www.oegb.at/servlet/ContentServer?pagename=OEGBZ/Page/OEGBZ_Index&n=OEGBZ_0.a&cid=1132731857624; ÖGB, 'Dienstleistungsrichtlinie', 14 November 2006, at: www.oegb.at/servlet/ContentServer?pagename=OEGBZ/Page/OEGBZ_Index&n=OEGBZ_Suche.a&cid=1163427807537

42. Wirtschaftskammer Österreich, 'Die Dienstlesitungsrichtlinie', Vienna: WKÖ, July 2006.

43. A summary of the LO position can be ascertained from the 2 September 2004 letter to Bolkestein himself.

44. See Svenskt Naringsliv, 'Europe Needs Modern, Simple Rules for Services Market', 22 October 2004, at: www.svensktnaringsliv.se/material/debattartikel/article3532.ece

45. See, for example, SIPTU, 'The Frankenstein Directive', 2006, at: www.siptu.ie/CampaignsandCurrentIssues/EUServicesDirective

46. See, for example, IBEC, 'Implementation Now the Issue for Services Directive', 2006, at: www.ibec.ie/sectors/ibb/ibbdoclib3.nsf/wvEAIICCC/B1A95CC81BA8A9728025723D003FA747?OpenDocument

47. [Irish] Department of Enterprise, Trade and Employment, 'Directive on Services in the Internal Market', 2006, at: www.entemp.ie/trade/marketaccess/singlemarket/servicesdirective.htm

48. Available at www.dgb.de

49. See, for example, 'Arbeitgeberpräsident Hundt: Europäischer Rat muss den Weg für eine Dienstleistungsrichtlinie mit klaren Regelungen ebnen', Press Release 20/2006, Berlin: BDA, 23 March 2006.

50. This was the original BDA position, as is, for example, documented in its president's pronouncements: 'Arbeitgeberpräsident Dr Dieter Hundt: Vorrang für Wachstum und Beschäftigung in Europa – Binnenmarkt für Dienstleistungen schnell vollenden', Press Release 76/2004, Berlin: BDA, 8 December 2004.

9

The Primacy of Domestic Politics: Neo-liberal Restructuring, the EU's Crisis of Governability and Social Imperialism

Otto Holman

It has become rather a matter of commonsense to depict the postwar process of European integration as fundamentally elite-driven. In a 1982 article, Martin Slater found that the member states' citizens were generally in support of integration while simultaneously showing little interest in, or knowledge of, the European Community. In the absence of popular involvement, a coalition of national elites and a 'pan-Europeanist political elite' had free reign to form the Communities in the course of the 1950s. In the 1960s and 1970s this coalition fell apart, mainly as a result of the resurgence of national rivalries.[1] Writing in 1982, Slater could not foresee the remarkable relaunch of European integration from the mid-1980s onwards. With hindsight we may conclude that the two decades following the publication of his article, that is, the period 1983–2003, witnessed a comfortable consensus among national and European elites again, this time centred around the complete unification of markets and monetary policies. And again, one might add, without the mass public having any idea of its consequences. This time, however, things turned out differently.

Recent events have profoundly disturbed national and European elites and have caused the elite-driven process of European integration to grind to a halt. The French and Dutch referenda in May and June 2005 were the start of a prolonged constitutional crisis. One year later, at the European Council summit of 16–17 June 2006, the European leaders of government (and the French head of state) were unable to reach an agreement other than to extend the period of reflection until 2008. Meanwhile, in the course of 2007, the once European Constitution – already rephrased as Constitutional Treaty – turned into a Reform Treaty, then usually referred to as the Lisbon Treaty. Most governments, notably in France, Great Britain and the Netherlands, defended the new Reform Treaty as being essentially different from the Constitutional

Treaty, in the process effectively bypassing popular scrutiny. Oppositional forces in these countries were almost unanimous in evaluating the changes as mere window dressing, as basically symbolic in nature. In June 2008 the Irish people voted against the Lisbon Treaty, further postponing a solution to the EU's crisis of governability. In finding an explanation for these recent 'no' votes it is not enough to refer to the reasons given by Irish respondents in a recent flash Eurobarometer. A lack of understanding or knowledge of the issues at stake came up as the main reason for voting against the Treaty (or for not voting at all).[2] But this in itself can not explain the recent upsurge in Euroscepticism – here defined in its soft variant as the 'contingent or qualified opposition [...] to the process of European integration'[3] – among the constituencies of both old and new EU member states. A lack of knowledge is no longer the mirror-image of popular indifference, and it is this last phenomenon – manifested in contingent or qualified opposition – that needs to be explained.

Two main reasons for the emergence and subsequent rise of Euroscepticism stand out in the literature.[4] First, the post-Maastricht acceleration in polity-building, together with the unprecedented widening of the EU from 12 to 27 member states, strengthened rival political elites which opposed certain characteristics or consequences of European integration without being opposed to membership per se. the future membership of Turkey played an important role in the 'no' campaign in the Netherlands and France, whereas the perceived loss of identity and sovereignty inspired many Irish 'no' voters. In both cases, Euroscepticism was cued by these rival political elites. Second, Euroscepticism is correlated with economic downturn per se and/or to a negative balance between (perceived) costs and benefits of European integration. In this explanation, European integration is, first and foremost, evaluated on the basis of its social and economic effects.

In this chapter, I will argue that the extended relaunch of European integration, that is from the decision to complete the Single Market in the mid-1980s to the establishment of Economic and Monetary Union (EMU) in the period 1998–2002, was an intended strategy to change the postwar European landscape of welfare-state structures and corporatist interest mediation. Concomitant to this strategy was the introduction of new modes of governance and regulation at the transnational level which effectively bypassed democratic accountability at the national level. It will be argued that a highly influential and exclusivist branch of organised business, the European Round Table of Industrialists, together with the representative par excellence of a pan-Europeanist political elite, the European Commission, can be held responsible for initiating the process of neo-liberal restructuring through Europeanisation, and for restoring the active and effective role of big business in the formation of public policy. The outcome of this strategy, a multilevel governance system based on asymmetrical regulation, is at the very heart of the upsurge of Euroscepticism. In a final section it will be argued that the present crisis of governability, of which the 'no' votes in recent referenda are just surface symptoms, can no longer be confronted by oversimplified soundbites such as 'competitiveness' or 'flexibility'. In this context we have to understand recent attempts by the European Commission to develop a more comprehensive approach in order to restore momentum in the process of European integration, among other things by focusing on the EU's global role as soft power.

The primacy of domestic politics: class and agency

In a way, this recent development in EU strategy reflects a burgeoning literature on empire in general, and on European empire or Europe as soft power (or related concepts) in particular. Much talk about American hegemony or, indeed, empire goes hand in hand with (or is gradually replaced by, one might add) a growing body of literature assuming American decline and – following a rigid zero-sum logic – speculating about potential successors. If American power has been weakened under President George W. Bush, what then will fill its space, Mark Leonard asks himself.[5] He and other exponents of the 'American demise, European rise' thesis proclaim a Europe-led 21st century in which the European Dream – with its emphasis on 'quality of life, sustainability, and peace and harmony' – will gradually replace the exhausted American one.[6]

Such optimistic assessments of Europe's role in the 21st century are evidently not in line with the picture of a crisis-ridden European Union described above. This points at a more general problem: many of the recent studies dealing with the EU's would-be superpower role in global affairs fail to theorise foreign actorness on the basis of its internal structures and contradictions. In a similar way, most of the literature on European governance pays no attention whatsoever to its consequences for the EU's foreign relations. Mark Pollack rightly points out that early strands of European integration theory were dominated by international relations (IR) scholars who focused in practice only on the European case, that is on the internal dynamics of European integration. With the extended relaunch of European integration, IR scholars have, paradoxically, begun to analyse the European case with the help of more general (and generally applicable) theoretical frameworks. Pollack distinguishes two broad approaches: a dominant, rationalist one and a (less developed) constructivist one. The rationalist research programme (which stems from an emerging consensus between realist, idealist and institutionalist approaches) 'assumes fixed preferences and rational behaviour among all actors in the EU (including individuals as well as member governments and supranational organizations) and examines the ways in which member governments adopt institutions which subsequently constrain and channel their behaviour'.[7] I am not sure whether Andrew Moravcsik's liberal intergovernmentalism (LI) can be fully subsumed under the second part of this rationalist research programme, but he is certainly one of the very few 'rationalists' who try to distil some foreign policy conclusions from general integration theory. Ironically, this brings him to a rather pessimistic assessment of the possibility of strengthening the EU's foreign actorness beyond its international economic and diplomatic relations (and beyond American hegemony):

> Little has come of schemes for a powerful European military, however – and little will. A common European force with the capacity to wage high-intensity, low-casualty war around the globe remains a pipe dream. Whatever they may tell pollsters, European publics will not tolerate the massive increases in military spending required to come anywhere near the American level, and more efficient use of current European resources, although desirable, will achieve only modest gains.[8]

There is only one military superpower, the United States, and that leaves Europe no other role than to use its instruments such as aid, trade, peace-keeping and international monitoring in the shadow of America's military might. That is why Moravcsik distinguishes between a bipolar world in terms of soft power and a unipolar world in terms of hard power, the former clearly being subordinated to the latter. It is not the intention here to elaborate on Moravcsik's thoughts about the desirability of a new transatlantic bargain along these lines. The point I want to make here is that his assessment of the EU's foreign actorness is an extrapolation of his European integration theory.

Echoing some of the propositions of neo-realism and using the insights of related, pluralist theories of complex interdependence, Moravcsik's LI emphasises the primacy of inter-state bargaining and the convergence of the policy preferences of major member states toward the lowest common denominator. European institutions have no other role to play than to guarantee a system of credible commitments at the European level. Watchdog functions are bottom-up delegated to the European Commission and the European Court of Justice. This implies that these institutions have no competences whatsoever to initiate new policy initiatives, for instance in the domains of foreign and security policies. These initiatives can only come from member governments; these governments in turn act on the basis of fixed, economic interests and not geopolitical ones. It is therefore highly unlikely that these governments, representing sovereign member states, will reach out for more than mere coordination in the field of high politics.[9]

This state-centric approach of LI may be questioned on several grounds. States are not ontologically primitive, as liberal intergovernmentalists wanted to have it. On the other hand, however, it is most unlikely that the present Union will turn into some kind of superstate as neofunctionalists and supra-nationalists sometimes suggested. The mainstream middle-course solution is represented by the multi-level governance (MLG) literature. MLG focuses on how the formal structures of European governance are functioning, without raising the questions of why this multilevel system has emerged and what kind of EU it seeks to promote. In short, MLG does not address issues like the social and political purpose of this hybrid polity. Here I attempt to problematise both the more general shift from government to governance and the more EU-specific emergence of multilevel governance as concomitant to the crisis of the postwar Fordist-Keynesian growth model and the subsequent shift towards neo-liberal restructuring. The current situation (which many new institutionalists tend to look at as the mature stage of the European polity at which European integration should be no longer seen as a dependent variable) can be best characterised as transnational governance without supranational government.[10] It is my contention that this new mode of transnational integration has come into existence by conscious design. Already in the mid-1970s, intellectuals such as Samuel Huntington were addressing the issue of the ungovernability of Western democracies due to the equation of democracy with equality, on the one hand, and the uncontrolled rise of welfare expenditure, on the other. Both threatened to destabilise 'bourgeois democracy' from within.[11] The extended relaunch of European integration, from Single Market to EMU, together with unfolding patterns of transnational governance and regulation, were instrumental in restoring bourgeois democracy from without. Business and governments were represented by a unique public-private partnership at the European level, while labour and national parliaments were successfully bypassed. The point to be made here is that MLG, in focusing on polycentric decision-making structures without taking notice of social purpose, is unable to fully grasp the contradictions this process generates. The intended consequences of the extended relaunch have resulted in a number of unintended consequences, like reform fatigue and Euroscepticism, which in turn threaten to reverse the intended ones. Moreover, political elites in Europe seem to be more aware than MLG scholars that the current political stalemate can only result in 'spill-back' and disintegration unless a new *raison d'être* for the EU can be found. Such a new *raison d'être* may very well boil down to a flight forward, reasserting the EU's role as a global power.

In this chapter I propose to reach beyond the rigid state-centrism of LI as well as the institutionalism of MLG, by premising both domestic social forces and supranational political entrepreneurs. I take a position similar to what David Harvey calls historical-geographical materialism or what Kees van der Pijl refers to as the interrelationship of modes of production and modes of foreign relations, the latter combining 'definite patterns of occupying space, protecting it, and organising exchange'.[12] The ontological position taken in this chapter is that the unequal distribution of power and welfare in time and space is independent of cultures and common within, across and between communities of all sorts (be it tribes, nations, civilisations or, indeed, religions). As such, this real world of unequally distributed power and welfare is the most important 'dependent' variable. Following this language, integration is one of the most important 'independent' variables: this chapter tries to explain how European integration has altered existing power relations and patterns of socio-economic inequality. At the same time, however, we have to unpack 'integration' as well and try to answer why the extended relaunch of European integration followed the course and direction it actually did. The notions of class structure, class formation and class agency will be used to give a deeper meaning to the process of European integration. Without identifying its internal social structure and the class strategies resulting from it, integration will remain an empty abstraction.

Erik Olin Wright distinguishes two conditions for a genuine class society: 1) ownership and control of the economically relevant assets or income-generating productive resources (such as land, capital [including shares, stock options, etc.], skills, information, labour power) by a small minority in society; and 2) the consequences of this unequal distribution of income-generating assets for the material wellbeing of the people. Or to put it the other way round: 'the more egalitarian the distribution of assets and the less a person's material wellbeing depends upon their relationship to those assets, the lower the classness of a society'.[13]

We have to keep in mind, first, that the income-generating nature of capital assets is anchored in the labour process. Or better, that the level of income inequality (whether or not the result of direct ownership or control of capital assets) is related to the level of exploitation of labour power and the price it fetches in the market, like other commodities. In this sense, it can be argued that the postwar period of de-commodification came to an end in the course of the 1970s and has turned into a period of accelerated commodification of labour since the early 1980s.[14] This indeed is the real meaning and objective of the flexibilisation of labour markets in Europe, one of the centrepieces of neo-liberal restructuring. Second, we have to realise that both the ownership and control of economically relevant assets, and their income-generating nature, are increasingly transnational phenomena. That is, transnational class formation implies the reproduction and transformation of class structures at the transnational level. In Europe, the dominant trend of transnational production and finance and the ever-closer integration of capital markets are obvious vehicles of this transnationalisation of class structures.

If we subsequently move from class structure to class agency, we have to emphasise that it is not agency of class but agency reproducing or transforming class structures that is at stake. Class is not an actor. But class formation (both nationally and transnationally) does not take place spontaneously (by accident) or unhindered either. As Stephen Gill argues, 'it needs leadership and action based on a highly developed political consciousness' to reproduce or transform class structures.[15] This can be best illustrated by briefly looking at the neo-liberal turn of the 1970s and 1980s. David Harvey has convincingly shown that the rise to hegemony of neo-liberal theory and practice was part of an intentional and conscious strategy to restore what he calls class power (without properly defining class, however). In our language, it was about restoring the power of capital ownership and about increasing income inequality, in short, about tackling the two main components of the crisis of governability mentioned above. In the United States this was orchestrated by leading members of the Reagan administration in cooperation with chief executive officers (CEOs) united at the American Business Roundtable.[16] In (continental) Europe, the turn to neo-liberalism was much more difficult to realise, particularly because of the much stronger position of trade unions in defending welfare-state structures. As a result, neo-liberal reforms were introduced much later than in the US, and quite unevenly among the member states, the United Kingdom being the first mover. Most importantly, however, in most countries neo-liberal restructuring took the form of a revolution from above, described in the jargon of mainstream integration literature as 'Europeanisation'. Here it took 'leadership and action based on highly developed political consciousness' in a much more subtle and indirect way, using the extended relaunch of European integration as the main vehicle. To this we turn now.

The viceroys of Europe and the European Risorgimento

Like so many novels written in the second half of the 19th century, Federico de Roberto's magnum opus *I Viceré* (The Viceroys) is about social and political change, about the erosion of traditional, feudal patterns of domination and the rise of capitalist class structures, about the so-called 'social question' and the rise of mass movements, about the first chaotic experiments with democracy and, indeed, about modern state formation. The novel narrates the story of the Uzeda family and the princes of Francalanza, descendants of the viceroys who reigned over Sicily on behalf of the Spanish King from the beginnings of the 16th century. It is a story about greed, envy, deception, but at a higher level it is about Italian unification and the rise of a bourgeois mode of domination. At first sight, the struggle between the members of the Uzeda family is about inheritance, but at a deeper level it is about the best way to prevent 'our kind of people' from degenerating. It turns out that some members manage to successfully adjust to the new circumstances and to increase their welfare and power. In the end, the famous last words of Tancredi Falconieri, protagonist of that other famous novel dealing with 19th-century Italy, Giuseppe Tomasi di Lampedusa's *Il Gattopardo* (The Leopard), come true: 'for everything to remain the same, everything has to change.'

Having been in power for many centuries, and having appropriated large sums from their capital assets on the island, the viceroys were now forced to participate in the Italian Risorgimento in order to defend their privileged position. With all the pitfalls (and obvious differences) of such historical metaphors in mind, the strategy of the most enlightened elements of the

Uzeda family is comparable to the role played by a European business aristocracy more than a century later. A group of large European companies,
primarily but not exclusively from the so-called Fordist industries, organised
in the ERT, took the initiative to relaunch the idea of a European Risorgimento. Threatened by competition abroad and social unrest at home, they
saw the completion of the Single Market and the move to a single currency as
the perfect solution to both problems. And in very much the same way as the
viceroys started to align themselves with the new political forces striving for
Italian unification, the European business aristocracy was actively involved
in setting up new, informal and formal, structures (or networks) at the European level where CEOs of European capitalist enterprises, politicians and high
representatives of the European cadres could meet each other. It was particularly the agenda-setting and policy-planning capacity of these networks
that was of importance here. And this was as much about decision-making
as it was about non-decision-making: keeping specific policy areas or topics
off the European agenda was as important as maintaining the momentum
of neo-liberal restructuring and disembedding free-market capitalism (under
the banner of competitiveness).

The public-private partnership between the European Commission and the
ERT must be singled out as most active and decisive element, particularly
during the two decades between 1983 and 2003. From the perspective of
European business, the Commission was of particular importance because
of its role as executive (and 'guardian of the Treaties') and co-legislature
at the European level. The Commission, on the other hand, operated in
close co-operation with organised business to bolster its right of initiative.
The ERT was seen as a privileged agenda-setting and policy-planning group,
privileged in its access to member-state governments and in its capacity to
influence the European agenda. The relationship between the two could best
be described as a 'symmetrically interdependent' one: the Commission and
the ERT needed each other in the realisation of their respective goals. Already
in the early years of its existence, a member of the Delors cabinet referred to
the ERT in the following way: 'We see this group as a very useful bunch of
people. These men are very powerful and very dynamic. They seed us with
ideas. And when necessary, they can ring up their own prime ministers and
make their case.'[17] In other words, the Commission could use the members of
the ERT in its attempt to strengthen its position *vis-à-vis* the member states,
both in its policy-initiating and innovating capacity.

It has now been convincingly documented, though not generally acknowledged in mainstream literature, that the ERT played an important role in
the relaunch of European integration in the 1980s, both with respect to the
completion of the internal market and the development towards EMU.[18]
After Maastricht, the agenda-setting and policy-planning activities of the
ERT shifted from a more comprehensive approach (including all the major
issues of European integration) to an approach focused on the much more

limited competitiveness discourse. Most of the reports of the ERT published after 1991 had European competitiveness as a central theme, with a strong emphasis on deregulation and labour-market flexibilisation. In the words of the former Secretary General of the ERT, Keith Richardson, 'the competitiveness of European business must be strengthened by making it possible to build an integrated free-market economic system, with a maximum of flexibility and a minimum of regulation'; and more explicitly,

> ... jobs cannot be created by laws or by writing some new clause or chapter into the Treaty of Maastricht. What is urgently needed is the deregulation of labour markets and better education and training. New jobs will then follow from economic growth and the creation of wealth by business.[19]

In 1995, then, the relationship between the European Commission and the ERT was institutionalised with the creation of the Competitiveness Advisory Group (CAG). As a co-initiative of the then German Commissioner for industry, Martin Bangemann, and the ERT, the CAG would 'act as a watchdog, by subjecting policy proposals and new regulations to the test of international competitiveness'.[20]

In referring to MLG, it was argued that few representatives of this literature talk about the social purpose of this hybrid polity. Did the EU as we know it today come about by accident or was it intentionally designed to impose neo-liberal restructuring on reluctant societies? In the next section we will look at the extended relaunch (and competitiveness and labour-market flexibilisation as its main offsprings) from the perspective of its consequences. By introducing the notion of asymmetrical regulation we can better understand the social purpose behind MLG.

The extended relaunch of European integration and asymmetrical regulation

The concept of asymmetrical regulation intends to grasp a phenomenon that mainstream multilevel governance literature fails to take into account, that is, the fact that some policy areas are moved to the supranational arena while other policy areas are strictly reserved to national authorities claiming national sovereignty. Concretely, asymmetrical regulation not only refers to the discrepancy between European economic and monetary free-market regulation on the one hand, and the lack of social regulation (or harmonisation) at the European level on the other, but – more importantly – to the adverse impact of economic and monetary integration at the European level on social cohesion at the national level. In fact, economic and monetary regulation at the supranational level and social deregulation at the national level are two sides of the same coin.[21] The key to this is Economic and

Monetary Union. What can national governments do to correct macro-economic imbalances? They no longer can use the mechanism of interest rate adjustment to counteract slackening growth. Indeed, the recent interest rate policy of the European Central Bank clearly shows the primacy of Eurozone price stability over national concerns with economic growth. The same goes for government spending to steer demand. Due to the Stability and Growth Pact this neo-Keynesian strategy is severely limited. Needless to say, competitive devaluations through the Exchange Rate Mechanism are history. Austerity measures, regime competition and microeconomic supply-side structural adjustment are the only policy measures left to national governments to correct macroeconomic imbalances. Part and parcel of the underlying shift from demand-side corporatism to supply-side corporatism is the full-blown labour-market flexibilisation programme, which in turn is an integral part of the attempt to make Europe the most competitive economy in the world by the year 2010 (the so-called Lisbon strategy).

The correlation between economic and monetary regulation at the European, supranational level and social regulation at the national level is not an unintended consequence of previous decisions to further integrate the different European economies. In a similar way as European monetary integration has been used by Italian modernising forces to break up the post-war Italian social and political system (starting with Italy's membership of the European Monetary System),[22] European monetary integration has been the conscious, intended strategy of transnational business to modernise the 'rigid' social systems at the national level. Elsewhere I have argued that governance and government are inextricably bound up, though not necessarily at the same level of decision-making. The novel, multilevel polity that emerged in the context of the so-called extended relaunch of European integration in the 1980s and early 1990s can be best described as transnational governance without supranational government. The privileged partnership between the European Commission and the European Round Table of Industrialists shows that transnational informal practices of governance have (had) an impact on formal practices at the national level. This is at the heart of what is referred to as asymmetrical regulation: supranational regulation in the context of the Single Market and Economic and Monetary Union is limiting the national capacity to act, notably in the field of social regulation. While keeping up the illusion of self-determination, it is national government that is in charge of reforming labour markets.[23] This is the real meaning of the fashionable concept of Europeanisation, that is, the process by which domestic policy areas become increasingly subject to European policy-making. And this is the very reason why governments handed over sovereignty to supranational institutions such as the European Central Bank: to compel compliance by future domestic governments and, more importantly, by domestic social forces.

The political mechanism underlying this system of asymmetrical regulation comes close to what Stephen Gill calls 'new constitutionalism': the separation of 'economic policies from broad political accountability in order to make governments more responsive to the discipline of market forces, and correspondingly less responsive to popular-democratic forces and processes'.[24] New constitutionalism within the European Union can not only be illustrated by, for instance, the interest-rate policy of the ECB, but is also very much related to the completion of the single market in the 1980s and early 1990s. One particularly strong example is the principle of mutual recognition that was originally formulated by the European Court of Justice (ECJ) in the Cassis de Dijon case (1979) but introduced as a general principle to complete the internal market. According to this principle – which was intended to abolish technical barriers (such as national regulations related to health, safety and environmental standards, and to consumer protection) – products that are lawfully manufactured in one country must be admitted into other member states, irrespective of whether they comply with existing legislation in that member state or not. In more general terms, the political significance of this judgement of the ECJ boils down to the primacy of European law over national parliaments, of the Community's *acquis communautaire* over national legislators. In the words of Fritz Scharpf: 'By judicial fiat [...] the freedom to sell and consume had achieved constitutional protection against the political judgement of democratically legitimised legislatures.'[25] The ECJ is first and foremost the European institution that guarantees a fair economic playing field or – in less neutral terms – ensures the free movement of market forces in a deregulated single market. It plays a central role in compelling compliance by member-state governments with respect to the Community's *acquis communautaire* (which in turn is mainly concerned with the completion of the single market, and its institutional underpinnings).

At this point, the 'normative' difference between efficient and redistributive regulatory policies, as introduced by Simon Hix,[26] comes to mind. Long-term collective interests, such as price stability, are best guaranteed if governments are made less responsive to popular-democratic forces and processes. This is one of the reasons why national sovereignty with respect to monetary policy was transferred to the politically independent European Central Bank. The same can not be said, however, for activities in the field of social policy. Guaranteeing a certain degree of social protection, for instance, can no longer be regarded as desirable to society as a whole. This is why these highly politicised policy areas 'need to made through the normal channels of majoritarian parliamentary and electoral policies'. Hence redistributive regulatory policies can only be implemented in the EU through soft mechanisms such as the Open Method of Coordination 'in which elected politicians are given ultimate freedom to change, block or renege on commitments'.[27] The problem is, however, that 'efficient' (re)regulation at the European level in terms of single-market and monetary integration is severely limiting the national capacity to act in social terms. The adverse impact of economic and monetary regulation at the European level on social protection at the national level is not taken into account in Hix's normative distinction. The same goes for the impact of the disciplinary competitiveness discourse on elected politicians and trade union leaders alike. Industrial relations, after all one of the classical cases of private governance and self-regulation at the national level, are no longer determined independently, but embedded in less transparent and accountable structures of transnational public-private governance.

From competitiveness to security: the double meaning of Europe as empire

The shift from redistributive to efficient regulatory policies, concomitant with the extended relaunch of European integration, points exactly to the very essence of the turn to neo-liberalism: restoring the power of capital ownership and increasing income inequality, in short, tackling the two main components of the crisis of governability (see above). As to the latter, it has been convincingly documented that income inequality has substantially increased in the majority of OECD countries since 1979, partly because of excessive pay levels at the top (including non-wage financial rewards), partly because of flexible wage levels and stagnant benefits at the bottom, and partly because of a switch from income taxes to regressive indirect taxes.[28] These measures were, without exception, legitimised by referring to global competition. In this reading, the objective of increasing competitiveness actually boils down to increasing income inequality.

If we look at the role of organised labour since the crisis of Fordism in the 1970s and 1980s, we see a dramatic decline in union power and union recruitment. Overall, union density rates in 2002–3 were lower than in 1970, partly as a result of global competition, partly as a result of rising service-sector employment and declining government employment, and partly as a result of labour-market flexibilisation.[29] The decline of union power together with the incapacity of national trade-union leaders to shift their loyalties to the transnational level (a would-be case of political spillover indeed) has created a true participatory void. In the absence of a strong institutional representation of labour at the European level, European capital has been optimally using the 'multilevel playing field' that has been created within the European Union to fully restore its dominance.

Inasmuch as the principle of mutual recognition, and more generally the subordination of national legislators to the European free-market *acquis*, implied a loss of national sovereignty, it can be held responsible for the rise of Euroscepticism in many a member state. It may be remembered that the 'no' vote in the French referendum was very much inspired by the Commission's attempt to apply the principle to the service sector (the proverbial Polish plumber). Second, Euroscepticism seems to be correlated with a general sense of insecurity which stems from 'globalisation'. Loss of identity and national sovereignty were among the most important reasons for voting against the

Lisbon Treaty in Ireland. If we look more closely at the socio-demographic indicators in the flash Eurobarometer survey (see endnote 2), we see that 58 per cent of the unemployed, 58 per cent of people who left education at an age below 15, and 74 per cent of manual workers voted 'no'. It seems as if the EU has become the more tangible scapegoat – that is, regionalisation (through European integration) has made the invisible hand of global free markets visible. Third, recent research has made it clear that the upsurge of Euroscepticism since the early 1990s was in part caused by Economic and Monetary Union, and particularly its (austere) budgetary and welfare-state implications.[30]

The consequences of this popular dissent are much more serious than just not having an operational Constitution or even a Reform Treaty. If it is true that Euroscepticism is first and foremost fuelled by the neo-liberal under-pinnings of the extended relaunch, or in more abstract terms by a higher classness of European society, a new crisis of governability may be the ulti-mate outcome, this time at the European level, however. The more that national constituencies become aware of the twin deficits of the EU – the democratic and the social – the more likely a return to economic and political nationalism will be. At the present conjuncture, disintegration has become a concrete and real alternative.

In this context, the agenda-setting and policy-planning role of the ERT has gradually diminished in the last couple of years, partially because of its landslide success in putting the notion of competitiveness at the fore-front of European decision-making, partly because of the Euroscepticism this in turn generated at the member-state level and partly because of the 'emergence' of new (security) challenges that can no longer be dealt with by enhancing competitiveness alone. In an attempt to save capitalism from the capitalists, a new comprehensive strategy has been developed consist-ing of two interrelated components. First, an inward strategy centred around the new concept of flexicurity aims at striking 'a balance between flexibil-ity and security on the labour market and (helping) both employees and employers to seize the opportunities globalisation offers'.[31] A closer look at the new buzzword suggests that it is about old wine in new bottles. Labour-market flexibility at the enterprise level is going hand-in-hand with proactive labour-market policies (and, if necessary, temporary social security arrange-ments) and, above all, practices of lifelong learning. Job security is past history, employment security is what counts. Being unemployed should be rephrased as 'in-between jobs' from now on, in the process shifting the bur-den of risk from the employer to the employee and taxpayer. Meanwhile, the new Community Lisbon Programme 2008–2010 has been launched as part of a more comprehensive attempt to present globalisation no longer as a challenge or, worse, as a threat, but as an opportunity, as a race to the top. To this end, a number of reports were commissioned by José Manuel Barroso in a bid to convince Europeans that globalisation is a positive force. These reports are part of a (partially) new European discourse that is intended to neutralise Euroscepticism and reform-fatigue among European constituencies.[32]

Second, an outward strategy of proactively promoting the EU's role in global governance is currently at the forefront of the Commission's agenda, and one of the cornerstones of the EU's Reform Treaty. This project no longer just focuses on making the EU the most competitive economy in the world – the so-called Lisbon agenda – but now tries to enhance Europe's leading role in comprehensively attacking all kinds of new real and imagined external security threats, ranging from global warming and energy security to the global food crisis. A recent example is offered by the joint report of the High Representative for Common and Security Policy and the Commission on 'climate change and international security'. The report suggests a European role that is in line with the civilian or soft-power capabilities attributed to it in the literature (as discussed at the beginning of this chapter):

> The EU is in a unique position to respond to the impacts of climate change or international security, given its leading role in development, global climate policy and the wide array of tools and instruments at its disposal. Moreover, the security challenge plays to Europe's strengths, with its comprehensive approach to conflict prevention, crisis management and post-conflict reconstruction, and as a key proponent of effective multilateralism.[33]

One way of interpreting this kind of sweeping statement is to positively assess the EU's role as a would-be empire. Following this argument, the EU indeed possesses all the necessary political and economic ingredients to lead the world in tackling the so-called new security dilemmas. On the other hand, however, the present crisis of governability in the EU suggests a new meaning to its famous expectations-capabilities gap. The soft-power expectations illustrated in the above quote are no longer in line with the EU's capabilities to uphold a necessary degree of internal social cohesion. This in turn suggests an alternative interpretation according to which the aspired-to widening of Europe's role in global affairs is merely a strategic attempt to neutralise social opposition at home and to mobilise popular support for a single, comprehensive project. Such an interpretation would come close to what Hans-Ulrich Wehler – referring to a totally different epoch and setting – coined 'social imperialism' – 'an ideology of integration which would be deliberately applied from above to combat the antagonisms of [...] class society'.[34] In analysing German imperialism, and more specifically the Bismarckian diversionary strategy of using foreign policy excursions to neutralise domestic social opposition, Wehler concluded that social imperialism

> emerges as a strategy and means for defending and stabilising political domination, and must be seen against a background of conflict generated

by attempts of either upholding or changing the system. In this respect, domestic and foreign policy become two facets of one and the same national policy.[35]

It was through this work on German social imperialism that Wehler became identified as one of the leading proponents of the so-called 'Primat der Innenpolitik' (primacy of domestic policy) thesis. In the EU of today, some keep up the illusion that European policy has become 'Innenpolitik' and that European 'domestic' and foreign policy have become two facets of one and the same 'national' policy. This may very well turn out to be a very dangerous (and counterproductive) illusion indeed.

The credit crunch and the EU's crisis of governability. Some concluding remarks

It is true that it has been frequently argued that the member states of the EU need crises in order to get their act together and deepen their integrational commitments. This is a variant of the so-called 'external threat' thesis, which attempts to explain upsurges in European integration in relation to commonly perceived external threats. The similarity lies in the commonality of the threat or crisis, on the one hand, and its immediacy, on the other. A closer look at the history of European integration, however, shows that crises can explain little. The one institutional crisis of the 1960s, the 'empty chair crisis', was solved by a compromise that basically boiled down to 'an agreement to disagree'. The global economic crisis of the 1970s and early 1980s was concomitant with a period of economic disintegration in Europe (as a result of the so-called 'New Protectionism'), aptly referred to as the period of eurosclerosis. It was only from the mid-1980s onwards, that is, after the crisis (and more than a decade after its very start), that the extended relaunch could take place.

As a result of the global credit crisis, the EU is suddenly faced with a double crisis: its post-referenda institutional crisis and the financial crisis. This chapter has argued that the extended relaunch of European integration in the period 1985–2005, and particularly the strategy of asymmetrical regulation used for it, can be held responsible for growing inequality and socio-economic insecurity on the one hand, and a sharp rise in Euroscepticism among European constituencies on the other. It is very unlikely that the second crisis will do much good in solving the EU's ongoing crisis of governability. The first reaction was quite characteristic; each member state tried to find its own short-term solution, in the process resurging national rivalries. Then, in October 2008, the 15 Eurozone countries plus the UK agreed upon a common strategy that was subsequently adopted by the European Council on 15 and 16 October. A concerted action indeed, but one of a strictly intergovernmental nature. As the *Financial Times'* Gideon Rachman rightly commented, '(the) institutions of the EU itself – the parliament, the commission – were largely irrelevant, as was the mighty body of EU law'.[36] In fact, it may very well turn out that the two European institutions responsible for upholding asymmetrical regulation par excellence, the independent ECB as guardian of austerity against government spending and inflation and the European Commission as guardian of the internal market against state intervention, will face growing pressure to curtail their powers. If the gloomy 2009 growth predictions, and particularly their unequal implication for individual member states, come out, this pressure may become stronger and stronger, moving the EU into a new period of eurosclerosis.

It may then take until after the crisis before new integrational initiatives can be expected, if at all. Faced with crisis at home, bold statements about the EU's leading soft-power role in the world of tomorrow seem rather premature.

Notes and References

1. See Martin Slater, 'Political Elites, Popular Indifference and Community Building', *Journal of Common Market Studies*, 21 (1, 2), 1982, 69–87.
2. Eurobarometer, 'Post-referendum Survey in Ireland. Preliminary Results', *Flash Eurobarometer*, 245, 18 June 2008, 3, 7.
3. Paul Taggart, 'A Touchstone of Dissent: Euroscepticism in Contemporary Western European Party Systems', *European Journal of Political Research*, 33, 1998, 366.
4. For an overview, see Liesbet Hooghe and Gary Marks, 'Introduction: Sources of Euroscepticism', in Liesbet Hooghe and Gary Marks (eds), *Understanding Euroscepticism*, special issue of *Acta Politica*, 42 (2, 3), 2008, 119–28.
5. Mark Leonard, *Why Europe will Run the 21st Century*, New York: PublicAffairs, 2005, x.
6. Jeremy Rifkin, *The European Dream. How Europe's Vision of the Future is Quietly Eclipsing the American Dream*, New York: Tarcher/Penguin, 2004, 7. See also Charles Kupchan, *The End of the American Era: US Foreign Policy and the Geopolitics of the Twenty-first Century*, New York: Vintage, 2003; T. R. Reid, *The United States of Europe: The New Superpower and the End of American Supremacy*, New York: Penguin, 2004; Stephen Haseler, *Superstate: The New Europe and its Challenge to America*, London: I. B. Tauris, 2004; and John McCormick, *The European Superpower*, Basingstoke, Palgrave Macmillan, 2007.
7. Mark Pollack, 'International Relations Theory and European Integration', *Journal of Common Market Studies*, 39 (2), 2001, 222.
8. Andrew Moravcsik, 'Striking a New Transatlantic Bargain', *Foreign Affairs*, July/August 2003, 83.
9. For a full account, see Andrew Moravcsik, *The Choice for Europe. Social Purpose and State Power from Messina to Maastricht*, Ithaca: Cornell University Press, 1998.
10. See Otto Holman, 'Transnational Governance without Supranational Government: The Case of the European Employment Strategy', *Perspectives on European Politics and Society*, 7 (1), 2006, 91–107.
11. Samuel Huntington in a report to the Trilateral Commission, quoted in Kees van der Pijl, *Global Rivalries. From the Cold War to Iraq*, London: Pluto Press, 2006, 110, 159.

12. David Harvey, *The New Imperialism*, Oxford: Oxford University Press, 2005, 1; Kees van der Pijl, *Nomads, Empires, States*, London: Pluto Press, 2007, 18.

13. Erik Ohlin Wright, 'The Continuing Relevance of Class Analysis – Comments', *Theory and Society*, 25, 1996, 699.

14. On the postwar de-commodification of labour, see Gosta Esping-Andersen, *The Three Worlds of Welfare Capitalism*, Princeton: Princeton University Press, 1990.

15. Stephen Gill, *American Hegemony and the Trilateral Commission*, Cambridge: Cambridge University Press, 1990, 45.

16. David Harvey, *A Brief History of Neoliberalism*, Oxford: Oxford University Press, 2005.

17. Quoted in G. Merritt, 'Knights of the Roundtable: Can They Move Europe Forward Fast Enough?', *International Management*, 26, July 1986, 22.

18. See, for instance, Maria Green Cowles, *The Politics of Big Business in the European Community: Setting the Agenda for a New Europe*, PhD dissertation, Washington, DC: American University; Bastiaan van Apeldoorn, *Transnational Capitalism and the Struggle over European Integration*, London: Routledge, 2002.

19. Keith Richardson, 'Het Primaat van Concurrentievermogen: het Europese Bedrijfsleven en de Intergouvernementele Conferentie van 1996', in Otto Holman (ed.), *Europese Dilemma's aan het Einde van de Twintigste Eeuw. Democratie, Werkgelegenheid, Veiligheid, Immigratie*, Amsterdam: Het Spinhuis, 1997, 64–5.

20. ERT, *European Competitiveness. The Way to Growth and Jobs*, Brussels: ERT, 1994, 3.

21. For a more detailed account, see Otto Holman, 'Asymmetrical Regulation and Multidimensional Governance in the European Union', *Review of International Political Economy*, 11 (4), 2004, 714–35.

22. Vincent della Sala, 'Maastricht to Modernization: EMU and the Italian Social State', in Andrew Martin and George Ross (eds), *Euros and Europeans. Monetary Integration and the European Model of Society*, Cambridge: Cambridge University Press, 2004, 126–49.

23. See Otto Holman, 'Transnational Governance without Supranational Government: The Case of the European Employment Strategy', *Perspectives on European Politics and Society*, 7 (1), 2006, 91–107.

24. Stephen Gill, 'Constitutionalising Capital: EMU and Disciplinary Neo-Liberalism', in Andreas Bieler and Adam D. Morton (eds), *Social Forces in the Making of the New Europe. The Restructuring of European Social Relations in the Global Political Economy*, Basingstoke: Palgrave Macmillan, 2001, 47.

25. Fritz Scharpf, *Governing in Europe. Effective and Democratic?* Oxford: Oxford University Press, 1999, 56.

26. Simon Hix, *The Political System of the European Union*, Basingstoke: Palgrave Macmillan, 2005.

27. Ibid., 248–9.

28. See Andrew Glyn, *Capitalism Unleashed. Finance, Globalization, and Welfare*, Oxford: Oxford University Press, 2006, particularly Chapter 7.

29. See Jelle Visser, 'Union Membership Statistics in 24 Countries', *Key Workplace Documents*, Cornell University: Federal Publications, 2006.

30. Richard C. Eichenberg and Russell J. Dalton, 'Post-Maastricht Blues: The Transformation of Citizen Support for European Integration, 1973–2004', in Liesbet Hooghe and Gary Marks (eds) *Understanding Euroscepticism*, special issue of *Acta Politica*, 42 (2, 3), 2008, 128–52.

31. European Council, Brussels European Council, March 2008, Presidency Conclusions (7652/08), 10.

32. David S. Hamilton and Joseph P. Quinlan, *Globalization and Europe. Prospering in the New Whirled Order*, Baltimore: Johns Hopkins University Press, 2008; *European Commission, Global Europe, Competing in the World. A Contribution to the EU's Growth and Jobs Strategy*, Brussels: European Commission, External Trade, 2008.
33. High Representative for CFSP and European Commission, Climate Change and International Security. Paper from the High Representative and the European Commission to the European Council, Brussels, 14 March 2008 (S113/08), 2.
34. Hans-Ulrich Wehler, *The German Empire, 1871–1918*, Leamington Spa: Berg Publishers, 1985, 173.
35. Ibid., 171.
36. Gideon Rachman, 'Super-Sarko's Plans for the World', *Financial Times*, 21 October 2008, 11.

10
National or European Social Models? Contesting European Welfare Futures

Ben Clift

This chapter looks at the changing nature of 'social Europe', analysing Europe's social models and their relationship with the Lisbon agenda of 'competitive Europe' within the European political economy. The discursive framing of the interactions between domestic welfare politics and European economic governance is situated in relation to the 'European social model' (ESM). For policy elites within the EU, the ESM was a crucial and 'central organising concept' throughout the 1980s and into the 1990s.[1] It continues to play a significant role in the 21st century, first within the Lisbon process and more recently in the context of 'Lisbon II'. Yet the ESM, a convenient organising concept that encompasses (perhaps conceals) a forbiddingly complex reality, *continues* to defy clear definition.

The term ESM is used by EU-level policy elites to gloss over (or assume away) profound differences between diverse sets of economic, social and welfare policies and the institutions, programmes and mechanisms that deliver them across Europe. The ESM succeeds in being all things to all people, drawing attention away from enduring diversity. Furthermore, the idea of convergence towards a singular ESM presumes a degree of coherence and a harmonising capacity on the part of EU institutions and actors such as the European Commission (EC), which does not exist. In reality, an anachronistic blend of prevailing national peculiarity and isolated instances of European conformity characterises the (very) hesitant harmonising of European social policies.

Discussions of European social policy, and its reform, are framed around the nature of (and conceptions of necessary reform to) the ESM. In this there is clear commonality between the UK social model and the EC's desired direction of travel for labour market reform. British governments have asserted the superiority (in terms of economic performance, and degree of 'fit' with the global economy) of aspects of the British model, which successive UK governments have sought to export to the EU for their benefit. New Labour governments have been quick to claim credit for those points of intersection between UK policy and the Lisbon agenda committed to making the EU 'the most dynamic and competitive knowledge-based economy in the world capable of sustainable economic growth with more and better jobs and greater social cohesion, and respect for the environment by 2010'.[2] The Blair governments recognised the opportunities presented by the Lisbon process for 'uploading' social and employment policy ideas, and sought to be the source, rather than recipient, of policy learning. New Labour continued to drive home a particular framing of European economic problems and challenges, and a (British) solution, placing 'Britain at the leading edge of EU development, shaping its form, not "taking" policies shaped elsewhere'.[3] This informs UK governments' civilising mission, seeking to transform the European political economic space in its own image as a means to improve European economic performance, modernise the European political economy, and 'respond' to challenges of the 'new global economy'.

This chapter charts debates about 'necessary' reforms to the current ESM (in terms of labour-market deregulation and flexibility), and assesses competing conceptions of 'modernisation', and of acceptable minimum welfare provision and labour market regulation standards. These are situated in relation to assumptions about the kind of political economy compatible with globalisation. The chapter challenges the analysis and assumptions underpinning the prevailing prescription (diagnosis and cure) for the ESM within the EC. We focus on the debates surrounding 'flexicurity' and its place within the implementation, successes and failings of the 'Lisbon agenda'.

The European social model

The term 'ESM' seeks to capture the essence of the different sets of economic social and welfare policies, and the institutions and mechanisms that deliver them, in different European countries. Ross and Martin conceive of the ESM as 'the institutional arrangements comprising the welfare state (transfer payments, collective social services, their financing) and the employment relations system (labour law, unions, collective bargaining)'. The general term 'social model' is, they continue, a Weberian ideal-type, involving 'conceptual abstractions of distinctive and central commonalities derived from a variety of empirical situations [...] elucidating the underlying similarities and differences across a range of complex social phenomena'.[4]

The tendency in much of the literature to avoid conceptual interrogation beyond this suggests scholars prefer either this level of 'taken as read' generality, or discussion of particular national cases. This is because, always infused with a strong normative element, the ESM's beauty lies in the eye of the beholder. Each discussion has in mind a particular configuration and trajectory for its evolution. Each intervention in debates about the future of the ESM smuggles in distinct understandings of the nature of that model, and more importantly of necessary reform to it.

Many scholars have sought to offer more precision, frustrated with the arguably empty meta-category of the ESM, and opt for a meso-level categorisation by identifying and typologising welfare-state 'families' in Europe. Just as there are different varieties of capitalist institutions, so there are several 'worlds' of welfare-state institutions,[5] or clusterings of national social-model variants into 'families of welfare'. The number of different clusters identifiable within Europe is disputed, but oft-identified types include the 'Nordic', 'Contental/Bismarckian', 'liberal' and 'Southern' or 'Mediterranean' poles.[6] We explore the fortunes of these various families of welfare further below.

The EU and social policy harmonisation

Dissonance between 'European' and national welfare agendas has a long pedigree. The relation between economic and social policy elements within the Treaty of Rome was 'ambivalent'.[7] It was not clear whether social progress and cohesion was assumed to follow automatically from economic development, or whether it was a separate goal. Initial aims at welfare-state harmonisation between founder members were 'articulated only weakly' in the Treaty of Rome, and were 'rapidly abandoned'.[8] Today, a 'deep tension' exists between national social protection and the logic of European integration,[9] presenting challenges to national social sharing, leading to a 'tug of war' over the control, trajectory and logic of social policy and a potential spatial reorganisation of social provision. The outcome varies according to national conditions and welfare state properties and to defensive institutional engineering.[10]

However, the influence of European integration is not at its strongest in the field of social policy. The differentiated labour market and welfare institutions, programmes and histories are sedimented into their national landscapes, and neither the EU nor any single member-state government within it is a geological force powerful enough to erode these national and subnational particularities. Questions must be raised about how effective, and how powerful, the EU is as a social policy change-inducing actor. Attempts to shape the future form of the ESM, whether articulated by the EC, or by opinionated member-state governments such as New Labour since 1997, face competition from other European visions and models. In practice no amount of enthusiasm for any of these models is likely to induce a high degree of convergence in social-policy and labour-market institutions and programmes across Western Europe. Given the range of intervening variables (including domestic electoral and political structures, veto players and points within welfare-state institutions and programmes), bold assertions that EMU and the Stability and Growth Pact, for example, 'impose' a particular evolution pattern on the ESM should be avoided.[11] The argument here is twofold. Firstly, that commonalities in the direction of travel within European welfare detailed below *do not* amount to or equate to convergence (the degree of difference and distance between the various national welfare states remaining too vast, and the likelihood of divergent outcomes remaining great). Secondly, such common-ality in direction of travel is not caused by or due to the EU as a policy actor, but results from the changing ideational and institutional conditions within the European economy (and its demographics) more broadly.

The stricture imposed on European welfare states by EMU's fiscal archi-tecture can be overstated. Martin conjectures that EMU is driving Europe towards the US social model, but he underspecifies *how* this will occur.[12] Focusing on EC and European Central Bank (ECB) pressure through multi-lateral surveillance[13] risks underplaying domestic resistance to supranational influence. Further 'softening' of the stability and growth pact's soft law in March 2005,[14] and the institutional crisis of the EU following the 'May events' of that year, make a reshaping of welfare institutions at the behest of over-bearing EU institutions appear less likely. Many analyses of the evolution of social policy and social models in Europe highlight the limitations of the EU as a convergence-inducing social-policy actor.[15] The impact of Europeanising pressures of EU economic governance on the ESM involves the complex and contingent interplay of endogenous and exogenous pressures. There remains enduring significant policy autonomy within the parameters set by EMU and the Single Market, with domestic ideational and institutional variables playing a key mediating role.[16]

In the absence of sanctions to ensure compliance with a given vision, the prevailing depiction is of a differentiated 'hybridisation' of Europe's welfare and labour-market institutions, programmes and policies. This is perhaps best illustrated in relation to the Lisbon Agenda and its methodology. The EC has sought to achieve Lisbon's objectives not through 'hard' law (directives and treaties), but the 'open method of co-ordination' (OMC), a 'soft'-law approach involving moral suasion, reporting, disseminating best practice and benchmarking. The OMC sees policy-making as involving 'problem-solving and policy development and learning through peer review, dialogue, soft incentives, normative reflection and experimentation'.[17] Underlying the Lisbon process, at least for those enthusiasts and advocates of the potential for policy learning, are assumptions about the 'suitability of national welfare state configurations' for meeting the 'challenge' of the Lisbon agenda.[18] EU-level social-policy actors argue that, if not already aligned and configured to facilitate the Lisbon strategy's success, then it is incumbent on national-level policy-makers to engage in the difficult task of restructuring national welfare-state and labour-market institutions in order to improve the goodness of fit with this agenda.

Even where there is a general consensus on the direction of travel, for exam-ple in relation to 'employment-centred social policy', the degree of social and labour-market policy change induced by the EC is limited. Activation elements in welfare and labour-market reform are fairly widely shared across the pre-enlargement member states. Yet the Lisbon process is an exercise in what Campbell calls 'bricolage' or 'translation' – 'the combination of locally available principles and practices with new ones originating elsewhere'.[19] As one looks closer, it becomes clear that commonalities of direction of travel mask widely divergent starting points,[20] and differential degrees of commitment to activation. The result is differences in how much of the pre-existing (protected, less reformed) labour market remains, and in the different relative importance of 'new' activation-oriented contracts and programmes. Social minima, welfare programmes, and labour-market institutions continue to differ widely.

The limitations of the OMC's non-coercive approach to delivering the Lisbon agenda of inducing harmonisation become all the more apparent in areas where the diagnosis and cure for social and economic policy problems remain hotly disputed. Not all share the same analysis of appropriate or 'necessary' welfare and labour-market institutions, programmes and policies (and minimum standards, and levels of provision) compatible with the global political economy in the pursuit of the Lisbon agenda. The nature of the OMC affects how constrained national policy elites are to 'download' social-policy measures advocated at the EU level. Many point to the lack of 'teeth', and change-inducing mechanisms within the OMC[21] and dissonance between the weakness of the Lisbon method and the very ambitious Lisbon agenda.[22] Indeed, the OMC is arguably little more than a 'discursive bandwagon'.[23] Within the OMC, Europeanisation takes on a 'voluntary form',[24] and national policy elites choose to 'learn' those policy elements that align closest with their existing practice.

As Wincott points out, much Europeanisation literature is 'too ready to identify the EU – ontological – level as ordered, coherent and consistent, providing a clear basis from which to develop claims about "Europeanisation"'.[25] This is not the case for economic and social policy and their interrelationship within European integration. The diverse elements within the project of European construction generate ongoing political contests and struggles. Talk of *an* ESM obscures the political struggles over the nature and direction of reform. In reality, the ESM has always been surrounded by a 'contested politics of competing "European" projects'.[26] There are liberal market-oriented elements akin to the UK model, many enshrined in the Single European Market. Yet there remain social solidarity and redistributive elements, more reminiscent of continental European models of regulated capitalism.

The European social model and economic performance

In the 1980s, as the process of European integration was re-energised, Jacques Delors entered the fray and campaigned for his vision of what he termed the 'European model of society'.[27] Politically, Delors' articulating of a particular vision of how to reconcile economic liberalism and social justice contrasted a European approach to welfare institutions and labour markets with an Anglo-Saxon neo-liberal Thatcherite British 'other'.[28] Both the 'social' and 'economic' elements have been present within the EU integration process that was re-energised in the early 1980s, but their relation has always been ambiguous.

Normative contestation surrounds the relative importance of and relation between social justice and economic efficiency (and the best way to achieve both). This ongoing political struggle is illustrated in the most thorough attempt to 'operationalise' the concept of the ESM, the 'Lisbon agenda' and process launched in 2000 and relaunched in 2005.[29] Within the Lisbon process, the EC (and certain member-state governments) act as ideologues, pushing for particular framings of policy debates and charting specific directions for policy evolution. We will explore this process below with reference to the EC's very particular interpretation of 'flexicurity', where the relationships between employment and social-policy initiatives and economic and employment outcomes remain contested.

Important ammunition in this clash of social models is provided by stylised facts summarising relative economic and employment performance. Thus contemporary fascination with flexicurity (see below) is closely linked to an economic conjuncture in which the Dutch and Danish economies (the flexicurity poster children) have exceeded by roughly 10 per cent the EU–25 average employment rate.[30] Similarly, higher growth and lower unemployment in the 1990s and 2000s in Britain (and the US), compared to most of continental Europe, nourishes assertions that the more nimble, flexible, liberal model adapts quicker and better to international competition. This feeds British assertions of the superiority of its social model in terms of economic performance and degree of 'fit' with the global economy.

The European economy tends to be weaved into the narrative in UK political economy debates as an undesirable 'other' in terms of the organising principles of its political economy. On the back of this, there is a proselytising desire to re-describe the European political economic space in the UK image. Yet New Labour's 'hubristic interpretation of the domestic record'[31] requires some interrogation. Such interpretations, especially when told by policy elites advocating a particular course of action, require careful unpicking because often they are painted with broad brushstrokes and tend to be selective in their inclusion of relevant facts and yardsticks by which success is judged. Blair played fast and loose with his comparative statistical evidence, noting for example that European productivity is inferior to US levels, neglecting to mention French and German *superiority* to UK productivity levels.[32]

The standard characterisation of the European continent as stagnating and ridden with high unemployment because of excessive labour market rigidities does not do justice to the complexity of experience in Europe, nor is it likely to stand the test of time. These comparative economic-performance issues form the backdrop (often implicitly) to debates surrounding the ESM. Advocacy of a particular set of labour-market or employment and social policies at a given point in time tends to be intimately related to the perceived economic health (or otherwise) of the broader variety of capitalism from which particular sets of policies, programmes or institutions are drawn. As Blanchard's impressive survey of the policy discussion about solving unemployment problems in Europe notes: 'the history of the last 30 years is a series of love affairs with sometimes sad endings, first with German and German-like institutions – until unemployment started increasing in the 1990s – then with the United Kingdom and the Thatcher-Blair reforms, then with Ireland and the Netherlands and the role of national agreements, and now with the Scandinavian countries, especially Denmark, and its concept of "flexisecurity".[33] It may be that if Dutch and Danish economic and unemployment performance takes a downward turn in the near future, the ardour with which European economic and social policy elites have embraced 'flexicurity' will be dampened.

European social model(s): 'modernisation' … and retrenchment?

It is argued here that the EU and EC are not driving a convergence in European welfare-state models, institutions and provision. However, that is not to say that the European welfare landscape is set in stone. Significant change *is* afoot. Yet that change is not driven primarily by European or Europeanisation pressures, nor is it leading to a convergence of European welfare provision. This all can be located within a broader set of debates about welfare states in the context of complex economic interdependence.[34] The identification above of four welfare state 'families'[35] begs the question whether there are specific trajectories in the changing global political economy for particular welfare families. Scholars have tried to assess the 'goodness of fit' between these different sets of welfare policies, programmes, institutions and histories and the changing conditions of complex economic interdependence. An initial hypothesis was that globalisation was bearing down on all welfare states with equal force, inducing retrenchment of programmes, reductions in generosity, and ultimately convergence of more minimalist liberal welfare norms.[36]

Lurking behind some of this analysis was the assertion that 'Anglo-Saxon' capitalism and its less generous, more flexible and increasingly deregulated labour market and welfare institutions, setting lower minimum standards, display compatibility with globalisation that is superior to all other variants. The accuracy of such assumptions has rightly been questioned. As Scruggs notes, 'by some conventional analyses, all of Scandinavia should have long ago collapsed under the weight of its public spending. Yet in 2005, three of the four most competitive economies in the world, according the *Global Competitiveness Index*, were in Scandinavia; the United States is the other one'.[37]

Closer empirical inspection showed that pressures for welfare-state retrenchment had been often overstated.[38] Subsequent studies suggested that such retrenchment as is occurring within European welfare states is distributed differently across different welfare-state clusters. This indicates *differential* vulnerability of extant EU welfare state 'clusters' to liberalisation pressures within the global political economy. The liberal model is, it seems, not alone in (fairly) successfully navigating the choppier waters of a more economically interdependent world. The (more generous and more egalitarian) Scandinavian or Nordic model seems to be fairing well, too. The 'continental' or 'Bismarckian' welfare states are, on the other hand, faced with greater retrenchment pressures.[39]

Social rights are at the core of any welfare-state regime. This apparently obvious observation generates a new take on the retrenchment debates that have been ongoing within comparative welfare states for some time. Paul Pierson, looking at overall welfare spending levels (which continued to rise in Britain from the 1970s to the 1990s), asserted that Margaret Thatcher's reputation for welfare-state retrenchment was unjustified. Anyone who lived in Britain in the 1980s and 1990s *knew* he was wrong. Work focusing on social rights and welfare-state retrenchment helps elucidate just *how* he was wrong.[40]

Looking at social rights to unemployment insurance, sick pay and public pensions, analysed in terms of *replacement rates* and *coverage*, this analysis assesses levels and duration of benefits, and conditions necessary to qualify for and gain access to benefits. In this way it unearths 'social programme dynamics' with more nuance than crude spending measures can, enabling a more fine-grained assessment of 'welfare state resiliency'.[41] Evolutions in aggregate spending levels can conceal significant changes in the logic and character of welfare-state provision. If the number of claimants increases significantly, then spending levels can increase, perhaps even substantially, whilst the *generosity* of benefits is reduced – which surely meets a commonsense notion of retrenchment. Indeed, this was precisely the case with unemployment insurance and pensions under Thatcher.[42]

Scruggs, while rejecting unambiguously the notion of a race to the bottom, does unearth 'tangible signs of replacement rate retrenchment in all three types of welfare states',[43] and notes that this retrenchment is greater in the most generous social-democratic welfare states. However, 'it is worth noting that all of these (social democratic) countries had higher expected benefits in 2002 than in 1972'.[44] The story is a complex one; 'while welfare state programmes are more generous than they were a generation ago, there has been a shift away from expanding entitlements and towards retrenchment'.[45]

This cross-national comparative quantitative study rings true with qualitative assessments of evolutions of social policy provision in Europe. While, to some extent, the different welfare-state 'families' have traceable trajectories, there are some general 'problems' and common priorities in terms of social policy reform. These include achieving cost-saving pension reforms (by means such as increasing contribution periods, de-indexing entitlements, reducing public-sector generosity), finding new ways to fund caring services (for childcare and the elderly), and trying to increase demand for low-skill workers through targeted subsidies and in-work benefits (which often works out cheaper than unemployment benefit). In similar vein, improving 'activation' incentives through reforms to the provision of employment services, and offering individual training and guidance, is another common phenomenon.[46]

These changes in the logic and nature of welfare-state provision are often framed in terms of the 'modernisation' of the ESM. Modernisation remains an ill-defined, nebulous concept: 'Like an epigram, the term "modernisation" carries with it an apparently self-evident truth ... the *definition* of the term is elusive.'[47] This mix of self-evidence and definitional vacuity is a dangerous blend. Modernisation's use imports a set of value judgements and dresses them up in the language of objective conditions and logical imperatives. The 'modern' is distinguished from the outdated by criteria taken from an analysis of decline or underperformance.

In the case of European welfare reform, that performance yardstick is, as noted above, the overall economic and unemployment record. Thus New Labour hubris about the UK's economic 'successes' for a decade after 1997 inform its ebullient, self-congratulatory self-image as an economic and social-policy model. Welfare-state modernisation (by which it understands emulation of the UK model) begins from the assumption that the UK has adopted the reforms necessary to survive in the 21st-century global economy. UK social minima and levels of labour-market regulation are seen as integral to UK competitiveness. The EC vision of ESM modernisation takes a similar view of the relation between social policy and economic competitiveness, and the appropriate degree of flexibility in the new global economy. As we shall see below, this is particularly true in relation to job security.

A common continental riposte to British (and EC) hectoring over labour-market reform is that not all accept that realigning labour-market institutions on the UK model is a necessary condition of globalisation, or the only means to the end of solving unemployment problems and achieving growth. On closer inspection, it becomes clear that good employment performance *can be* compatible with a variety of types of labour market, including those more regulated and incorporating higher minimum standards than the UK economy.[48] Sweden, the Netherlands and Denmark have all, at different times, been invoked in this context, and Germany's recent improving economic performance, should it continue, will add grist to this mill. Thus, processes of welfare-state 'modernisation', in the face of pressures (both perceived and real), notably demographic change and 'globalisation', are understood differently in different national social welfare contexts. Perhaps unsurprisingly, for those analysts and policy elites contemplating how to 'modernise' continental/Bismarckian models from within, the more generous and egalitarian Nordic model is a more attractive beacon than the UK's (even if, in reality, the likelihood of movement towards either is unlikely, given the complexity of welfare-state restructuring).[49]

The political economy of labour-market reform: institutions and unemployment

Given that full employment is central to the Lisbon agenda, and prioritised by many member-state governments as a goal of labour-market and social-policy reform, the remainder of this chapter will explore in more depth attempts to achieve high levels of employment within Europe, and the debates surrounding appropriate social and labour-market policy within member states and the EC in pursuit of this goal. Macroeconomic policy debates and orthodoxies are crucial in shaping the context within which such full employment objectives are pursued and the ESM evolves. Thus the discussion of social-policy and labour-market reform must first be placed in the context of developments in macroeconomic policy thinking in Europe.

Macroeconomic policy priorities have evolved in recent decades, with increasing priority afforded to 'stability' (low inflation), and a decreasing conviction on the part of policy-makers (in particular central bankers) that macroeconomic economic policy has an active role to play in securing full employment. The lessons drawn from earlier macroeconomic policy errors (such as the Lawson boom of the 1980s, or Swedish policy in the 1980s and early 1990s[50]) is that activist macroeconomic policy, whilst potentially beneficial, is also capable of doing considerable damage. Therefore, ambitions are modest, seeking to deliver stability as priority number one. One distillation of this approach is the ECB's view of the 'appropriate' (non-inflationary) growth rate of the Euro zone at 2 to 2.5 per cent, and the assumption that it cannot have a positive impact on unemployment without generating higher (and accelerating) inflation.[51]

This is often interpreted as an 'abandonment' of Keynesianism and an 'embrace' of neo-liberalism or monetarism. However, it makes sense to add more nuance, since elements taking inspiration from both approaches are present within European policy mixes, and the quantities put into the mix can vary cross-nationally. Many mainstream economists agree that macroeconomic policy *does* have an impact upon unemployment. Blanchard, for example, explains how monetary policy (first accommodating, then contractionary) helps account for the initial rise, and long-term duration of, European unemployment in the 1970s and 1980s.[52]

That said, the overbearing focus of some macroeconomic policy-makers on inflation objectives is compatible with a compartmentalisation of economic policy, whereby unemployment is interpreted as caused (exclusively) by labour-market institutions and social policies. This line of thinking aligns with another pillar of the dominant European macroeconomic policy orthodoxy in the 1990s crystallised in the policy consensus around the 1994 *OECD*

Jobs Study.[53] This prevailing 'wisdom' identified institutions, and specifically 'labour-market rigidities' as *the* cause of persistent high unemployment in certain continental European countries, notably France, Germany, Italy and Spain.[54] Layard et al.[55] had previously placed considerable emphasis on the role of institutions in explaining high unemployment, yet it is the focus on labour-market institutions (and rigidities) *to the exclusion of all else* which is striking. The ECB explicitly aligns with such a compartmentalisation of economic policy, seeing 'structural reforms' to excessively rigid labour-market institutions as the only possible avenue for activism.[56] There is a denial of the role for macroeconomic policy (or demand-side policy) in securing increased or full employment.

In the UK, New Labour, although they conceive of a combination of demand and supply-side approaches in securing full employment,[57] nevertheless anachronistically align with the labour-market-rigidities consensus in diagnosing prescriptions for European unemployment.[58] Yet, as noted above, the empirical record by no means lends unequivocal support to this simplistic reading. Even *Financial Times* economists question this view, noting that it is excessively complacent to interpret all unemployment as resulting from labour-market rigidities, and to ignore the possibility that macroeconomic policy errors may be part of the story.[59] Other analysts convinced of the wisdom of the *OECD Jobs Study* also note the need for monetary expansion to accompany labour-market reform to help offset (temporary) job losses.[60]

A variety of employment experiences across Europe (good and bad) in the past 20 years have been seen in a variety of different labour-market contexts (both more and less regulated). Assumptions about higher unemployment associated with more regulated labour markets are confounded by research offering little evidence of continental labour-market institutions increasing aggregate unemployment levels,[61] with differences in unemployment protection 'largely unrelated to differences in unemployment rates across countries'.[62] Martin's analysis finds that labour-market institutions did not have the impact on the NAIRU (the non-accelerating inflation rate of unemployment) that some economics literature credits them with. He finds 'no consistent relationship … between economic outcomes and labour market institutions',[63] and little correlation between the extent of labour-market reforms and changes in the NAIRU. Labour-market reform *may*, he concludes, help reduce unemployment, alongside demand explanations. It is these interactions between institutions and macroeconomic factors, assessing the relative weight to attach to each, which are crucial.

Thus it is erroneous to assert that a rigid labour market 'equals' poor economic performance and high unemployment. That is not to say that labour-market institutions may not benefit from reform, and that they may well be one of many contributing factors to unemployment performance. Yet views differ as to what extent labour-market reform should erode the generosity and automaticity of benefits, and job security (see below). In short, how much social justice can be retained whilst seeking to reinvigorate economic efficiency? The kind of labour and welfare institutions seen by the EC as 'necessary' in a global economy are regarded as threatening cherished norms and *acquis sociaux* in many European countries. Their defenders are comforted by countries like Sweden and Denmark that have achieved success in a global economy without the root-and-branch retrenchment of welfare and the labour-market flexibilisation seen in the UK since the early 1980s.[64]

Beyond the *OECD Jobs Study* approach

The issue of how to marry economic efficiency to social justice has been the underlying fault line of the ongoing debate surrounding social and labour-market policy reform in Europe and is one source of 'tensions between the EMU policy regime and the ESM'.[65] The ECB's myopic analysis of the causes of unemployment and economic problems in Europe is part of the problem. Not all accept this analysis, and indeed over time fewer do. Thus member states and policy actors are decreasingly willing to internalise the ECB's dogmatic 'structural reform' discourse, with labour-market rigidities understood as *the* problem.

Many argue that the EU has to acquire institutions ensuring a monetary and fiscal policy mix without a deflationary bias.[66] Part of the reason for high Eurozone unemployment may well lie with the political-economic underpinnings of the euro, and the restrictive monetary policy stance holding back growth.[67] Blanchard also questions assumptions of the ECB that low European inflation 'proves' that European unemployment is at its 'natural' level, on which expansionary macroeconomic policy cannot have a beneficial effect, except at the expense of (substantially and accelerating) rises in inflation; 'it may be that, in fact, an expansion of demand might decrease unemployment without leading to steadily higher inflation'.[68]

In this light, the British model of an independent Bank of England with a *symmetrical* inflation target (in theory at least, the central bank has to *reflate* the economy if inflation falls too low) may be a step in the right direction. The rebalancing of priorities between inflation and growth could alleviate the deflationary pressure of the ECB.[69] By contrast, arguments for a 'growth spurt' induced in part by macroeconomic policy to give an impulse to growth (and employment),[70] are not considered by the ECB – its statutes enshrine neo-liberal orthodoxy on this point. There have been many calls (from political parties, trade unions and employers' organisations) for the ECB to change its statutes to incorporate a priority for jobs and growth alongside its constitutional obligation to keep inflation low. These calls continue to fall on deaf ears, and such a reform agenda would in all likelihood fail in the face of formidable collective action problems and considerable opposition to the change. However, while rewriting ECB statutes is decidedly off the political agenda, articulating a Europe-wide labour-market policy-reform agenda is very much on the Lisbon agenda.

From flexibility to flexicurity?

The ECB view of labour-market rigidities seems somewhat outdated at a time when, as Keune and Jepsen note, 'even the OECD itself retracted many aspects of its radical stance; in particular it had to admit that there is no clear relation between the level of employment protection in a country and its level of unemployment'.[71] The OECD's recent, more nuanced approach aligns with a wider body of European thinking.

The Lisbon process has been interpreted as an 'interrogation of the orthodox assertion that a "big trade-off" exists between equity and efficiency'.[72] There is a broad consensus on the need to scale back 'passive' welfare provision spending which makes no discernable contribution to economic growth.[73] However, not all welfare spending, or labour-market and social policy, is tarred with the same brush. Ideas of 'activation' within employment-policy and social-policy reform became much more widespread throughout Europe in the 1990s and early 2000s and are at the heart of the Lisbon agenda.[74] In fact, 'on the ground' similar activation-oriented or 'employment-centred' social policies were being pursued in many European countries, including Denmark,[75] France,[76] the Netherlands[77] and Portugal[78] to name but a few, in the mid-to-late 1990s.[79] This emphasis on 'active' welfare spending, seen as an investment that contributes to human capital formation through education and training, suggests a very different set of priorities for social and labour-market policy than the *OECD Jobs Study*.

The Lisbon process has political-economic foundations in ideas such as 'supply-side egalitarianism', 'competitive solidarity',[80] and 'competitive corporatism'.[81] Slightly removed from the rigidity/flexibility dichotomy, the approach is more nuanced as to the kind and degree of labour-market reform desired, as well as its interrelationship with other reforms. A widely shared 'Lisbon' consensus has emerged that economic and social-policy reform should seek to prioritise employment, encourage adults into employment, make work pay by ensuring welfare and labour markets work in tandem, address poverty traps, facilitate the reconciliation of work and family commitments, and generate incentives to seek work, and to hire.[82]

More familiar social-policy objectives, such as redistribution, are 'at best implicit' in the objectives that underpin the Lisbon process.[83] Some see the social element, whose role alongside the economic focus was always ambiguous, as further marginalised in 'Lisbon II' since 2005. This is a process of 'market-making' regulatory social-policy reform. The emergent consensus noted above accepts 'the market and employment' as 'the primary *loci* of integration' to solve social exclusion.[84] It is, in welfare-state literature terms, concerned with recommodification (returning citizens to the labour market) not decommodification.[85] However, this consensus does not extend to the blend between activation and the distributive consequences of welfare-state institutions. Thus while all advocate activation, some remain more committed to redistribution than others.

Drawing on Dutch and, more recently, Danish experience, the mooted combination of flexibility and security within 'flexicurity' has been the central focus of 'market-making' regulatory social-policy reform in recent years. The EC in particular has seized on this term to frame its social and labour-market policy agenda. The following discussion of the EC's selective interpretation of flexicurity draws extensively on Keune and Jepsen.[86] This is an instance of what Rosamond calls the 'social construction of "Europe" as a valid economic space'.[87] The EC's role within the OMC identifying and disseminating 'best practice'[88] gives it significant discursive power. The EC seeks to rhetorically and discursively shape how aspects of European political-economic reality are structured and understood through a deliberate and narrow framing of debates about 'flexicurity'-oriented labour-market and social-policy reform. In imparting a particular meaning to crucial terms in the European social and economic-policy reform debate, the EC seeks to mould 'emergent inter-subjectivities' surrounding economic reform in Europe. Through such a 'discursive construction of Europe',[89] particular reform trajectories are prioritised, others marginalised. This is how best to interpret the process undertaken by the EC since October 2006[90] – seeking to develop a common set of flexicurity principles across the EU.[91]

The idea of a 'balance between flexibility and security' had been part of the European Employment Strategy since 1998, and the notion of social policy as a productive factor was integral to the Lisbon strategy.[92] In longer historical perspective, combining flexibility and security has affinities (in being activation and market-oriented) with the earlier Rehn model in Sweden. However, the attraction of the term for the EC is that 'the empirical content of flexicurity is, in principle, open'.[93] The EC interpretation involves a very particular understanding of 'security'. This in turn rests on a distinctive conception of the ESM, and the relation between competitiveness, flexibility, and social cohesion within it.

That said, EC efforts take place in the context of 'a consensus among the main players at the European level that the European labour market needs flexicurity'.[94] One source of this consensus is the correlation between those states with high employment rates, and those pursing flexicurity-style policies (Denmark and the Netherlands). The support from academic studies, imparting causal significance to this correlation, served to add a scientific, technical quality to EC discourse on flexicurity. However, its appropriation and deployment by the EC was in truth a deeply political process. What is significant here is precisely *how* the EC conceives of the connection between markets, social cohesion, flexibility and economic efficiency, within its particular (singular) understanding of flexicurity. This, in concert with a wider European consensus that flexicurity (in a broad sense) is a 'good thing', makes flexicurity a 'powerful discursive tool for the Commission'.[95]

The EC's flexicurity agenda is framed, like New Labour's, by the perceived flexibility imperatives of labour-market policy and its reform in the global economy. The EC calls this 'the increasingly transitional nature of today's labour market',[96] referring to frequent movement into and out of employment, unemployment and inactivity. Flexicurity's role is to provide bridges between these different labour-market situations, whilst tackling problems of labour-market segmentation and job precariousness.[97] The key elements for delivering this are work contracts providing adequate flexibility (that is, facilitating hiring and firing), active labour-market policies, lifelong learning and social security systems providing support during absence from the labour market and facilitating transition and mobility.[98]

Significantly, job security is *not* a priority from an EC perspective, and dismissal protection is deemed damaging to flexibility. It is people, not jobs, that are to be protected. What the EC takes as the core of flexicurity is to prioritise increased mobility, use of non-standard employment, and *reduced* job protection. In the process, 'old' security will reduce, supplanted by 'new' security. The EC has redefined security no longer as 'protection against risk' but rather as 'the capacity to adapt to change by means of a process of constant learning'.[99] Lifelong learning, skills upgrading and activation-oriented social security systems are prioritised. The notion of 'adequate support' during absences from the labour market is not defined or elaborated upon. This silence on levels of minimum provision is important.

The EC vision *contrasts* in a number of important respects from Danish 'flexicurity', which is supposedly its inspiration. What is striking is the stronger redistributive commitments within Danish flexicurity policies. The Danish version combines three elements in a context of increasing flexibility of work contracts and work practices, as well as the institutional decentralisation of wage bargaining. Firstly, there is limited private-sector employment protection (hiring and firing), and thus high job mobility. Secondly, there are generous universal unemployment and health insurance and other welfare benefits. These were increasingly closely tied to employment-seeking, levels were reduced, and eligibility was restricted through reforms in the 1990s. The levels of benefits remain, even post-retrenchment, much higher than UK standards.[100] Thirdly, there are extensive retraining opportunities to help workers acquire new skills, as well as assistance and support in locating new employment opportunities.[101] This model's combination of welfare generosity with an 'activating' role for the state attracts admiring interest from other European countries with high unemployment, such as France.

The EC understands flexibility primarily in terms of hiring and firing (internal/external numerical) rather than functional or working-time flexibility. The agenda that flows from this is 'a tightening of benefits schemes where they are "generous", and a reduction of employment protection'.[102] This arguably erodes security (certainly 'old' security) without a 'compensatory' bolstering of redistributive provision mitigating the effects of labour-market transition. Since the Lisbon relaunch, adapting and specialising education and training systems and raising employment and employability have been increasingly central to the agenda.[103] As with 'Lisbon II' more broadly, social and redistribution commitments are decreasingly visible and present within the EC's flexicurity agenda. Given the redefinition of security, the 'balance' between flexibility and security is decisively skewed towards the flexibility side. The irony is that, at the same time that the OECD departed from its myopic flexibility-obsessed interpretation of labour markets and their relation to employment performance, the EC has moved on to precisely the terrain the OECD has vacated.

Conclusion

How should we understand the ESM, and what impact are Europeanising pressures of the single market, the EU competition regime, and EMU having on its evolution at the national level? Different histories, institutions, programmes and policies generate 'national variants of the ESM'.[104] Talk of *an* 'ESM' overstates the commonalities of programmes, histories and trajectories of welfare states and social policies. It also assumes away the difficulty reconciling these different social models, encompassing different redistributive and regulatory commitments.

Real ESMs are historically contingent phenomena, and thus the 'European' story entails the interplay of endogenous and exogenous pressures in the reshaping of Europe's social models, mediated by intervening 'domestic' ideational and institutional variables.[105] Ferrera's 'tug of war' between national and supranational 'ownership' policy areas is still being won more often than it is being lost by national policy elites in social-policy and labour-market reform. While there has been some welfare-state retrenchment, its scale should not be overstated.[106] Its cause is more likely related to international factors (globalisation) and domestic factors (demographic change) than European pressures, be they from the EC, ECB, Single European Market or EMU. Furthermore, the outcome is likely to be continued differentiation of national social models, rather than convergence.

The EC's particular interpretation of how, in terms of social-policy and labour-market reform, to achieve the Lisbon agenda's ambitious goals, as exemplified in its very flexibility-oriented take on 'flexicurity', may not fall on receptive ears. This is because there is ambiguity about how much of the UK's comparative economic success results from the flexible and deregulated labour-market institutions it tries not terribly successfully to foist on the rest of Europe. New Labour hubris and EC hectoring conceal assumptions about a 'necessary' scaling back of welfare-state generosity and redistribution (and an abandonment of job security) which not all European policy-makers and publics share. This difference of view is of fundamental importance, because the Lisbon process lacks the mechanisms to induce the convergence that the EC exhorts.

The UK model's relative success in terms of growth and employment in the decade after 1997 was, some felt, bought at too high a price in terms of social equality. Wincott and Hopkin's analysis indicates that the UK uniquely has an extremely poor inequality score, and that 'the UK remains an unusually unequal society by general European (never mind Nordic) standards'.[107] This is a gremlin hindering the smooth uploading of British social policy to the EU 'mainframe'. This undermined the effectiveness of Blair and Brown, each a latter-day 'fishwife Britannia',[108] who emulated (in style if not content) Margaret Thatcher in haranguing European policy elites about their failure to share New Labour's vision of the kinds of flexibility-oriented economic and labour-market institutions compatible with the new global economy.

The likely future trajectories of European economic and social policy involve cross-fertilisation and hybridisation of models. Indeed, the OMC makes this a *more* likely impact of Europeanisation. The UK's export record of political-economic ideas to the European continent is considerably better than its actual economic performance in terms of exports in the last decade. Yet even here international competition is stiff, with Denmark and Sweden cornering a sizeable market share of the economic and social-reform agenda. Economic performance and political-economic institutions display a more complex interrelation than the flexibility-obsessed EC, or New Labour, with its superiority complex, chooses to admit. There may even be, if German economic improvement continues, another rebalancing in the protean comparative-capitalisms debates between the relative merits of 'regulated' versus 'neo-liberal' capitalism (in favour of the former).

Notes and References

1. D. Wincott, 'The Idea of the European Social Model: Limits and Paradoxes of Europeanisation', in K. Featherstone and C. M. Radaelli (eds), *The Politics of Europeanisation*, Oxford: Oxford University Press, 2003, 295.
2. A. Blair, Speech to the European Parliament, 23 June 2005, available at www.number-10.gov.uk/output/Page7714.asp; G. Brown, *Global Europe: Full Employment Europe*, London: HM Treasury, 2005; R. Taylor 'Mr Blair's Business Model – Capital and Labour in Flexible Markets', in A. Seldon and D. Kavanagh (eds), *The Blair Effect*, Oxford: Oxford University Press, 2005, 184–206.
3. Wincott, op. cit., 297.

4. A. Martin and G. Ross, 'Introduction: EMU and the European Social Model', in G. Ross and A. Martin (eds), *Euros and Europeans: European Integration and the European Model of Society*, Cambridge: Cambridge University Press, 2004, 11.

5. G Esping-Andersen, *The Three Worlds of Welfare Capitalism*, Cambridge: Polity, 1990; L. Scruggs, 'The Generosity of Social Insurance, 1971–2002', *Oxford Review of Economic Policy*, 22 (3), 2006, 349–64.

6. P. Pierson (ed.), *The New Politics of the Welfare State*, Oxford: Oxford University Press, 2001; A. Hemerijck and M. Ferrera, 'Welfare Reform in the shadow of EMU', in Ross and Martin, op. cit., 248–77; M. Ferrera, A. Hermerijck and M. Rhodes, *The Future of Social Europe*, Oeiras: Celta Editoria, 2000.

7. M. Daly, 'EU Social Policy after Lisbon', *Journal of Common Market Studies*, 44 (3), 2006, 468.

8. C. Annesley, 'Americanised and Europeanised: UK Social Policy since 1997', *British Journal of Politics and International Relations*, 5 (2), 2003, 150.

9. M. Ferrera, *The Boundaries of Welfare: European Integration and the New Spatial Politics of Social Protection*, Oxford: Oxford University Press, 2005, 221.

10. Ibid., 8.

11. K. Featherstone, 'The Political Dynamics of External Empowerment: the Emergence of EMU and the Challenge to the European Social Model', in Ross and Martin, op. cit., 226.

12. A. Martin, 'The EMU Macroeconomic Policy Regime and the European Social Model' in Ross and Martin, op. cit., 20–49.

13. A. Sbragia, 'Shaping a Polity in an Economic and Monetary Union: the EU in Comparative Perspective', in Ross and Martin, op. cit., 51–75.

14. See B. Clift, 'The New Political Economy of Dirigisme: French Macroeconomic Policy, Unrepentant Sinning, and the Stability and Growth Pact', *British Journal of Politics and International Relations*, 8 (3), 2006, 388–409.

15. Daly, op. cit.; A. Sapir 'Globalisation and the Reform of European Social Models', *Journal of Common Market Studies*, 44 (2), 2006, 369–90; Hemerijck and Ferrera, op. cit.; M. Smith, *States of Liberalization*, New York: SUNY Press, 2005; Featherstone, op. cit.

16. Featherstone, op. cit.

17. Wincott op. cit., 283; Daly, op. cit., 466.

18. Daly, op. cit., 466.

19. J. Campbell, *Institutional Change and Globalization*, Princeton: Princeton University Press, 2004, 65.

20. C. Hay, 'Common Trajectories, Variable Paces, Divergent Outcomes? Models of European Capitalism under Conditions of Complex Economic Interdependence', *Review of International Political Economy*, 11 (2), 2004, 231–62.

21. C. Annesley, 'Lisbon and Social Europe: Towards a European "Adult Worker Model" Welfare System', *Journal of European Social Policy*, 17 (3), 2007, 195–205; Wincott, op. cit.

22. Daly, op. cit., 478; Sapir, op. cit., 386.

23. C. Radaelli, *The Open Method of Co-Ordination: a New Governance Architecture for the European Union?*, Stockholm: Swedish Institute for Policy Studies, 2003, 32.
24. Wincott, op. cit., 297.
25. Ibid., 300.
26. Ibid., 297.
27. J. Delors, *Our Europe?*, London: Verso, 1992, 157–8.
28. Wincott, op. cit., 288.
29. Daly, op. cit.; Annesley, op. cit., 195–6.
30. M. Keune and M. Jepsen, *Not Balanced and Hardly New: the European Commission's Quest for Flexicurity*, European Trade Union Institute for Research, Education and Health and Safety (ETUI-REHS), Working Paper 2007.01, 2007, at: http://etui-rehs.org/research/publications
31. J. Hopkin and D. Wincott, 'New Labour, Economic Reform, and the European Social Model', *British Journal of Politics and International Relations*, 8 (1), 2006, 50–68.
32. Blair, op. cit., fn 2; contrast with HM Treasury, *European Economic Reform: Meeting the Challenge*, London: HMSO, 2001, 20; Taylor, op. cit., 200–1.
33. O. Blanchard, 'European Unemployment: The Evolution of Facts and Ideas', *Economic Policy*, January 2006, 5–59, 45.
34. C. Hay, 'What's Globalisation Got To Do With It? Economic Interdependence and the Future of European Welfare States', *Government and Opposition*, 1, 2006, 1–22.
35. Hemerijck and Ferrera, op. cit., 252.
36. For a discussion and critique, see H. Schwartz, 'Round Up the Usual Suspects! Globalisation, Domestic Politics, and Welfare State Change', in P. Pierson (ed.), *The New Politics of Welfare*, Oxford: Oxford University Press, 2001, 17–44.
37. Scruggs, op. cit., 349.
38. Hay, op. cit.; D. Swank, *Global Capital, Political Institutions, and Policy Change in Developed Welfare States*, Cambridge: Cambridge University Press, 2002.
39. Hay, op. cit., 9–13; Sapir, op. cit.; P. Palier, 'A Long Goodbye to Bismarck?', Seminar at the CEVIPOF, Science Policy, Paris, March 2007.
40. Scruggs, op. cit.
41. Ibid., 349–50.
42. Ibid., 352; Esping Andersen, op. cit.
43. Scruggs, op. cit., 355.
44. Ibid., 362.
45. Ibid.
46. See, for example, Hemerijck and Ferrera, op. cit.
47. J. Gaffney, *France and Modernisation*, Aldershot: Avebury, 1988, 1.
48. Blanchard op. cit.; Hopkin and Wincott, op. cit.
49. See P. Pierson, *Dismantling the Welfare State?*, Cambridge: Cambridge University Press, 1994.
50. See M. Ryner, 'Swedish Employment Policy after EU-Membership', *Osterreichische Zeischrift fur Politikwissenschaft*, 29 (3), 2000, 341–5; and M. Ryner, *Capitalist*

Restructuring, Globalisation and the Third Way: Lessons from the Swedish Model, London: Routledge, 2002, 150–3.

51. Martin, op. cit., 24.
52. Blanchard, op. cit., 21–3.
53. OECD, *The OECD Jobs Study*, Paris: OECD, 1994; M. Dostal 'Campaigning on Expertise: How the OECD Framed EU Welfare and Labour Market Policies – and Why Success Could Trigger Failure', *Journal of European Public Policy*, 11 (3), 2004, 440–60.
54. Blanchard, op. cit., 26.
55. R. Layard, S. Nickell and R. Jackman, *Unemployment: Macroeconomic Performance and the Labour Market*, Oxford: Oxford University Press, 1991.
56. Martin, op. cit., 24–7.
57. B. Clift and J. Tomlinson, 'Credible Keynesianism?: New Labour Macroeconomic Policy and the Political Economy of Coarse Tuning', *British Journal of Political Science*, 37 (1), 2007, 47–69.
58. For a critique, see Hopkin and Wincott, op. cit, 53–5 and Taylor, op. cit.
59. W. Munchau, 'Commentary on European Unemployment: the Evolution of Facts and Ideas', *Economic Policy*, January 2006, 55–9.
60. Sapir, op. cit., 385–6.
61. S. Nickell and R. Layard, 'Labour Market Institutions and Economic Performance', in O. Ashenfelter and D. Card (eds), *Handbook of Labour Economics*, Amsterdam: North Holland, 1998.
62. Blanchard, op. cit., 30–1.
63. Martin, op. cit., 40.
64. Taylor, op. cit., 198.
65. G. Ross and A. Martin, 'Conclusions', in G. Ross and A. Martin (eds), *Euros and Europeans: European Integration and the European Model of Society*, Cambridge: Cambridge University Press, 2004, 310.
66. J. Pisani-Ferry, 'Only One Bed for Two Dreams: A Critical Retrospective on the Debate over the Economic Governance of the Euro Area', *Journal of Common Market Studies*, 44 (4), 2006, 823–44.
67. Martin, op. cit., 32–41; L. Ball, 'Aggregate Demand and Long-Run Unemployment', *Brookings Papers on Economic Activity*, 2, 1999, 189–251.
68. Blanchard, op. cit., 47.
69. Pisani-Ferry, op. cit.; P. Lamy and J. Pisani-Ferry, 'The Europe We Want', in L. Jospin, *My Vision of Europe and Globalization*, London: Policy Network/Polity, 2002, 109–16; Martin, op. cit. 29.
70. Ball, op. cit.
71. OECD, *Employment Outlook. Boosting Jobs and Income*, Paris: OECD, 2006, 96–100; OECD, *Main Economic Indicators*, March 2007, Paris: OECD, 2007, 6.
72. Hopkin and Wincott op. cit., 51.
73. Annesley, op. cit.; G. Bonoli, V. George and P. Taylor-Gooby, *European Welfare Futures: Towards a Theory of Retrenchment*, Cambridge: Polity, 2000.
74. F. Vandenbroucke, 'Foreword', in G. Esping-Andersen, with D. Gallie, A. Hemerijck and J. Myles, *Why We Need a New Welfare State*, Oxford: Oxford University Press, 2002.
75. J. Campbell and O. Pedersen, 'The Varieties of Capitalism and Hybrid Success: Denmark in the Global Economy', *Comparative Political Studies*, 40 (3), 2007, 307–22.

76. J. Clasen and D. Clegg, 'Unemployment Protection and Labour Market Reform in France and Great Britain in the 1990s: Solidarity versus Activation?', *Journal of Social Policy*, 32 (3), 2003, 361–81.

77. C. Green-Pedersen, K. van Kersbergen and A. Hemerijck, 'Neo-liberalism, the "Third Way" or What? Recent Social Democratic Welfare Policies in Denmark and the Netherlands', *Journal of European Public Policy*, 8 (2), 2001, 307–25.

78. M. Costa Lobo and P. Magalhaes, 'The Portuguese Socialists and the Third Way', in G. Bonoli and M. Powell (eds), *Social Democratic Party Policies in Europe*, London: Routledge, 2004, 91–3.

79. Ibid.

80. W. Streeck, 'Competitive Solidarity: Rethinking the "European Social Model"', MPIfG Working Paper 99/8, September 1999, at: www.mpi-fg-koeln.mpg.de/pu/workpap/wp99-8/wp99-8.html

81. M. Rhodes, 'The Political Economy of Social Pacts: "Competitive Corporatism" and European Welfare States', in Pierson op. cit., 165–98.

82. Annesley, op. cit.; F. Vandenbroucke, 'European Social Democracy and the Third Way: Convergence, Divisions, and Shared Questions', in S. White (ed.), *New Labour and the Future of Progressive Politics*, London: Macmillan, 2001; Vandenbroucke, 'Foreword', op. cit.

83. Daly, op. cit., 470.

84. Ibid., 469.

85. Esping-Andersen, *Three Worlds of Welfare Capitalism*, op. cit.

86. Keune and Jepsen, op. cit.

87. B. Rosamond, 'Imagining the European Economy: "Competitiveness" and the Social Construction of "Europe" as an Economic Space', *New Political Economy*, 7 (2), 2002, 158.

88. Keune and Jepsen, op. cit., 10; B. Casey and M. Gold. 'Peer Review of Labour Market Programmes in the European Union: What Can Countries Really Learn from One Another?, *Journal of European Public Policy*, 21 (1), 2005, 23–43.

89. Rosamond, op. cit., 158.

90. See, for example, CEC, *Employment in Europe 2004*, Luxembourg: CEC, 2004.

91. Keune and Jepsen, op. cit., 8.

92. Ibid., 12.

93. Ibid, 7.

94. Ibid., 9.

95. Ibid., 12.

96. CEC, *Employment in Europe 2004*, op. cit., 159.

97. CEC, Proposal for a Council Decision. Guidelines for Employment Policies of the Member States (presented by the Commission) COM (2006) 32, Brussels, 25 January 2006, 39; Keune and Jepsen, op. cit., 12–13.

98. CEC, Proposal for a Council Decision, op. cit., 31; Keune and Jepsen, op. cit., 13.

99. Keune and Jepsen, op. cit., 15.

100. Scruggs, op. cit., 354, Table 1.

101. Campbell and Pedersen, op. cit., 316–9.

102. Keune and Jepsen, op. cit., 15.

103. Daly, op. cit., 466.

104. Martin and Ross, 'Introduction', op. cit., 17.

105. Ibid., 16; Featherstone, op. cit.
106. Scruggs, op. cit.
107. Hopkin and Wincott, op. cit., 59–61, 65.
108. P. Clarke, *A Question of Leadership: Gladstone to Thatcher*, London: Hamish Hamilton, 1991, 317.

11

European Economic Policy: Protectionism as an Elite Strategy*

Vo Phuong Mai Le, Patrick Minford and Eric Nowell

What would we say if the EU, instead of being an engine of ever-widening free markets, became a mechanism by which those of its members who could not reform their economies forced on other hitherto free-market members a programme of protection? In a recent analysis, Minford et al. argued that this indeed was what the EU had become.[1] Their conclusion was that if Britain could not, with whatever free-market allies it could find, divert this process back onto the original free-market agenda of the EU, then it would be forced to leave or incur massive and increasing net costs of membership. They also found that where they could calculate them the net costs to EU citizens other than Britain's was roughly as high in percent of GDP as ours.

Protection is a word that refers primarily to trade. But at the heart of the political economy of the current 'sick men of Europe' (Germany, France and Italy) lies the fear of unemployment; so protection also extends to the labour market and to the welfare system designed to buy off the unemployed. In the labour market this protection covers limits on hours (designed to share work around), strong powers for unions, minimum wages, high unemployment benefits of potentially indefinite duration, workers' councils designed to stop job cuts, and much else. Because this protection is not enough to stop firms closing factories, if they could not be controlled somehow by local politicians, it has led to protection against takeover by foreign firms. It is now usual to hear worries about 'economic nationalism' breaking up the single market.

Labour and product-market interference by these EU governments is now so well-known and so widely attacked by commentators and international bodies such as the OECD, the IMF and even the EU Commission, that we spend no space here discussing it further. The focus of this paper will be instead trade where the extent of EU protectionism has yet either to be

---

* We are grateful for helpful comments to David Collie, Michele Fratianni, Andrew Gamble, Max Haller, Kim Huynh, David Lane and other participants at the Indiana University 2006 conference in Fratianni's honour and at the Cambridge CRASSH seminar.

appreciated or evaluated. Again, as agricultural trade and the CAP have been well crawled over, we concentrate on trade in manufactures and in services. For manufactures we have updated previous estimates for 2002 and a wider group of countries. Our aim is to produce some estimates of the extent of protection and to evaluate the welfare costs of it. We conclude with some broader comments on the general protectionist disease of the EU, how it might relate to the role of elites in Europe, and whether it can be cured.

Protectionism in manufactures

It is usually assumed that since the various GATT and WTO rounds have brought manufactured trade tariffs down across the world including the EU, that EU protection is light in this sector. However, in the wake of retreating tariffs, governments have been given wide discretion to reach agreements on trade quotas, to impose anti-dumping duties or to threaten them and negotiate pre-emptive price rises by importers. Furthermore, these processes reinforce the power of cartels to be established and to survive;[2] thus what starts as temporary protection against 'dumping' ends as the equivalent of a permanent tariff. Tariffs are transparent; but these measures are hard to monitor. While we know how many duties have been imposed and what trade agreements have been made, we cannot easily find out what pre-emptive measures have been taken, nor can we tell whether agreements that have notionally lapsed have done so effectively (especially if a cartel of producers has been implicitly allowed to perpetuate it, as noted above). Calculating the tariff-equivalent has to be done by looking at the price-raising effect of all the various interventions.

Fortunately there is data on prices now on a wide scale owing to the purchasing-power-parity calculations being done by international organisations. A pioneering study by Bradford of the price differentials between major OECD countries and their least-cost OECD supplier suggested that the EU was substantially more protectionist in impact than the USA even though the latter has resorted to a similar number of anti-dumping duties.[3] Averaging across the EU countries studied (Germany, the Netherlands, Belgium and the UK) Bradford's figures, which are adjusted for distribution margins, tax and transport costs, are 40 per cent tariff-equivalent for the EU against 16 per cent for the USA. These percentages are not much different if one looks at 1999 instead of his original 1993.

We have updated these figures to 2002 and extended the comparison more widely now that OECD membership has risen to include South Korea in particular; we also cover all EU countries and have made an attempt to update the figures relative to China. The figures for the EU weighted average against lowest-cost non-EU trade partners are somewhat lower in 2002; the USA, followed by South Korea, are the lowest price alternatives. Bradford presented new measures of final goods trade protections in eight developed countries.[4]

Table 11.1:   Estimates of tariff-equivalents on manufactured goods due to all trade barriers (per cent)[6]

	1990	1996	1999
Belgium	42	65	42
Germany	39	60	29
Italy	38	36	21
Netherlands	42	58	41
UK	41	41	50
USA	16	14	15

Note: Data are expenditure-weighted average ratios of imputed producer prices to the landed prices of goods from the country with the lowest level of price in the sample.

He argued that the barriers to arbitrage between countries are barriers to trade. To measure the trade barriers, one needs to allow for unavoidable costs associated with shipping goods between countries. Once this is done, if there is a price gap for equivalent goods in two different countries, then the higher-price market is protected. To measure the protection barriers, one needs to use the factory prices of the good, not the retail prices. These factory/producer prices show which industries in which countries are most efficient.[5] For the EU as a whole the 2002 figure comes out at 21 per cent, against 30 to 40 per cent on the narrower basis for the 1990s. For the USA, which has also embraced policies of non-tariff protection, the 2002 figure is 6.5 per cent, against middle double-digit percentages in the 1990s.

If one attempts to include China, possible in a crude way for 2002, the implied protection estimates become much larger – 68 per cent for the EU and 48 per cent for the USA. These numbers should be treated cautiously because we do not have prices in separate commodity categories for China and indeed China as yet does not produce for export a whole range of advanced products competing with Western countries. The estimates rely on the manufacturing-wage cost comparisons made by the US Bureau of Labor Statistics (which estimates Chinese manufacturing wage costs per hour at 7 per cent of South Korea's); we also assume that unskilled labour represents 30 per cent of total costs, a percentage deliberately put on the low, cautious side. Nevertheless, even these crude estimates indicate just how China's products are being kept at bay by various means, at least in finished form. Even as protection may be coming down on the products of the more developed emerging market countries such as South Korea, we can see that it is rising in response to the penetration of Chinese products.

Protectionism in services

Throughout the UK debate on the EU it has been implicitly assumed that somehow the UK would gain from the Single Market in services. We are after

Table 11.2:   Survey indicators of service barriers (scale 0–6 from least to most restrictive)[7]

	1978	1988	1998
UK	4.3	3.5	1.0
REU	5.4	5.1	3.4
USA	4.0	2.5	1.4
Australia	4.5	4.2	1.6
Canada	4.2	2.8	2.4
Japan	5.2	3.9	2.9
Switzerland	4.5	4.5	3.9

Note: Simple averages of indicators for seven industries – gas, electricity, post, telecoms, air transport, railways and road freight. Depending on the industry the following dimensions have been included: barriers to entry, public ownership, market structure, vertical integration, price controls. For the Rest of the EU, simple averages of individual EU countries.

all large net exporters of services. It might therefore seem that we must benefit from a customs union in services where we are net exporters just as we lose from one in food and manufactures where we are net importers.

However, there is little parallel between the arrangements in food and manufacturing on the one hand and services on the other. There is no EU customs union in the vast mass of service sectors. Instead there is a patchwork of national protectionism, with the UK having relatively free markets within it. Some survey-based measures of the extent of protectionism across countries and industries are presented in Table 11.2 above.

The idea of the Single Market is to replace this patchwork with a free deregulated market across the EU; in principle this might be accompanied by some sort of barrier against non-EU service companies which could parallel the customs union in food and manufactures. However service markets within the EU are individually often penetrated by foreign (notably US) firms through FDI and other arrangements (especially in the UK which in practice has liberal access for US firms). Hence once there was EU-wide deregulation it would inevitably allow free access to foreign firms lodged in national markets which cannot be practically distinguished from their national counterparts, indeed in many cases have merged with them.

Moreover EU-wide deregulation would, independently of such penetration, unleash strong competition between a large swathe of European national firms. Such competition would be deliberately boosted by EU competition authorities whose aim would of course and rightly be to ensure that prices were pushed down to competitive levels. Indeed they would welcome any assistance in that regard from foreign competitors located in the EU.

Hence the prospects for services sectors would appear to consist of two main possibilities:

1) The single market fails to make much progress at all in the face of strong producer vested interests in national markets; national protection thus remains as now.
2) It is highly successful in the end and produces competitive price levels.

The aim of the EU Commission (the latest services directive, currently being blocked by France and Germany) appears to be to move steadily towards the second by the progressive dismantling of national service barriers.

What of a third option where the EU established a customs union in services? Under this the Single Market would establish EU-wide regulative barriers which put EU-wide prices somewhere between the most liberal and the most restricted regimes currently in place – that is, typically somewhere between the restricted REU average and the current liberal UK regime. We find that such a service customs union would involve substantial transfers to the UK from the rest of the EU as UK service producers displaced REU home producers within the customs union. UK producers of services would receive higher than world prices, this amount on UK net exports being paid for by REU loss of tariff revenue. Such a transfer is unlikely to appeal to the REU majority within the EU's Council of Ministers. If protection is to fall, they would prefer it to fall without a customs union being formed.

Assessing the costs to the UK of these arrangements is rather easy in cases 1) and 2) and those between them. Under both of them the UK's leaving would make no difference on the assumption the UK's regime is already liberal. Under 1) the UK continues in its liberal regime if out just as when in; the REU too carry on as now. Under 2) if the UK stays in it is part of a competitive market; but if it left it would also enjoy a competitive market – exactly the same situation for its consumers and producers. Thus, contrary to the popular perception, the UK faces no prospective gain from being within the EU Single Market in services; it would be as well off under free trade.

On the other hand it is plain that other EU countries would gain considerably from the reduction of national protection of services since this would usher in competitive prices for consumers and either a rise of efficiency in service production or a displacement of resources out of services into other areas of greater productivity.

The cost of EU protection

In this section we use these estimates of protection to estimate their welfare implications for the UK and for the EU. For this, we use a CGE world model built by Minford et al. to generate estimates of changes in trade that result from this protection.[8] We calculate from these changes the welfare effects in the normal manner: these consist of the terms of trade gains/losses of real income, the customs union transfers effected through trade-diversion of ROW sourcing to customs union partners, and the consumer surplus lost through higher internal prices.

We decided to use for our central estimates the usual calculations of consumer surplus, measured in equivalent income variation, but applied to the general equilibrium results of our four-bloc world trade CGE model. For this purpose we disregarded all effects of increased output and income, solely counting the substitution effects of protection; the reason for this is the standard one that income effects are compensated or compensatable, whereas the substitution effects cause costs via misallocation. Such a standard calculation is illustrated in the well-known diagram of a customs union, where the supply and demand curves can be considered as the result of substitution effects in general equilibrium.

We did also consider a calculation using the CGE model alone as the basis and allowing full effects on all industries and land/labour use. We discuss this later.

The calculations fall into three parts for any given trade policy change:

1) The transfer effect of customs union protection whereby one partner pays more than the world price for imports from another partner.
2) The resource misallocation effect whereby output and demand is switched between sectors – this is the usual 'triangle' of lost consumer surplus. For this we use only the substitution effects predicted by the model.
3) The terms of trade effect whereby the changes brought about by the policy change in net world supplies alters world prices. For this calculation we use the full changes predicted by the model.

We look at the net gains/losses to the UK and to the EU from two basic sets of policy changes:

1) If the UK withdraws from the EU trade arrangements in favour of unilateral free trade.
2) If the EU also moves to unilateral free trade.

We are interested in knowing whether it would pay the UK and EU for the UK to withdraw from the EU's trade arrangements; and whether it would pay the EU to liberalise its trade arrangements. In all our calculations we take the status quo, existing trade arrangements, as the benchmark.

What we find is that it would indeed pay the EU to move to unilateral free trade in goods and services; the gain for the rest of the EU (REU) would be a substantial few per cent of REU GDP and for the UK much the same – these figures become greatly magnified to middle double-digit percentages if one assumes liberal planning laws allowing land to be diverted from farming to service and non-traded industries. However, if we assume that because of the power of existing institutions and vested interests, the EU does not change from its existing protective setup, then we find that the UK would still gain a similar percentage of GDP from withdrawing alone to unilateral free trade, while there would be some essentially trivial loss to the REU.

A dilemma resides in these two estimates for UK policy: does it stay within the EU and fight on in the hope of EU trade liberalisation from which it would derive the same benefits as from unilateral free trade and without the trauma of leaving the EU, or does it leave in the expectation of the same gains but more certainly and immediately? There is also an interesting choice for the rest of the EU: does it benefit its citizens generally by going to free trade or does it accept that this is impossible because of the way that EU politics is conducted? If it assumes this impossibility, then should it welcome the departure (at rather small cost) of a UK that is fundamentally at odds with it over both the costs of the trade arrangements and the moves to a more federal politics? We return to these policy issues in the conclusion.

We now consider each product category in turn and go through the detail of the figures.

Agriculture

According to Bradford, whose tariff-equivalent estimates we follow for all goods trade, EU agricultural protection is on average 36 per cent.[9] The model, as we have implemented it, prevents agricultural land from responding to price change, in line with planning and CAP restrictions on planting. Also, consumer spending on food is assumed to be highly inelastic. Hence we observe no effects on the terms of trade as net trade volumes are essentially unaffected. Thus the cost of the CAP consists purely of the transfer cost to the UK which is an equal gain, of course, to the rest of the EU.

As UK net imports of food are some 0.8 per cent of GDP this is 0.3 per cent of UK GDP and 0.06 per cent of EU GDP.

Other studies mostly allow for more trade volume effects; certainly our assumption stretches plausibility as undoubtedly farming interests have had ways of achieving acreage increases which must surely be partially reversed by a 26 per cent (36/136) fall in prices. However, because agriculture is a very small part of GDP – less than 1 per cent in the UK – even adding in more volume effects does not change the size of the estimate unduly as a fraction of GDP.

Basic manufacturing

Bradford's estimate here is of a 16 per cent average tariff-equivalent; our latest estimates for 2002, without China, are similar, at 20 per cent.[10] Against

China the figure exceeds 100 per cent but at this stage of our research we are unwilling to put too much weight on this figure. So we have stayed with Bradford's estimate. The spread of tariff-equivalents across products is very high. But the reason the average is low is that many of these products (such as textiles) have been subject to competition from cheap-labour sources for so long that the domestic industries in the West have largely disappeared as their capital has depreciated; the vested interests pushing for protection have accordingly little power.

Here the UK is twice as large a net importer as it is of food, at 1.7 per cent of GDP. The model's estimated trade effect of the UK eliminating this tariff is that it would effectively eliminate this industry's production (14.4 per cent of GDP). There would be no terms of trade effect however, given the small size of this effect in terms of the world market. Thus UK withdrawal would save the customs union transfer effect of 0.3 per cent of GDP (= 1.7×0.16), which is worth 0.06 per cent of GDP to the rest of the EU; and also the consumer surplus burden of 1.1 per cent of GDP (= $14.4 \times 0.16 \times 0.5$) – a total saving of 1.4 per cent.

Were the EU to liberalise, then its net exports would contract by 13.7 per cent of GDP against the current GDP share of basic manufacturing at 17.6 per cent. This is large in terms of the world market and induces a rise in world prices of basic manufactures by 4 per cent. Since both the UK and the REU would be, after liberalisation, large net importers of these, the terms of trade cost would be 0.6 per cent of GDP for the UK and 0.5 per cent of GDP for the REU. However the consumer surplus gain to the REU would be 1.1 per cent of GDP as for the UK. For the REU liberalisation would thus bring a net gain of 0.5 per cent of GDP (= $1.1 - 0.5 - 0.06$). For the UK the gain would be less than going to free trade on its own: because of the terms of trade effect, it would fall to 0.8 per cent of GDP.

High-tech manufacturing

Bradford's estimate of protection for high-tech manufacturing (which includes the large transport-equipment industry as well as electronics, both of them areas where emerging-market countries in the Far East and elsewhere have made recent penetration) is 58 per cent.[11] On the updated 2002 figures the figure we obtain is lower at 22 per cent if we exclude China and higher at 77 per cent using China as the comparable world price. Here we rely somewhat on the Chinese estimates since they are across a broad range of products and so again leave Bradford's estimate unchanged for the welfare calculations. The model estimate of the trade effect of the UK withdrawing from this protection is the effective elimination of the UK's existing modest-sized industry, currently 3.6 per cent of GDP; of course with the decline of such industries as cars and computing equipment, this has already contracted greatly. The consumer surplus gain to the UK from withdrawal would thus be 1.1 per cent of GDP ($=3.6 \times 0.58 \times 0.5$). The UK would also gain from not paying the customs union transfer on its net imports for the REU; these net imports run at 0.8 per cent of GDP, hence the transfer is 0.5 percent ($=0.58 \times 0.8$). Therefore the total gain for the UK from leaving the customs union in high-tech manufactures would be 1.6 per cent of GDP. For the REU the cost would be the loss of the UK's transfer, worth 0.1 per cent of REU GDP.

For the REU, high-tech manufacture output constitutes 7.9 per cent of GDP, and net exports 1.5 per cent. Clearly certain of these industries have strong comparative advantage and require no protection while others are weak and under attack from emerging-market competition. This latter portion, the model indicates, would be wiped out by the elimination of the protection; we have no good figures for what this portion is but we assume it to be the existing industry minus net exports (6.3 per cent of GDP). Thus the REU would make a consumer surplus gain of 1.8 per cent of GDP ($=6.3 \times 0.58 \times 0.5$). However, it would lose the 0.1 per cent customs union transfer it gets from the UK. Furthermore, the model suggests (after allowing for the capping of the output effect at 6.3 per cent of GDP) that the prices of high-tech manufactures would rise by 4.2 per cent as REU supplies were withdrawn from world markets. Since both the REU and the UK would have become net importers after liberalisation (the REU to the tune of 4.8 per cent, the UK 4.4 per cent, of GDP) the terms of trade cost would be 0.2 per cent of GDP for both the REU and the UK. Thus for the REU the total net gain of moving to free trade would be 1.5 per cent of GDP ($=1.8 - 0.2 - 0.1$).

Services

In this area our estimates of protection are particularly uncertain. The various pieces of evidence we looked at on service trade suggest that it is quite a lot higher in the REU than in the UK. This is supported by the net export figures. The UK's net exports are 3.4 per cent of GDP and 12.4 per cent of service production, suggesting that a large part of the industry must be competing on world markets and hence with no protection. The REU has a rough trade balance.

Available studies, though largely qualitative, suggest that REU protection is rather high – we put it at 30 per cent which seems to be in line with these estimates.[12,13,14] On the other hand, given its very large rate of net exports, UK prices are likely to be driven by competition to supply world markets down to world price levels; thus we assume that protection in the UK is effectively nil, we also assume that the protection is carried out by states and not at the EU level; there has been very little penetration of common standards across the EU in services. In consequence the EU is assumed to have no customs union in services, with free trade inside the union; each country instead has the same barriers against all other countries, including those in the REU.

Table 11.3:   Net gains to the UK and to the REU if the UK withdraws from status quo trade arrangements and adopts unilateral free trade (per cent of GDP)

	UK	REU
Agriculture	+0.3	−0.06
Basic manufacturing	+1.4	−0.06
Hi-tech manufacturing	+1.6	−0.1
Traded services	−	−
Total	+3.3	−0.22

Under these assumptions it is easy enough to work out the effect of the UK withdrawing from the EU protective system. Since the EU has only state-level protection and the UK is assumed to have no protection in the first place, the effect is simply nil. (Were we to have assumed that the UK had some protection in place, we would have found an additional gain from higher consumer surplus, as this protection was eliminated. However, of course eliminating protection that is not due to the EU does not require withdrawal from the EU; so again we would not attribute this gain to 'withdrawal from the EU's protective system' as there is no such system in place.)

For the REU matters are different. Reducing each country's protection of 30 per cent on services would theoretically reduce output of services substantially; according to the model, were the REU to do this service output (20 per cent of GDP) would fall to zero. However we must recall the assumption here that this policy is applied on its own; this is highly unlikely given that traded services are where most rich countries now think the future lies for their new industrial activity. Given this assumption, however, the estimate is not unreasonable, with internal prices falling by 23 per cent (= 30/130) on this traded activity. On this assumption, the gain in consumer surplus is 2.3 per cent of GDP (= 20 × 0.23 × 0.5). However, the prices of services would rise on world markets by 6 per cent according to the model; with net imports now of 20 per cent of GDP, the REU would lose 1.2 per cent on the terms of trade, making its total gain 1.3 per cent of GDP. The UK as a net exporter would gain 0.2 per cent of GDP (= 3.4 × 0.06).

Gains and losses from separate acts of policy compared with the status quo

We can now use these calculations to draw up a table of gains and losses were the UK to withdraw from various parts of the EU's trade arrangements (see Table 11.3).

This table is relevant to the decision of the UK to withdraw or not from individual parts of the trade treaties. We note that the UK has a strong incentive

Table 11.4:   Net gains to the UK and to the REU if the EU replaces status quo trade arrangements with unilateral free trade (per cent of GDP)

	UK	REU	REU*
Agriculture	+0.3	−0.03	−
Basic manufacturing	+0.8	+0.54	+0.6
Hi-tech manufacturing	+1.4	+1.5	+1.6
Traded services	+0.2	+1.3	+1.3
Total	+2.7	+3.3	+3.5

* REU if UK has already gone to free trade; this is column 2 plus transfer effects (these are already eliminated by UK liberalisation)

to withdraw. For the REU the UK's withdrawal creates marginally negative effects.

We can also ask whether the UK and REU have any incentive to liberalise EU markets and move to free trade, with the UK remaining a member of these common arrangements. For this we show in Table 11.4 the net gains and losses for the UK and the REU, comparing a post-liberalisation situation with the assumed benchmark.

Here we can see that there is a strong incentive on welfare grounds for the REU to liberalise.

Examining policies as a group

Notice, however, that if we want to know what the sum total is of doing all these things together we have to re-examine the estimates under that precise assumption. In practice UK withdrawal would occur across all the areas of trade; to leave one area would probably not be negotiable. Essentially you must 'leave or not leave'; having left, certain treaty areas might be restorable under a completely new relationship.

As for EU liberalisation it is difficult to know the stages by which it might proceed. Currently service liberalisation is actively proceeding under the new services directives, though plainly progress differs greatly between industries. But there is no activity at all in the area of manufacturing; no official discussions yet entertain the possibility of dropping anti-dumping actions and of breaking down cartels in order to allow free entry at world prices by low-cost emerging-market producers. Nor in agriculture is any change in CAP protection rates actively on the agenda. Hence in evaluating the possible gains of reform in the REU we assume two stages: first, a liberalisation of services, and second, a possible liberalisation of agriculture and manufacturing.

Thus in this section we examine the above policies as packages of reforms, substituting the full CGE model estimates coming from their joint implementation. To calculate these we have taken the CGE model's total predictions of sectoral change with the complete packages.

Table 11.5:   UK and the REU simultaneously move to free trade

	UK	REU	REU*
Sum of partial effects	+2.7%	+3.3%	+3.5%
CGE full estimate	+17%	+14%**	+14.2%

* REU if UK has already liberalised
** does not include liberalisation of services

We now discuss more fully the meaning of this full CGE model simulation. It is carried out on the assumption that the market for land is like the markets for skilled and for unskilled labour: it has a price that sets supply of land (assumed to emerge from a process of owner supply as moderated by the planning process) equal to demand. Thus, for example, as agricultural protection falls the price of land falls with it, reducing the use of land overall; there is also a switching of land use from agriculture into services and non-traded industry.

The gain of welfare to the UK here is dramatically larger at 17 per cent (this amount is not greatly affected by whether the REU simultaneously liberalises or not). What is going on is that with agricultural prices at home greatly lowered by the elimination of the CAP tariffs, land prices drop substantially (26 per cent) as demand for land in agriculture contracts sharply, and land is switched into traded services and non-traded activity (with the implicit permission of the planning authorities). These latter two sectors are therefore able to expand considerably – services by 35 per cent, non-traded by 15 per cent. Notice that both agricultural output and manufacturing fall by about a quarter. One may legitimately have doubts about the political feasibility of this solution, which is why we do not use it as our central estimate. However, it does indicate that, in the presence of some planning flexibility, the central estimate we have used, based on partial substitution effects only, could be a significant underestimate – how much so depending naturally on the extent of such planning flexibility.

In this case of the EU as a whole, we have not attempted to assess liberalising services alone in the first step using our CGE model. The reason is that the outcome depends on a complex of factors, not merely the drop in general external protection but also the role of inward investment in services, reconstituting local suppliers with the help of external expertise. An example would be the effect of the liberalisation of airlines on airline provision by continental European airlines; this has resulted in a steep drop in prices but also a surge in domestic operators, drawing on the experience of low-cost airlines from outside the European continent. Thus, based on such an example, one might expect liberalisation to strengthen local service providers through competition and expand the market. Our CGE model assumes that competition already exists, albeit at high prices, and that the industry's structure is given; both assumptions are unlikely to hold.

With the liberalisation of services EU protection then becomes identical with that of the UK, consisting entirely of the EU's external tariff-equivalents. We can now assess the effects of removing protection in an orthodox way. Thus turning to the liberalisation of trade in the EU the effects are naturally highly similar to those in the UK as is the rise in welfare at 14 per cent (or 14.2 per cent if the UK has already liberalised by leaving). Again we find that there is the same large drop in land prices and a switch of land use into services (up by 35 per cent) and non-traded industries (up by 10 per cent). Politically, as in the UK, this raises questions of realism, in particular with planning consent. Planning is a highly complex phenomenon in the REU, differing both across countries and across regions within countries. On the other hand, given the huge pressures to create employment under the REU conditions of generally high unemployment, the popular pressure might be greater for liberalisation. The essential point we make here is not that the full simulation should be believed but that it reminds us that the central-case calculation based on partial substitution effects alone is a minimum which could be added to depending on the extent of land liberalisation.

Assessing the overall economic costs and benefits of UK membership of the EU

In this final section we briefly consider the broader economic costs and benefits of membership of the EU. We do it from the UK's viewpoint because we have the relevant data for it. However, the argument can be generalised to other EU members with suitable data. There is every reason to believe that the EU as a whole is being damaged in particular by excessive social intervention, which has caused both unemployment and slow growth. In considering the economics of the EU, we interpret the thrust of future EU policy in the light of recent policy actions by the EU (for example the decision by France and Germany to scrap reform of the CAP) and of the general thrust (in favour of protectionism and social rights) of proposed new policies, such as those recently envisaged in the draft constitution and its successor, the Lisbon Treaty.

Using the Liverpool Model of the UK economy, we have examined what might be the effects of the social policies, which amount to the reversal of the reforms brought in by the UK government from 1979. On the assumption of rather moderate changes (a minimum wage raised to 50 per cent of male median wages, union power restored to mid-1980s levels, social cost rises worth 20 per cent of current wages), the model predicts that they would raise unemployment by 5.7 per cent – that is, 1.8 million – and cost 6.4 per cent in reduced output. It could of course be either more or less depending on just how extensively this harmonisation was pursued; but the draft constitution indicates clearly enough that what we have seen so far – including the Working Time Directive, the Social Chapter and the Works Council Directives – is just a beginning.

A further ('bail-out') cost comes from potentially insolvent state pensions on the continent. Extensive estimates were made of these pension deficits in an OECD study in the middle 1990s. Recent attempts to recompute these prospects suggest little change.[15] If we take these 1995 OECD projections as illustrative at least, the deficits projected are: for Germany 10 per cent of GDP by 2030; for Italy about the same; and for France a little bit less. Add up these deficits as a percentage of UK GDP, which is of similar size to each of these countries, and you come to some 30 per cent. If the UK were to pay a quarter of that, for example via some federal system of burden-sharing, then the bill would be some 7 per cent of GDP. Again, like harmonisation, the extent of this is rather uncertain; it could be a lot more or a lot less, depending on both the extent of reforms undertaken by these countries and the extent to which the progress of federalism enables burden-sharing between countries. But this is certainly a burden the UK does not want to risk sharing, at even a modest level.

When one asks what the countervailing benefits are, one finds that they are hard to identify on the economic side. The Cecchini Report claimed that there would be large benefits in greater specialisation and exploitation of scale economies because of the Single Market: the logic was that lower barriers within the EU would encourage a better adjustment to market forces.[16] The evidence has not supported gains on the scale predicted by Cecchini; our CGE model by construction does not impute scale economies but it does include any gains (the majority according to studies of UK Cecchini-style effects) from greater competition within the Single Market, whatever in practice they may have been. Free trade with the whole world (facing whatever unilateral barriers each country chose to levy) would permit the UK to exploit the same processes but in a way that is consonant with its comparative advantage. The gains we have identified from leaving the EU relate to the UK's exploitation of its true comparative advantage in services essentially; most studies agreed that in services scale economies are unlikely.

The NIESR claimed that there are gains of foreign direct investment (FDI) from membership of the EU.[17] FDI is related to technology transfer and where it occurs it depends on the structure of the economy. As we have seen above, that structure changes dramatically if the UK leaves the EU. Whether FDI as a method of technology transfer is as needed when the economic structure shifts to its true comparative advantage, we simply do not know. But if it is, it will occur equally in the new structure. The essential point concerns whether the economy's technology is at its maximum in the new structure as compared with the old: given that all industries will be competing on a level with the best in the world, the pressure at least will be maximal. But of course we have no real way of measuring this matter in practice. Thus to summarise, the NIESR rightly observed that in the old structure there was a high FDI level, much of it in manufacturing; and it conjectured that there would be less FDI outside the EU and concluded that this would reduce productivity. However, as our argument indicates, this conclusion is a non-sequitur: less could occur because the technology level in the new structure is higher, in which case productivity too would still be higher.

European elites and their role in protectionism

This paper has focused on the costs and benefits of EU policies to its citizens and to those of the UK in particular. However elites only care about these things if their own interests are aligned with them. It is a well-known result in political economy that minorities with much to lose generate much bigger pressure on governing elites because they are able to command substantial votes and cash budgets, compared to ordinary citizens who each individually have little to lose, even if their total loss is greater than that of the minorities by a large margin.[18] That is the situation here. Protection brings big gains to small groups such as the protected industries, and widespread costs across the citizenry that are relatively small for each citizen. The situation is often aggravated by ignorance on the part of the general citizenry; indeed that ignorance is individually rational since the costs of acquiring technical knowledge will greatly exceed the possible gains, especially net of the organisational efforts required to deploy it. Again that is true here; ignorance about the true costs of protection is general and indeed the use of non-transparent methods (such as anti-dumping and industry agreements) to produce protection aggravates the problem of discovery.

The problem of getting support for reform is further aggravated by the existence of short-term costs during the transition to the long-term improvement in industrial allocation. Existing industries that cannot compete in the long term must contract, causing unemployment, while the new industries that will take their place may take time to grow and absorb the unemployed. There is a substantial net gain when these two are balanced off but this net gain is not easily seen, and requires popular education. Again, this is hard to achieve in the face of minorities that will vociferously argue that there is a net loss.

Inside a nation the political process can produce mechanisms to get around these problems. Think-tanks can explain problems and mobilise support for solutions, acting as middlemen between the technical issues and the public and politicians. Sometimes a coalition can be built around a reform policy that raises general living standards while causing damage to particular groups; the latter can in these policies be sufficiently compensated out of general taxation that they are willing to go along with the reforms or at least not to obstruct them. However, this process is much more difficult at the EU level because while the EU has certain powers – for example, to set commercial policy – it does not have others, such as taxation, that can be used to compensate losers. (True, it has some regional and social funds but these are tightly allocated to other uses than such ad hoc compensation.) Thus, for example, liberalising trade policies that cause national losers in certain industries are impossible for the EU to pursue without enlisting national support for those policies – which will in practice mean nations raising taxes to compensate the losers.

As it happens, the current EU Commission is in favour of liberalisation of trade, as well as the deregulation of services. However, it has proved powerless to get such policies enacted. They have been effectively vetoed by the nations whose principal industries would be damaged – even if their citizens would benefit from the reforms by more in total. The same nations have been equally unable to reform domestic institutions to reduce unemployment, for example. It is therefore no mystery in political economy why we observe the national elites in the EU finding protection to be in their interest.

Nor is it easy to see how the situation can be changed. One possibility would be to give the EU power to raise extra taxes ad hoc. But this would clearly be resisted by many member nations, if not all. Another possibility is to spread popular education in these issues more widely among EU citizens. Better information about the trade-offs would then begin to influence debates on domestic reform; these in turn could enable support to form for liberalisation at the EU level, with necessary compensation at the national level.

It is easier therefore to understand what is wrong than it is to see ways for solutions to be advanced with any speed. At best the EU seems condemned to suffer poor policies for a long time to come, with reforms arriving glacially if at all.

A word about the attitude of the UK elite to the EU: in the face of considerable evidence that the UK would be better off under free trade and accompanying free-market policies outside the EU, why is there no agenda on the part of any of the three major UK political parties to leave the EU? Again the answer can be given in terms of the powerful groups ranged against such action – both agricultural and manufacturing industry lobbies are strongly against it for obvious reasons, while the general citizenry is ignorant of the economic case. (There is a debate about political aspects of EU membership focusing on sovereignty; but UK public opinion is ambivalent on this.) The elites of none of the major UK parties show much willingness to engage against these lobbies, or indeed to press for much in the way of further free-market reform within the EU. It is as if there is policy exhaustion after the massive reforms of the 1980s and 1990s.

Finally, can one say anything yet about the effect of the current banking crisis on these elite attitudes? The policies that separate EU governments have pursued towards their banking systems have been chosen nationally but after a bad-tempered start in which the French were forced by German opposition to deny their proposals for joint action, there has been consultation, with several EU summits, and cooperation has occurred on general principles. The crisis has strikingly underlined the ECB's lack of a single fiscal authority with which it could coordinate actions. But there is no willingness as yet to pool any further fiscal powers within the EU.

At the same time, some protectionism is already evident, notably in Italy where Prime Minister Berlusconi is taking powers to prevent hostile takeovers of Italian companies by foreign ones; he has pumped state money into Alitalia, with the object of passing it on to some Italian entrepreneurs. As the recession worsens, we may well see more of this intra-EU protectionism as well as stronger demands for action against non-EU products. Such action would cohere with the elite strategy we have seen in this chapter.

The crisis has also reinforced widespread suspicions of market forces within the EU elites. These will further set back attempts to liberalise markets. So all in all the banking crisis is likely to delay even further any progress in economic policy.

Conclusions

In this chapter we have attempted to estimate the costs, both to the UK and the Rest of the EU (REU), of the EU's protectionist trade policies in agriculture, manufacturing and services. Contrary to the popular impression that the EU is a mechanism for creating a 'competitive single market', it turns out that the EU is levying costs in wasted resources of the order of 3 per cent of GDP (or under favourable planning assumptions a large multiple of this) by protecting its industries from world competition. These costs apply to UK and REU citizens more or less alike and on a similar scale. The economic damage created by the EU does not however stop there: because of the widespread welfare lobbies within member countries on the continent, the majority coalition within the EU has pressed for social protection and spending to be 'harmonised' at a fairly high level. It also faces a prospective pensions crisis, in the sense that it cannot be assumed that necessary cuts in pensions promises or rises in the taxes to pay for them will be politically feasible. Thus those member states whose pension plans are affordable and whose social regulations are the least burdensome on business, face the prospect of a potentially severe burden from the pensions problems elsewhere in the EU and from the pressure of harmonisation. We have been able to quantify this potential cost for the UK; but it is also a real threat to many other members, such as those recently joining from Eastern Europe.

We have discussed briefly how it is that European elites would find it in their interests to perpetuate this protectionist situation. Under the EU institutions minority groups have considerable power and incentive to block change and exercise this through their own national governments, as well as at the EU level. The EU commission has no tax resources with which it could buy them off in the interests of EU citizens in general; it relies on its member nations to do this since they have the taxation powers but even if one nation might to get enough support to do so, reform requires that many must have a pro-reform political consensus. Hence the prospects for change are dim in the short term. In the longer term they might very slowly improve if either the EU could raise its own resources for such ad hoc needs or there were a general move at the national level towards reform. Unfortunately the current banking crisis can only worsen these prospects.

Notes and References

1. P. Minford, V. Mahambare and E. Nowell, *Should Britain Leave the EU? An Economic Analysis of a Troubled Relationship*, London: Edward Elgar, 2005.
2. P. Messerlin, 'Anti-dumping Regulations or Pro-cartel Law? The EC Chemical Cases', *The World Economy*, 13 (4), December 1990, 465–92.
3. S. C. Bradford, 'Paying the Price: Final Goods Protection in OECD Countries', *Review of Economics and Statistics*, 85 (1), 2003, 24–37.
4. Ibid.
5. For details of the formula used and data see: www.cf.ac.uk/carbs/econ/workingpapers/papers/E2009_1.pdf.
6. Based on S. Bradford and R. Z. Lawrence, *Has Globalization Gone Far Enough? The Costs of Fragmented Markets*, Washington DC: Institute for International Economics, 2004.
7. G. Nicoletti and S. Scarpetta, 'Interactions between Product and Labour Market Regulations: Do They Affect Employment? Evidence from OECD Countries', Paper presented at the Banco de Portugal Conference on 'Labour Market Institutions and Economic Outcomes', 3–4 June 2001, Cascais.
8. Minford, Mahambare and Nowell, op. cit.
9. Bradford, op. cit.
10. Ibid.
11. Ibid.
12. Minford, Mahambare and Nowell, op. cit.
13. D. Nguyen-Hong, 'Restrictions on Trade in Professional Services', Productivity Commission Staff Research Paper, Ausinfo, Canberra, August 2000.
14. G. McGuire. and M. Schuele, 'Restrictiveness of International Trade in Banking Services', in C. Findlay and T. Warren (eds), *Impediments to Trade in Services: Measurement and Policy Implications*, London and New York: Routledge, 2000, 201–14.
15. OECD, 'Fiscal Implications of Ageing: Projections of Age-related Spending', OECD Economics Department Working Paper No. 305, Paris: OECD Economics Department, 2001.
16. Cecchini Report, *The Cost of Non-Europe*, Brussels: European Commission, 1988.
17. NIESR, 'Continent Cut Off? The Macroeconomic Impact of British Withdrawal from the EU', *NIESR Quarterly Economic Review*, February 2000.
18. M. Olson, *The Logic of Collective Action – Public Goods and the Theory of Collective Groups*, Cambridge MA: Harvard University Press, 1971.

12
The European Union: A Player in World Energy Politics?

Simon Bromley

Speaking at the launch of the European Union Commission's proposals for an integrated energy and climate change package in January 2007, Commission President Jose Manuel Barroso stated that:

> Today marks a step change for the European Union. Energy policy was a core area at the start of the European project. We must now return it to centre stage. The challenge of climate change, increasing import dependence and higher energy prices are faced by all EU members. A common European response is necessary to deliver sustainable, secure and competitive energy.[1]

Together with the Energy Commissioner, Andris Piebalgs, and the Competition Commissioner, Neelie Kroes, President Barroso has sought to put climate change, energy security and the liberalisation of energy markets in the EU and beyond at the centre of the Commission's work. The EU's ambitions in the field of energy policy, including foreign energy policy, are certainly high and they represent an ambitious attempt both to position the Commission at the core of a key agenda for the member states of the European Union and to make a claim for EU leadership in a key arena of world politics.

In this chapter, I aim to use a discussion of key aspects of the EU's proposed foreign energy policy in order to examine the coherence of the ambitious agenda launched by the Commission and what kind of role the EU might play in this key arena of world politics. In Section 1, I briefly outline the key features of the Commission's agenda in order to establish its implications for the idea of a European foreign energy policy. Section 2 steps back from current developments to take a brief look at the extent – minimal I argue – to which the European Community shaped earlier European energy policies as this casts a revealing light on the distance that current proposals would have to travel to make a substantial impact. Section 3 considers the key role of natural gas in EU energy policy as this raises questions about both the internal-market project and future relations with a Russia that shows no signs of conforming to liberal notions of markets and property rights. Section 4 considers the prospects for higher oil and gas prices and the idea of a transition to a low-carbon energy future while Section 5 takes a brief look at the prospects for nuclear power. A brief conclusion suggests grounds for caution in expecting too much from the EU in these respects.

A common EU energy policy?

The January 2007 communication on an energy policy for Europe from the EU Commission to the European Council and the European Parliament emphasised the need to:

- establish the internal energy market, recognising that effective internal gas and electricity markets 'are not yet in place';
- ensure a secure energy supply, in a context where the 'risk of supply failure is growing';
- reduce greenhouse-gas emissions, against a background in which 'present energy policies within the EU are not sustainable';
- develop energy technologies, especially renewable energy technologies, and the technologies of carbon capture and storage from fossil-fuel power generation;
- consider the future of nuclear energy; and
- implement a common international energy policy, in which 'energy must become a central part of all external EU relations'.[2]

This followed the Green Paper on a European Strategy for Sustainable, Competitive and Secure Energy in March 2006 and the call by the Brussels European Council (23–24 March 2006) for an 'Energy Policy for Europe, aiming at effective Community policy, coherence between Member states and consistency between actions in different policy areas and fulfilling in a balanced way the three objectives of security of supply, competitiveness and environmental sustainability'.[3] And in March 2007, the European Council adopted an energy Action Pan for the period 2007–9.

The strategy was premised on the idea that 'business as usual' was not an option. In the first place, the Commission reckoned that 'business as usual' would see final energy consumption increase by 25 per cent over 2000 levels by 2030 and energy import dependence rise from 50 per cent of total consumption to 65 per cent by 2030. Natural gas import dependence would increase from 57 to 84 per cent; and crude-oil dependence rise from 82 to 93 per cent. Given the rapid increases in crude-oil prices from 2000, the continued indexing of gas prices to oil prices and the consequent impact on electricity prices where, as in most European countries, gas is the marginal fuel, these trends would represent significant economic and security-of-supply risks.

Business as usual would also mean that the EU would fail to meet its Kyoto commitments – energy use accounts for some 80 per cent of greenhouse gas emissions in the EU – because while carbon dioxide emissions in the EU-25 decreased by 3 per cent between 1900 and 2000, most of this was in the early 1990s and accounted for by dramatic falls in the new, transition countries, and emissions in the old EU-15 slightly increased. Projections by the Commission show future carbon dioxide emissions exceeding the 1990 level by 5 per cent in 2030 if present policies continue. Given the need to bring the rapidly industrialising developing world into future global climate-change arrangements, the Commission argued that 'policies for containing and eventually reducing fossil fuel consumption in industrialised countries seem to be a prerequisite for global moderation'.[4] By 2030, the EU might account for just 15 per cent of the increases in carbon dioxide emissions and less than 10 per cent of world energy consumption.

In order to deal with these problems, the EU plans to reduce its total primary energy consumption by 20 per cent by 2020 as well as reducing its carbon emissions by a similar amount as compared with the 1990 (Kyoto) baseline. Ambitious targets, described by the Commission as 'truly ambitious', have been set for renewable energy: 20 per cent of energy consumption by 2020, 10 per cent from biomass alone. The EU also aims to lead a 'post-industrial' revolution based on the technologies of a low-carbon economy. It claims to be a world leader in renewable technologies and the Energy Commissioner, Andris Piebalgs, has stated that Europe is poised to make breakthroughs in carbon sequestration that will enable the exploitation of internal coal reserves without compromising environmental commitments. The Commission 'believes that by 2020 all new coal-fired plants should be fitted with [carbon dioxide] capture and storage and existing plants should then progressively follow the same approach' and it plans for 10 to 12 industrial-scale demonstration projects to be built.[5]

The Commission further emphasised the need to review the future of nuclear power: in 2006, it accounted for 15 per cent of EU energy consumption (30 per cent of electricity generation) in 152 reactors spread across the EU–27. With the future of nuclear power uncertain, replacement of this capacity by fossil-fuel electricity generation (in the absence of carbon sequestration) would add to climate change problems and further increase dependence on gas imports. 'Any development' of electricity generation 'consistent with present EU Climate policy will need either to force solid fuels consumption in electricity much down compared to the baseline scenario or to ensure broadly applied carbon sequestration in order to reduce emissions'.[6] Aside from carbon sequestration and renewable energy, nuclear power is the obvious choice, though the Commission is formally agnostic on its future, perhaps because this is so clearly a responsibility of member states.

The Commission recognised that despite two decades of focus on the completion of the European energy market, particularly the liberalisation of the electricity and gas markets, there is still no integrated European market. Rather, there is what Dieter Helm describes as 'a string of national markets with bilateral connections'.[7] While this did not matter overly in the 1980s and 1990s 'because most member states had excess capacity, and world energy prices were very low', now 'the majority of European electricity assets are based upon fossil fuels, and most are old and coming up to replacement'; 'renewables technologies have proved expensive relative to fossil fuels'; and 'the first generation of nuclear power stations are coming towards the end of their lives, taking out significant zero carbon emissions capacity'. In short, 'both security of supply and the climate change challenges need to be met with major new investment'.[8] The Commission maintained that completing the internal market in energy would not only deliver competition and efficiencies for consumers but also stimulate 'higher investment'.

Further progress on the completion of an internal energy market required: unbundling of energy distribution and production, which could be achieved either by regulation or (better according to the Commission) ownership unbundling; harmonisation of national regulatory regimes and the insertion of a Community dimension into national approaches; the development of sufficient electricity generation and gas storage capacities; and rapid development of trans-European physical infrastructure to connect markets, the most important of which are 'the Power-Link between Germany, Poland and Lithuania; connections to off-shore wind power in Northern Europe; electricity interconnections between France and Spain; and the Nabucco pipeline, bringing gas from the Caspian to central Europe'.[9]

And finally, the Commission emphasised the need for the EU 'to speak with a single voice on the international stage'. The extension of the EU *acquis* to neighbouring countries and the Energy Charter Treaty process and its further development are viewed as central to this endeavour. The scale of the task in this respect should not be underestimated as even the Commission staff accept that 'the external dimension of the EU security of energy supplies is, for the time being, neither coherently identified nor under any EU control'.[10] While Council documents and texts do not directly contradict this language about the need for a common external policy, they also make constant reference to taking account of member states' situations, the principle of subsidiarity and specifically the idea of 'member states' sovereignty over primary energy resources and choice of energy-mix'.[11] That said, some of the priorities laid out included that:[12]

- 'The EC and its member states should be a key driver in the design of international agreements, including the future of the Energy Charter Treaty and the post-2012 climate regime';
- 'The EU aim to build up a wide network of countries around the EU, acting on the basis of shared rules or principles derived from the EU energy policy';

- The EU enhance relations with Russia 'based on market principles and those of the Energy Charter Treaty and draft Transit Protocol';
- The EU 'continue to develop closer energy relations with other major consumers, in particular through IEA and G8 or through intensified bilateral cooperation';
- The EU 'deepen dialogue and relations with key energy producers and transit countries, whether through OPEC and the Gulf Cooperation Council or fully implementing the Memoranda of Understanding with Azerbaijan and Kazakhstan and moving on to establish new ties with other important Central Asian producers like Turkmenistan and Uzbekistan. In addition, it is imperative to facilitate the transport of the Caspian energy resources to the EU';
- The EU lead on the development of 'an international agreement on energy efficiency';
- The EU develop a 'comprehensive Africa-Europe Energy partnership'; and
- The EU should 'promote non proliferation, nuclear safety and security, in particular through a reinforced cooperation with the International Atomic Energy Agency'.

European Community energy policy: a brief sketch

In the light of these ambitions – and in the light of Barroso's claim that 'energy policy was a core area at the start of the European project' – it may be worth recalling something of the history of energy policy in the European Union in order to situate current developments. Although it is true that the European Coal and Steel Community (ECSC) was an important forerunner to the development of the European Community, there has in fact been little common energy policy-making among the member states. The Paris Treaty (1951) determined that coal would come under the auspices of the ECSC; nuclear power was covered by Euratom (1957); and the Treaty of Rome (1957) gave oil, natural gas, hydropower and electricity to the Commission. But none of these instruments included provisions for the development of a common energy policy. This was hardly surprising since most of the components of Western Europe's energy industries were state-owned or -regulated, nationally based companies. Any attempts at rationalisation on a community-wide basis, whether as a result of administrative means or market forces, would have run into strong obstacles in terms of regional unemployment and national claims to sovereign control over resources. Indeed, given the priority accorded to national reconstruction during the 1950s, and the subsequent moves towards corporatist planning in the 1960s, many states regarded energy as a key sector for dirigiste coordination.

However, perhaps the most important reason for the absence of anything approaching a common energy policy was that no such thing appeared to be necessary. In the 1950s and 1960s the central concerns in Western European

Table 12.1:   Shares of coal and petroleum (oil and gas) in energy demand (per cent)

	1955		1980	
	Coal	Petroleum	Coal	Petroleum
Britain	85	14	37	58
France	61	28	18	65
West Germany	88	9	30	64
Italy	25	44	8	85

Source: Adapted from Nigel Lucas, *Western Energy Policies*, Oxford: Clarendon Press, 1985, Table 4.1, 141.

energy matters were the unemployment and regional implications of the rundown of the coal sector and the security of supply of rapidly rising crude-oil imports from the Middle East. After the cautious outlook of both the Armand (1955) and Hartley (1956) reports, the Robinson Report of 1959 foresaw an energy surplus and took a sanguine view of oil imports. And when the oil companies demonstrated that their worldwide distribution systems could cope with the supply disruptions of the Suez Crisis (1956) and the 1967 Arab-Israeli War, lingering worries about security of supply were dissipated. (Even such emergency planning as did take place – around the security of oil supplies in times of conflict – did not take place through Community institutions or processes but rather in NATO councils. The most powerful members of the Community – West Germany, France and Italy (and later the United Kingdom), as well as Belgium, Denmark and the Netherlands – were also members of NATO and while the community aspired to a common political definition, it played little role in foreign policy.)

The displacement of coal by oil was dramatic: in 1950 coal accounted for 75 per cent of the Community's total primary energy requirements and oil some 10 per cent; by 1966 the corresponding figures were 38 per cent and 45 per cent and in 1971 20 per cent and 60 per cent – see Table 12.1. The Community's energy import dependence increased in parallel: in 1950 imports amounted to 13 per cent of requirements, by 1960 this rose to 30 per cent and in 1970 it stood at 63 per cent.

As to the longer-term, it was widely assumed that oil would provide a bridge to an energy future centred on nuclear-generated electricity. Under these circumstances and assumptions, the main community policies related to the regularisation of coal subsidies, the harmonisation of taxes and the promotion of competition. Then came the first oil shock of 1973. The state of energy balances in the four largest members of the Community prior to the oil crisis of 1973–4 can be seen in Tables 12.2 and 12.3 below.

In response to the crisis of 1973–4, the Commission presented the Council of Ministers with a long-term strategy paper on problems and resources

Table 12.2: Total energy demands by fuel in 1973 (per cent)

	Oil	Natural gas	Coal	Others
Britain	52.1	13.2	33.6	1.2
France	72.5	8.1	16.1	3.2
West Germany	58.6	10.1	30.1	1.3
Italy	78.6	10.0	8.6	3.2

Source: Adapted from Romano Prodi and Alberto Clo, 'Europe', in Raymond Vernon (ed.), *Daedalus*, no. 104, special issue, *The Oil Crisis*, 1975, Table 4, 95.

Table 12.3: Domestic production as a proportion of domestic consumption by fuel in 1972 (per cent)

	Oil	Natural gas	Coal	Total
Britain	2	97	98	51
France	1	54	69	23
West Germany	7	64	115	50
Italy	1	93	5	15

Source: Adapted from Romano Prodi and Alberto Clo, 'Europe', in Raymond Vernon (ed.), *Daedalus*, no. 104, special issue, *The Oil Crisis*, 1975, Table 5, 95.

of energy policy for the decade 1975–1985,[13] in which it made the case for a unified internal energy market for energy alongside policies to cope with security of supply. It suggested that the latter could be pursued by increasing electricity's share of final consumption from 25 per cent to 35 per cent, by a general increase in the use of nuclear power, coal and natural gas, and thus a reduction of oil's share from some 60 per cent to nearer to 40 per cent of total energy requirements. Although the Commission advocated a unified internal energy market, it also urged the coordination of a 'flexible system of concertation' among energy companies and the Committee of Energy; however, none of these proposals was backed by a concrete programme of action.

In November 1973, the Community also issued a joint declaration calling for a cease-fire in the Arab-Israeli war and an eventual Israeli withdrawal to its pre-1967 borders and France argued for an independent EC dialogue with the oil-producing countries. West Germany, Denmark and the Benelux countries also sought a common Community policy towards the oil producers but did not support the anti-US stance of the French; and Britain, Italy and Ireland favoured no action at all. France also increased the stakes in these discussions by raising the question of an independent European security posture based on coordination in the West European Union (WEU) permanent weapons committee but West Germany insisted that any such discussions had to take place in the Eurogroup in NATO.

At the same time, the United States was sponsoring the creation of an International Energy Agency (IEA) to counter the apparent power of OPEC. All the member states of the Community except France were reluctant to compromise transatlantic unity and therefore at the Washington Conference of February 1974, they all – except France – aligned themselves with the United States. At these founding talks of the IEA, President Nixon linked the stationing of US troops in Western Europe to better political and economic cooperation across the Atlantic, a point that was reiterated by his Secretary of State, Henry Kissinger. Indeed, Jeffrey Pryce has argued that: 'The Washington Energy Conference was a turning point in relations among the allied countries. By uniting against France and with the Americans when the crux finally came, the other Europeans expressed disapproval of transatlantic confrontation'.[14] Specifically, West Germany proposed and Kissinger and Nixon agreed that after EC political directors reached a common position, but before the Community's foreign ministers took decisions, Washington would be consulted.

In this way, 'only after the Europeans established a consultation procedure and relations with Washington improved could the Euro-Arab dialogue proceed'.[15] In the event, the dialogue ran into other problems of Palestinian representation and the Arab League's refusal to compromise the position of OPEC. To be sure, this whole discussion was complicated by, and cannot be understood apart from, Cold War, East-West rivalries and Europe's growing energy trade with the Eastern bloc, but it is also evidence of what Robert Lieber called 'fierce American opposition' to independent European initiatives towards Middle East oil.[16]

In practice, whatever the economic effects of the 1973–4 oil crisis, security of supply was never really an issue for the European Community. Neither Western Europe as a whole, nor Community members, suffered shortages:

> So far as Europe was concerned, the oil crisis did not bring on an overall shortage in either oil or energy. The difficulties of the crisis were mainly the result of disturbances in the internal distribution of oil products, which were triggered by the resistance of governments to the price increases imposed by the oil companies, and which led to delays in delivery, discrimination against independent companies, and the speculative hoarding of stocks.[17]

Indeed, notwithstanding the second oil crisis prompted by the Iranian Revolution of 1979, movements in international oil markets in the 1980s and 1990s were relatively benign. The combination of structural change in the main OECD economies, as services displaced manufacturing, and increased oil prices meant that demand for crude oil fell sharply. Moreover, OPEC production fell and non-OPEC production increased – see Table 12.4.

Table 12.4: Oil production and consumption, 1978 and 1985

	Millions of barrels per day		Change (per cent)
	1978	**1985**	
Non-communist world consumption	50.3	45.3	−10
Non-OPEC production	18.6	25.3	+36
OPEC production	29.8	15.4	−49
Saudi Arabia	8.3	3.2	−61
Iran	5.2	2.2	−58
Iraq	2.6	1.4	−46

Source: Adapted from Ian Skeet, *OPEC: Twenty-five Years of Prices and Politics*, Cambridge: Cambridge University Press, 1988, Tables 11.1 and 11.2, 211–12.

In 1979 production was only 12 per cent higher than in 1973 and by 1985 it was 12 per cent lower than in 1979; by 1991–2 production had just recovered to the 1979 level; since then the industry has seen a steady but lower increase of around 2 per cent annually, falling to just over 1 per cent in times of recessions such as the period after the 1997–8 financial crises in Asia and elsewhere. The 1980s were characterised by plentiful supplies of oil (relative to demand), rapidly expanding supplies of natural gas and a major expansion of international trade in steam coal – EC consumption of steam coal rose from 41 to 95.8 million tons between 1975 and 1988, while European production of coal fell by some 50 million tons between 1975 and 1985 – so that real energy prices fell. By the end of the 1980s, the Commission was emphasising the need to complete the internal market in the energy sector and to consider relaunching nuclear power early in the new century.

With the dissolution of Eastern European communism (1989–91) and the disintegration of the Soviet Union (1991–2), the Commission proposed a European Energy Charter and a concluding document was signed at The Hague in December 1991. The Energy Charter Treaty was signed in Lisbon in December 1994 by all the Charter signatories except the United States and Canada and it came into force in 1998. While respecting the sovereign rights of states over their energy resources, the Energy Charter Treaty seeks to promote market-based, transparent cooperation and competition through legal guarantees concerning investments, transit and trade in the energy sector. The EU and the IEA have seen the Energy Charter Treaty and its Transit Protocol as the basis for East-West – that is, former Soviet Union-EU – energy cooperation.

Europe and the regional market for gas

For the EU, gas increased its share of total primary energy supply from 2.5 per cent in 1965 to 25 per cent by 2005. EU–27 gas supplies are currently as follows: own production 37 per cent; Russia 29 per cent; Norway 17 per cent; Algeria 13 per cent; 83 per cent comes by pipeline from Russia, Norway and Algeria and 17 per cent by LNG from Algeria, Nigeria and the Middle East. Own production is expected to fall by 50 per cent over the next two decades. As to the future, the largest proven reserves in 2006 were as follows: Russia 26.3 per cent; Iran 15.5 per cent; Qatar 14.0 per cent; Saudi Arabia 3.9 per cent; UAE 3.3 per cent; USA 3.7 per cent; Nigeria 2.9 per cent; Algeria 2.5 per cent and Venezuela 2.4 per cent – by contrast, the EU–25 have 1.3 per cent. Unlike oil, there is no world market and price for gas, which is largely a regional rather than global commodity. And whereas the future growth of oil consumption is primarily linked to the transport sector, future growth of gas consumption – some 70 per cent of the growth over the next 20 years – will be for electricity generation.

To date, EU policy has focused on internal liberalisation, without being able to ensure that the requisite physical connections are in place on a pan-European basis to make the internal market a reality, and on increasing competition in national markets, while allowing European-wide levels of competition to diminish. At the same time, the EU has pursued an external policy which has given a central role to getting external suppliers to enter a single regulatory space based on the extension of the relevant EU *acquis* and the Energy Charter and its associated Protocols in order to facilitate integration with the EU's internal energy market.

As far as Europe itself is concerned, this means that, in addition to the EU–27, Albania, Bosnia and Herzegovina, Croatia, Norway, the Republic of Macedonia, Serbia and Montenegro, Switzerland and Turkey are all involved. This 'Europe–35' currently imports about 45 per cent of its gas consumption but this is also expected to rise sharply in the next several decades. Relations with countries of the European Economic Area, Turkey and Ukraine extend EU influence:

> Most EU legislation and regulation also applies to the European Economic Area (EEA) countries – Norway, Iceland and Liechtenstein – through the Treaty between the two organizations. The ratification of the European Energy Treaty in June 2006 requires another eight countries to implement the key EU Directives and Regulations by July 2007 [Turkey is invited to join once the relation of the Treaty to its accession timetable is clarified and Ukraine is an observer]. The EU energy acquis is therefore on the verge of becoming pan-European, encompassing virtually all European nations, stretching from Belarus in the east, to North Africa and the Middle East in the south.[18]

Further afield, regional energy dialogues with countries in the Black Sea and Caspian Sea region, in Central Asia, the southern Mediterranean, the

Maghreb, Mashrek and the Gulf and Africa all seek to extend cooperation and integration.

As noted above, both the EU and the IEA have seen the Energy Charter Treaty (ECT) as central to building 'East/West' energy integration in the wake of the Cold War and the dissolution of communism. 'At its core,' says Debra Johnson, 'the ECT reflects the principle of comparative advantage whereby substantial economic gains are obtained through trade between energy-poor but technology-/capital-rich Western Europe and the energy-rich but technology-/capital-constrained economies of Russia and other former Soviet republics.'[19] Since the October 2000 EU–Russian Summit there has also been a less formal process of an Energy Dialogue. However, Russia has not ratified the Treaty and its Transit Protocol and the EU's external strategy in this area has been described by one informed analyst as 'almost hopeless'.[20] Yet, as recently as 2006, the European Council said that: 'Decisive efforts should be made to complete the negotiation of the Energy Charter Transit Protocol and secure Russia's ratification of the Energy Charter Treaty'.[21] The EU–Russia Summit in Samara (May 2007) postponed negotiations on a new trade and political agreement as Russia rejected the politico-economic model embedded in the EU's *acquis* and nor did Moscow's G–8 Presidency lead to any movement in this respect.

Meantime, Gazprom, which exports all of Russia's gas destined for Europe, has been successful in striking deals with big European (largely national) energy companies. Gazprom has nationalised reserves, controlled pipelines, has developed a special relationship with Germany – the focus of Germany's gas policy has been 'security of supply, seeking greater partnership with Gazprom, its largest supplier'[22] – and undermined potentially competitive pipeline proposals from the Caspian. According to the *Petroleum Economist*:

> Gazprom now has everything in place to execute its strategy of increasing gas exports: the gasfields of Sakhalin Island, Shtokman, Kovykta and the Yamai peninsula, and two pipelines to Europe. Its success in developing this formidable list of projects is matched by mastery over the various parties that now depend on the company and its gas: consumers in the EU; the former-Soviet transit countries; and the foreign companies that have taken stakes in the big gasfields and pipelines.[23]

The obvious response on the part of the EU 'is to ensure a continued high level of diversification of supply. Combined with an expansion of the interconnection between different national or regional markets within the EU, supply diversification would be the most important security of supply measure'.[24] Specifically, additional regasification capacity for liquefied natural gas (LNG) would act as a cap on piped gas price increases. 'But the LNG will only come if buyers can compete with rivals in other parts of the world – forcing up

LNG prices and, in turn, putting the price of this cap even higher'.[25] To the extent that the EU or Europe–35 can diversify sources of supply, even a company as large as Gazprom has a lot to compete for: 'gas export revenues in 2005 were around 55 per cent of the company's total receivables and around 17 per cent of total Russian foreign trade earnings outside CIS countries.'[26] As Johnson notes, more generally, 'whilst Europe is seeking security of energy supply, Russia is also searching for security of energy markets and there is a mutuality of interests on both sides'.[27]

The Commission continues to push for change on the part of Russia, for example, by suggesting limiting ownership of assets in the EU by foreign firms unless reciprocal arrangements are in place for EU firms to do the same. It is not obvious that this is a sensible course of action for several reasons. First, it appears to overlook the fact that overall there is far more EU investment in Russia than vice versa – in any case, sectoral reciprocity is not a principle recognised under international economic law. Secondly, it might further divide EU members between those that have chosen to work with Russia from those who have not – some commentators speak of an 'unholy alliance' between Russia, France and Germany to derail the Commission's liberalising agenda. Thirdly, it seems to underestimate the determination of the Russian leadership – first under President Putin and now under his successor Medvedev – to reverse the appropriation of oil and gas assets by the oligarchs, to insist on the state's right to regulate the use of natural resources, in Putin's words 'independent of on whose property they are located', and to use resource and pipeline diplomacy to reassert a degree of Russian influence in and control over its 'near abroad'.[28] After all, it is hard to resist the conclusion that President Putin used his former KGB networks to neutralise sources of opposition among the oligarchs, regional governors, the media, parliament, opposition parties and NGOs. And fourthly, it overlooks the basic economic fact that the relatively high fixed and sunk upstream costs in the industry, as well as the need for capital-intensive infrastructure to get gas to market, create considerable pressures for long-term contracts or vertical integration, especially given that gas markets are mainly regional as a result of the cost advantages of pipelines over LNG. A better strategy, as Helm points out, would be to license strategic assets and place special conditions in the licenses 'in respect of conduct, obligations and financial security'.[29]

Prices, 'scarcity' and the transition to a low-carbon economy

If European attempts to reduce consumption falter, and if oil and gas import dependence increases, is there a genuine danger of conflicts arising from resource scarcity? The first point to note is that price increases 'may help us see if a finite resource like oil is becoming scarcer – if the price increases from resource depletion exceed the rate at which discovery and technological change lower production cost – but it does not tell us about the absolute magnitude of the resource'.[30] It is highly likely, in fact, that the current rise in oil prices represents the run-down of excess capacity in the system (from some 15 per cent of global demand in 1986 to perhaps 2 or 3 per cent in 2005), rapidly rising demand in emerging markets (especially China), inadequate refinery capacity worldwide (but especially in the United States), geopolitical risks (Venezuela, Iraq, Nigeria, Iran, and others) and natural disasters (such as hurricanes). The truth is that until very recently the oil industry world-wide has been living off finds made in the 1950s and 1960s, capitalised and developed in the 1970s; and the OPEC producers have been scared to develop potentially excess capacity following the price collapse in the mid-1980s.

Taking oil and gas reserves together, 14 of the top 20 companies are nationally owned companies (NOCs) or newly privatised NOCs, and state monopolies represent the top ten. In 2005, of total reserves of 1,158 billion barrels, NOCs that didn't allow foreign equity participation accounted for 77 per cent of proven reserves (886 billion barrels) and Russian companies another 6 per cent (69 billion barrels); the major international oil companies (IOCs) – such as ExxonMobil, BP, Shell, Chevron, Total, ENI and ConocoPhillips (which account for just under three-quarters of all oil and gas reserves controlled by private companies) – had less than 10 per cent of the world's oil and gas reserves.

The key concern about the NOCs is that they will not make sufficient investment in new capacity to meet demand either deliberately to keep prices high or because they are starved of investment resources because of other priorities in the states' budgets. Equally, changes in the ways IOCs are run have resulted in falling investment, as Paul Stevens explains:

> The IOCs began to adopt value-based management systems. Thus, based upon capital asset pricing methodology, if the company cannot earn a rate of return on its capital at least as great as the equities in the sector and the market more generally, then it should return funds to shareholders via dividends or share buy-backs rather than investing itself. A consequence ... is that during the high prices experienced since 2000, increased sums of capital have been draining out of the industry's investment pot. This contrasts with the aftermath of the second oil shock of 1978–81. High prices led to sharp increases in investment in the upstream, creating a large expansion of capacity which, by the mid-1980s, undermined the high oil prices resulting in the 1986 oil price collapse.[31]

For the large IOCs, the repurchase of equity rose from 1 per cent of spending in 1993 to 37.1 per cent in 2006, while expenditure on exploration fell from 13.8 to 5.8 per cent over the same period. In 2006, the exploration expenditure of the big five US firms was roughly the same as that of the next 20 independent firms, despite the operating cash flow of the former ($155 billion) being over three times that of the latter ($50 billion).[32] Whether sustained high prices will begin to reverse these trends remains to be seen but there are already signs of substantial movement.

Looking to the longer-term, if we focus not on proven reserves of conventional oil but on ultimately recoverable reserves, including unconventional oil – that is, oil sands, heavy oil and oil shale – then, according to the US Geological Survey, not only does the Middle East lose its global centrality (having around one-third to one-half of the world's total oil), but also the peak of world production moves well beyond, say, 2030, when conventional oil output may reach a plateau. For example, Canada's oil sands, with currently proven reserves of 175 billion barrels (some two-thirds the size of total declared Saudi reserves), have production costs of around $15–20 per barrel. At a price of $50 per barrel, deeper and more dispersed formations may be economically exploitable, raising reserves to as much as 314 billion barrels. Venezuela claims 1.2 trillion barrels of recoverable reserves of heavy oil in the Orinoco basin, oil that is unconventional only because with existing refineries it costs more to refine than lighter Middle East crudes.

It is against this background, finally, that we need to consider the possibilities of substitution away from conventional oil. The sticking point as far as conventional oil is concerned is the transport sector and particularly the ever-expanding demand for individual, personal or family mobility via cars. Where will all the fuel come from? The answer is that it doesn't have to come from conventional oil at all. Technologically speaking, it is feasible to manufacture fuel from other hydrocarbon sources than crude oil such as unconventional oil, or even natural gas or coal. The critical question is one of cost. Mark Jaccard estimates that:

> substantial additions to conventional oil can be brought on stream at full production cost (which includes exploration, development and extraction) of less than $20 per barrel while unconventional oil from oil sands has a full production cost of about $25. Synthetic substitutes for refined petroleum products produced from natural gas and biomass are also economic when oil prices are in the $25 per barrel range. Finally, new investments in coal plants that produce refined petroleum products are profitable once oil is above $35 per barrel.[33]

The Economist is somewhat less sanguine, reckoning that tar sands and gas- and coal-to-fuel technologies are economical around $40 per barrel and shale oil at $50 per barrel. Either way, these are figures substantially below the price of oil in 2005/6/7/8. The clear implication, then, is that if the major oil producers continue to be 'locked out of the Middle East' as those states continue to sit on their 'virtual' reserves, 'the new era of manufactured fuel will further delay the onset of peak [conventional oil] production'.[34] And as the major energy companies substitute away from conventional oil either to unconventional oil outside the Middle East or to manufacturing fuel from other sources, so the costs of these alternatives will set a ceiling to the sustainable long-run price of conventional oil.

In short, the depletion of conventional oil matters little, as long as there are substitutes for the secondary energy it produces. The key question is whether the back-stop alternatives to conventional oil cost a lot more and whether they can be brought on-stream in reasonable time. The answers seem to be that the alternatives are not that costly and can be made available in a matter of decades. So, the real danger for the world economy is not that it will run out of oil any time soon, let alone the technically viable substitutes, but that price and investment cycles in the international oil and energy industries make a smooth transition beyond conventional oil more difficult than it need be. This means that the scenario sketched by the Commission of using gas (and to a lesser extent oil) as a bridge to a low-carbon energy economy is technically achievable, even achievable at an acceptable economic cost – and certainly achievable at lower cost than current (2008) oil and gas prices.

However, it will not happen if long-term investment decisions are left to liberalised markets and if long-term planning decisions remain uncoordinated on a regional – that is, EU – and an international level. The Commission appears to believe that completing the internal energy market, and properly pricing carbon dioxide's environmental externalities through the EU's Emissions Trading System, will be enough to steer energy industries towards a low-carbon path of development. There is little evidence that this will be sufficient. The one EU national market that has fully liberalised its energy sector is the United Kingdom and it has been clear that the short-term contracts that dominate the electricity and gas sectors have done very little apart from strengthen the hold of gas over the power-generation sector. Only determined regulation of those markets will make clean coal and nuclear power viable. But if this can be achieved on an EU-wide scale, then the idea, advanced by the Commission, that 'for 2050 and beyond, the switch to low carbon in the European energy system should be completed, with an overall energy mix that could include large shares for renewable, sustainable coal and gas, sustainable hydrogen, and, for those member states that want it, Generation IV fission power', is not impossible to believe.[35]

A future for nuclear power in Europe?

As nuclear power may yet play a significant role in any such transition, let us briefly review its prospects in Europe. The turn towards liberalisation and privatisation of energy markets undermined the command-and-control approach to nuclear power that was characteristic of decisions in the 1950–70 period. Leaving to one side concerns about safety, the disposal of radioactive waste and public acceptability, nuclear power has much greater capital costs than fossil-fuel plants and much lower fuel costs. This means that in the absence of guaranteed long-term contracts, the risks and thus the target rate for investment returns are much higher. Nuclear power is thus inherently uncompetitive – irrespective of average costs of the lifetime of the plant – in flexible markets dominated by short-term contracts.

It is no accident that the European country where the future of nuclear power seems most assured is France. According to the IEA Country Review (2004), the French 'centralised, nation-based approach with strong government involvement' has been 'largely successful, it has produced some of the cheapest energy prices in the OECD, security of supply for all energy sources is sound and the country has one of the lowest levels of greenhouse gas emissions ... per unit of GDP in the world'.[36] Before the first oil crisis in 1973 France generated 43 per cent of its electricity from oil, 32 per cent by hydropower and 10 per cent from coal. As a result of a political decision to sustain a large number of plants in the national market and by standardising on a single model of reactor, by 2001 France had 58 nuclear power stations accounting for 41 per cent of total primary energy needs and 77 per cent of electricity generation, in a national market where EDF generated 90 per cent of the electricity. Another model that might be capable of establishing the long-run connections between supply and demand and the economies of scale that are necessary to facilitate the economics of nuclear power would be a European-wide company or consortium that was big enough to sustain a part of its portfolio in long-term investment projects.

Although Belgium, Spain and Sweden are committed to ending nuclear power, these decisions may yet be reviewed. Switzerland is reconsidering its position and even Italy, which phased out nuclear power in the 1980s, may change its mind. Germany, where 12 per cent of total primary energy needs and one-quarter of electricity generation are accounted for by nuclear power, is also committed to phasing it out. In 2006, Chancellor Merkel indicated that a rethink might be necessary and the IEA Country Review (2007) said: 'we strongly encourage the government to reconsider the decision to phase out nuclear power'.[37]

Across the Atlantic the Bush administration has been a supporter of nuclear power as a means of reducing energy import dependence and, as Malcolm Grimston notes: 'Whether the USA moves to new nuclear construction or not is likely to be a major influence on nuclear development in other countries'.[38] More widely still, even though nuclear power stalled in Europe and the United States in the 1980s and 1990s, 'it continued elsewhere, notably in the Asia Pacific region'.[39] Looking forward, the US Energy Policy Act (EPAct 2005), the first comprehensive energy policy since 1992, provides expanded R&D programmes for the next generation of nuclear power stations and the IEA's Country Review (2007) concluded that 'a nuclear renaissance in the United States is now not only possible, but likely'.[40]

Conclusions

This review has only sketched the contours of the EU's emerging energy policy and its foreign policy dimensions but I hope that it makes clear a number of significant limits. The emphasis on completing the internal energy market and extending this beyond the orbit of the EU is a necessary but by no means sufficient response to the challenges of sustainability and security that have been rightly identified. In the first place, the transition to a low carbon fuel economy will require much more extensive regulation and market-making than the Commission seems to acknowledge, both internally and externally, and the principal agents of that must be the member states. Secondly, while the idea of extending the EU framework to many of its neighbours has merit, it is very unlikely to be the basis of a productive relationship with Russia and other major powers. And finally, rather than press for an ever greater definition of the Community interest, and hence Commission involvement, it would be better to recognise the continuing reality of member-state sovereignty in much of energy policy (and questions of energy security) and seek to coordinate the main states inter-governmentally. In all these respects, the many good ideas and proposals in the 'energy policy for Europe' need to be pursued with a great deal of political realism about what Community methods and institutions can and cannot achieve if they are to amount to an effective EU response to this key set of issues in world politics.

Notes and References

1. EU Commission President, Jose Manuel Barroso, 10 January 2007, IP/07/29, available at http://europa.eu/
2. Communication from the Commission to the European Council and the European Parliament – An Energy Policy for Europe, SEC (2007) 12.
3. Presidency Conclusions of the Brussels European Council, 7775/06, 15.
4. Commission Staff Working Document, Annex to the Green Paper, *What Is At Stake* – Background document on the Green Paper – *A European Strategy for Sustainable, Competitive and Secure Energy*, SEC (2006) 317/2, 6.
5. Communication from the Commission to the European Council and the European Parliament – An Energy Policy for Europe, SEC (2007) 12, 12.
6. Commission Staff Working Document, Annex to the Green Paper, *What Is At Stake* – Background document on the Green Paper – *A European Strategy for Sustainable, Competitive and Secure Energy*, SEC (2006) 317/2, 28–9.
7. Dieter Helm, 'European Energy Policy: Securing Supplies and Meeting the Challenge of Climate Change', in D. Helm (ed.), *The New Energy Paradigm*, Oxford: Oxford University Press, 2007, 440.
8. Ibid., 440, 442–3.
9. Communication from the Commission to the European Council and the European Parliament – An Energy Policy for Europe, SEC (2007) 12, 7.

10. Commission Staff Working Document, Annex to the Green Paper, *What Is At stake – Background document on the Green Paper – A European Strategy for Sustainable, Competitive and Secure Energy*, SEC (2006) 317/2, 47.
11. Ibid., 16.
12. See the Communication from the Commission to the European Council and the European Parliament – An Energy Policy for Europe, SEC (2007) 12, especially Annex 1.
13. Commission of the European Communities, *Problems, Resources and Necessary Progress in Community Energy Policy 1975–1985*, Brussels: Commission of the European Communities, 1975.
14. Jeffrey Pryce, 'The Atlantic Alliance and the Yom Kippur War', *Cambridge Review of International Studies*, 1 (1), 1986, 28.
15. Elizabeth Heneghan, 'Acrimony and Alliance: European Political Cooperation and the Middle East', *Cambridge Review of International Studies*, 1 (1), 1986, 34.
16. Robert Lieber, 'Cohesion and Disruption in the Western Alliance', in David Yergin and Martin Hilenbrand (eds), *Global Insecurity*, Harmondsworth: Penguin, 1982.
17. Romano Prodi and Alberto Clo, 'Europe', in Raymond Vernon (ed.), *Daedalus: The Oil Crisis*, 104, 1975, 103.
18. Anouk Honoré and Jonathan Stern, 'A Constrained Future for Gas in Europe?', in D. Helm (ed.), *The New Energy Paradigm*, Oxford: Oxford University Press, 2007, 243.
19. Debra Johnson, 'EU-Russian Energy Links: A Marriage of Convenience', *Government and Opposition*, 40 (2), Spring 2005, 273.
20. Dieter Helm, 'The Russian Dimension and Europe's External Energy Policy', September 2007, 3. At: www.dieterhelm.co.uk
21. Presidency Conclusions of the Brussels European Council, 7775/06, Annex III, 31.
22. IEA, *Country Policy Review: Germany*, Paris: IEA, 2007, 7.
23. 'Bullish Gazprom Plots Way Forward', *Petroleum Economist*, January 2008, at: www.petroleum-economist.com
24. Commission Staff Working Document, Annex to the Green Paper, *What Is At Stake – Background document on the Green Paper – A European Strategy for Sustainable, Competitive and Secure Energy*, SEC (2006) 317/2, 25. There is, of course, another dimension of 'security' of supply to do with the geopolitics and control of oil and gas transportation routes, including their military protection, which the EU is not well placed to address, notwithstanding its support for the Nabucco pipeline proposal. The significance of this dimension was underscored by the August 2008 Russian invasion of Georgia and the (temporary) closing of the BTC pipeline. This is an area that NATO began to address at its Riga Summit in November 2006 but it is beyond the scope of the present chapter.
25. 'Bullish Gazprom Plots Way Forward', *Petroleum Economist*, January 2008, at: www.petroleum-economist.com
26. Honoré and Stern, op. cit., 240.
27. Johnson, op. cit., 261.
28. Putin is quoted in Martha Brill Olcott, 'The Energy Dimension in Russian Global Strategy: Vladimir Putin and the Geopolitics of Oil', The James A. Baker III Institute for Public Policy, Rice University, October 2004.
29. Helm, 'The Russian Dimension …' op. cit., 57.
30. Mark Jaccard, *Sustainable Fossil Fuels*, Cambridge: Cambridge University Press, 2005, 14.

31. Paul Stevens, 'Oil Markets and the Future', in Dieter Helm (ed.), *The New Energy Paradigm*, Oxford: Oxford University Press, 2007, 128–9.
32. See Amy Myers Jaffe and Ronald Soligo, 'The Changing Role of National Oil Companies in International Markets' and 'The International Oil Companies', The James A. Baker Institute for Public Policy, Rice University, April and November 2007, respectively.
33. Jaccard, op. cit., 238.
34. 'Steady as She Goes', *The Economist*, 22 April 2006, 82.
35. Communication from the Commission to the European Council and the European Parliament – An Energy Policy for Europe, SEC (2007) 12, 11.
36. IEA, *Country Review: France*, Paris: IEA, 2004, Executive Summary, 7.
37. IEA, *Country Review: Germany*, Paris: IEA, 2007, Executive Summary, 9.
38. Malcolm Grimston, 'Nuclear Energy', in D. Helm (ed.), *The New Energy Paradigm*, op. cit., 409.
39. Ibid., 410.
40. IEA, *Country Review: the United States of America*, Paris: IEA, 2007, Executive Summary, 13.

Part IV
Whither the European Union?

13
European Elites on the European Union: What Vision for the Future?

Vivien A. Schmidt

What is the EU, what should it be, how far should it expand, and what should it do? These are questions European elites are now asking themselves. But there is little agreement. The problem is not just that the political elites of the 27 member states differ in their ideas about what the European Union is and their countries' role in it. They also have very different visions of what the EU should be, how far it should go in terms of territory, and what it should do in the world.

Member states' visions for the EU can be related to four basic discourses: the pragmatic discourse of the EU as problem-solving entity promoting free markets and regional security; the normative discourse of the EU as values-based community ensuring solidarity; the principled discourse of the EU as rights-based post-national union promoting democratisation;[1] and the strategic discourse of the EU as global actor 'doing international relations differently.'[2] These discourses are also related to ideas about the objectives of the EU and the reach of enlargement, from problem-solving free market without borders to community of values with clear borders to post-national union of rights free of borders to global actor based on free markets, community values, and/or human rights with or without borders.

Informing these visions are nations' senses of identity as member states of the EU.[3] These identities have been forged over the course of their membership and reflect such things as the conditions and history of their accession, the patterns of their participation, their ideas about their place in the EU, and their views of the impact of the EU on nation-state identity. Such identities influence how member states imagine the EU institutionally, as an inter-governmental or supranational governance body; economically, as a free market completely open to globalisation or intent on regulating it; territorially, with regard to whether and where the enlargement process will end, with or without clearly established borders; or strategically, as a global actor that projects its power more through 'soft' than 'hard' means and engages the world multilaterally rather than unilaterally. Moreover, national identities, in the sense of national frames based on history, culture and interests, also have a significant impact on how member states construct their identities in the EU.[4] The result is that member states' sense of identity in the EU entails 27 very specific visions about the country in the EU – not to mention the divisions within the countries contesting those visions.

Lately, in particular light of the problems surrounding the ratification of the Constitutional and Lisbon Treaties on institutional reform and concerns involving enlargement to the east, political elites have been trying collectively to define a new common vision for the EU. But here, the difficulties in building such a common vision stem not only from the differences in national identities in the EU and visions for the EU but also from European member states' divisions over the policies that would define the EU as a global strategic actor and the practices by which the EU governs itself.

Are there any generalisations that can be made about where elites stand on their member-state identity in the EU and their visions for the future? New states versus old states? Big states versus small states? Liberalising states versus more economically conservative states? States with left-leaning governments versus states with right-leaning governments? States that have traditionally played a leadership role versus states that have long followed? These are all factors that contribute to an explanation of divisions on identities and visions. This chapter assesses the applicability of these factors through an examination of European leaders' ideas and discourse as found in speeches made (what they say) and positions taken (what they do) against a background of past ideas and discourse about member-state identity in Europe and visions of Europe. The chapter shows that no one factor can capture the complexity of the divisions among member states within as well as across the four basic visions of the EU. It argues, moreover, that the only way for these visions to be reconciled is for European elites to start developing new ideas together, thinking collectively about a new vision for the EU – what it is, how far it can go and what it could do – and then reinvent their discourse about their countries' relationship to the EU in the terms of this new vision. In the conclusion, the chapter also offers a preliminary vision of what the EU is that could serve to reconcile continuing division over visions of the future, by seeing the EU as a 'regional state' that accommodates differing levels and degrees of membership.

The methodological approach used herein is what I call 'discursive institutionalism', which analyses the substantive content of ideas and the interactive processes of discourse in institutional context.[5] This approach is very close to the 'constructivism' of international relations and the identity and discourse analyses of European studies.[6] For the explanation of European elites' visions of the future, discursive institutionalism takes us beyond the path-dependence of institutionalised identities and visions described by historical institutionalism, the strategic rationality of interest-based identities and visions defined by rational choice institutionalism, and the cultural framing of norms-based identities and visions depicted by sociological institutionalism to explore how elites, separately as well as together, through imagination and deliberation, discursively (re)construct their ideas about member-state identity in Europe and visions for Europe's future against a background of national histories, interests and cultures.

The pragmatic discourse of a borderless problem-solving free market

The discourse about the EU as problem-solving entity tends to be pragmatic, with membership seen as a question of efficiency and utility, and often linked to arguments about extending the free market or, more recently, to reinforcing security.[7] It tends to envisage the EU as optimally without borders, opening to successive countries when and if they meet the criteria of membership, thereby expanding free markets as well as ensuring regional security. It is the view stereotypically ascribed to the UK, but also to the member states of recent enlargements, in particular the CEECs and to some extent the Scandinavian countries. Elites in all member states, however, use this discourse at different times to some extent, and even those member states in which this discourse predominates do not use it exclusively.

With regard to enlargement to the CEECs, in particular for EU member states in the early 1990s, the pragmatic problem-solving discourse was all about guaranteeing stability and avoiding the descent into authoritarianism (post-communism), although it was also about extending the single market. Those who subscribe to this kind of pragmatic discourse also mostly tend to favor Turkish membership, or even that of Georgia and Ukraine, with the assumption that the problems of trade and security are best solved by continuing to enlarge. This view of enlargement beyond the current borders has predominantly been the view expressed by British elites, not only by political leaders but the quality press.[8] Swedish elites have also been vocally in support of such enlargement, in particular with regard to Georgia and Ukraine, as have the CEECs with regard to their neighbours to the east. With regard to Turkey, however, the pragmatic argument can cut both ways. On security issues, for example, the answer could be yes to Turkey because it enhances European security, or no because the EU would have borders with unstable Middle Eastern states such as Iraq, Syria and Iran. On economics, it could be yes because it would become a market for other European countries and a source of dynamism, or no because it could be a financial drain as a result of the economic backwardness of much of the country.

The United Kingdom

For the UK, a latecomer in 1973, membership was all about economic interests, and about becoming a member of an economic community that was to be little more than an intergovernmental union of states. In the early 1960s, the Conservative Prime Minister Harold Macmillan had presented membership as a 'commercial move' to protect national economic interests,[9] and the EU (or the EEC, as it then was) itself as a kind of confederation or commonwealth along the lines of de Gaulle's *'Europe des patries'* (Europe of fatherlands, or nations) – which would retain the great traditions and the pride of individual nations while working together in clearly defined spheres for their common interest.'[10] Later in that decade, the Labour Prime Minister Harold Wilson saw membership as 'defending the national interest against interfering foreigners'.[11] In the 1980s, the Conservative Prime Minister Margaret Thatcher, who insisted time and again that she would 'fight tenaciously for British interests',[12] cast the EU as a 'free enterprise *Europe des patries*'.[13] Her 1988 Bruges speech warning about the dangers of 'a European super-state exercising new dominance from Brussels', moreover, became the main rallying cry for the Eurosceptics. Their message, picked up and amplified by the Fleet Street press, depicted the EU as a threat to parliamentary sovereignty and identity, as well as against Britain's economic interests.

After 1997, the 'New Labour' Prime Minister Tony Blair did little to counter the Eurosceptic discourse, since he barely talked about the EU in Britain, but when he did, addressed economic rather than sovereignty or identity issues. Moreover, having promised a referendum on the euro when the 'economic tests' were met, Blair then switched to promising a referendum on the Constitutional Treaty instead. He was lucky not to have had to have the later referendum once the French and Dutch 'no' votes were tallied. This is because, even had he cast the debate as 'Britain in or out of the EU', it would have been almost impossible to win, given political elites' lack of pro-EU legitimating discourse related to sovereignty and identity over the course of EU membership. Since Gordon Brown took over as New Labour Prime Minister in June 2007, even Blair's minimal amount of pro-EU discourse has largely vanished. On the Lisbon Treaty, all he did was to insist repeatedly that British national interests were defended and all its red lines maintained.[14]

Small West European states

The smaller West European states which also had the pragmatic vision of the borderless market and security zone – Ireland and Scandinavian countries – tended to articulate very different discourses from the British. Most importantly, as smaller states, they felt much more strongly both the limits to formal sovereignty and the difficulties of economic development in an increasingly globalising world. But while Ireland was a less developed country at its moment of entry, and benefited tremendously from the structural funds, the Scandinavian countries had already prospered as small states with open economies in the world market.[15] And yet, despite sharing similarly pragmatic visions of the EU, the Scandinavian countries each responded to it in very different ways, having joined at different times for different reasons, having opted in or out of different policy areas, and even organising their day-to-day dealings with the EU in very different ways.[16] Whereas Denmark, like Ireland, entered the EU in 1973 largely to follow the UK, in which it had a large share of trade, Sweden and Finland entered in 1995. For Sweden the request for membership followed upon a major internally driven economic crisis in the early 1990s which spelled the end of its neo-Keynesian macroeconomic policy experiment. For Finland, economic reasons for membership were joined by security issues related to the collapse of the Soviet Union. Economic interest also played a major role for Norway, contributing to the 'no' vote in the referendum which kept it out of the EU – in particular the resistance of fishermen and farmers – although sovereignty and identity issues were equally important. Public rather than elite resistance also explain the failures of Denmark and Sweden to join the euro. But these votes were all based on fears about the EU's impact on the highly generous welfare state, along with sovereignty and identity concerns.[17]

Ireland, although also largely pragmatic in its vision, has equally strong elements of the values-based community discourse. From the beginning, national leaders presented membership not only in terms of economic interest – as a way of reducing dependence on the British market while gaining a large liberalising market for Irish products – but also in terms of national identity – since joining the EU was a way of being on a par with the UK, enabling the country to determine its future independently from its former colonial master. Unlike the British, in fact, the Irish saw the EU as enhancing national sovereignty rather than diminishing it, and as 'a place we belong', in the words of Taoiseach Bertie Ahern in 2000.[18] There was also a normative element, resonating with Catholic Ireland, in terms of rejoining Europe. Add to this the miracle of economic growth, largely underwritten by the EU structural funds, in which Ireland went from a 'less developed country' and one of the 'peripherals' in Europe along with Greece, Iceland and Turkey, as defined by the OECD in 1957, to the second richest member state – and we can easily explain general Irish enthusiasm for the EU.[19]

More difficult to explain is Ireland's 'no' votes on the Nice Treaty and again for the Lisbon (Reform) Treaty. These resulted not from any deep-seated currents of Euroscepticism about the EU of the kind that have flourished in the UK. Rather, they point to the problems of referenda generally, and the dangers of holding them when governments are unpopular or the economy is going down. But it also points more specifically to the failure of Irish political leaders to make the case. In the Nice Treaty, they mainly said that the public 'had to vote for it'. In the Lisbon Treaty, politicians at first told the public not to bother reading the document, that it was 'unreadable', before then trying to respond in mind-numbing detail about its content. In the meantime, the 'no' campaign capitalised on voters' disparate worries about the loss of their low corporate tax or of farm subsidies as well as fears that the treaty would legalise abortion or undermine Irish neutrality. This, together with the fact that a large majority of the public voted 'no' because they wouldn't vote for a treaty they couldn't understand (and who could?), spelled its demise.

Central and Eastern European countries

Even greater differences characterise the CEECs, despite similarities in visions with regard to the EU as a free-market and security zone. The CEECs all underwent significant neo-liberal market reform under pressure from the EU as well as international economic institutions subsequent to the fall of the Berlin wall. Security issues, however, were complicated by the Atlanticist preferences of the accession countries, which in the early years in particular made them see the European Security and Defense Project (ESDP) as being in direct competition with NATO and the US alliance. Moreover, much of the EU hard-bargaining in the accession negotiations were bruising to the national sense of sovereignty of countries that had newly regained it. Thus, although becoming members of the EU was in some sense sovereignty and identity-enhancing, it was at the same time a threat to the newly developing identities of these newly sovereign nations. This may help explain the backlash we have seen in recent years by CEEC elites against European integration, with the rise of populism accompanying anti-European discourse in some such countries. The most noteworthy have been the Kaszynski twins in Poland, who proved to be uncooperative hard-bargainers on voting rights related to the Constitutional Treaty, and then threw monkey-wrenches into the ratification of the Lisbon Treaty. President Vaclav Klaus in the Czech Republic has been a bit more diplomatic, but no less negative in his pronouncement about the EU's impact on national sovereignty.[20]

Normative discourse of a bordered values-based community

The discourse focused on the EU as a values-based community has little to do with pragmatic interests about markets or security, and instead derives from ethics and moral commitments that assume a specific kind of community held together by feelings of solidarity or 'we-feeling'. Such solidarity can be generated by the EU's building a community of peace and prosperity, of tolerance and mutual respect, but also by the 'we-feeling' resulting from a common history, fought through civil wars, or even religious tradition.[21] This normative discourse tends to justify actions in terms of the common good, and allows for uneven distribution of the costs and benefits of membership – as in the case of Germany footing a large proportion of the bill for European integration. It is also connected to projects focused on making the EU a 'political union', as opposed to only a free market.

Political leaders who adopt normative, values-based discourses tend to envisage the borders of the EU stopping before Turkey – and excluding Georgia and Ukraine as well – because they assume that these countries would not fit their underlying conception of a values-based community. They subscribe to the notion that 'deepening' Europe, or creating a 'political Europe', is only possible within the confines of 27 member states, or 33–34 at most (whenever the countries of the Balkans are ready). These discourses have been characteristic of both Germany and France, by political leaders as well as by the quality press,[22] but Austria, Belgium, the Netherlands and Luxembourg also fit. Although there are those who would go so far as to argue for a 'Christian Club', most of the arguments have very little to do with Turkey and a lot to do with 'feeling European', with nostalgia for the original 'core Europe', or with the desire for a 'political union' of Europe with real borders and clear goals.

For those who hold this normative discourse about the EU, the pragmatic vision of the EU as a borderless free market is anathema, and conjures up what they are most afraid of, an EU that is an engine of soulless economic liberalism.[23] On top of this, many see the argument for no fixed borders and unending enlargement as a cynical ploy by the British to destroy the EU as a values-based community and/or future political union. For the British, by contrast, this normative discourse of a values-based community and/or political union is tantamount to declaring in favour of a superstate. They worry, moreover, that it will stop enlargement, while too much deepening will produce too much juridical rigidity, therefore also negatively affecting the free market.[24] For other countries with a pragmatic vision, however, such as Poland under the Kazyncski twins, the problem may be that the 'wrong' values are emphasised in this values-based community.

France

For all the commonality of vision among Continental elites on the EU as a values-based community, member states have constructed their discourses of nation-state identity in the EU quite differently. French elites' discourse was all about leading an intergovernmental union. The discourse of membership in a free market was secondary. De Gaulle's foundational paradigm focused on the country's political leadership in Europe, with the EU a 'multiplier of power' that was to bring gains not only in regional power and economic interest but also in identity, by enhancing the country's *grandeur* as it projected its universalist human-rights values on to the rest of Europe. And no need to worry about sovereignty or identity issues, because the state would defend republican values and remain sovereign in a Europe which, rather than federal, was to be 'a Europe of nations'.[25] The economic issues came up later, under Mitterrand, who updated de Gaulle's vision of the EU by casting the EU as a shield against globalisation.[26] As for enlargement, Mitterrand initially seemed hesitant about admitting the CEECs to the EU club, although he quickly shifted once faced with a *fait accompli*, and he then supported the accession process. On Turkey, moreover, French elites are generally opposed to membership. But in the quality press, which spoke for most political elites, while the conservative newspapers focused on values and identity issues, the progressive ones wrote of the problems of deepening in a Europe not yet adjusted to its enlargement to the CEECs, and expressed a fear that this would dilute European construction and go against the hopes of founders of the EU for ever closer political union.[27] The former French President and head of the Constitutional Convention, Valéry Giscard d'Estaing, summed up the general view when he stated that opening doors to Turkey would mean no less than 'the end of the European Union'.[28]

France itself, however, could be blamed, along with the Netherlands, for halting the process to a values-based political community when the citizens voted 'no' in the referendum on the Constitutional Treaty in 2005. Part of the problem for French political leaders during the referendum process was that they remained trapped in the longstanding discourse that proclaimed French leadership in an EU that was good for the economy and identity, when the public clearly saw that France was no longer leading Europe, felt in crisis over national identity, and increasingly blamed EU neo-liberalism for the country's economic difficulties.[29] Moreover, while the 'yes' campaign spoke to the (boring) European institutional questions, the 'no' campaign garnered votes from those on the left who worried that the Treaty would threaten abortion rights, that mentioning 'free trade' was a call to neo-liberalism, and that the imaginary 'Polish plumber' would challenge the French social model, and from those on the right who saw EU-facilitated immigration and enlargement to the east as a threat to French identity.[30] Although the mainstream right, and in particular President Chirac, was unable to muster convincing arguments, it was the split in the left's political leadership that was the real blow to the chances for passage. It was not until two years later, after the presidential elections, that there was a renewal of the French discourse about Europe when President Sarkozy insisted that 'the identity of Europeans is our identity' and promised that France was back in Europe while reiterating that the EU stopped before Turkey and that it was not a future nation-state and certainly not a superstate but rather a 'Europe of nations exercising their sovereignty in common [that decide] to stay themselves'.[31]

Germany

Germany, although sharing France's commitment to a values-based political community, has a very different sense of identity in Europe. In German elites' discourse, 'Europeanness' as 'Germanness' was the way in which German national identity was reconstructed in the early postwar period – although 'Atlanticist' was also a component of that identity. But this did little to hinder its willing partnership with France in building an integrated Europe. Konrad Adenauer's 'Rhineland' vision in which European integration would enable Germany to slowly regain its sovereignty and, ultimately, its unity, became the founding vision upon which his successors built, and which was expanded by Helmut Kohl in 1989 to accommodate unification.[32] Since unification, however, differences among policy elites have developed with regard to how Germany should act in Europe,[33] while European integration itself has become more contested as its effects have been felt on national policies and the economy (in particular with regard to public disenchantment with losing the Deutschmark). From 1998, moreover, somewhat more assertive approaches to Europe emerged. Prime Minister Gerhard Schroeder wanted Germany to be freer to pursue its national interests and get some of its money back (although he failed). The Foreign Minister, Joschka Fischer, wanted Germany to free itself from some of the 'burdened' aspects of its identity and to move the EU forward in a more federal direction, which is why he launched the constitutional debates.[34] The current Chancellor Angela Merkel has charted her own course, with a communicative discourse that emphasises the common and fundamental values of Europe, including human dignity, solidarity, liberty and tolerance[35] and 'shaping globalisation'.

Unlike the French, the Germans generally agreed on enlargement to the CEECs, and were the first in the early 1990s to call for quick integration of the Eastern European countries – much to the concern of Mitterrand at the time – because this was about a history-centred values-based community, focused on reuniting Europe and the need for reconciliation.[36] German leaders have been much less enthusiastic on further enlargements, in particular with regard to Turkey. The arguments against Turkey, however, have been split between the conservative quality press, which tended to emphasise the cultural and identity aspects of incompatibility, and the more progressive press, which focused mostly on the issue of how 'widening' the EU to Turkey would undermine the deepening of the EU.[37]

Italy

Italian leaders been even more positive about all aspects of European integration than the Germans, although they too are reticent on further enlargement. Italian leaders' discourse since Alcide de Gasperi presented Italy as the enthusiastic follower, with an Italian-as-European identity serving as a source of national pride, and with the EU itself serving as the rescue of the nation-state.[38] Italy in the postwar period was a country riven by vast cleavages – politically between right and left, territorially between north and south, and religiously between practising Catholics and non-believers – and suffering from political immobilism and state incapacity despite a flourishing economy and a vibrant society. European integration was therefore key to overcoming state incapacity and parliamentary inefficiency with reforms that, without the EU, could not have passed. The Italian vision of Europe, as a result, is one in which Europe is the opposite of Italy, and therefore to be embraced for its effective governance, rule of law, transparency with regard to decision-making, and more. National pride also mattered with regard to European integration, and was intimately linked to the identity issues. While Germany found itself at the heart of Europe, not only economically and geographically but also as a central motivating factor, Italy was more on the margins, and very afraid of not belonging to the club. Its heroic efforts to join the euro, by finally getting the public budget under control and even instituting a eurotax (the only in Europe), was not only about economics; it was also about identity.[39] Italy's euroenthusiasm remains, despite its bad record of implementation and its more recent soft, creeping Euroscepticism, in particular from right-wing politicians.

Benelux and Austria

In the three smaller founding members, Belgium, the Netherlands and Luxembourg, plus latecomer Austria, national leaders presented the EU as the means for small countries to participate as equals in the decisions affecting their future and in the markets vital to their economic success. Moreover, their vision of the EU tends to be primarily one of a values-based community, resistant to further enlargement to the east, although they all embrace the vision of the EU as global strategic actor doing international relations differently. Even here, however, there have been significant differences. Most notably, the Belgians have remained very pro-European not only because of the benefits that have followed from having Brussels as the capital of the EU but also because they have looked to Europe to solve their problems of identity and regional differences, instead of seeking remedies on their own. The result is that they are in a national identity crisis that has brought them to the brink of dissolution.

The Dutch, although also largely pro-European, voted 'no' in the referendum on the Constitutional Treaty, three days after the French vote, by an even larger margin (61 per cent vs. the French 55 per cent). The reasons, as in France, had to do with the ability of the 'no' camp to galvanise members of the electorate on the right and the left opposed to a disparate range of policies, in this case mainly about immigration, the perceived impact of the euro on inflation, plus the desire to punish an unpopular government. And for the 'yes' camp, it again was unable to deliver a persuasive message in what was the country's first-ever referendum. The problem was not only a lack of experience but also an absence of ideas about what to say, given that politicians had long assumed that it was the EU's role to legitimise Europe, and when they talked (rarely) about the EU, they tended to use technocratic language, making it even more alien from the citizens and not of interest for the media to report on. All of this, together with the usual blame-shifting and credit-taking of politicians, as in other member states, ensured that what the EU did was largely invisible to the public.[40]

Principled discourse of a border-free rights-based post-national union

The discourse focused on a rights-based post-national union evokes legally entrenched fundamental human rights and democratic procedures rather than feelings derived from culture or history. This principled discourse, then, is all about the constitutional order of the EU and its universalistic commitment to human rights, justice and democracy. It tends to be supported by 'liberal' or 'cosmopolitan' elites across Europe as well as by European Union-level officials, and is exemplified by the arguments of Habermas and Beck and Grande.[41] At the European Union level, the discourse of accession for the CEECs has been squarely located here, in the emphasis on conditionality, and letting the accession countries in only once they had democratised as well as liberalised sufficiently, with respect for human rights the primary issue. Importantly, once this argument was made, it would have been difficult to back out of accession without tremendous loss of credibility and legitimacy.[42] This was equally the case for Greek accession for which, once the issue had been turned into a question of democracy, rejection for economic or administrative reasons was no longer acceptable.[43] And thus it could similarly be applied to Turkey since accession discussions have been underway. But here, the outcome remains contingent upon Turkish fulfilment of the conditions for membership in terms of democratisation and respect for human rights.

Many supporters of enlargement, including those in the UK, legitimate the 'no-borders' argument not so much on grounds of its pragmatic utility and efficiency as of those of rights-based post-national union. They fear that setting borders will in fact destroy what the EU has done best, in enlargement after enlargement, which has been to ensure the democratisation of its ever-expanding borders through its extremely strong 'power of attraction'.[44] Moreover, countries that benefited from the democratising pull of the EU have continued to emphasise the principled discourse. This includes both the 1980s enlargement countries that emerged from authoritarianism, including Spain, Portugal and Greece, in which political leaders focused mainly on the promises of democracy, as guaranteed by the EU and the demands of the accession process, and the 2000s enlargement countries that emerged from communism, that is, the CEECs. But in the latter countries, although political leaders made democratisation their central theme, their discourse was also much more closely linked to market liberalisation, and security and defence, with divided loyalties between NATO and the EU, and the EU and the US, given strong transatlantic ties.

The strategic discourse of a global actor doing international relations differently

Finally, the discourse focused on the EU as global actor is all about the EU's role in the world, and how it may further its strategic interests. These interests, however, need not necessarily be defined only in terms of the pragmatic, utility-maximising entity that promotes free trade or regional security. They may just as easily be defined in terms of the norms of an EU values-based community or of the commitments to human rights and democratisation of an EU rights-based post-national union. This vision of the EU may be just as much about bringing the CEECs in to the EU to stabilise its borders as about the EU exercising its 'normative power'[45] and maintaining its 'power of attraction'.[46] The strategic discourse about the EU as a global actor is all about its doing international relations differently – in particular by contrast with 'sovereign' nation-states such as the US – by engaging the world through multilateralism, by emphasising peacekeeping and the Petersburg tasks, by promoting democracy through conditionality and the EU's power of attraction in its neighborhood, and by linking trade more generally to conditionality and the respect for human rights. In terms of the EU's active engagement with the rest of the world, moreover, this discourse is for the most part focused on humanitarian intervention and nation-building, and emphasises the gradual move to a post-Westphalian order based on the rights of individuals as much as the rights of states.[47] Thus, it is primarily about creating a community based on values of global humanitarian intervention in a post-national, rights-based order. As Tony Blair said in his April 1999 Chicago speech: '… through humanitarian intervention, interests and values become inextricably intertwined.'[48]

This vision of the EU as a global strategic actor is relatively new. Although the EU engaged the world in myriad ways in increasing amounts over time, its sense of itself as an actor with a major role to play in the world is recent. Only for the French has the idea always been there, ever since the European Defence Community was voted down (by the French Parliament) in 1953. But it was to be an unfulfilled dream, mainly because the British consistently torpedoed any later attempt to resurrect something like it. Only with the Saint Malo agreement in 1998, negotiated by British Prime Minister Tony Blair and French President Jacques Chirac, did the discourse of the EU as global strategic actor doing international relations differently (through the Petersburg tasks of peacekeeping) begin to take shape.

National and EU leaders' speeches about the EU as global actor reflect not only the newness of the ideas but also a mix of the three other visions. All pay homage to the human rights vision as they emphasise the free market or values-community vision, albeit not one to the exclusion of the other. The British and French discourses are particularly illustrative of the differences.

Despite the fact that British leaders have in mind primarily a borderless problem-solving free market when they speak of Europe, they have increasingly referred to the EU's common values, its importance for human rights, and its role as a global actor. This was most evident in Prime Minister Blair's rousing speech to the European Parliament subsequent to the rejection of the Constitutional Treaty in France and the Netherlands (23 June 2005), when he insisted that the EU was a 'union of values, of solidarity between nations and people, of not just a common market in which we trade but a common political space in which we live as citizens … [a] political project'.[49] More recently, however, Prime Minister Brown has said little about the EU other than to tout the importance of projects such as combatting climate change. But his Foreign Secretary, David Miliband, has been more voluble. Thus, Miliband noted that rather than a 'superstate', the EU was a 'model regional power' notable not only for its 'openness' (as a free market) but also for its 'triumph of shared values'. This, he went on to suggest, made it ideally placed to share its values even more widely, with no end to potential enlargement, which in turn would only enhance the EU's role as global strategic actor focused on international law and human rights, engaged in humanitarian intervention and environmental leadership.[50]

French leaders have similarly been mixing visions, albeit with a different spin. Although they continue to have in mind a bordered values-based community when they speak of Europe, they accept that the EU is a free market open to globalisation with a major role to play as a global actor. President Nicolas Sarkozy promised that France was back in Europe to promote a 'political Europe' defined by what it does, which is about 'projects' rather than 'process'. By calling Europe 'a project of civilisation' as opposed to 'just procedure', he suggested that it was to preserve its values-based and rights-supporting heritage involving centuries of civilisation and of European humanism – and to have borders that stop before Turkey. As a global actor, moreover, the EU was to do all good things regarding defending itself against terrorism, mastering immigration, engaging in projects focused on energy, space, civilian protection, judicial cooperation and a 'Mediterranean Union'. But it would not promote 'pure competition which banishes all voluntarist politics' because Europe 'refuses globalisation without rules' and 'opens itself to globalisation and free trade but only in reciprocity'.[51]

Significant differences remain in British and French visions then, but speaking of the EU as a global strategic actor seems to sing from a very similar hymn book. This can be generalised across the EU. Of late national and EU elites have sought to reinsert some dynamism into the EU since the calm after the Constitutional Treaty storm by speaking of the EU as a global strategic actor. Everyone now repeats that the EU is all about 'projects' rather than 'process', involving concrete proposals for remedying world problems. Although there are certainly differences among leaders on how to solve the problems – in particular on whether to try to regulate global forces or not – there is at least agreement on which are the problems and a willingness to sit down at the table to deliberate about them. Moreover, because for the time being the enlargements to Turkey, Ukraine and Georgia are still years away, and depend upon these countries' ability to meet the requirements of conditionality related to the Copenhagen criteria – democracy, open economy, *acquis communautaires* and rule of law – the issues of borders is moot. And the enlargement debates, so divisive in the run up to the Constitutional Treaty, have therefore been conveniently taken off the table by all and sundry.

Reconciling visions?

One final question: Is it possible to conceptualise the EU in ways that allow different visions of Europe – borderless problem-solving entity, bordered values-based community, border-free rights-based post-national union, and global actor – to coexist? Can we maintain a sense of the 'we-feeling' of values-based community without giving up on the rights-based post-national union? And can we at the same time meet the needs of the utility-maximising problem-solving discourse linked to trade and security?

There is one way: if the decision-making processes and future boundaries of the EU were thought about differently. For the moment, the future is conceived of much like that of nation-states, with reasonably clear boundaries, membership as a question of 'in' or 'out', uniform rules for all, and unanimity for treaties that decide on major institutional reforms, policy initiatives and enlargement to new members. This worked well in the past, when the member states numbered six, nine or even 12. But at 27, this is a recipe for disaster, as we witnessed with the referenda on the Constitutional and Lisbon Treaties. Today, the unanimity rule, designed for an intergovernmental union of six nation-states, stops the treaty process dead in its tracks while the uniformity ideal imposed by a Commission dreaming of a federal state chokes off differentiated integration. The only real possibility of moving forward while reconciling the differing visions of the EU is for member states to recognise what the EU is and to change the decision rules accordingly.

The EU is a 'regional state' which has state-like qualities and powers in an ever-growing number of policy domains, with variable boundaries due to its ever-enlarging territorial reach and its member states' increasingly differentiated participation in policy 'communities' beyond the Single Market.[52] To make this work today, the EU needs to give up on unanimity on EU decisions and uniformity in their application, as well as to abandon the absolute demarcation line between who is 'in' and who is 'out'.[53]

This is easier to do than one might think. With regard to unanimity, the EU has already breached the principle in the wide range of areas covered by qualified majority voting and in the occasional opt-outs for member states with regard to treaties. It need only make a general rule for this, in which opt-outs substitute for vetoes in the treaties and in areas not covered by qualified majority voting, to get out of the EU decision-making paralysis. With regard to uniformity, the EU has also already given up on it in areas other than the Single Market. These include the single currency (with 15 of 27 member states), Schengen (minus the UK and Ireland but with Norway and Iceland), ESDP (without Denmark but with the participation of Norway in the Nordic Battlegroup), and the Charter of Fundamental Rights (with opt-outs for the UK and Poland). Such differentiated integration is only increased by the 'outside-insiders' such as Norway, Iceland and Switzerland which participate in the Single Market as well as in a range of other EU policy communities such as Schengen and ESDP but don't have a vote. The Lisbon Treaty's initiatives on 'permanent structured cooperation' for defence and security policy and 'enhanced cooperation' for all other policy areas (just proposed in divorce law under the Nice Treaty but potentially useful in a wide range of social-policy sectors) will only increase such differentiation further. The only thing yet to be floated is the concept of graduated membership rather than 'in' or 'out' for countries on the EU's periphery, which would ensure socialisation for those in the accession process while maintaining the EU's power of attraction for those still outside. But it would only be attractive to prospective members, as well as outside insiders, if it were to come with institutional voice and vote in the sectors in which they participate.

Once the principles of unanimity and uniformity are abandoned, membership in the EU will no longer be an all-or-nothing proposition. Beyond certain basic membership requirements – being a democracy that respects human rights and participates in the Single Market – member states will increasingly come to pick and choose the policy 'communities' of which they wish to be a part. The result is differentiated membership in the EU regional state in which some countries would envision the EU as a borderless free-market and security area while participating in the Single Market and ESDP; other countries might envision the EU as a values-based community while participating in most policy areas; and yet others would envision the EU as a political union by participating in all sectors in a more deeply integrated way using enhanced cooperation. This is not to suggest, however, that the EU is now to be '*Europe à la carte*', as the free-marketers might wish. Nor is it to encourage the communitarians to retreat to a 'core Europe', with one dish for all. Rather, this is an elaborate '*menu Europe*', with a shared main dish (the Single Market), everyone sitting around the table, and only some choosing to sit out one course or another.[54]

Notes and References

1. Following Helen Sjursen, 'Enlargement in Perspective: The EU's Quest for Identity', Recon Online Working Paper 2007/15, 2007 at: www.reconproject.eu/projectweb/portalproject/RECONWorkingPapers.html
2. Jolyon Howorth, *European Security and Defence Policy*, Basingstoke: Palgrave Macmillan, 2007.
3. See J. Schild, 'National vs. European Identities? French and German in the European Multi-level System', *Journal of Common Market Studies* 39, 1975, 331–51; R. K. Herrmann, T. Risse and M. B. Brewer, *Transnational Identities: Becoming European in the EU*, New York, Rowman & Littlefield, 2004; L. McLaren, *Identity, Interests and Attitudes to European Integration*, Basingstoke, Palgrave Macmillan, 2006.
4. Juan Diez Medrano, *Framing Europe. Attitudes to European Integration in Germany, Spain, and the United Kingdom*, Princeton: Princeton University Press, 2003; Sophie Duchesne, Elizabeth Fraser, André Paul Frognier, Florence Haegel, Guillaume Garcia and Virginie van Ingelgom, 'European Citizenship Revisited, Session Two: Enduring National Differences in Citizens' Talk about Europe.' Paper presented to the Politics Department, Oxford University, 23 June 2008, at: http://erg.politics.ox.ac.uk/projects/discussion_political/index.asp#publications; Martin Marcussen, Thomas Risse, Daniela Engelmann-Martin, Hans Joachim Knopf and Klaus Roscher, 'Constructing Europe? The Evolution of French, British and German Nation State Identities', *Journal of European Public Policy* 6 (4), 1999,

614–33; Thomas Risse, 'A European Identity? Europeanization and the Evolution of National Identities', in M. Cowles, J. Caporaso and T. Risse (eds), *Transforming Europe*, Ithaca: Cornell University Press, 2001, 198–218.

5. See Vivien A. Schmidt, *The Futures of European Capitalism*, Oxford: Oxford University Press, 2002, 275–7; Vivien A. Schmidt, *Democracy in Europe: The EU and National Polities*, Oxford: Oxford University Press, 2006; Vivien A. Schmidt, 'A "Menu Europe" will prove far more palatable.' Comment in the *Financial Times*, 22 July, 2008

6. See, for example, Marcussen, et al., op. cit.; Markus Jachtenfuchs, Thomas Diez and Sabine Jung, 'Which Europe? Conflicting Models of a Legitimate European Political Order', *European Journal of International Relations* 4 (4), 2000, 409–45; Thomas Risse, '"Let's Argue!" Communicative Action in World Politics', *International Organization*, 54 (1), 2000, 1–39; Thomas Diez, 'Europe as a Discursive Battleground: European Integration Studies and Discourse Analysis', *Cooperation and Conflict* 36 (1), 2001, 5–38; Ole Wæver, 'Identity, Communities and Foreign Policy. Discourse Analysis as Foreign Policy Theory', in Lena Hansen and Ole Wæver (eds), *European Integration and National Identity. The Challenge of the Nordic States*, London and New York: Routledge, 2002, 20–49; Henrik Larsen, 'British and Danish European Politics in the 1990s: A Discourse Approach', *European Journal of International Relations* 5 (4), 1999, 451–83.

7. See Sjursen, op. cit.

8. Andreas Wimmel, 'Beyond the Bosphorus? Comparing German, French and British Discourses on Turkey's Application to join the European Union.' Working Paper, Institute for Advanced Studies, Vienna, Political Science Series 111, 2006.

9. Stephen George, 'Cultural Diversity and European Integration: The British Political Parties,' in S. Zetterholm (ed.), *National Cultures and European Integration*, Oxford: Berg, 1994, 55, 59.

10. George Smith, 'Britain in New Europe', *Foreign Affairs*, 71 (4), 1992, 5.

11. George, op. cit.

12. Speech to the Conservative Party conference in Blackpool, 14 October 1983.

13. Margaret Thatcher, *The Downing Street Years*, London: HarperCollins, 1993, 536.

14. Statements to Parliament, 11 and 22 October 2007.

15. Peter Katzenstein, *Small States in World Markets*, Ithaca: Cornell University Press, 1985.

16. Jacobsson, Laegreid and Pedersen, op. cit.

17. Hansen and Wæver, op. cit.

18. Speech on 21 March 2000.

19. Brigid Laffan, 'Ireland and the European Union', in William J. Crotty and David E. Schmitt (eds), *Ireland on the World Stage*, Pearson Education, 2002.

20. Jacques Rupnik, 'East-Central Europe Backsliding? From Democracy Fatigue to Populist Backlash', *Journal of Democracy*, 18 (4), 2007, 17–25.

21. Sjursen, op. cit.

22. Wimmel, op. cit.

23. Vivien A. Schmidt, 'Trapped by their Ideas: French Elites' Discourses of European Integration and Globalization', *Journal of European Public Policy*, 14 (4), 2007, 992–1009.

24. Schmidt, *Democracy in Europe*, op. cit.

25. Risse. op. cit., 1–39; Henrik Larsen, *Foreign Policy and Discourse Analysis*, London: Routledge, 1997, 97.

26. Schmidt, *Futures of European Capitalism*, op. cit.
27. Wimmel, op. cit.
28. *Le Monde*, 9 November 2002
29. Schmidt, 'Trapped by Their Ideas ...', op. cit.
30. Annie Laurent and Nicolas Sauger (eds), 'Le Référendum de Ratification du Traité Constitutionnel Européen du 29 Mai 2005: Comprendre le 'Non' Français', *Cahiers du Cevipof*, 42, 2005, 42–73; A. Cole and H. Drake, 'The Europeanization of the French Polity', *Journal of European Public Policy*, 7 (1), 2000, 26–43.
31. Speech to the European Parliament in Strasbourg, 2 July 2007.
32. William Paterson, 'Helmut Kohl, "The Vision Thing" and Escaping the Semi-Sovereignty Trap', *German Politics*, 7 (11), 1998, 20–1.
33. Jonathan P. G. Bach, *Between Sovereignty and Integration: German Foreign Policy and National Identity after 1989*, New York: St Martin's Press, 1999.
34. Charlie Jeffery and William Paterson, 'German and European Integration: A Shifting of Tectonic Plates,' *West European Politics*, 26 (4), 2003, 71–2.
35. For example, speech on the 50th anniversary of the EU, Berlin, 25 March 2007.
36. Zaborowski, op. cit.
37. Wimmel, op. cit.
38. See Schmidt, *Democracy in Europe*, op. cit., Chapter 4.
39. Alberta Sbragia, 'Italy', in Maria Green Cowles, James Caporaso and Thomas Risse (eds), *Transforming Europe: Europeanization and Domestic Change*, Ithaca: Cornell University Press, 2001; Claudio M. Radaelli, 'The Italian State and the Euro', in Ken Dyson (ed.), *The European State and the Euro*, Oxford: Oxford University Press, 2002.
40. WRR (Scientific Council for Government Policy), *Rediscovering Europe in the Netherlands*, Amsterdam: Amsterdam University Press, 2007.
41. U. Beck and E. Grande, *Cosmopolitan Europe*, Cambridge: Polity, 2007.
42. Sjursen, op. cit.
43. S. Verney, 'Justifying the Second Enlargement: Promoting Interests, Consolidating Democracy or Returning to the Roots?', in H. Sjursen (ed.), *Questioning EU Enlargement: Europe in Search of Identity*, London: Routledge, 2006.
44. Mark Leonard, *Why Europe Will Run the 21st Century*, London: Fourth Estate, 2005.
45. Ian Manners, 'Normative Power Europe: A Contradiction in Terms?', *Journal of Common Market Studies*, 40 (2), 2002, 235–58; Zaki Laïdi, *EU Foreign Policy in a Globalized World: Normative Power and Social Preferences*, London: Routledge, 2008.
46. Leonard, op. cit.
47. Howorth, op. cit.
48. Speech to the Economic Club, Chicago, 24 April 1999, at: www.number10.gov.uk/Page1297
49. Speech to the EU Parliament, June 2005, at: www.number10.gov.uk/Page7714
50. Speech at the College of Europe in Bruges, 15 November 2007, at: www.euractiv.com/29/images/bruges%20speech_tcm29-168458.doc
51. Speech to the European Parliament, Strasbourg, 2 July 2007.
52. Schmidt, *Democracy in Europe*, op. cit.
53. The following draws on Schmidt 'A "Menu Europe"...', op. cit., 13; Vivien A. Schmidt, 'Envisioning a Less Fragile, More Liberal Europe', *European Political Science*, 2009 (forthcoming).
54. See Schmidt 'A "Menu Europe"...', op. cit.; 'Envisioning a Less Fragile ...', op. cit.

14
Towards a European Identity?

Montserrat Guibernau

Introduction

In several respects the EU represents both a novel system of quasi-supranational governance and a novel form of political community or polity. But it is also a fragile construction for it remains a community still in the making with an ambiguous sense of identity and within which powerful forces are at work. This paper has three main aims:

First, to stress the shifting nature of Europe's geographical frontiers and assess whether cultural frontiers have remained more stable throughout time. In particular, it examines the main criteria which have traditionally been employed when having to decide who should be included and excluded from Europe. A different question concerns the requirements for EU membership and the monopoly of the adjective 'European' by the EU, which somehow has come to be identified with Europe.

Second, to explore contemporary sources of European cultural diversity. Here I argue that European identity stands as a 'non-emotional identity' in sharp contrast with traditional forms of national identity.

Third, the emergence of a European identity requires the political will to build a common project for the future, a vision encompassing socio-economic progress, commitment to liberal democracy and the pledge to replacing conflict by consensus among EU members. The paper concludes by considering what are the main challenges currently faced by a still incipient European identity.

The cultural frontiers of Europe

Europe is a cultural reality that spreads well beyond the boundaries of the European Union. In recent times, it has become common practice to identify Europe with the EU. Yet when people refer to 'European integration', 'European citizenship and laws', 'European institutions' or the generation of a 'European identity', they usually employ the term 'European' to refer to the processes of consolidation and greater integration led by the European Union.

On geographical boundaries

Europe is generally understood to include the western portion of the Eurasian landmass, together with a number of islands not far from the mainland (Iceland, Corsica, Malta, Sardinia, Sicily, Crete and Ireland as well as Great Britain), however, this does not provide a clear-cut idea of where Asia stops and Europe begins.

Precisely where the division between Europe and Asia lies is a matter of some debate. To understand Europe as a geographical area involves awareness of Europe's shifting boundaries. The Greeks conceived a water-bound Europe whose borders lay on the Black Sea and its northern extension, the Sea of Azov, as far as the banks of the river Don. From the 18th century, though, Europe has often been understood to end (or begin) with the Ural Mountains and the river that takes its name from them and flows into the Caspian Sea. But this carries some ambiguities. Following the dissolution of the Soviet Union in 1991, it leaves the Transcaucasus and the newly independent states of Armenia, Azerbaijan and Georgia in an uncertain relation with regard to Europe, while Turkey also lies to the west of the Urals.

The geographical boundaries of Europe have suffered dramatic changes throughout time, even the most recent past offers different examples that illustrate the shifting character of European borders. The post-1989 uni- fication of Germany, the separation of Czechoslovakia, the break-up of Yugoslavia, the independence achieved by the Baltic Republics and the dis- membering of the Soviet Union illustrate dramatic border changes within European countries taking place in the last 15 years.

Further to this, we should consider the claims of countries such as Turkey, which are currently asserting their European character and demanding the right to be included within the European Union. The 2004 and 2007 enlarge- ments of the EU strengthen the idea that the boundaries of Europe are not fixed and that the boundaries of the EU, which is often identified with 'Europe', are not fixed either. It follows from this that the definition of Europe and indeed who is included and who is excluded from Europe tends to change throughout time. The description of Europe, or any other territory, as a 'geographical' entity invariably implies the absence of more elevated claims associated with the embodiment of some general values and a sense of shared identity, as loose as it may be, among its citizens.

But, how useful are geographical boundaries in defining Europe? Is Europe a merely geographical space? In the light of the evidence provided above, the answer to these questions seems to be a negative one.

But, what about history? Is it possible to identify any clear elements of historical continuity pointing at a pre-existent idea of Europe? In my view, this is extremely difficult and controversial since Europe's history is fraught with confrontation and war. This seems to indicate that geography and history appear to be insufficient criteria to decide who should and who should not be included in Europe. What other criteria may then be applied to shed some light into the commonalities shared by those who call themselves 'Europeans'? Many scholars and politicians have turned to defend the idea that what unites Europeans is the sharing of a certain culture and values which differentiate them from other peoples, more crucially from Eastern peoples. This argument is based upon the assumption that 'there has always been a different way of life between East and West, between the full and half European ... between real Europeans, and those caught in a nether world between the European and Asian'.[1]

Some scholars consider Europe as a system of values and mention the impact of Christianity and the rise of a set of ideas including those of freedom, humanism and material progress as key elements in the construction of an incipient European identity.

The 'idea of Europe' did not begin by reference to geographical or historical divisions. Instead, it emerged as a term connected to a specific cultural and political heritage embodied in Athenian democracy. It was not until the 19th century that George Grote, a radical banker and historian, located the origin of European civilisation in Greek democracy, rather than in the establishment of Christianity towards the end of the Roman Empire.

But if the idea of Europe has a cultural basis connected to Athenian democracy and some common traditions and consciousness, is it then possible to refer to the cultural frontiers of Europe? What are the main criteria to decide on where to draw the line? Furthermore, if we were to agree on the existence of a certain European culture, no matter how incipient this might be, would this be sufficient to account for the existence of some embryonic European identity?

On culture

Culture is formed by values, beliefs, customs, conventions, habits and practices which give rise to a particular identity uniting those who have been socialised within a particular society.[2] From a symbolic perspective, 'culture is the pattern of meanings embodied in symbolic forms, including actions, utterances and meaningful objects of various kinds, by virtue of which individuals communicate with one another and share their experiences, conceptions and beliefs'.[3] The process of identification with the elements of a specific culture implies a strong emotional investment. Individuals are born within cultures that determine the way in which they view and organise themselves in relation to others and to nature.

Two major implications deriving from this possess a particular significance for the analysis of whether we can refer to a distinctive European identity based upon a shared culture. First, a common culture favours the creation of solidarity bonds among the members of a given community and allows them to imagine the community they belong to as separate and distinct from others. Solidarity is then based upon the consciousness of forming a group, outsiders being considered as strangers and potential 'enemies'.

Second, a common historical past which includes memories of war, deprivation, victory, repression, success and a future common project reinforce the sense of a shared identity among members of a given community. There is a strong connection between history and culture, since crucial elements in the culture of any given community, such as symbols, language, sacred places, heroes, anthems, legends and traditions, are inextricably bound up with the community's history.[4] For our purposes here, the key question concerns whether Europeans share some cultural elements capable of uniting them and making them different from 'others'. This is, is there a sense of solidarity among Europeans which goes back to medieval times? Where are to be found the symbols, holy places, heroes, and traditions that unite Europeans? What are Europe's shared values? In a nutshell, what are the criteria for establishing the cultural frontiers of Europe?

At present there is a substantial body of literature that examines the historical origins of contemporary Europe and argues that some common 'traditions' and a somewhat unspecified sense of common 'consciousness' have united the peoples of Europe since the Middle Ages. Such accounts highlight European unity above the diversity that has traditionally defined European peoples. The search for a common past and traditions responds to the need to identify or invent some elements capable of acting as pillar blocs in the construction of a shared sense of European identity which, ideally, should go hand-in-hand with greater EU integration. In spite of considerable efforts to define such elements it is proving quite difficult to agree on them, particularly since the history of European peoples is fraught with memories of war. In addition, the status of Europe as a cultural unit and a system of values at the dawn of the 21st century remains problematic. There is a clear contrast between Europe's strengthening institutional structures and more intensive processes of governance on the one hand (at least so far as the EU is concerned), and the relative weakness and uncertainty of the values that underpin it on the other.

Religion as an inclusion-exclusion mechanism

Samuel Huntington in his most celebrated book, *The Clash of Civilizations*,[5] argues that religion provides the best common means of historically distinguishing between Europeans and the rest, which in particular refers to the Judeo-Christian tradition confronting Islam. This argument, however, seems to ignore that, in the Middle Ages, most intra-European wars had a religious character. In turn, it could be argued that such wars did not imply the existence of different civilisations within Europe, rather they consisted of wars between countries defending different and revised 'versions' of a religion that had a unique origin. It is precisely from this perspective that it seems plausible to point to religion as a key feature in constructing what we now term as an embryonic European identity. Following this line of argument, Anthony Smith stresses that 'there is a clear sense, going back at least to the Crusades and probably even to Charles Martel, in which Europeans see themselves as not Muslims or as not Jews'.[6] Should we then conclude that European culture is based upon Christianity and that the cultural boundaries of Europe are determined by religion? This raises two main issues.

First, is the appeal to a shared religion a recent invention? Were Charles the Great and the crusaders convinced that the religious divide between those who believed in God and those who did not was to reflect a further division between Europeans and the rest? Would they have defined themselves as Europeans? Probably not. Furthermore, early Europe as Christendom already contained significant religious minorities (Jews and Muslims) – and barely included the rural masses whose peasant status was closely linked with a 'pagan' (and thus non-Christian) outlook which presented a constant challenge to the consolidation of any regional Christian realm.

Second, if we were to assume that religion, and Christianity in particular, is the key criteria for inclusion in Europe, what do we make of the religious wars in which European countries fought each other since the Middle Ages? Reflecting on these issues, Adam Burgess writes:

> it is only with the Ottoman challenge, coupled with the social and religious crises of the fourteenth and fifteenth centuries, that Europe became the Christian continent, and therefore distinct limits were drawn [...] Significantly, however, this unity was more apparent than real. Christian Europe was moving into the schisms of those centuries, and the heresies of the sixteenth.[7]

A further point concerns whether religion operates as an inclusion/exclusion mechanism in contemporary Europe. This raises some questions, for instance, if religion were to be considered as the key criteria in determining a particular country's European character. Could it then be argued that some of the EU member states' opposition to Turkey's accession to the EU derives from the latter's Muslim allegiance rather than from the economic and geopolitical concerns often openly invoked by these countries? This is a highly sensitive and controversial issue. The 2004 EU decision to initiate the process of Turkey's accession – subject to a set of conditions – seems to indicate that contemporary Europe is not based upon a religious divide arising from a pre-modern religious outlook on the world. Yet, this is not to deny that religions play a major part in the cultural make-up of their followers and that most elements of Europe's secular culture to be explored in the following section have, at some point, developed in opposition, debate, confrontation and/or dialogue with prevailing religions in different European countries.

On Europe's secular culture: the impact of the Enlightenment and the Industrial Revolution

But, if religion is not an appropriate criterion to define Europe, are there any alternative secular traditions which might be relevant when deciding where to draw the cultural boundaries of Europe? Machiavelli's work offers an incipient notion of Europe based upon secular principles. However, the idea of Europe did not acquire real meaning until the age of the Enlightenment.[8]

During that period, a primarily elitist consciously felt European identity came to the fore. This stronger 'European' consciousness retained a Christian outlook but was now associated with other values, particularly those of a novel and a fast-developing European civilisation embodied in a rapidly changing Europe turned into a champion of freedom, humanism and the growing ideas of material progress. According to Pim den Boer, it was not until the 19th century and specifically after the break with tradition prompted by the revolutionary years that the concept of Europe was historicised and politicised. He writes:

> At the beginning of the nineteenth century the idea of Europe was projected back much further in history. A search was instigated for the roots of European civilization. Europe, which in the Middle Ages had in fact hardly existed as a geographical expression, became an accepted historical category. The historical writings of the nineteenth century romantics made it appear that in the Middle Ages there had been a conscious idea of Europe: The notion gained ground that out of the ruins of the Roman empire (the Latin element), the Barbarian peoples (the Germanic element), led by the Christian church, had been amalgamated to form the true European civilization.[9]

The ideas embodied in the Enlightenment took a specific political form in the democratic explosion of the French Revolution. Napoleon's dissemination of revolutionary ideas throughout the European mainland contributed further to the radical transformation of European societies by prompting a series of dramatic changes that would progressively affect the peoples of Europe. These transformations challenged the so-called *ancien régime* and fostered the emergence of an early convergence among European national elites. This was a factor that emphasised the wide gap separating the mass of the population from Europe's cultural, political and economic elites. These transformations involved:

a) The decline of the aristocracy and the advent of the bourgeoisie, which was to become the leading component of elites throughout Europe;

b) The separation between state and church which, in turn, was to initiate a process characterised by the progressive weakening of mass allegiance to traditional religions. This would evolve in partnership with the rise of secular values grounded upon humanist principles;

c) The rise and consolidation of the nation-state as the main political institution whose power should be rooted in popular consent and whose aim was to accomplish the cultural homogenisation of its citizens. This framework facilitated the rise of modern nationalism, a device that proved to be exceedingly useful for refocusing a people's loyalty away from the monarch. The nation, personified through symbols and rituals that symbolically recreated a sense of 'people', became the focus of a new kind of attachment;

d) The emergence of the concept of citizenship as a mechanism to translate ideas of popular sovereignty into universal adult suffrage. Citizenship had to be struggled for, and although it was ideally conceived as embracing all inhabitants of any given nation state, in most European countries, enfranchisement was limited to male citizens owning a certain amount of property – France in 1830 had a population of some 30 million while boasting an electorate of a mere 90,000.

Religion could also disenfranchise a man, particularly if he were a Catholic in a Protestant state, or a Jew. In Britain, Catholics had to wait until 1829 and Jews until 1858 for the right to vote. Full enfranchisement, however, often did not take place until well into the 20th century. For instance, in most European nation-states, universal suffrage was achieved after the First World War. Women usually acquired democratic rights some time after men – in Switzerland spectacularly so (1971).

e) A great emphasis on the importance of universal education fed into most nation-states' decision to create national education systems capable of attaining the cultural and linguistic homogenisation of an otherwise diverse population. Further to this, education should teach the population how to become good citizens loyal to the nation state.

Recent literature suggests that the Enlightenment opened a fissure between the 'civilised' West and the 'uncivilised' or 'barbarian' East. It would be misleading, however, to ignore the fact that the Enlightenment also affected the empires of Central and Eastern Europe, a feature that once more stresses the difficulty of drawing a clear-cut cultural boundary of Europe.

Enlightenment ideas triggered dramatic socio-political transformations in European societies, but they also prompted the adoption of rationality as a method and progress as an objective. It is in this sense that a connection between the Enlightenment and the Industrial Revolution could be established. Rationality involved the end of alchemy and magical arguments and fostered a scientific revolution that culminated in the Industrial Revolution. Both the Enlightenment and the Industrial Revolution challenged traditional social, political and economic patterns and prompted profound transformations in European societies.

The Industrial Revolution originated in England and Scotland in the mid-18th century and expanded from there to the continent. Already by 1850 more people in England were working in industry than in agriculture, a situation that would be reached in southern Europe, including France, only a century later.[10] The social and economic development prompted by the Industrial Revolution transformed the West and established a radical division between industrialising countries and those that were primarily based upon rural economies, as was the case in most of Central and Eastern Europe, but also in Greece, Portugal, most of Spain (excluding Catalonia and the Basque Country) and Italy. Burgess argues that:

> With European development, especially through the nineteenth century, the Ottoman Empire, a part of which later came to constitute the border of 'the East' of today, became not only 'the sick man of Europe' in Western eyes, but the embodiment of torpor and decay. The change here was not so much in the Ottoman Empire. Certainly it had stagnated, but it was hardly unrecognizable. Rather, the change was relative to the newfound dynamism of the West.
>
> It was the vantage point of the great powers that had really been transformed. They now looked down on those who had failed to reproduce their own astonishing rate of progress and innovation.[11]

The advent of industrialism transformed national landscapes. It created large factories, prompting rural migration to urban centres, re-shaping and enlarging cities, greatly improving transport and communications, developing the media and, in particular, favouring the proliferation of newspapers and magazines, and producing a vast range of mass-produced goods.

Industrialism signalled a turning point in European societies by causing massive social change. It was based upon the division of labour and the separation between home and the workplace. In many instances, industrialism is associated with the spread of capitalism. A fundamental difference between the two should be established. Thus while industrialism is based upon the mechanisation of mass-produced goods while remaining 'neutral' in respect of wider institutional alignments, capitalism is a type of production system dominant in a given society which presupposes an alignment of the 'economic' and the 'political' focused through private property and the commodification of wage-labour.[12] Only when the conjunction between capitalism and industrialism is well advanced does it become plausible to speak of the existence of 'capitalist societies', and it is precisely the constitution of such capitalist societies which could be taken as a point of reference when distinguishing between European societies and those which remained outside the industrialised world.

To sum up, after the Enlightenment, competing versions of Europe emerged; liberal and conservative, for or against revolution, with constitutional or absolutist forms of government. This process of incipient European convergence initiated by the Enlightenment was greatly enhanced by the almost simultaneous emergence and spread of the Industrial Revolution. It was from that moment that European societies began to share certain features which would accentuate the difference between them and those societies 'towards the East', which remained untouched by industrialism.

In spite of this, it was not until the 20th century and after suffering the devastating effects of two world wars that we can locate the surfacing of the coherently defined idea of Europe which has served to inspire the European Union. In this process, the division of Europe into two halves during the Cold War dramatically contributed to re-define its cultural boundaries. In most cases, contemporary criteria for inclusion and exclusion are connected to the role played by countries during the Second World War and even more crucially by the position held by them either within or without the area of Soviet influence.

After the Second World War, Western Europe (although strongly underwritten by the United States) was clearly regarded as more 'European' than the Soviet-dominated East, a view that supported the special role played by the EU and its predecessors in the region as a whole. The EU's economic success sustained democracy and its overall stability strengthened this conception, which still prevails after the disintegration of the Soviet Union.

At a time when the EU is moving towards further political and economic integration we are confronted with the question of whether Europe is becoming more united in cultural and social terms or whether, on the contrary, greater divisions are emerging among EU member states. Currently, different voices are arguing that any new Europe has to be imagined afresh and constructed as a conscious plan of action rather than deduced from existing values. There are, undoubtedly, differing 'projects for Europe'. Again, Europe is often conflated with the EU, and although some non-EU countries claim their European credentials, the EU seems to monopolise the idea of Europe as a project, which still remains largely undefined.

Towards a European identity?

The European Union was created by nation-states after the Second World War. Its main objectives were avoiding war, strengthening state power and overcoming the poverty and destruction caused by two world wars.

The EU is a dynamic political institution, which since its inception has experienced a dramatic expansion and growth in terms of territory and citizen numbers coupled with increasing wealth, productivity and international presence. Right now, the EU seeks economic and political integration and in so doing it stands up as the most ambitious project promoted by any supranational political institution worldwide. The creation of a single market, the free movement of people and goods across its frontiers, the introduction of the Euro in 2001, and its latest enlargement to include ten new member states in 2004 and two more in 2007, have turned the EU into a major global political actor – although it is one still struggling to offer a united voice in some areas, for instance, in international relations, foreign policy and security. The EU embraces a considerable number of nation-states prepared to relinquish some aspects of their own jealously guarded sovereignty in order to benefit from membership of an economically prosperous and dynamic internal market, which has turned the EU into a successful global economic player.

But, how do its own citizens perceive the EU? Do they identify with it? What enables identification to take place? Previous experience shows that identification with the nation-state emerged only after a considerably long period involving the linguistic and cultural homogenisation of citizens, the fighting of wars, taxation, the establishment of citizenship rights and duties, the construction of a certain image of the nation endowed with its own symbols and rituals (instilled by the state), the existence of common enemies and the progressive consolidation of national education and media systems.[13]

At sub-state level, the construction of autonomous political institutions also tends to generate a sense of belonging. For instance, when considering regional identity, the study of devolution in Britain, Canada and Spain proves that the establishment of autonomous political institutions with sufficient power and resources to rule a territory, and make a difference to the peoples' lives, tends not only to strengthen pre-existing identities but also to breed a sense of belonging and shared identity where it did not previously exist:[14] this is particularly so, for instance, among the citizens of newly created autonomous communities in post-1979 Spain. In Western Europe, devolution does not tend to weaken national identity, and compatibility between national and regional identity often leads to the coexistence of dual identities invoked at different times.

If compatibility between national and regional identity goes hand-in-hand with multilayered government, should we then conclude that a further layer of identity, on this occasion of a supra-state nature, would automatically emerge among European citizens once they feel the political weight of the EU upon their own lives? The response depends on how we are to define such a new form of collective identity, that is, on what type of attachment we imagine. In my view, European identity cannot be expected to follow the pattern of national identity, simply because the EU is not a nation-state but a new genre of political institution born out of a new socio-political and economic environment shaped by globalisation.

The EU is a novel political institution created out of the free will of sovereign nation-states, which continue to establish a sharp distinction between 'communitarian' and 'domestic' affairs in terms of policy and decision-making. For instance, recognition of national and ethnic minorities as well as devolution models are considered as 'internal affairs' and remain in the hands of each particular nation-state.

Ultimately, nation-states set up the aims and structure of the EU while funding and deciding on its budget. In some cases, nation-states employ the EU as an excuse for action or inaction within the domestic arena and, sometimes, they even refer to the EU as a scapegoat, thus fuelling nationalism and reinforcing national identity. Bearing this in mind, I believe that nation-states are only partially interested in promoting a European identity focused on EU membership, since 'too much Europe' could potentially weaken national identity and eventually result in refocusing a people's loyalty away from the nation-state.

European identity, as well as national identity when instilled by the state, is a top-down institutionally generated identity designed to foster solidarity bonds among a diverse population. It is also aimed at nurturing feelings of loyalty towards the EU yet, in my view, this is more of a project for the future than a reality.

On how Europeans regard the EU

Currently, Europeans are split concerning support for EU membership. In 2004 those considering membership of the EU as a 'good thing' scored 85 per cent in Luxembourg, 77 per cent in Ireland, 72 per cent in Spain and a mere 38 per cent in the UK. In contrast, those who considered the EU a 'bad thing' amounted to 33 per cent in the UK, 43 per cent in Latvia, 42 per cent in the Czech Republic and 37 per cent both in Slovakia and Poland.[15] Sizeable changes were recorded in 2005 when the view that EU membership is a 'good thing' decreased from 54 to 50 per cent[16] to increase again to 53 per cent in 2008.

In 2008 membership of the EU was still regarded as a good thing by an absolute majority of Europeans (53 per cent) while only 15 per cent of Europeans considered their country's membership as a bad thing. In 25 of the 27 member states the majority view was positive. In 2008, those considering membership of the EU as a 'good thing' scored 80 per cent in the Netherlands, 71 per cent in Luxembourg, 67 per cent in Ireland, 65 per cent in Poland, 64 per cent in Germany, 62 per cent in Spain and 32 per cent in the UK. When compared with 2004 data, this signals a slight decline in Luxembourg, Ireland and Spain.[17]

'A neutral stance toward membership is voiced in Latvia (49 per cent) and Hungary (45 per cent) while citizens in Greece, Austria, Italy and Cyprus are more equally divided between positive views and neutrality.'[18] In the UK, where the majority of the population used to view EU membership as negative, currently we encounter a population divided between those holding positive, neutral and negative views. Among candidate countries, support for potential membership has weakened. Respondents in the Former Yugoslav Republic of Macedonia continue to be most positive about their country's potential membership (62 per cent 'a good thing'; down 10 points) compared with Turkey (42 per cent 'a good thing'; down 7) and Croatia, where the majority view now is that potential membership would be a bad thing (38 per cent; up 13).[19]

Scores for the perceived advantages of EU membership have improved. In 2005, 52 per cent of Europeans considered that their country had benefited from EU membership while in 2008, this view reached 56 per cent (up 4 points). In 2005, 36 per cent felt that their country had not benefited from EU membership, this declined to 31 per cent in 2008 (down 5 points). 'The majority view in nearly all Member States is that EU membership has on balance been beneficial. Exceptions to this are Hungary (51 per cent 'not benefited'), the United Kingdom and Cyprus (46 per cent each) where the highest proportions think that the negative aspects of membership outnumber the benefits.'[20]

A further decline was identified. It involved a decrease in feeling that the image of the EU is positive, from 50 per cent (Autumn 2004) to 44 per cent (Autumn 2005) rising to 46 per cent (Autumn 2006) and reaching 52 per cent (Spring 2007). Since then, the image of the EU has followed a steady decline, reaching 45 per cent in Autumn 2008. The proportion of Europeans with a neutral image of the EU is 36 per cent; 17 per cent have a negative view. Only 26 per cent of British, 28 per cent of Finnish and 29 per cent of Latvians and Austrians declare a positive image of the EU. This contrasts with 63 per cent of Romanians, 59 per cent of Irish, 54 per cent of Polish, 51 per cent of Spaniards and 48 per cent of Germans holding a positive view.[21]

Undoubtedly, a decline in the perception of a positive EU image combined with a decrease in support for EU membership does not contribute to strengthening an incipient European identity. On the contrary, if such trends were to continue, they would signal the inability of the EU to focus on what unites Europeans rather than a denoting of a deepening of existing differences. A sustained decline in the perceived advantages of EU membership holds the potential to weaken the emergence of a cohesive European identity.

Currently, the expectations of some new member states are not being fulfilled at the speed that they had initially been envisaged; if this continues to be the case it will generate resentment and the construction of deep divisions within the EU. Simultaneously, enlargement is having a considerable impact upon the socio-cultural structures and public opinion of the 15 old member states. The latest enlargements are certainly extremely recent, but the consequences of opening up markets by expanding the territorial boundaries of Europe are likely to exert a powerful socio-economic impact upon European societies – some signs of it are already visible. Enlargement further problematises existing visions for greater political and social cohesion within the EU.

The strengthening of a still incipient European identity is further complicated by the accession of the largest contingent ever to join the EU at one time since its foundation.

Support for the EU is mixed and, critically, different percentages are obtained when analysing overall attitudes and feelings across the 25, and now 27, member states, and when studying country-by-country surveys that reveal deep differences among citizens of various member states.

The EU: a 'non-emotional' identity

But, what constitutes European identity? What are or could be its main components? European identity cannot be founded upon the cultural and linguistic homogenisation of its citizens, a mistake too often made by nation-states seeking to annihilate internal diversity to create a homogeneous citizenry. National and ethnic minorities claiming the right to cultural and linguistic survival and, in some cases, the right to self-determination, are now contesting such homogenisation attempts. In a similar manner, European identity cannot claim to rely upon a common past and it cannot even boast clear-cut geographical or cultural boundaries.

In contrast, a still embryonic European identity relies on the shared consciousness of belonging to an economic and political space defined by capitalism, social welfare, liberal democracy, respect for human rights, freedom and the rule of law, prosperity and progress. In my view, these are the pillars of a European identity, primarily defined by the sharing of a specific political culture and the desire to benefit from the economic advantages derived from EU membership. But are these sufficient to generate loyalty to the EU? Would support for the EU dwindle if an economic crisis were to hit it hard?

As I see it, a major economic crisis would undoubtedly question the purpose of the EU at a time when the economic prosperity associated with the Union has become of paramount importance to the EU-15 while simultaneously acting as a magnet for those nation-states that joined the EU in 2004 and 2007, as well as for those currently applying for membership. It is also true that avoiding Russian influence by firmly placing themselves within Western political and military structures – such as the EU and NATO – is regarded as a guarantee of independence by the former Soviet republics that are now independent nation states.

The EU is still a fragile institution and to make it work, nation-states need to believe that they would not get a finer deal by abandoning the Union. Economic prosperity is driving EU integration and a major failure in this area would bring the EU's capacity to bring political integration to a standstill.

At the moment, the economic incentives of EU membership are enormous, but the determination to protect national interests is so robust that, if a major economic crisis were to affect the EU, this could prompt some member states to believe that they could do better on their own or by establishing alternative partnerships. Under those circumstances, a still feeble and incipient European identity would suffer a major blow.

In my view, at least while in its early stages, European identity is best defined as an emergent 'non-emotional' identity, in contrast with the powerful and emotionally charged national identities of our time.

In its present form, I do not expect European identity to arouse feelings comparable to those inspired by national identity. In a similar manner, I do not anticipate the emergence of a European nationalism powerful enough to mobilise the masses in the name of Europe; it would be problematical to find common causes and interests uniting Europeans and prompting them to sacrifice their own lives in the name of the EU. So far, the nation-state retains the emotional attachment of its citizens and when it becomes alien to them or too broad and distant, individuals turn to regional, ethnic, local and other forms of identity that tie them to more appropriately sized communities than the EU.

Challenges to a EU identity

In addition to economic success, several other key challenges to the consolidation of a European identity should be mentioned, among them a widening gap between the elites and the masses regarding perceptions and attitudes towards the EU (although it must also be said not even European elites share a coherent vision of the EU). Rather, there exist substantial differences concerning their ideas about the institutional shape the EU should progress towards as well as the degree of political and economic integration it should aim at. Max Haller highlights the lack of a single project for an EU identity by signalling the existence of 'significant differences in their ideas, both among political leaders and elites in different European nation states, and between different political parties, as well as between economic, political and cultural elites'.[22]

Up to a point, the gap between elites and the masses has materialised in the opposition to the draft Constitution that received a 'no' vote in France and the Netherlands in 2005 and the failure of Ireland to sanction the Revised Constitution – or Reformed Treaty – thus opening up a significant crisis at the heart of a EU that, once again, has seen its political integration project halted.

Dissatisfaction with the EU's democratic deficit, concern about the future of social welfare, disagreement on the institutional model propounded for the EU, lack of representation (voice and vote) for constitutional regions such as Catalonia, Scotland and Flanders, opposition to what is perceived by many as a growing hyper-bureaucratic entity distant from ordinary citizens, inability to speak with a single voice at crucial moments (intervention in the wars of the former Yugoslavia and Iraq), post-enlargement economic adjustments of EU subsidies and discontent about their own national governments have prompted a large number of citizens to vote 'no'. Saying 'no' to the Constitution and the Reformed Treaty, among other issues, implies that, for some, the brand of European identity emerging from the EU's magna carta does not fulfil their aspirations. At the dawn of the biggest enlargement ever experienced by the EU, it is of crucial importance to pause and reflect on the message being sent by French, Dutch and Irish citizens.

In my view, the emergence of a European identity requires the political will to build a common project for the future, a vision encompassing socioeconomic progress, commitment to liberal democracy and the pledge to replace conflict by consensus among EU members. When constructing such a project we should be wary of grand ventures, which in the past have resulted in conflict and destruction. Mazower cautions us: 'It was thus not preordained that democracy should win over fascism and communism, just as it remains still to be seen what kind of democracy Europe is able and willing to build'.[23] Yet, he adds, 'we should certainly not assume that democracy is suited to Europe'.[24]

A further challenge to the EU derives from the rise of populist right-wing nationalism in the shape of political parties fully integrated within the democratic system that tend to exploit fears of economic and cultural takeover by immigrants (legal and illegal), refugees and asylum-seekers attracted by the EU's wealth. Fear of diversity, feelings of being worse-off than newcomers regarded as benefiting from social welfare, cultural clashes, prejudice and difference in lifestyles, all these generate anxiety and encourage some sectors of the population, many of whom are to be found among the working class, to support right-wing, often populist, parties that are prepared to be 'tough' and place the interests of their own citizens first.

Current debates on whether assimilation, integration or multiculturalism should prevail are causing heated confrontations in European societies. Evidence of ghettoisation, the existence of parallel societies which do not interact with each other, discrimination, racism, clashes between some members of ethnic groups, and confrontation between migrants from different origins have ignited resentment and violence. The outburst of violence registered in France during November 2005 exemplifies this. In addition, the 7 July 2005 London terrorist attacks perpetrated by British citizens of migrant origin have shaken British society to the bone.

Mazower's idea that '[t]he real victor in 1989 was not democracy but capitalism, and Europe as a whole now faces the task which Western Europe has confronted since the 1930s, of establishing a workable relationship between the two'[25] expresses one of the EU's greatest challenges, because it is capitalism and the need to stand up as a global economic player that prompted European integration in the first place.

Furthermore, the EU's will to assert its identity as a global political actor through the implementation of a common foreign and security policy, including the eventual framing of a common defence policy as envisaged in the Maastricht Treaty for the EU (Article B), is proving a challenging object-ive. Lack of accord among EU leaders has resulted in the absence of a unified EU response to profound crises such as the occupation of Kuwait by Iraq and the subsequent Gulf War (1991), civil war resulting in the disintegration of Yugoslavia in the early 1990s, the recognition of new independent states such as Slovenia, Croatia and Kosovo, and the US-led invasion of Iraq.

To assume that an emotional attachment to the EU should follow suit underestimates the complexity and strength of national identity, which still continues to act as the immediate frame of reference for the majority of citi-zens. Even accepting that the nation-state is re-casting its nature, I do not think we can announce that it is fading away. In my view, European identity will remain an abstract concept in the medium term and its future will cru-cially depend on the socio-economic and political consequences of adopting a single currency, successfully managing enlargement and dealing with mass immigration as well as the cultural, social and political questions associated with it.

Notes and References

1. A. Burgess, *Divided Europe*, London: Pluto Press, 1997, 67.
2. M. Guibernau, *Nationalisms*, Cambridge: Polity Press, 1996, 75.
3. J. B. Thompson, *Ideology and Modern Culture*, Cambridge: Polity Press, 1990, 132.
4. A. D. Smith, *National Identity*, London: Penguin Books, 1991.
5. S. P. Huntington, *The Clash of Civilizations and the Remaking of the World Order*, New York: Simon and Schuster, 1996.
6. Quoted in Burgess, op. cit., 67.
7. Ibid., 69.
8. Enlightenment humanism emerged in France and involved establishing a dis-tinction between those parts of the world engaged in the pursuit of the ideas of rationality and progress, which lie at the heart of the Enlightenment, and those enmeshed in pre-rational practices and beliefs. In spite of the superiority, which the *philosophes* attributed to their revolutionary way of thinking, the Enlight-enment that they represented did not result in a diminished interest in other philosophies around the world.
9. P. Den Boer, 'Europe to 1914: The Making of an Idea', in K. Wilson, K. and J. van der Dussen (eds), *The History of the Idea of Europe*, London: Routledge, 1995, 70.
10. C. Crouch, *Social Change in Western Europe*, Oxford: Oxford University Press, 1999, 20.
11. Burgess, op. cit., 91.
12. A. Giddens, *The Nation-State and Violence*, Cambridge: Polity Press, 1985, 140.
13. M. Guibernau, 'Anthony D. Smith on Nations and National Identity: A Critical Assessment', *Nations and Nationalism*, 10 (1/2), 2004, 125–41.
14. M. Guibernau, *The Identity of Nations*, Cambridge: Polity Press, 2007, Chapter 2.
15. *Eurobarometer 62/* fieldwork Oct/Nov 2004. Publication December 2004. At: http://europa.eu.int/com/public-opinion/indez-en.htm (accessed 3 December 2005), 8.

16. *Eurobarometer 64/* fieldwork Oct/Nov 2005. Publication December 2005. At: http://europa.eu.int/com/public-opinion/indez-en.htm (accessed 8 November 2006), 9.
17. *Eurobarometer 70/*, fieldwork Oct/Nov 2008. Publication December 2008. Brussels: European Commission, 31.
18. Ibid., 32.
19. Ibid.
20. Ibid., 35.
21. Ibid., 48.
22. Max Haller, 'Voiceless Submission or Deliberate Choice? European Integration and the Relation between National and European Identity', in H. Kriesi, K. Armingeon, H. Siegrist and A. Wimmer (eds), *Nation and National Identity: The European Experience in Perspective*, Chur/Zürich: Rüegger, 1999, 263–96. See also Sonia Puntscher-Riekmann, *Die kommissarische Neuordnung Europas*, Berlin: Springer Verlag, 1998.
23. Mark Mazower, *Dark Continent: Europe's Twentieth Century*, London: Allen Lane, The Penguin Press, 1998, xii.
24. Ibid., 3.
25. Ibid., 405.

Index